Doctors
in the
Movies

BOIL THE WATER AND JUST SAY AAH

Doctors
in the
Movies

BOIL THE WATER AND JUST SAY AAH

Peter E. Dans

M

MEDI-ED PRESS

Printed in the United States of America. All Rights Reserved.
ISBN 0-936741-14-7

Reviews of the following films appeared in "The Physician at the Movies" column in *The Pharos*, the Alpha Omega Alpha honor medical society journal, and are reprinted in part with permission of the editors of *The Pharos*: *Article 99, As Good As It Gets, Awakenings, Beyond Rangoon, The Citadel, City of Joy, The Doctor, Eve's Bayou, Extreme Measures, The Fugitive, The Last Angry Man, Like Water for Chocolate, Lorenzo's Oil, Malice, Mary Shelley's Frankenstein, Medicine Man, Not As a Stranger, Outbreak, Patch Adams, Playing God, The Prince of Tides, The Third Man, and What About Bob?"*

Graphics by Horizon Prepress and Design

Library of Congress Cataloging-in-Publication Data:

CIP data pending

MEDI-ED PRESS
#5 White Place
Bloomington, Illinois 61701
1-800-500-8205

Contents

Acknowledgment .... *ix*

About the Author .... *xi*

Introduction .... *xiii*

    "The Golden Age of Medicine" .... *xv*

    "Doing Better and Feeling Worse" .... *xvii*

    Medicine Disorganizes and Doctors Get Knocked Off the Pedestal ...*xviii*

1 Hollywood Goes to Medical School 1

    Of Human Bondage 3

    Miss Susie Slagle's 5

    Doctor in the House 8

    Not As a Stranger 10

    Gross Anatomy 15

    Flatliners 19

    Patch Adams 21

2 The Kindly Savior: From Doctor Bull to Doc Hollywood .. 29

    The Dedicated Solo General Practitioner 31

        Doctor Bull 32

        The Country Doctor 34

        Meet Dr. Christian 37

        Doctor Jim 39

        Welcome Stranger 40

        People Will Talk 42

        The Last Angry Man 48

        Doc Hollywood 51

3 Benevolent Institutions 55

    Surgeons As the "Golden Boys of Medicine" 56

        Men in White 56

        Society Doctor 59

        Internes Can't Take Money 64

THE DIAGNOSTICIAN 66
   Young Dr. Kildare 67
   Dr. Kildare's Crisis 70
   Dr. Kildare's Wedding Day 72
THE TWILIGHT OF THE GOLDEN AGE OF MEDICAL MOVIES 74
   The Young Doctors 74
   The Interns 76

4 The Temple of Science 83
  THE PRICE OF HUBRIS 84
   Doctor X 84
   Arrowsmith 85
   Dr. Jekyll and Mr. Hyde 93
   Mary Shelley's Frankenstein 96
  THE GLORY OF SCIENCE: PASTEUR, EHRLICH, AND THE CURIES ... 98
   The Story of Louis Pasteur 98
   Dr. Ehrlich's Magic Bullet 101
   Madame Curie 107
  MEDICAL SCIENCE IN POSTWAR FILMS 110
   Medicine Man 111
   Lorenzo's Oil 112

5 "Where Are All the Women Doctors?" 121
   Mary Stevens, M.D. 124
   Dr. Monica 127
   Woman Doctor 130
   Spellbound 132
   The Girl in White 134
   Coma 139
   The Prince of Tides 143
   Beyond Rangoon 145

6 Blacks, the Invisible Doctors 149
   Lost Boundaries 152
   No Way Out 155
   Guess Who's Coming to Dinner 160
   The Heart Is a Lonely Hunter 162
   Outbreak 165
   Eve's Bayou 168

7 The Dark Side of Doctors 173

The Citadel 173

Kings Row 179

Sister Kenny 182

Dead Ringers 186

The Doctor 189

Malice 193

Playing God 195

8 The Institutions Turn Evil 199

M*A*S*H 199

The Hospital 203

One Flew Over the Cuckoo's Nest 210

The Verdict 212

Article 99 214

THE NEW VILLAINS: HMOS AND INSURERS 218

As Good As it Gets 218

The Rainmaker 220

Critical Care 222

9 The Temple of Healing 229

Symphony of Six Million 230

The Green Light 234

Magnificent Obsession, 1935 237

Magnificent Obsession, 1954 238

THE SEPARATION OF MEDICINE AND RELIGION 240

Extreme Measures 243

10 More Good Movie Doctors and Other Personal Favorites . 249

House Calls 250

What About Bob? 253

The Third Man 256

Doctor Zhivago 260

Like Water for Chocolate 262

The Fugitive 265

City of Joy 270

Awakenings 276

Appendix A: Recurring Medical Themes and Stereotypes 283

Appendix B: Filmography 299

Sources of Photographs 375

Index 377

Acknowledgment

Acknowledgments usually begin at the outer circle of acquaintances and move inward, ending with the family. I'm reversing the order. As my mentor Doctor David Seegal used to say, the best thing a doctor could do was marry well. Because I was fortunate to have done so, I must first thank Colette, my wife of thirty-three years and truly my better half, as many will attest. Her love transformed my life and she has tolerated this mad obsession with movies when I could have been occupied in more financially productive pursuits. A first-generation American, she grew up in Woonsocket, a Rhode Island mill town with a heavy French Canadian population. Her careers have included being a chemist (which she credits for her excellence as a chef), a mother, and now a French immersion teacher. Many readers comment on how much they enjoy the down-to-earth insights she contributes to my reviews.

She also made me aware of the need to reset my priorities. In 1975, I was already a tenured associate professor at the University of Colorado, either spending long days at the hospital or flying around the country giving lectures. She told me "we have four children and they don't know you." The next year I took a sabbatical in Washington as a health policy fellow at the Institute of Medicine and made sure to have dinner at home and to spend weekends going to museums and on other family outings. On returning to Hopkins, I arranged my work so that I could be involved in parents' programs (a practice which continued from middle school through their graduate school years), attend important events, and not miss many evening and weekend meals at home. This allowed me to enjoy the children as they grew up and to keep abreast of what was "happening."

True, I never became a full professor at Hopkins, but then again I didn't neglect my family. So, thanks to Maria, Paul, Tom, and Suzanne, who are establishing themselves in medicine, law, and investment banking, but more important are "good kids." Seeing through their eyes and those of Laura and Scott, who have joined the family, has helped leaven my thinking and keep it from entirely fossilizing. I am particularly indebted to my grandmother, parents, and uncles for making me feel loved. I must also acknowledge special teachers like Sister Mary Berchmans Flynn, who tried vainly to teach me penmanship, and Brother Walter O'Rourke, who made history come alive. Thanks also to Drs. David Seegal, Arthur Wertheim, Ed Leifer, Anna Southam, Katie Borkovich, Max Finland, Bob Chanock, Paul Beeson, Gordon Meiklejohn, Mac Harvey, Victor McKusick, and Richard Ross, who had faith in me and showed me what being a doctor was all about.

I must also acknowledge the help and support of the initiator of "The Physician at the Movies" column, Ralph Crawshaw; the former editors of *The Pharos*, Bob and Helen Glaser, who asked me to write the column when Ralph resigned; Carolyn Kuckein, who makes sure that *The Pharos* sees the light of day; and Ted Harris, its current editor. Without the encouragement of John McPhee, Pete Riley, Janet Worthington and other readers of the column who wrote to tell me that they enjoyed it, the book would not have been written.

Researching it was made easy through the gracious assistance of Nancy Chambers, Christine Ruggere and other information specialists at the Welch Library of the Johns Hopkins School of Medicine. Dick May, vice president for preservation at Warner Bros. helped me to select films and obtain those not available on video by facilitating contacts at Turner Classic Movies (especially the ever cooperative Dennis Millay) and other studio archives. Finally, I must also thank Michael Shortland whose resource on medicine and the movies proved invaluable as a starting point for my research; and Professors John Burnham, Jo Banks, Suzanne Poirier, and Naomi Rogers for their helpful critiques of various chapters.

Finally, most editors who looked at my manuscript said they "personally enjoyed the work" or that it was "amusing and interesting," "engaging and well-written," "witty and incisive," but alas, "not for us" or unlikely to find "an audience" or "a market." So, thanks to William and Sherlyn Hogenson at Medi-Ed Press for being interested in the book and for their help along the way.

I apologize to anyone I may have inadvertently left out. As John Donne said, "No man is an island, entire of itself; every man is a piece of the continent." To those mentioned and not mentioned with whom I have been continentally "connected" in the sense that E. M. Forster advised that we be, a sincere "thank you."

Peter E. Dans, M.D.
Cockeysville, Maryland

Addendum: It's customary in acknowledgments to add a disclaimer to the effect that all errors are the author's. That's certainly true in my case, but let me add a personal request. During our second-year medical school course in surgical pathology, the excellent instructor Dr. Virginia Kneeland Frantz craftily promised that for any errors we found in her textbook, she would give us anywhere from a nickel to a quarter, depending on how egregious it was. The princely sums say something about the times. I think I made thirty cents. I can't offer anyone remuneration, but I certainly would like to hear about things I got wrong as well as those I got right.

About the Author

PETER E. DANS, M.D.

Dr. Dans is an internist with special interests in infectious diseases, health policy, and ethics. He graduated from Manhattan College and in 1961 from Columbia University College of Physicians and Surgeons. Dans trained at the Johns Hopkins Hospital, Presbyterian Hospital in New York, the Laboratory of Viral Diseases at the National Institutes of Health, and the Thorndike Memorial Laboratory at Harvard Medical School. He also spent three months caring for cholera patients at Calcutta's Infectious Disease Hospital.

From 1969 to 1978, Dans was on the faculty of the University of Colorado Medical Center, where he helped found a migrant health clinic, a sexually transmitted diseases clinic, and an adult walk-in clinic, while directing the student and employee health services. In 1976–1977, he was named a Robert Wood Johnson health policy fellow and then staffed an Institute of Medicine committee studying what physicians are taught about aging.

In 1978, Dans returned to Johns Hopkins to establish an office of medical practice evaluation aimed at improving patient care and decreasing costs and directed it until 1991. He also directed the required Ethics and Medical Care course. Now part-time, he continues as an associate professor of medicine and associate professor of health policy and management at Johns Hopkins University and is also a clinical professor of medicine at Marshall University.

He was appointed by Maryland's governor to the state board of physician licensure and discipline from 1988 to 1992 and was deputy editor of the *Annals of Internal Medicine* from 1991 to 1994. After spending a year working for a health-related computer software firm, he became an independent consultant in 1996, specializing in issues related to medical ethics, geriatric polyphamacy, and disease management.

Dans is a fellow of the American College of Physicians and a member of the Alpha Omega Alpha honor medical society, for whose quarterly publication, *The Pharos*, he writes the column, "The Physician at the Movies." He is the author or coauthor of more than one hundred scientific articles, book chapters, and essays.

Introduction

Myth, like denial, is central to human existence. History may tell us what we have been, but myths tell us what we could have been and still might be, as well as what others think we are. In this century, the most influential mythmakers have been moviemakers. The so-called "Hollywood dream factory" has inspired, educated, frightened, and entertained us. It has shaped how we think about ourselves and those around us by reinforcing old stereotypes and creating new ones.

This book is about how movies have portrayed medicine. It arises from a life-long love affair with the silver screen. Growing up in a cold-water flat on the lower east side of New York in the 1940s, I eagerly anticipated being taken to the now-extinct Tribune Theater, near the statues of Ben Franklin and Horace Greeley on Printer's Square. After we were moved to the Dyckman Housing Project, the "air-conditioned" Alpine Theater became the destination. Films like the U.S. Cavalry trilogy, *Fort Apache, She Wore a Yellow Ribbon*, and *Rio Grande*, transported me to a world of breathtaking beauty where a premium was placed on honor and country. That the cavalry was never so glamorous mattered little to me then or now. Those films became a part of my psyche just as *Casablanca, Mr. Smith Goes to Washington, Top Hat, It's a Wonderful Life*, and *The Seventh Seal* later did.

My interest deepened while directing separate film series for adults and children at the University of Colorado Medical Center in the 1970s. In 1990, I replaced psychiatrist *cum* Renaissance man, Ralph Crawshaw, as "The Physician at the Movies" for *The Pharos*, the Alpha Omega Alpha (AOA) honor medical society journal. My charge was to review films through a physician's eyes in a quarterly column that my son Paul said should have been renamed "The Physician at the Videostore," given the speed with which movies now disappear from theaters.

I'm almost ashamed to say that this book is the product of thousands of hours of movie watching and reflecting on how the medical profession is and has been seen by those we serve. It is not a history of medicine, but rather a look at the ways movies have mirrored the changes in medical care and in society's attitudes towards doctors, ranging from laudatory to highly critical.

During our sixty-year tour of medical movies, we will encounter many recurring events and themes that screenwriters would have us believe are part and parcel of medicine. As Spears says in his book, *Hollywood: The Golden Era*,[1] "Few groups have been so consistently distorted and maligned by Hollywood as the medical profession." He cites stereotypic portrayals as "the dedicated research scientist, the in-humane quack, the Lothario with pretty nurses and other men's wives, the flashy plastic surgeon and Park Avenue psychiatrist, the crazed cre-ator of monsters, the bumbling country practitioner with a heart of gold, and the brilliant young intern who puts his stodgy superiors to profes-sional shame."

At the outset, it is important to note that criticism of doctors is as old as history. It achieved the status of an art form in the eighteenth century, when Voltaire acidly wrote: "Doctors are men who prescribe medicine of which they know little to cure diseases of which they know less in human beings of which they know nothing."[2] The nineteenth cen-tury caricaturists, Rowlandson, Cruikshank, and Daumier, portrayed physicians as pompous, greedy quacks who hid their ignorance under a veneer of Latin phrases.[2] Of all the lay indictments of the profession, George Bernard Shaw's *The Doctor's Dilemma*,[3] written in 1906, remains the severest. He accused doctors of profiting from the misfortunes of others, an inevitable consequence of the nature of the profession and the state of the art at the time.

Critics were not lacking within the profession. Oliver Wendell Holmes, author and physician at Harvard Medical School, reflecting on the heroic practice of his day, said that after excluding wine, opium, and a few other drugs derived from nature, "if the whole materia medica as now used could be sunk to the bottom of the sea, it would be all the better for mankind—and all the worse for the fishes."[4] In 1902, medical education was such that William Root, a medical student at the Univer-sity of Chicago, started AOA because, in his words, "the name 'medical student' was associated with rowdyism, boorishness, immorality and low educational ideals."[5] It took the Flexner report[6,7] in 1910 to crystallize the development of uniform professional standards in medical training. Flexner's advocacy of Johns Hopkins, which had recruited a distinguished faculty (fig. 1) and had unified science, clinical care and training under one roof, helped foster the development of academic medical centers. Nonetheless, as shown in Sir Luke Fildes's portrait of the kindly doctor helplessly sitting by the bedside of the dying child (fig. 2), doctors could

FIGURE 1. *The Four Doctors* by John Singer Sargent. Welch, Halsted, Osler, and Kelly, the founders of the Johns Hopkins University School of Medicine.

still do little for their patients. The noted physician/writer Lewis Thomas captured this in his reminiscences about accompanying his father on house calls in the 1920s: "What troubled him most all through his professional life was that there were so many people needing help, and so little that he could do for any of them. It was necessary for him to be available, and to make all those calls at their homes, but I was not to have the idea that he could do anything much to change the course of their illnesses."[8] All that was about to change.

"THE GOLDEN AGE OF MEDICINE"[9]

The earlier films to be discussed were made during a period that Burnham has called "The Golden Age of Medicine" when doctors attained an "admiration for their work that was unprecedented in any age."[9] Public opinion polls from the 1930s to the 1950s consistently ranked physicians among the most highly admired individuals, comparable to or better than Supreme Court justices.[10] As Burnham notes, "Highbrow and mass media commentators alike associated medical practice with the 'miracles' of science and made few adverse comments on the profession."[9] This era of good feeling is captured in Norman Rockwell's *Saturday Evening Post* magazine covers, the Metropolitan Life Insurance Company's pamphlets on health heroes, and a series of prints titled *Great Moments in Medicine* commissioned in the 1950s by Parke Davis Pharmaceuticals for display in doctors' offices.

This tendency for the public to put doctors on a pedestal was in large part due to a remarkable string of scientific breakthroughs. Anesthesia and antisepsis made once-fatal surgeries, like appendectomies and Caesarean sections, routine. The production of antitoxins, antisera, and vaccines (a consuming passion for dedicated researchers in 1930s movies) led to the control of major killers of the young, such as diphtheria, rabies, and tetanus. In 1910, Ehrlich manufactured Salvarsan, an arsenical compound to treat syphilis; this was followed by the introduction of sulfa drugs in the 1930s, penicillin in the 1940s, and other antibiotics in the 1950s. These drugs enabled the conquest of pneumonia, meningitis, strep throat, and ear infections that had claimed the lives of many children or left them ravaged by rheumatic fever, mastoiditis, or permanent retardation.

Banting and Best's discovery of insulin in 1922 saved thousands of young diabetic patients from a premature death. Relatively healthy women who suffered from anemia could be helped by iron, folic acid, and vitamin B_{12}. The ability to transfuse blood, plasma, and blood components rescued patients who otherwise would have died of hemorrhage and blood disorders. Hench's discovery of ACTH in the 1950s and the subsequent development of steroid drugs helped patients with asthma and allergic conditions and especially those with Addison's disease, a deficiency of the adrenal glands that affected John F. Kennedy and may have resulted in Jane Austen's early demise.[11] Salk's and Sabin's vaccines for polio liberated parents from their dread of summer and their children's use of swimming pools. In short, in Burnham's words, "By the 1940s, virtually everyone had heard of miracle drugs and many people knew they owed their lives to them."[9]

As we shall see, movie doctors in the Golden Age were not all paragons; there were arrogant egotists, handsome womanizers, and villains. Still, Malmsheimer estimates that physicians appeared in half of eight hundred films made in 1949 and 1950, with "only twenty-five instances where the doctor was portrayed as a bad person."[12] Thus, the images that predominated in America's psyche were the earnest Doctor Kildare, the kindly Doctor Christian, and the driven scientist, Arrowsmith. Their names were in the titles of their films and the first

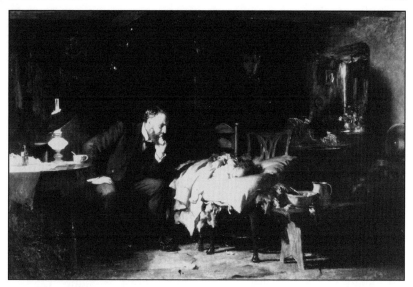

FIGURE 2. *The Doctor*. Sir Luke Fildes's portrait of a kindly doctor helplessly sitting by the bedside of a dying child.

two were easily transposed to the new medium of television where they were joined by such sympathetic figures as Marcus Welby and Ben Casey. The television show *Medic*, based on case histories drawn from the files of the Los Angeles County Medical Association, referred to the doctor as the "guardian of birth, healer of the sick, and comforter of the aged."

"DOING BETTER AND FEELING WORSE"[13]

The second half of the films to be discussed were made during medicine's fall from grace, which was due in large part to its successes.[14] Health status improved greatly, not just for the affluent, but, with the advent of Medicaid and Medicare, for the poor and elderly as well. Fewer families had children with birth defects or the residua of polio that had forged a bond of shared misfortune between young and old, rich and poor. As acute life-threatening diseases declined, they were replaced by chronic diseases less amenable to the administration of a "magic bullet." A generation that hardly knew serious illness came increasingly to view good health as a right rather than a fragile blessing.

At the same time, the bond between patients and their physicians weakened as doctors no longer made house calls or saw patients in their home offices. House calls, which constituted 40 percent of all patient/physician encounters in 1930, fell to 10 percent in 1950 and to

0.6 percent in 1980.[15] By contrast, hospitals, which in the nineteenth century had been avoided as pesthouses for the sick poor, became, with the advent of surgery, a principal venue for medical care.[16] In 1942, very few counties, outside of the Northeast and California, had hospitals (fig. 3) and many 1930s movies showed doctors "fighting the establishment" to get them built. In 1947, enactment of the Hill Burton Act subsidized a hospital building boom that radically changed the medical care landscape and its cost.[17]

Although spectacular health care advances continued, as in the treatment of once fatal leukemias and lymphomas, most of the new developments after 1960 were what Lewis Thomas called "halfway technologies."[18] Such techniques as cardiopulmonary resuscitation, artificial respiration, kidney dialysis, and long-term intravenous feeding, although not curative of the underlying condition, saved many from premature death. However, as intensive care units (ICUs) proliferated and these technologies were more widely applied to prolong the life of the terminally ill,[19] a backlash was created as shown in Sidney Lumet's angry 1997 film, *Critical Care*. He pictures ICUs as places where unscrupulous doctors keep insured terminally ill patients alive on numerous life supports in order to run up exorbitant bills.

The introduction of transplantation made it necessary to define when someone was officially dead in order to harvest viable organs. In 1968, a group at Harvard published elaborate criteria for "brain death"[20, 21] that contrasted sharply with the old movie doctor's use of a mirror held up to the person's mouth to see if it became fogged or simply checking the pulse and respiration. The advent of assisted reproduction, genetic engineering, and the report of sheep cloning have eerily conjured up Aldous Huxley's *Brave New World*.[22] The accumulated societal concerns about these new technologies are reflected in films like *Coma* and *Extreme Measures*, in which unscrupulous doctors and scientists exploit the unwary for scientific fame or profit.

MEDICINE DISORGANIZES
AND DOCTORS GET KNOCKED OFF THE PEDESTAL

At its birth in 1850, the American Medical Association (AMA), representing clinical medicine, was closely tied to the public health and academic medical communities through one of its founders, Oliver Wendell Holmes. William Welch, immortalized in John Singer Sargent's *Four Doctors* (fig. 1), was a president of the AMA as well as a founder of both the medical school and the School of Hygiene and Public Health at Johns Hopkins. As the relationships among these communities weakened in this century, the AMA's physician membership dropped from a

FIGURE 3. Percentage of Counties without Registered General Hospital Facilities in 1942, by State*[17]

State[†]	Percent	State	Percent
Alabama	45	Nebraska	42
Arkansas	56	Nevada	47
Arizona	0	New Hampshire	0
California	18	New Jersey	6
Colorado	46	New Mexico	32
Connecticut	0	New York	2
Delaware	0	North Carolina	31
Florida	42	Ohio	27
Georgia	63	Oklahoma	39
Idaho	45	Oregon	25
Illinois	32	Pennsylvania	15
Indiana	33	Rhode Island	40
Iowa	27	South Carolina	37
Kansas	49	South Dakota	59
Kentucky	71	Tennessee	54
Louisiana	50	Texas	42
Maine	0	Utah	52
Maryland	17	Vermont	8
Michigan	18	Virginia	45
Massachusetts	0	Washington	28
Minnesota	15	West Virginia	38
Mississippi	43	Wisconsin	13
Missouri	63	Wyoming	19
Montana	43		

* Tuberculosis and mental disease hospitals are not included.

† There are no entries for Alaska, Hawaii, North Dakota, and Washington, DC.

Adapted from the Proceedings of the Hearings before the Committee on Education and Labor. U.S. Senate Bill S-191. February and March 1945. Washington, DC: Government Printing Office. Reprinted with permission from Annals of Internal Medicine.

high of 80 percent of American doctors in the 1950s to under 40 percent today. Full-time academic physicians and many subspecialists stopped joining, feeling more kinship with specialty and research organizations. The rift with public health was in part because it emphasized prevention, whereas organized medicine characteristically focused on diagnostic and therapeutic interventions. However, the major point of contention, as Burnham notes,[9] was political and involved the issue of universal health care insurance. Beginning in the 1940s, the AMA, whose early leaders had supported the concept, vigorously opposed what it called "socialized medicine," with considerable help from the growing health insurance industry.

When the AMA agreed to drop its opposition to Medicare and Medicaid in the 1960s, it exacted a promise that the new laws would incorporate its "usual, customary, and reasonable" fee system. This paid disproportionately for hospital visits, surgery, and technologic procedures for treating acute illnesses, as opposed to office visits for maintenance treatment of chronic illnesses or for prevention. The legislation also accommodated hospitals by agreeing to pay all their costs plus 2 percent. This favored the development and use of costly technology and instrumentation in larger and more complex institutions. Medical care, once considered a "cottage industry,"[23] became "corporatized,"[24] or, in the words of Arnold Relman, editor of the prestigious New England Journal of Medicine, a "new medical-industrial complex."[25] No longer could the profession's ethos be set by a Hippocrates, Sir William Osler, or the few distinguished leaders and institutions that dominated it until the 1950s.[26]

Over time, the AMA's public image declined[9] to the point where, in the 1971 film *The Hospital*, it is referred to as the "American Murder Association." During my stint as a health policy fellow in 1977 when a health care cost "crisis" was being proclaimed, some key Congressional staffers were contemptuous of the AMA's views and listened more favorably to representatives of public health and specialty societies. Nothing captures medicine's fragmentation better than the cacophony of voices that purported to speak for doctors during the "health care reform" debate of the 1990s. The endorsement of a physician union by the AMA at its annual meeting in 1999 is not likely to heal the breach or to enhance medicine's status as a profession.

As the new millennium dawns, medical care is in the midst of turbulent cost-cutting changes, with the reigning philosophy being "managed care." Market forces are determining the how, what, where, when, and who of care. In the 1950s, we were taught that the business side of medicine was somehow unseemly; medical students now ignore it at their peril. Medical education and research, once idealized, are now threatened by public indifference and an obsession with the "bottom line."

These changes, which should concern the public, not just the profession, have evolved over decades as we will see in the movies. It will probably take another decade before the smoke clears and the "health care system" is re-humanized. When that happens, my guess is that good doctors will be as essential as ever. The 1998 Academy Award winner, *As Good As It Gets*, which is highly critical of managed care and insurance companies, seems to recognize this.[26] The very professional, gray-haired doctor who makes a home visit to treat an asthmatic child is as positive an image as any movie doctor in "the Golden Age."

Even so, the shattering of the doctor myth has been good for both doctors and patients. The myth set impossible expectations and often led to burnout and disillusionment for those doctors who tried to live up to it. Being available twenty-four hours a day often led physicians in solo practice to neglect their families, their health, and their own needs.[27] The myth also tended to hide what everyone knew, namely, that doctors were like everyone else. Individually and sometimes simultaneously, they could be good and bad, selfish and selfless, greedy and altruistic, competent and incompetent. Another upside is that the emphasis on individual autonomy and personal choice has made today's patients more in charge of their own health care, as they should be.

On the flip side, the loss of respect for medicine bodes ill for doctors and patients alike. Doctor-bashing does little to enhance personal and professional esteem or to engender a sense of trust. The patient/doctor relationship is a covenant,[28] not simply a contract for a technical service. Most doctors strive to do good and avoid harm. They may not always know best, but many know a great deal. In short, there must be what Siegler calls a "patient-physician accommodation."[29] As my wife puts it, she doesn't want to be on a first-name basis with her doctor; she's not looking for a friend. Sure, she wants her physicians to be caring, but she doesn't want them to pretend to feel her pain or say "I know what you're going through." For the most part, doctors are a healthy lot and generally don't know all that their patients are going through until, as in *The Doctor*, they themselves become ill.

Leveling doctors may be seen as democratic, but I have my doubts about the utility of such tactics. I helped found a clinic for Chicano migrant farm workers in 1970,[30] a time when it was the rage for medical students and residents to eschew the white coat and, instead, to dress casually in jeans and an open shirt. One day, a student told me that his appearance was important for the people to feel that he was close to them. The ironic thing was that I, who had come from poverty, had dressed up to care for the migrants and he, who had come from affluence, had consciously dressed down. Unsolicited, the "consejero," the advisor or wise one to whom the community turned for guidance, pointed to the student and said that what he was doing was insulting. "If I had his money and education, I would dress better." He then went on to say that the young man was showing little respect for his patients who expected doctors to look, as well as act, the part.

As doctors have been leveled, their names have been replaced on movie marquees by institutions such as *M*A*S*H* and *The Hospital* and on television by *MASH*, *St. Elsewhere*, *ER*, and *Chicago Hope*, where they have become ensemble players. The notable exception is *Doctor*

Quinn, Medicine Woman, an Old West throwback to Doctors Welby and Kildare, and even her television show got canceled despite a devoted following. The change reflects a societal shift away from the image of righteous professional paragons to a belief that individuals are both flawed and powerless. Notable exceptions are the action heroes portrayed by Eastwood, Willis, and Stallone, who take the law into their own hands using violence rather than laboratories and knowledge to solve mankind's problems.

As noted, the change may be for the better because the portrayals are more honest and less hokey. As a former member of Maryland's board of medical discipline, I can vouch that there are enough scoundrels in the profession to justify the harshest criticism. Still, there is value to the perception of medicine as a noble profession dedicated to the service of others, an ideal that unless reinforced is easily overwhelmed by commercialism and self-interest. People of whom much is expected rise to the occasion, not always, but often. Conversely, those of whom little is expected invariably fail to disappoint.

For this reason, a part of me longs for more uplifting portrayals of doctors, such as in *As Good As It Gets*, recalling the power of movies to convey images that stay with us long after the details fade. You may not remember much from *Shane*, but the young boy's plaintive call for his hero stays with you. The wonderful dynamic between the proud Black worker and the equally proud White mother superior in *Lilies of the Field*, the indomitable Mrs. Miniver, the dedicated Mr. Chips, the majestic Miss Pittman, and the honorable Atticus Finch inspire us and help us dig down for the best that's in us and, as the song says, "hang on." We need to believe that we and the world can be better. With that in mind, don't be surprised if you detect a bias towards medical counterparts of Capra's Mr. Smith and George Bailey, who exhibit the underlying values and verities that continue to ennoble the profession.

Trying to convey the movies' characterizations of patients, doctors, and other caregivers over the years presents many challenges. First and foremost, the book should be interesting and fun. Second, it should be coherent. I have elected to blend a chronologic approach with a thematic perspective. In addition to the usual clichés and stereotypes, societal issues such as racism and sexism will be considered. Indeed, some of the most interesting though lesser known films involve the struggles of women and Blacks in a profession traditionally dominated by White males and now undergoing a remarkable demographic change. Finally, because the few available doctor books have been by or about psychiatrists,[31-34] I have chosen to focus on other specialties of medicine.

It is important to confess that I have not been schooled in film technique or filmography and in this respect I feel more kinship with everyday moviegoers. Furthermore, commenting on movies has been, and still is, a hobby taking a back seat to medicine and my family, who have tolerated my enthusiasm for black-and-white movie hokum. Many readers have told me that this naiveté is a plus. Others may see it as a handicap. To paraphrase the old Romans, "Caveat lector," or let the reader beware. Now, let's go to the movies and have some fun.

NOTES

1. Spears J. Hollywood: The Golden Era. Cranbury, New Jersey: A. S. Barnes & Co, 1971.
2. Helfand WH. A Less than Loving Look at Doctors. In: Encyclopedia Brittanica Medical and Health Annual, 1991, p 22–39.
3. Shaw GB. The Doctor's Dilemma, with preface on doctors. New York: Brentano's, 1909.
4. Holmes OW. Address to the Massachusetts Medical Society (May 30, 1860). In: Bartlett's Familiar Quotations, 12th edition, ed. C Morley and LD Everett, 1951, p 454.
5. Dans PE. Is Alpha Omega Alpha still relevant? The Pharos 1994; 57: 7–10.
6. Ludmerer KM. Time to Heal: American Medical Education from the Turn of the Century to the Era of Managed Care. New York: Oxford University Press, 1999.
7. Ludmerer KM. Learning to Heal: The Development of Medical Education. New York: Basic Books, 1985.
8. Thomas L. The Youngest Science: Notes of a Medicine-Watcher. New York: Viking Press, 1983.
9. Burnham JC. American medicine's golden age: What happened to it? Science 1982; 215: 1474–1479.
10. Gallup GH. The Gallup Poll: Public Opinion, 1935–1971. New York: Random House, 1972, pp 1152 and 1774–1780.
11. Cope Z. Jane Austen's last illness. BMJ 1964; 2: 182–183.
12. Malmsheimer R. Doctors Only: The Evolving Image of the American Physician. New York: Greenwood Press, 1988.
13. Wildavsky A. Doing better and feeling worse: The political pathology of health policy. In : Doing better and feeling worse: Health in the United States. Daedalus 1977; 106: 105-123.
14. Gruenberg EM. The failures of success. Milbank Mem Fund Q Health Soc 1977; 155: 3–24.
15. Meyer GS and Gibbons RV. House calls to the elderly—a vanishing practice. N Engl J Med 1997; 337: 1815–1820.
16. Martensen RL. Hospital hotels and the care of the 'worthy rich." JAMA 1996; 275: 325.
17. Dans PE. Perverse incentives, statesmanship, and the ghosts of reforms past. Ann Intern Med 1993; 118: 227–229.
18. Thomas L. On the science and technology of medicine. Daedalus 1977; 106: 35–46.
19. Hellerstein D. The slow, costly death of Mrs. K—. Harper's 1984; 268: 84–89 (March).
20. Landmark Article Aug 5, 1968: A definition of irreversible coma. The report of the ad hoc committee of the Harvard Medical School to examine the definition of brain death. Reprinted in JAMA 1984; 252: 677–679.

21. Wuermeling HB. A change of heart and a change of mind? Technology and the redefinition of death in 1968. Soc Sci Med 1997; 44: 1465–1482.
22. Huxley A. Brave New World. London, Chatto & Windus: Hogarth Press, 1984.
23. Ramsey P. Ethics of a cottage industry in an age of community and research medicine. N Engl J Med 1971; 284: 700–706.
24. Starr P. The Social Transformation of American Medicine: The Rise of a Sovereign Profession and the Making of a Vast Industry. New York: Basic Books, 1982.
25. Relman AS. The new medical-industrial complex. N Engl J Med 1980; 303: 963–970.
26. Halberstam MJ. The decline and fall of medicine's golden age. Prism 1975; 2: 15–19 (July-August).
27. Martensen RL. On the mortality patterns of physicians. JAMA 1996; 275: 1541.
28. Crawshaw R, Rogers DE, Pellegrino ED, et al. Patient-physician covenant. JAMA 1995; 273: 1553.
29. Siegler M. The physician-patient accommodation: A central event in clinical medicine. Arch Intern Med 1982; 142: 1899–1902.
30. Dans PE and Johnson S. Politics in the development of a migrant health center: A Pilgrim's Progress from idealism to pragmatism. N Engl J Med 1975; 292: 890–895.
31. Fleming M and Manvell R. Images of Madness: The Portrayal of Insanity in the Feature Film. Rutherford, NJ: Associated University Presses, 1985.
32. Gabbard K and Gabbard GO. Psychiatry and the Cinema. Chicago; University of Chicago Press, 1987.
33. Schneider I. The theory and practice of movie psychiatry. Am J Psychiatry 1987; 144: 996–1002.
34. Shortland M. Screen memories: Towards a history of psychiatry and psychoanalysis in the movies. BJHS 1987; 20: 421–452.

1

Hollywood Goes To Medical School

There is no film comparable to *The Paper Chase* for portraying what it takes to become a doctor. In the few that do focus on under-graduate medical education, students are portrayed as hard-working and serious, boisterous and frisky, or cynical and "on-the-make." In early films, they appear destined to marry a nurse or a rich patient, if they marry at all. They spend a lot of time discussing their career objectives which seem to be in descending order of merit: (a) driven scientist search-ing for "The Cure" for cancer; (b) kindly impoverished country doctor; (c) public health hero; (d) rich surgeon or highly-paid specialist tooling about in a fancy convertible. The films generally focus either on techno-logic symbols or on extracurricular activities, probably because the reality of medical education is fairly mundane. The tremendous advances in medicine in the last six decades are reflected in the changes seen in medi-cal school props from the ubiquitous skeleton in the early films to first-year students exploring the limits of cardiac resuscitation in a re-cent film.

As Ludmerer points out,[1] the majority of students through the early 1950s were unmarried White males whose lives revolved around school and competing for coveted internships. Many joined fraternities where adolescent hijinks relieved stress. Ludmerer quotes a faculty member as saying that, in order to master an ever-expanding curriculum, stu-dents were expected "to fit 25 hours into a 24-hour day."[1] Failing to cope with stress or to pass muster was considered to be the individual's failing. By the 1960s, changes were beginning to be seen. Over half of graduating students were married. Many lived off-campus and spent considerable time away from the academic center during their clinical years. Medical school classes became less homogeneous in the 1950s as barriers to the entry[1-5] of Jews and Catholics (especially those of Italian descent[3]) began to be lifted, followed in the 1970s by the dismantling of quotas against women, Blacks, and other minorities. To cope with the stress of medical school, students no longer relied solely on their peers; for example, by 1966, 30 percent of Harvard's first-year class were seeking psychiatric help. Many educators began to point a finger at the environment as being unnecessarily stressful. As the cost of tuition skyrocketed, there were demands for increased financial aid. Over time, a relatively placid, cohesive, and regimented community became more turbulent, diverse, and individualistic.

This progression toward turbulence and diversity and the societal changes that prompted it are visible in the movies to be discussed in this chapter. The earliest students are portrayed as naifs. Philip Carey in 1934's *Of Human Bondage* is sensitive to the point of weakness and is ashamed of being a "cripple." "Pug" Prentiss in 1945's *Miss Susie Slagle's* is an awestruck and insecure lad who earned his medical school tuition working in a lumber mill. He and his cohorts are respectful to their professors and to the rules established by their landlady and surrogate mother. They relieve their stress with practical jokes and lab alcohol. The earnest and likable student in 1954's *Doctor in the House* with the rather meek-sounding name, Simon Sparrow, joins his peers in chasing student nurses and hanging out in the local pub. By contrast, 1955's *Not As a Stranger* features Luke Marsh, who is all business. While still an idealist, he is cocky enough to challenge the chief of surgery and not above marrying a nurse he doesn't love to get his tuition paid. Fast forward to 1989's *Gross Anatomy* and we meet Joe Slovak, who drives up to his interview in his father's fish delivery truck and proceeds to demonstrate to one and all that he is God's gift to the world. He berates the deans when they expel his roommate for cheating and generally acts like a self-righteous horse's tail. The championship for insufferable self-righteousness goes, however, to the lead character in 1998's *Patch Adams*, a so-called "true story."

In *Miss Susie*, medical students are "medical monks" forbidden to socialize with nurses or to marry before they complete training. Their "aw-shucks" behavior contrasts sharply with the 1992 *Flatliners* student who is engaged to one girl while secretly videotaping steamy sexual escapades with any girl who falls for his line. Later movies also reflect the slowly changing gender and racial composition. Nurses and nursing students are replaced as objects of affection by other medical students or those outside the profession, but not the rich socialites of the 1930s films. This transformation from naive idealists to street-wise cynics is due more to enormous societal changes and the removal of the movies' censorship code than any shift in Hollywood's attitude towards medicine. The enormity of the change in screen persona will be obvious as we progress from the earliest films through *Gross Anatomy*, *Flatliners*, and *Patch Adams*.

Of Human Bondage (1934)

The first of three adaptations of Somerset Maugham's book, this film's reputation as a "classic" rests largely on Bette Davis' breakthrough performance as a tough Cockney tart, Mildred Rogers, who captures the heart of doctor's son Philip Carey. Carey has just returned to London to attend medical school after a brief fling as a struggling and mediocre artist. He reasons that, "If one can't be great, one can at least be of some use to people." Leslie Howard plays Carey with a weak and effete persona that worked well in *The Scarlet Pimpernel* and in *Gone with the Wind*, but is hard to take here.

Philip, who undoubtedly saw George Bernard Shaw's *Pygmalion* once too often, is intent on remaking Mildred. With characteristic Leslie Howard gentility, he delivers such lines as, "You have a lovely smile; you ought to use it more often." Mildred repays Philip's doting attention by laughing at his "hang-dog" manner and marrying a worldly salesman (Alan Hale). When a pregnant Mildred returns after her husband kicks her out, Carey tells his friends that he wants to marry her, mainly to give the child a name. Griffiths (Reginald Denny), Philip's fellow student and best pal, asks, "What kind of a practice can you have with a wife like that?" Later he himself has an affair with Mildred. The relationship really goes south when Carey refuses to have sex with Mildred (a good call, as she later turns out to have syphilis in the book, but tuberculosis in the film[6]) (fig. 1). Philip's refusal to have sex with her elicits what would become classic "Bette Davis" venom when she screams at him: "You dirty swine! I never cared for you! Not once! I was always making a fool of you! You bored me stiff! I hated you! It made me sick when I had to let you kiss me! I only did it because you begged me! You hounded me! You drove me crazy! And after you kissed me, I wiped my mouth. WIPED MY MOUTH!" If it were a play, the scene would be a showstopper.

In the 1950s remake starring Kim Novak as Mildred and Laurence Harvey as Philip, the same scene is much sexier but less dramatic. In that one, Mildred coos at Philip as the camera lingers on a nude picture of Novak. She then retreats to her bedroom and positions herself seductively in a state of *dishabille* before summoning Philip. His response is: "You disgust me!" I'm sure some viewers disagreed.

FIGURE 1. *Of Human Bondage.* Medical student Philip Carey (Leslie Howard), studying in his suit and tie, refuses to abandon his books to accompany Mildred Rogers (Bette Davis) to bed.

Philip spends very little time studying, so the medical school visuals are few. The old standby human skeleton makes an appearance, accompanied by a rather saucy line for the time, as one student says it's a woman because, "you can tell by the pelvis." All the students are old White males; indeed, Reginald Denny looks like he should be on the faculty. The major medical theme, Carey's clubfoot and limp, reminds us of how something that can be easily repaired today was catastrophic only a few generations ago. There's a scene in which a boy with a club foot is examined by a particularly insensitive instructor, Doctor Jacobs (Desmond Roberts). As the students crowd around Jacobs, he singles out Carey to examine the boy because he "is particularly suited to do so." The boy tells Carey that he finds his clubfoot to be "no trouble." Carey says, "That's wonderful. I always did." The boy replies, "That's because you let them go on at you." (Out of the mouths of babes). Impatiently, Jacobs intervenes and declares that the boy's foot is "one of the less interesting examples." After asking Carey to take off his socks, he says patronizingly, "He keeps his feet nice and clean. Hmm, pelipes equinus, interesting example, I must say, of congenital clubfoot." This is just what Carey needs to bolster his self image, after being told by Mildred that she "could never love a cripple."

Carey's recurring dream is to be able to dance gracefully. To Norah (Kay Johnson), the wealthy and cultured woman who loves him, he whines, "If only I could take you dancing!" "Stop thinking about your feet," she replies. Meanwhile, Carey manages to neglect his studies, to get thrown out of school (after Mildred, in a fit of pique, burns the bonds he needed for his tuition), and to turn his back on Norah and a second love, Sally (Frances Dee). Before leaving school, the head doctor convinces him to get his feet operated on.

In short, this is soap opera with medical student as good-hearted, spineless chump. Fortunately for us and him, Sally rescues him after he gets thrown out of his apartment, and he completes his studies. When Mildred, who keeps turning up like a bad penny, dies, our hero is freed (we think) to be happy. Still, having seen what a twit he has been through most of the film, I wouldn't bet the ranch on it.

Miss Susie Slagle's (1945)

Produced by John Houseman and based on Augusta Tucker's 1939 novel, the film is a period piece about a boardinghouse where Miss Susie (Lillian Gish) acts *in loco parentis* to Johns Hopkins Medical School students. It reflects a time when almost all doctors were men; all nurses were women; and most servants in the very southern town of Baltimore were Black. As an aside, segregation persisted at Johns Hopkins Hospital until 1960 when separate wards for Blacks and Whites were abolished; the first Black student didn't graduate from Johns Hopkins Medical School until 1967.

The film opens as Pug Prentiss (Sonny Tufts), fresh from his train trip and full of naiveté and a sense of wonder, knocks on a door asking, "Is this Miss Susie Slagle's?" Hizer, the "Negro" butler (J. Louis Johnson), responds: "Shore is. Step right in, Doctor." Pointing to photos of previous residents, he says, "I called them all 'Doctor' when they first came and when they left, too. Some were wild; some wasn't. Some were smart; some wasn't. In the end, they were all doctors and good ones, too." Pug is escorted to his room where he sees a heart over his bed, drawn by someone who is now "a big heart man." Hizer says that he was "the roughest talking boy, now he's wearing spats and riding around in a big limousine." Moving to the window, Pug views the school's dome. This prompts the following exchange: Hizer: "You've wanted to come here a long time." Pug: "How did you know?" Hizer: "The way you looked at it." Parenthetically, although the dome is meant to signify Hopkins, the institution refused to let its name be used in the film, reportedly because the script was not altered sufficiently to meet its demands.

Miss Susie's rules and philosophy are simple: "At no time smoke in bed." "It's a stag house." "None of my boys have ever failed" (fig. 2). The student group includes Silas Holmes (Lloyd Bridges), the son of a former resident of Miss Susie's; Bert Riggs (Pat Phelan), a missioner's son from China; a Jewish student, Irving Asrom (Michael Sage), who doesn't figure much in the story; and Pug, the All-American boy. They are joined by the son of the physician-in-chief and professor of medicine, Elijah Howe, Jr. (Bill Edwards). After failing his exams, Junior tells his father, "You've wanted me to be a doctor since I was five. I'm getting out of medicine and out of your shadow." Fortunately Pug takes him to Miss. S, who makes him one of her "boys." She sends up warm milk and orders him to bed when he threatens to pull an "all-nighter"— try that trick on a medical student today! The next day, with his father hovering in the background, he passes his orals by throwing around a lot of medical terms, such as "cirrhosis."

The picture is "corny," reflecting the deferred adolescent status that characterized most medical students at the time. The antics are rather innocent, such as references to drinking "C_2H_5OH," a pretty snappy name for alcohol in those days. Even the faculty members act like adolescents when they hide the mint juleps from Miss Susie at an

FIGURE 2. *Miss Susie Slagle's.* Miss Susie (Lillian Gish) poses proudly with her "boys" and her butler, Hizer (J. Louis Johnson), on the medical school graduation day.

Easter celebration and then play along when she offers them sherry in what is supposed to be an alcohol-free house. While the mandatory skeleton is visible (it must be a male since it sports a derby), the principal prop is "Little Elize," an anatomic specimen over the bathtub with whom all students fall in love permanently. Billy De Wolfe, who plays third-year man Ben Mead and provides the requisite comic relief, tells the students: "From now on when you look at a woman that's what you'll see—a heart, kidney, spleen, blood vessels, a tibia, a fibula." Later, the students and faculty alumni of Miss Susie's sing of Little Elize's "thoracic aorta, brachial plexus and all."

The main roles for women in this movie involve becoming nurses and marrying doctors. Margaretta Howe (Joan Caulfield) tells Pug that her mother was "a perfect doctor's wife." He asks: "That's what you want to be?" When she answers "yes," he says "Listen, lady, I'm just a poor medical student." "That's OK," she says, "that's how all doctors begin. I'm young, I'll wait." Later, on their way to a medical school fancy dress ball, Margaretta asks her father if it's all right to kiss a boy. He answers, "Kisses are to love what thermometers are to a fever. You can't tell how bad you have it without them." Then he adds, "Like thermometers, if you use them too much they tend to become inaccurate." The other romance is between nursing student, Nan Rogers (Veronica Lake) and Bert, the missionary. Nursing and medical students are strictly forbidden to "fraternize," so they meet secretly and plan to go off to China together where she will take care of him as well as do the nursing.

Women medical students are relegated to two brief walk-ons; in one scene a "full of himself" first-year man tries to impress a dance partner, who turns out to be a fourth-year medical student. The irony of their relative invisibility is that Johns Hopkins Medical School was able to be opened in 1893 only because Mary Garrett, daughter of the owner of the Baltimore and Ohio Railroad, donated the necessary money, under the stipulation that women had to be admitted. Their numbers varied from 1 percent to almost 20 percent of the class until the 1970s when the proportion began to climb to its current level of about 45 percent.

In contrast to *Of Human Bondage*, this picture does emphasize hard work and sacrifice in medical school and beyond. Mead shudders as he tells the new arrivals: "When I think of what's ahead of you—Anatomy, Pathology, Histology, Neurology, Pharmacology, Physiological Chemistry." Later, a student grouses: "When do they expect us to sleep?" The answer is: "They don't." One doctor's son reflects: "My father died of a bad heart. He didn't have a vacation in twelve years." Another theme is the crisis in confidence that many students endure. In the old-time surgical amphitheater, Pug and his cohorts watch as Dr. Fletcher (Morris Carnovsky), described as the best surgeon in the country who makes a quarter of a million," removes a gall bladder. When the patient's pulse increases and the blood pressure falls, Pug runs out. Later, he tells a fellow student, "It's pretty bad for a doctor—to be afraid." The student tells Pug a story about Dr. Fletcher taking a piece of steel out of a young man's heart, and asks: "Don't you think he was afraid? It just made him stronger." PS: Both patients survived.

Pug's final crisis of confidence occurs after Bert gets diphtheria. As Pug sits by him, Bert feels his pulse slowing and realizes that his heart is affected. He tells Pug, "You know what that means. You saw that diphtheria heart in the lab. Nobody can live with it." Pug runs out again and his friend dies asking for him. Afterwards, the hospital director presses the fourth-year students into service because there are eight new cases of diphtheria among members of the staff. This reminds us that doctors regularly contracted illnesses to which they were exposed in the line of duty. Miss Susie tells the recalcitrant Pug: "A doctor can't accept or refuse calls depending upon his moods." After agreeing to deliver a baby, he makes a house call where the husband tells him: "I did everything they told me at the clinic. I got the water boiling." When the baby's heart slows, Pug is again ready to bolt, but the mother urges him on. Finally, he tells Nurse Rogers, "Prepare for an emergency operation. Get the father in here so he can give the anesthetic." As they leave in the buggy with the baby crying in the distance, Rogers says, "You're going to be a fine doctor," and he replies, "You're going to be a fine nurse." Naturally, he interns with Fletcher and the movie comes full circle with a new arrival asking: "Is this Miss Susie Slagle's?" and Hizer responding: "It shore is. Step right in, Doctor."

Doctor in the House (1954)

Though not strictly a Hollywood film, this J. Arthur Rank production deserves comment. A lighthearted comedy about a group of medical students at St. Swithin's in London, it's more sophisticated than *Miss Susie Slagle's*, but just about as innocent. Drawn from all parts of the United Kingdom, the class has Blacks, East Indians, and women, but the student protagonists are all White males. Kenneth More is superb as Grimsdyke, a fun-loving student who finds creative ways to fail so as not to lose the one thousand pound allowance contingent on his remaining in medical school. He is balanced by the earnest and naive Simon Sparrow, played by Dirk Bogarde. Grimsdyke, who deigns to make an appearance at the dean's welcoming lecture and proceeds to read the newspaper, reminded me of a fellow medical student from Harvard who read the *New York Times* rather obviously during lectures.

The dean (Geoffrey Keen) quotes Dickens to the effect that "medical students are a parcel of lazy, idle fellows who smoke, drink and lounge about." He tells them: "The nurses are here for the comfort of the patients, not yours." However, these students don't live up to this stereotype. They load up on heavy books and the requisite human skeleton, which Simon manages to have come apart on the bus. They practice on roommates to locate the retina and the eardrum as well as play rugby and carouse a bit after a win. The nursing school matron is determined to enforce the strict rules of separation between the rambunctious medical students and her charges. When the inevitable breaches occur, the students are defended by the influential Harley Street surgeon, Sir Lancelot Sprat, delightfully played by James Robertson Justice who continued to liven up the sequels such as *Doctor at Sea*. Sir Lancelot supports Sparrow after he is found in the nurses' residence, saying, "Medical students are medical students, you can't expect them to be choir boys!"

Bogarde, who also continued in the series, played the character with whom I most identified. Unsure of himself, bumbling at times (fig. 3), but sincere in his desire to help, he provides a nice touch of warmth to

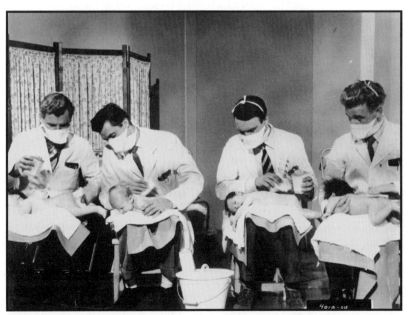

FIGURE 3. *Doctor in the House*. Medical students are introduced to pediatrics by powdering babies' bottoms.

the romp. Just before their first venture out on the wards, one student asks a classmate the proverbial question: "Do you think they'll know we never examined a patient before?" "No, they'll think we're doctors" is the response. Of course, the patients know they are students and are not above having some sport with them. The most poignant scene occurs when Simon succeeds without a midwife's help in his first delivery, while the assistant is "boiling the water." He discounts his responsibility for the successful delivery, but diffidently accepts the mother's decision to name the child after him. She says: "It must be wonderful to be a doctor." He replies, "Yes, it must." As he leaves, Simon projects that feeling of satisfaction all of us have felt when we seemed to have made a difference, a feeling that obliterates all sense of fatigue.

Not As a Stranger (1955)

If I had to choose only one film for a seminar on movies and medicine, this would be it. Based on a best-selling book by Morton Thompson,[7] the film follows idealistic and egomaniacal Luke Marsh (Robert Mitchum) from hotshot first-year student to dedicated country doctor obsessed with stamping out disease and medical errors. Stanley Kramer, in his directorial debut, manages to cram in enough doctor clichés, scientific jargon, and patients to justify a moviegoer's expectation of credit towards a medical degree. The medical advisor, Morton Maxwell, M.D., is undoubtedly responsible. Mitchum demonstrates a gamut of emotions ranging from stolid to impassive. Olivia De Havilland seems out of place with a fake Minnesota Swedish accent and dyed blond hair that clashes with her brunette eyelashes. Still, there are so many good lines that the film fits into the category of being so bad, it is good.

The movie opens with a body being wheeled into anatomy class. Dr. Aarons (Broderick Crawford) makes a speech about how medical students traditionally believe that joking about death makes it easier (fig. 4). He says there is nothing funny about death either in the abstract or in particular, noting that seven hours ago the body lying before them housed a human soul. "You are about to violate it," he says, "and when you do, you will help yourself immeasurably as physicians and healers if you do so tenderly and with love." He then follows the "method of Rokitansky" and makes a cruciate incision and, on cue, a medical student faints.

Lee Marvin (Brundage) and Frank Sinatra (Boone) play Luke's classmates. When Luke passes on the nurses' party, Brundage asks "what's he do for kicks?" "He wants to be a doctor," says Boone. "So what, do we want to be house painters?" Brundage replies. "He wants it more," says Boone. Later, Luke learns that his father Job (another biblical reference) has spent Luke's maternal inheritance, intended for his education, on booze. Job (Lon Chaney, Jr.) tells his son, who has wanted to be doctor since he was a kid, that he won't make it anyway, "Something was left out of you. It isn't enough to have a brain; you have to have a heart."

Faced with dropping out, he petitions Dr. Aarons for money and is told that Aarons had it worse. "You're not a Jew. I'm part of the 5 percent they let in because they were ashamed to keep us out entirely." After being casually introduced, this heavy issue is never heard from again. Aarons gives Luke seventy-five dollars and advises him to get the rest by telling "the bursar you're going to hold up a gas station. Pull out all the stops. Lie to them." This is followed by one of the movie's best lines when the bursar tells him: "This isn't a state institution. We have to be

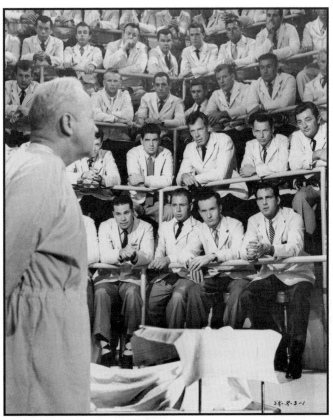

FIGURE 4. *Not As a Stranger*. Brundage (Lee Marvin), Boone (Frank Sinatra), and Marsh (Robert Mitchum) listen attentively to Dr. Aarons (Broderick Crawford) as he begins the gross anatomy course in the first-year amphitheater.

business-like about this." In the absence of a student loan program, Luke turns to the Yellow Pages for financial help and comes up empty.

Enter De Havilland as Kristina Hedvigson, who, Luke learns, has a three thousand dollar bank account. She wonders what he sees in her since she's not "sexy" like her fellow nurses. We know why, and she seems to, as well, when she says, "He wants to be a doctor. Everything is nothing after that. Maybe that's why I love him." When he tells his roommate of his marriage plans, Boone says (as only Sinatra could), "You're marrying Hedvigson, the OR [operating room] nurse? This is not the kind of dame you marry. A doctor's wife gets him patients, she went to the right schools, her folks belong to the right country club. She's charming. She was brought up that way. This dame oughtta marry a farmer." Luke and Boone end up in a pathetic fight, after Boone delivers a devastating indictment, "You know what kills me about you idealists is just how far you'll go. I'm supposed to be a cynic, but I could never do anything like this." He gets Luke to admit he doesn't love Kristina, but Luke says, "She'll never know." After the fight, though, Boone agrees to be his best man.

Back in school, Luke attends Aarons' lecture on the dangers of leukoplakia. When Boone loudly whispers, "Relax, they only expect you to learn 70 percent," an angry Aarons asks him to pick a page in the text and proceeds to recite verbatim the entry on the abducens nerve. Then he tells them, "To graduate, you will memorize fifteen thousand pages just like that" and adds ominously, "A doctor is memory. Those who succeed in this course will become members of the only group in society that is allowed to commit manslaughter with immunity from the law." Boone, the saving grace in this melodrama, asks: "Anybody for law school?"

Whereas Luke's concern about money is related to getting through school because he plans to be a family doctor, the others are more pragmatic. One student envies the Bentley owned by Dietrich, the chief of surgery. They discuss the pros and cons of dermatology (patients never die, never get well, and never get you up at night, but don't pay); obstetrics (patients pay, but get you up at night), etc. Brundage then says, "Lets join Dr. Kildare (referring to Luke) in surgery," where medical error and judgment are dealt with in a preposterous manner. Dietrich is directing a resident to sew up a patient following a gastrectomy for an ulcer. He tells the students, "Note that Dr. Radcliffe will suture with extreme care. This is a ward patient. There's no charge, of course. I get as much as a thousand dollars for this operation. For that kind of money, the patient is entitled to a handsome scar."

Luke, a second-year student by now, notes that Dietrich has failed to sever the vagus nerve. Unable to hold his tongue in front of the whole class, Luke refers to a recently published study that vagotomy lowers the rate of recurrent ulcers and then implies that more recurrences mean more surgeries. Later, he comments self-righteously, "Money, that's all they care about—all of them." His mentor Aarons urges him to apologize or Dietrich will ruin him and he won't be able to intern at University Hospital. His wife adds: "I'm in the operating room every day of my life. Sometimes I see things that make me want to scream. You expect too much. A doctor is like everybody else." Luke responds, "A doctor is not like anybody else. He deals in human lives. You're not too stupid to understand that! When a doctor makes a mistake, he must be stopped." Luke finally apologizes and is told by Dietrich, "We all make mistakes," something Luke clearly does not believe.

On to internship where the service chief wisely warns them, "Make friends with the nurses, they run the hospital." Today, that might be changed to "Listen to the administrators." There is an unbelievable scene at the nurse's station where Luke accuses Boone of casually removing a patient's mole and risking the release of cancer cells into the bloodstream rather than having it done in the operating room. Marsh is so sure it's a melanoma, he's ready to report his friend without even looking at the pathological specimen. He also attacks his wife for defending Boone and is told, "There are two people in the world who care about you, and that's one of them." People would be entirely justified coming away from this film thinking that being a dedicated physician is synonymous with being egomaniacal, manipulative, self-righteous, and friendless.

Aarons sends them on their way after internship with an intriguing line: "You're practicing physicians now....Don't endorse any cigarettes," the screenwriter's reference to a time when doctors were shown in cigarette ads. Later, Aarons discusses his protege's decision to practice in Greenville, which he calls "Hicksville" where "they never saw a thousand dollar bill. There are country roads and an old Ford for an ambulance, except it isn't an ambulance, it's a white horse and you're St. George, complete with spotless armor. You get to a farmhouse. There's a man bleeding to death. Alone with no instruments, you perform an impossible operation. Because your heart is pure, he is saved. Well, you're going to go down that road and what you'll find is a man with a boil on his backside. You'll lance it and go home." As Luke turns to leave, Aarons calls him one of his most brilliant students and says he'll be a great doctor, "but stop living your life like a Greek tragedy or you'll miss out."

The rest of the film goes on to devote considerable screen time to feeding the myth of the superhuman country doctor (see chapter 2). Following internship, Luke joins an old-fashioned, hard-working, small-town doctor, Dr. Runkleman (Charles Bickford). They remove open safety pins from the stomach, incise ingrown toenails, take out adenoids, treat "cardiacs," deliver hundreds of babies, lance boils, and repair aortic aneurysms. Dr. Runkleman tells Luke, "If they have a pain, treat it. If they think they have a pain, treat the pain they think they have. You can't practice medicine. You have to treat people." They don't get paid in money, but in trade. Luke passes out after seeing two hundred patients in a week. Although he's worried that some patient won't get enough attention, he doesn't seem concerned about neglecting his wife Kris. He's seldom home and when he is, he's barely awake, so she can't even find time to tell him she's pregnant, but he didn't want a family anyway. After learning of his affair with the local rich playgirl (Gloria Grahame), Kris finally "throws the bum out."

The film's early focus on medical error continues when an inept anesthetist almost loses a patient by letting a pentothal drip run too fast and during the subsequent intubation the patient develops laryngospasm. Luke saves the day by deftly injecting curare to reverse it. The anesthetist, Dr. Snider (Myron McCormick), is the head of the hospital and known to be incompetent. However, he's a political appointee, so the other doctors just keep an eye on him. A nurse shows Luke "a terminal pneumonia" patient on whom Snider has left no orders, saying, "When the time comes, Doctor lets the old ones cross over peacefully. This one won't last until morning." This scene has particular resonance today. Snider is incompetent, so his judgments about who can be helped and who cannot are suspect. The patient actually has a treatable condition. Luke detects a typhoid rash and isolates the patient. The patient is in shock and the hospital is so poorly equipped that they don't "even have shock blocks to raise the foot of the bed." Luke relies on levophed, an oxygen tent, pumping the patient's abdomen, and the then new antibiotic chloromycetin to save the patient. He then organizes a community-wide immunization campaign.

His triumph sets up the conclusion. Earlier, Luke had diagnosed an aortic aneurysm by examining Runkleman's chest, but his recommendation of elective surgery was refused. When Runkleman's aneurysm begins to rupture, Luke performs emergency surgery with the aid of a new "cathode ray tube oscillograph." He stops the leak but then tries to get too fine and ignores Snider's warning to leave well enough alone and to close up. As he tries to "wrap the aorta," it ruptures and his partner bleeds to death, despite a long resuscitation attempt. Luke over-reached and as he leaves the operating room in tears, Snider says "God help him, he made a mistake." He returns home distraught, calling to his wife, "Kris, help me. For God's sake, help me." The music comes up and curtain comes down.

The movie's title is hard to fathom even after knowing that it comes from the Book of Job 19:25: "But as for me, I know that my Redeemer liveth, and at the last, he will stand upon the earth, and though worms shall devour my flesh, and bones be as dust, yet shall I see God, whom I shall see for myself, and mine eyes shall behold Him, and not as a stranger."[7]

The focus in the 1960s and 1970s doctor films moved away from medical school to internship (see chapter 3). When Hollywood turned back to undergraduate education in the 1980s and early 1990s, it was for a harder-edged and even more cynical approach. The 1985 film, *Bad Medicine*, is the worst of this undistinguished lot and is only worth a brief mention. It stars Steve Guttenberg as the last in his family's line of doctors who is being forced into medicine against his will and does poorly enough in college to be rejected by all domestic medical schools. He goes to a fly-by-night offshore school whose dean is played by another wasted talent, Alan Arkin. Gross, unfunny, and studded with ethnic stereotyping, it represents one of the low points in the medical genre. The next film, while also characterized by a knowing smart-aleckiness, is a cut above.

Gross Anatomy (1989)

In this film, entirely devoted to first-year medical students who meet around the cadaver, few of the old stereotypes are recognizable. Gone are the innocent idealists working hard to reach a goal respected by society or the students mesmerized by the flashy cars. They have been replaced by different archetypes. There's Joe Slovak (Matthew Modine), the handsome wisecracking jock who covers his caring side with a street-wise cynicism. There is a know-it-all doctor's son, Miles Reed (John Scott Clough), an arrogant and sycophantic grade-grubber, not someone as in *Miss Susie's*, trapped in his father's shadow. There's the nervous nebbish, David Schreiner (Todd Field), who studies inces-santly. More importantly, there are two women. One is a self-assured surgeon's daughter, Laurie Rorbach (Daphne Zuniga), who seems to have it all together. The other is an Asian-American, Kim McCauley (Alice Carter), again reflecting this group's substantial presence in today's classes. She is married to a man who clearly is not happy about all her studying and who wants her to stay home and have a lot of children! She becomes pregnant for her second child, but continues to come to anatomy lab using a gas mask to protect the baby.

There are no nurses cavorting with students; instead, now that the percentage of women in entering classes is over 40 percent, medical students date one another or hang out at bars where "telephone sales agents" are all over the male medical students. Sloppiness is tolerated, although the two obsessive-compulsive grinds are neat-niks. There seems to be a test a minute with a heavy emphasis on grades, something that was not as prominent in the 1950s when we weren't told our grades unless we were in trouble and didn't have access to them. A 1970 law changed all that. Many schools still try to minimize grade anxiety by using a pass/fail system for all or part of the curriculum, but everyone knows he or she will be rated and ranked for those highly sought-after residency slots.

The pride and joy of a blue-collar family, Slovak drives up for his medical school interview in the family's fish delivery truck. He even leaves his "interview suit" at home, opting for more casual clothes. Slouching in the chair with a cocky air, he seems to be saying: "Hit me with your best shot." When asked why he wants to be a doctor, he first says the obligatory "I want to help people." Later, when urged to be honest, he smilingly declares, "I want to make lots of money," a Hollywood staple that may have to be jettisoned in the managed care era. Being a stud, he wants to be a gynecologist. His response to the question, "What would your college professor say about you?" is "the most brilliant student I ever had. I didn't teach him anything; he taught me." No self-respecting admissions committee would let this smart-aleck in, but then again, the moviemakers may have caught it right, in that some students may actually harbor such thoughts, while they mouth the expected platitudes.

The orientation lecture by the associate dean for students and gross anatomy professor Dr. Rachel Woodruff (Christine Lahti) provides an interesting contrast to the other films. Slovak comes in late and makes a maximum amount of noise, a "notice me, notice me" routine that becomes increasingly wearing as the film proceeds (fig. 5). If the medical students in *Not As a Stranger* thought they had it bad with their need to memorize fifteen thousand pages to get through, they should be glad they are not in this school. The dean tells the class that just in the next eight months "you will be required to memorize six thousand anatomical structures, read twenty-five thousand pages of text, attend two hundred lectures, and pass or fail forty examinations." How's that for upping the ante!

FIGURE 5. *Gross Anatomy.* Hotshot first-year student Joe Slovak (Matthew Modine) treats Dean Rachel Woodruff (Christine Lahti) to one of his smart remarks while his cadaver-mates watch.

She asks them to look to the left and the right and to be aware that one of their neighbors won't be back. This is a gross exaggeration. In my experience at four different medical schools, especially as the threat of litigation became greater, almost all graduated, even though a few students were skywriting that they shouldn't be doctors. Woodruff gives the students the option to check out right there and then, and when no one does, she sends them on their way with the cheery thought that they are committing themselves to a "profession with the highest rates of suicide, alcoholism, divorce, and drug addiction." While I am not sure this is completely true, it is sufficiently important to be dealt with preventively, as some of us have tried to do, and not simply, as a throwaway line. Then again, no other medical student film has even raised it.

Not surprisingly, the focus of the film is on gross anatomy, called "the thing you have dreaded most since acceptance" (really?), and the "centerpiece of the first year" (true in my time, but less true now when students in some schools can attend a simulated anatomy lab). Having spotted the lovely Laurie during orientation, Joe maneuvers to get assigned to her table by saying he can't dissect a female cadaver, because his mother just died (not true and raising questions about his integrity). Joe assumes Laurie's surgeon parent is her father (wrongo!, it's Mom). She jogs; he plays basketball. She avoids him until a study session in the motel where, after telling him that she has wanted to go to medical school ever since she can remember and that it is not a game for her, she succumbs to his charms such as they are. This leads to a poor excuse for an up-and-down romance that parallels the ups and downs of Joe's school year.

Miles Reed stakes his claim to being obnoxious student numero uno with smug lines like, "I've seen dead bodies before, lots of them; my father's a heart specialist." His specialty is, in the current parlance, "sucking up" to the teachers, or as he puts it: "Some people call it asskissing; I call it politics." The prototypic student concerned about appearances, he tells Joe that he's applying for a job as an orderly in the hospital in order to stand out among the 140 students. His cardiologist father told him: "Hold your nose and do it. It looks great on your resumé." This concern with resumé-building captures this era well, when what you say you did and how you say it seem more important than what you did and who you really are. Joe becomes an orderly, too, but for the money. This allows the filmmaker to inject the "blood and guts," "slam-bang" shouting and stretcher-running emergency room atmosphere, so popular now. While it may be exciting and has more dramatic film and television values, it tends to suggest that real doctors are those who react to emergencies, often involving violence and neglect of health. Cutting and reconstructing are more important than the anticipating, preventing, or quietly healing.

David, his worried roommate, estimates that they will actually need to read thirty-five hundred pages a week and is already studying before orientation. He records the lectures (not so possible in my time, but standard now with note-taking cooperatives). He regiments his studying and sleeping, but has to resort to taking amphetamines and cheating on exams, an important issue[8] that we haven't seen alluded to before. On David's dismissal, Joe treats us to one of his very self-righteous and public outbursts against the faculty. He then decides to check out of school, telling Laurie, "The truth is I really don't care about medicine. You do. Miles does. Why put up with all the bullshit!" So much for pathetic rationalization.

Joe's relationship with Dean Woodruff is a rather strange one. He sits on her desk and riffles through her charts. She gives him a chart to research and this first-year student makes the diagnosis of late-stage lupus. When she asks him what he would tell the patient, he says, "I'd say, 'Goodbye. Shit happens!'" This is probably the most asinine scene and epitomizes a 180-degree shift from the compassionate portrayals of medical students in the past. Later, on learning that the dean is terminally ill, Joe realizes that it was her chart that he was studying.

How patient identity and a diagnosis could be so masked is beyond me. We are also asked to ignore the fact that the chart was sitting on her desk. He confronts the dying dean in her home, and she puts up with his self-important and self-righteous nonsense, because she has tagged him as potential superstar. Instead of laying this jerk out, she blames herself, "I try to turn my best students into perfect doctors. I expect them to be more than human. They turn out to have minds for medicine and hearts for real estate. What would they say to one of their terrified patients who says, 'explain this to me, stay with me so I won't be so alone.' I didn't teach them that. People need healers." This is a pretty devastating indictment of medicine and of medical school faculty. While largely inaccurate, it represents what some of the public perceive—or at least the writers of this script—and as such must be reckoned with.

Commenting that she and Joe are too smart for their own good (an accurate diagnosis), Dean Woodruff tells him, "I want you to be better than you want yourself to be. I can't tell you how to be it." Joe waltzes back to school and into Laurie's arms. He manages to deliver their classmate's baby on the counter of a remote diner; yes, someone shouts "boil the water." This results in an epiphany about his desire to become a doctor, and he rushes to share it with the dean. Alas, she is dead and, as is true for most teachers, they only get to hear the "lip" and not how much they helped. Dr. Banumbra, the West African anatomy professor (Zakes Mokae), passes on to the students her final words, "She wished the very best for you. She expected the very best from you." He also gives out the best piece of advice in the movie as he prepares the students for a practical exam, "Don't change your answers, because your first instincts are almost always right." Joe goes on to ace the written exam, but Laurie beats him in the practical and a "star" is born (or should I say two stars).

Flatliners (1990)

A sharply different view of medical students is shown in this dark, scary film filled with religious and satanic imagery. Kiefer Sutherland, Julia Roberts, and Kevin Bacon play students who are not only streetwise and cynical, but seem to have lots of time for sex, philosophic bull sessions, and human experimentation. One of the first-year students, Labraccio (Bacon), is so good that while working as an orderly in the emergency room, he intubates and saves a woman before the resident arrives. Again, the scene allows for a slam-bang opening of "blood and guts" medicine, but is pretty dumb. To make it worse, instead of being praised, Labraccio is thrown out of school. Fortunately for his buddies, he hangs around as they seek a near-death experience to discover what it is like "on the other side." The ringleader, Nelson (Sutherland), steals a line from *Coma* (see chapter 5), when he declares, "Philosophy failed; religion failed; only the physical sciences can tell us truth." Rachel (Roberts), another rather precocious student, is inexplicably seen interviewing ward patients about their near-death experiences. Her reason is, "I've had people die that are close to me. I want to make sure they've gone to a nice place."

One by one, the four students challenge the limits of returning to full function after cardiac arrest by remaining in a flatline state for increasingly longer periods (fig. 6). Technologically sophisticated beyond their years (after all, they are still taking anatomy), they rig each other up in rotation to an electrocardiogram (EKG) monitor, an electroencephalogram (EEG), and a thermoregulating blanket. Using nitrous oxide, sodium pentothal, sodium bicarbonate, chilled glucose solution, and electric shock, they stop the heart for up to the five minutes generally considered to result in brain death, before attempting to restart it. They hope to prolong this limit by dropping the body temperature (hypothermia), which slows down metabolism and thus diminishes blood and nutrient requirements. The game of chicken gets a little out of hand as Rachel ups the ante. Then Nelson goes back for a replay and when no one is there to assist, he starts his own intravenous injection of potassium in order to stop his heart.

I know today's medical school faculty are very busy, but these folks are unsupervised and out of control. The only visible teacher, in what appears to be a broken-down school (ostensibly the University of Chicago), is an obnoxious anatomy professor who announces before the final that she is curving the grades to give "3 As, 5 Bs, 10 Cs, and the rest Ds and Fs." She expounds the absolute worst educational philosophy: "You're not in competition with yourself or with me, but one another, just as in life." No wonder they are willing to risk their lives for science. What their experiments first reveal is a flowing world of beauty and peace. They soon learn, however, that they shouldn't mess with Mother Nature as they bring their "unforgiven sins back from the dead." The most intriguing contrast with the past is the womanizing doctor-to-be, Joe (William Baldwin) who, after sweet-talking a string of women into having steamy sex, videotapes the proceedings without their knowledge. Doctor Video's punishment is to be besieged by images of the duped women chastising him and to have his fiancée, whom he has been assuring of his undying love, see the tapes when she rushes to his apartment concerned about his welfare.

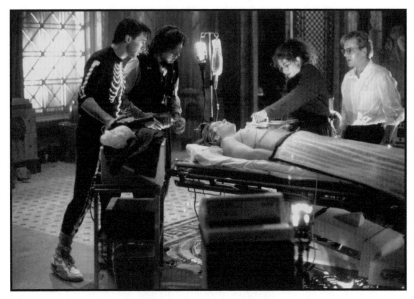

FIGURE 6. *Flatliners*. Rachel (Julia Roberts) flatlines Labraccio (Kevin Bacon), as classmates Joe (William Baldwin), Steckle (Oliver Platt), and Nelson (Kiefer Sutherland) wait their turn for a near-death experience.

Farfetched as it is, the film does articulate a message that not only concerns laypersons, but also scientists as to the hazards of scientific hubris (see chapter 4). This is summed up by Labraccio, the student who is already the equivalent of a chief resident, when he cries out, "I'm sorry, Lord. We stepped on your fucking territory." Later, he tells his fellow risk-takers, "We're being paid back for our arrogance." He prescribes "atonement" for sin and advises that they all seek forgiveness from those they have wronged in order to rid themselves of the demons their hubris has unleashed. Given his technical skill and his profound understanding of human nature, I found myself rooting for his readmission to medical school, unlike the character in the next movie who does get a degree.

Patch Adams (1998)

This preachy, self-indulgent, vulgar film, starring an out-of-control Robin Williams, elevates one doctor while demeaning the profession as a whole. It purports to be "based on a true story," just as *Road to Wellville*, Hunter Thompson's slam of the innovative Dr. John Kellogg, did.[9] Unfortunately, most of today's Hollywood types couldn't differentiate truth from their agenda-driven perceptions and extreme distortions of reality, even if they stumbled over it. While making some important, albeit hardly novel points, the filmmakers create a cardboard world of good guys and villains. The result is self-promotion being passed off as trenchant philosophy. It is important to note, however, that the film earned more than 125 million dollars at the box office and that many in our screening audience applauded the film's conclusion. One can either be alarmed that the public's esteem for the profession has sunk so low that they accept this drivel or simply write it off as yet another example of how tastelessness and half-truths sell in contemporary America.

The film opens with Patch Adams (Robin Williams) attempting suicide with pills and then committing himself to a mental institution. Adams is pictured as making breakthroughs with his disturbed brethren while managing to show up the psychiatrist, who, he says, "sucks" at helping people. For example, he connects with a wealthy patient who is said to have a "genius syndrome" by simply patching his leaky styrofoam coffee cup, thereby earning his nickname. After temporarily helping his disturbed psychotic roommate overcome a phobia, Adams realizes he has "the gift," escapes from the institution, and decides to apply to medical school. Entering "Virginia Medical University" (the real Hunter ["Patch"] Adams attended the Medical College of Virginia), he makes Joe Slovak, the know-it-all medical student in the film *Gross Anatomy* seem like a shrinking violet. Adams proceeds to teach the dean and all those other insensitive White male faculty members about compassion. Bob Gunton plays the dean with the same despicable persona he used as the warden in another boomer parable, *The Shawshank Redemption*. Just so we know whom to root against, we're treated to this line in the orientation lecture, "our mission here is to rigorously and ruthlessly train the humanity out of you and make you something better. We're going to make doctors out of you." Anyone recognize that?

As my wife noted, the filmmakers trot out a bevy of terribly outdated "truths" and clichés as if they discovered them. For example, the students are told that they will not see a patient for two years. Never mind that Case Western Reserve Medical School introduced first-year students to patients in the 1950s and that almost all schools followed suit thereafter. Carin (Monica Potter), the female medical student, says that there are only 8 women in a class of 163. That may have been true of Adams's entering class in the late 1960s, but this situation changed so radically, beginning in the 1970s, that now women constitute almost 50 percent of entering classes. There's the ubiquitous reference to the patient as a "disease" or "room" by nurses and attending physicians. This film would have viewers believe that the medical school faculty not only condoned this practice long after many had spoken out against it, but presumably encouraged it to aid in "distancing" and to guard against "transference." Fortunately, like Mighty Mouse, first-year student Patch is there to teach the faculty the folly of their ways and to "save the day."

Defying the dean, who is shown trumpeting his having trained at "The Brigham," Adams walks on the ward with a white coat he obtains at a convention of butchers, whom he had just wowed. Joletta (Irma P. Hall), a Black nurse, disdainfully calls him her "future boss" and adds that "in another five years, you'll be so full of yourself, you'll have to hang a cup out your ass just to catch the excess." Taking a liking to him though, she allows Patch to enter the pediatric oncology ward, where he brings smiles to one and all. But like the true bastard he is, the dean threatens to dismiss Patch for going to see patients. He also intimates that Adams cheats, because he gets grades of 98 without studying and with time left over to read Walt Whitman. The dean criticizes his enthusiasm and his desire to make people laugh, telling him, "Passion doesn't make doctors. I make doctors. Understand? Medical students, as a rule, have no contact with patients until the third year. Our way of doing things is a product of centuries of experience."

Guessing that it was his nerdy roommate Mitch who accused him of cheating, Adams confronts him. Played with icy hauteur by Philip Seymour Hoffman, the roommate is a descendant of doctors and believes that he has it in him "to be a great doctor." Consequently, Adams couldn't possibly get better grades than he. This situation leads to another heavy-handed sermon, as Patch responds to Mitch's assertion that doctors have to be "arrogant pompous pricks, not kindergarten teachers," especially when confronting a dying patient.

Adams is allowed to remain in school and, unbelievably, is asked by the dean to set up a welcome for the all-White male gynecologists' meeting at the university. He decorates the doorway to the conference center with a woman's legs on stirrups and a sign reading, "Welcome, Gynos, At Your Cervix." We are meant to see this unclassy act as another brilliant stroke by our hero. This scene was one of the "word-of-mouth" endorsements I overheard for this picture at a local haberdashery.

Wouldn't you know it, that nasty dean is enraged by this cute act and presumably tells Patch, "You want us to get down on the same level with our patients, to destroy objectivity." To which Patch replies, "When I was in the hospital, doctors didn't help me; patients did." Adams then walks out and again enters the hospital, to win over yet another patient whom those fool doctors can't seem to reach. He enters the room of an angry patient dying of pancreatic cancer and begins singing "Blue Skies." This scene is reminiscent of *What Dreams May Come*, another 1998 transcendental mess in which Williams starred. At first, Adams gets thrown out of the room, but his magic begins to work; as the patient lies dying, the family leaves and, with Patch in attendance still cracking tasteless jokes, the patient passes to the great beyond on a chorus of "Blue Skies." Silly me, I couldn't help thinking the patient would have been better off dying at home among his loved ones.

As Patch and his best pal Truman (Daniel London) eat in a diner, discussing yet another insensitive action by the hospital staff, there's the requisite grousing about bad doctors and health care costs. Every restaurant patron has a health care horror story. This leads our hero to start a free clinic. Now there's a novel idea. No one would suspect that concepts of community health and free clinics had been pioneered almost two decades before Patch entered medical school, by George Reader, Jack Geiger, Count Gibson, Sam Johnson, Art Warner, and others.[10-13] Adams's clinic is staffed by undergraduate medical students and dependent on stealing supplies from the hospital. Patients are their own doctors, and humor is the main therapy.

This drivel really got to me. As I learned from helping to establish free migrant health[14] and sexually transmitted disease clinics[15] in the early 1970s, the poor and underserved deserve better than untrained, albeit enthusiastic, caregivers who can volunteer in and also volunteer out. We didn't have to steal supplies but got them from the University of Colorado Medical Center authorities until we obtained funds to establish first-class facilities and staffing. Happily, the migrant health clinic evolved into a thriving community health center north of Denver, and the sexually transmitted disease clinic continued for twenty years before being folded into Denver General Hospital's clinic. Another interesting sidelight that the Chicano migrants taught us is that a token payment of even a dollar was useful in that it preserved patients' dignity and bonded them to the activity. Don't look for any such insights in Adams's story.

Indeed, the movie's key lesson, which is actually contrary to the movie's agenda, is obscured in sentimentality. It seems that Patch is smitten by Carin, who, after repeatedly rebuffing him, finally succumbs to his charms and joins him at the clinic. Arriving home late one evening, she finds a message on her machine calling her to the home of a patient, Larry (Douglas Roberts). It's important to note that on first meeting this frequenter of the emergency room, she had appropriately called him "weird." Patch's know-it-all response is, "I'm weird. If we don't show him compassion, who will?" (fig. 7). Patch goes on to tell her and us how much the patients are the doctors and proceeds to joke with the disturbed, reclusive, wealthy young man. Carin goes alone to the house, where the young man kills her and then himself in fulfillment of some bizarre delusion. What a great opportunity for a sermon on the hazard of hubris and that doctoring is not "un jeu d'enfant!" Never happens. Instead, we have a soap opera charade, wherein Patch vows to close the clinic and stays on the periphery at the gravesite during the burial. After everyone leaves, Patch falls on the bier, which has been conveniently left above ground, and apologizes to his dead friend. A lot of good that does her.

Later, Truman tries to dissuade Patch from closing the clinic by saying it's the best thing he has ever done because he is assisting Patch in a "pure and good purpose." Even Mitch, his pompous ass of a roommate, tells him, "I can outdiagnose any attending and surgeon in this hospital, but I can't make Mrs. Kennedy eat. You have a gift. You have a way with people. They like you." Adams blows them off and leaves for the mountaintop he and Carin loved, in order to attempt suicide again. Just then, he sees a butterfly, presumably the reborn girl friend. Or is it Shirley MacLaine? This experience prompts him to return to solve Mrs. Kennedy's eating problem. With adoring fellow students and

FIGURE 7. *Patch Adams.* Robin Williams plays the role of Patch Adams, a self-described "weird" medical student who defies the establishment.

nurses, he fills the hospital's outdoor pool with spaghetti to fulfill the patient's lifelong wish to jump into one.

Mrs. Kennedy is happy, but that terrible dean isn't. So Patch calls him a "dickhead" and is dismissed from school. On his way out of the dean's office, Adams steals his folder. Seeing that he is at the top of his class and that he has been accused of "being excessively happy," he resolves to fight expulsion at the state medical board. This development provides the opportunity for yet another long, gratuitous lecture directed at over-the-hill White men, about doctors thinking themselves superior ("O, Doctor, your flatulence has no odor"). He tells the students, "Don't let THEM anesthetize" the compassion out and advises them to cultivate friendships with the hardworking nurses (now there's a fresh insight!). He asks rhetorically, "At what point in history did a doctor become more than a trusted and learned friend who visited and treated the ill?" Ironically, this supreme egoist ends by saying, "No matter what your decision, I will still become the best damned doctor the world has ever seen." So much for humility.

As judgment is about to be passed, the pediatric oncology patients and their families appear, wearing Patch's trademark clown noses, and as expected, he is reinstated, to loud cheers. The head of the medical center tells him, "You carry a flame that should spread like brushfire through the profession." To cap it off, just when it appears that he is conforming by wearing a graduation gown, Patch moons the audience and walks out with his behind flapping in the breeze. Wow, that's class. Of course, the director, one-time stand-up comedian Tom Shadyac, whose emotional development seems to have been arrested in preadolescence, also directed *Ace Ventura: Pet Detective* and *The Nutty Professor*. The adoring filmmakers tell us that Adams was in family practice for fifteen years and is now building his Gesundheit Institute in West Virginia and that a thousand doctors have signed up to staff it. On a recent *Good Morning America*, Adams said, "There is no place in American medicine for compassion. I spend three to four hours with a patient and we are friends for life."

To quote the liner notes, "Compassion, involvement and empathy, Patch holds, are as great a value to physicians as breakthrough medicines and technological advancements. Radical thinking, then and now." Really? Director Shadyac adds, "Today we know about endorphins and the importance of the mind in the healing process. That knowledge didn't exist back in the 1960s and 1970s when Patch was forming his philosophy. It was a radical concept then. He's really a pioneer in the discovery of the medicinal value of laughter and compassion."

Too bad Francis W. Peabody[16] and Norman Cousins[17] aren't alive to set the record straight about how long those concepts have been around. And, of course, there's Jonathan Swift's aphorism that remains true despite the medical advances since his day, "The best doctors in the world are Doctor Diet, Doctor Quiet, and Doctor Merryman."[18] Unfortunately, this movie's self-righteous aggrandizement is falling on receptive ground, given the lack of a sense of history in the public at large, the turmoil in health care, and the disunity in the medical profession. It is another example of how entrenched the tactics of division and polarization are in societal discourse on the eve of the millennium.

That most movie portrayals of medical students have been off-base is clear from my experience with thousands of medical students in the past four decades. One is left to wonder whether the discrepancy between reality and the movies makes much difference. Probably not. As far as I can tell, life isn't imitating "art" (broadly defined). Still, it would be nice if someone got it close to right. Then again, it would be a documentary, and some excellent ones have already been made at Harvard and Penn.

NOTES

1. Ludmerer KM. Time to Heal: American Medical Education from the Turn of the Century to the Era of Managed Care. New York: Oxford University Press, 1999.
2. Starr P. The Social Transformation of American Medicine: The Rise of a Sovereign Profession and the Making of a Vast Industry. New York: Basic Books, 1982.
3. Rothstein WG. The demand for medical education in New York after World War II. Transactions & Studies of the College of Physicians of Philadelphia 1992; 14: 131-145.
4. Sokoloff L. The rise and decline of the Jewish quota in medical school admissions. Bull NY Acad Med 1992; 68: 497-518.
5. Juthani M. A comparison of Asian-American and Jewish involvement in the medical profession. JAMA 1997; 277: 768-69.
6. Lederer SE and Parascandola J. Screening syphilis: Dr. Ehrlich's Magic Bullet meets the Public Health Service. J Hist Med 1998; 53: 345-370.
7. Thompson M. Not As a Stranger. New York: Scribner, 1954.
8. Dans PE. Self-reported cheating at one medical school. Acad Med Suppl 1996; 71: S70-72.
9. Dans PE. The road to Wellville. The Pharos 1995; 58 (2): 49–50.
10. Goodrich CH, Olendzki M, Buchanan JR, Greenberg S, Erle H, Reader GG. The New York Hospital-Cornell Medical Center project: An experiment in welfare medicine. Am J Pub Health 1963; 53: 1252–59.
11. Hamlin RH, Kisch AI, Geiger, HJ. Administrative reorganization of municipal health services: The Boston experience. N Engl J Med 1965; 273: 26–29.
12. Geiger HJ. Tufts in Mississippi: The Delta Health Center. Tufts Med Alumni Bull 1966; 3: 3–9.
13. Warner AL. Problems in delivering comprehensive health care to the inner city. Arch Environ Health 1968; 17: 383–86.

14. Dans PE, Johnson S. Politics in the development of a migrant health center: A Pilgrim's Progress from idealism to pragmatism. N Engl J Med 1975; 292: 890–95.
15. Dans PE. Organization and operation of a facility for sexually transmitted diseases. Bull NY Acad Med 1976; 52: 955–69.
16. Peabody FW. The care of the patient. JAMA, 1927; 88: 877–82, reprinted in JAMA 1984; 252: 813–18.
17. Cousins N. Anatomy of an Illness as Perceived by the Patient: Reflections on Healing and Regeneration. New York: W.W. Norton & Co, 1979.
18. Swift J. Polite conversation. In Bartlett's Familiar Quotations, 16th edition, ed. J. Kaplan. Boston: Little, Brown & Co, 1992, p 290.

2

The Kindly Savior:
From *Doctor Bull* to *Doc Hollywood*

Over the years, movies have contributed to the myth of doctors as omniscient, omnipotent, kindly beings. This image of the profession and its later antithesis are best illustrated in a November, 1997, Sunday *New York Times* interview[1] of acclaimed director, Sidney Lumet prior to the opening of his bitter anti-medicine polemic, *Critical Care* (see chapter 8):

> Q: What's your earliest memory of doctors?
>
> A: Saviors. Kindly Jewish doctors on the Lower East Side who made house calls.
>
> Q: Now you depict them as creeps, potential murderers, drunks, heartless technocrats. Is it really that bad?
>
> A: They're not saviors anymore. Recently my son-in-law's sister had a terrible accident. She busted four ribs, suffered head contusions and was in intensive care for six days. But she was discharged without a neurological examination. Well, she had to go back to the hospital because she suffered severe headaches and every once in a while started talking gibberish. Episodes like that show that our system is in the toilet. I think people get a lot of their reality from "E.R." They get an abrupt awakening when something really goes wrong with them.

Lumet's fond remembrance of a kindly Jewish doctor on the Lower East Side of New York is captured in *The Symphony of Six Million* (see chapter 9). Still, his comments are ironic in that in 1924 when he was born, most physicians on the Lower East Side of New York could do much less to combat the serious illnesses afflicting their patients; certainly there would have been no intensive care unit (ICU) to care for the injured woman. Having been born there myself thirteen years later, I know that all too often doctors could merely confirm the patients' resignation to their ills as "God's will." Yet, these physicians were probably more likely to do something that may have been lost in the rush of available new cures, namely, offer compassion and comfort. Furthermore, it is extremely unlikely for someone to be admitted to an ICU with head injuries and not have a neurologic examination. However, taking the story at face value, it suggests that the diagnosis of a subdural hematoma might have been missed, which was probably more likely in the old days, given the lack of technology. Even so, as shown in films such as 1939's *Meet Dr. Christian*, physicians have been warned for decades to keep this possibility in the forefront when treating patients with head injuries. What Lumet's comments best illustrate is how medical hype and our vaunted technology have raised patients' expectations. When they are unmet, the effect can be devastating. Because doctor-patient contact has increased greatly since the spread of health insurance in the 1950s and 1960s, everyone has heard some horror story, even if the facts are not always as represented.

Lumet's comments also bring to mind how doctors were once seen as integral parts of their community, even in large cities. As they became better educated and better compensated and medical care moved out of doctors' homes into hospitals and large clinics, physicians came to be seen as belonging to a different class. This was often accentuated by their living in communities other than those in which they practiced, sometimes in physician enclaves dubbed "Pill Hills" by realtors. They were less likely to be seen as "one of the folks" as they are portrayed in some of the films to be discussed in this chapter.

Part of the nostalgia for a presumably simpler time is crystallized in the oft-lamented replacement of the generalist by the specialist. The enormous contribution of specialization to medical advancement is often overshadowed in the minds of the healthy majority by the impersonalization and overuse of technology that too often accompanied it. The generalist/specialist dialectic is well captured in the 1959 film *The Last Angry Man* in which the kind old generalist Dr. Sam Abelman rails, "They now have specialists for one toe and a specialist for another toe." Yet, to see how old this nostalgic sentiment is, compare it to the following passage from Dostoyevsky's *The Brothers Karamazov*, published in 1880.[2]

The medical faculty…have no idea how to cure you…. "We only diagnose," they say, "but go to such-and-such specialist, he'll cure you." The old doctor who used to cure all sorts of disease has completely disappeared, I assure you, now there are only specialists and they all advertise in the newspapers. If anything is wrong with your nose, they send you to Paris; there, they say, is a European specialist who cures noses. If you go to Paris, he'll look at your nose; I can only cure your right nostril, he'll tell you, for I don't cure the left nostril, that's not my specialty, but go to Vienna, there there's a specialist who will cure your left nostril.

That Dostoyevsky was recording a broadly-held belief is shown in the following lament by a Boston generalist in 1895, "The family doctor is dead and buried. The specialists have squeezed him out as the vines do the big trees."[3] As the French say, *Plus ca change, plus ca meme chose.* So, as you read this and other chapters, keep in mind that things were never as good as they were portrayed, nor are they now as bad. The truth is that today there are many down-to-earth, dedicated doctors who don't come close to resembling Lumet's description. Still, as they say in Hollywood and its sister city, Washington, D.C., "perception is reality."

THE DEDICATED SOLO GENERAL PRACTITIONER

As Spears notes in his book *Hollywood: The Golden Era*,[4] "the beloved country doctor was the protagonist of many silent movies" such as the 1909 film, *The Country Doctor*, as well as spoofs like Harold Lloyd's 1923 comedy, *Doctor Jack*. In the sound era, the dedicated doctor who cares more about patients than about money is best illustrated in such films as *Doctor Bull*, *The Country Doctor*, *Meet Dr. Christian*, and *The Last Angry Man*. While they celebrate, often effusively and unabashedly, the doctor as kindly savior, they also show his weaknesses and the struggle to maintain a posture of simplicity and common sense in a profession being transformed by new technology and specialization. Revisiting these films also illustrates how the move from solo practice in homes and offices into institutions radically changed things for good and ill. We will conclude with *Doc Hollywood*, a film that shows the struggle for a doctor's soul: "Will it be the easy life and big bucks of plastic surgery in L.A. or the hard life and small change of the rural G.P.?"

Doctor Bull (1933)

Directed by John Ford and based on *The Last Adam*[5] by James Gould Cozzens, this film starred Will Rogers. The title, *Doctor Bull*, is both self-mocking and a reference to his being trained as a "cow doctor." The scrolling introduction leaves no doubt about its desire to celebrate the old-fashioned family doctor: "Doctor Bull brings his neighbors into the world and postpones their departure as long as possible. He prescribes common sense and accepts his small rewards gratefully." His patients call him "Doc." The setting is New Winton, Connecticut, a "dull town" where the main topic of conversation is about how Doc spends an awful lot of time at Widow Cardmaker's (Vera Allen). Doctor Bull lives with his aunt who refuses to answer the phone and frequently leaves it off the hook (fig. 1). Doc highlights the growing importance of this relatively new fixture in rural settings as he admonishes her, "How are people who get sick going to get well if you keep doing a thing like that?"

The film does not see Doc through rose-colored glasses; he is rather ornery and at times callous. When he arrives late to the bedside of a dead seventeen-year-old, he responds to accusations of "improper medical attention" saying, "I've seen a hundred people die. None of them seemed to mind whether I was there or not. They were too sick to mind. There's only one way into this world and a thousand ways out. Thirty percent will die with this disease even with a good doctor." He then dismisses the hypochondriacal soda jerk, Larry Ward, played by Andy Devine, with the comment, "I've been up all night with real sick people and I don't want to hear you whine." Later, Ward tells him (with characteristic Devine nasality): "You're getting hard-hearted, Doc, and the people in town are talking about it."

Doc has a number of duties, including inspecting the water supply as public health officer; however, he neglects doing it and a typhoid outbreak occurs. Indeed, it's Aunt Emily (Nora Cecil) who smells the disease in their cook's breath and Bull asks if there are rose-colored splotches and runs to his 1933 textbook on clinical diagnosis. Later, when he takes a specimen to a specialist, he gets laughed at for suggesting the diagnosis. He admits that he's just a "cow doctor" and gives Aunt Emily full credit. When the rich town doctor Dr. Verney (Ralph Morgan) joins in the criticism, Doc puts him down saying, "I decided to learn medicine instead of being a diagnostician." Pointing to the doctor's fancy car, Bull says, "Many a tonsil in that." This comment in the era before antibiotics became available for strep throat and when almost everyone had

FIGURE 1. *Dr. Bull*. Dr. Bull (Will Rogers) lectures Aunt Emily (Nora Cecil) about leaving his home-office phone off the hook.

a tonsillectomy echoed an early indictment of the procedure's overuse and surgical faddism in general.[6] Later, he says, "Soon, spring sickness will be here and I'll load the whole town up on sulfur and molasses," the traditional spring tonic. This is also true to life; indeed, to her death at ninety-two, my mother-in-law, who lived in a small town in Rhode Island, swore by her spring tonic which was supposed to do for her body what her spring cleaning did for her house.

Bull becomes the subject of derision when he draws from his experience in curing a paralyzed cow to treat a man paralyzed after falling from a ladder. A specialist laughs at him because the condition is "incurable." Showing the fascination of the era's moviemakers with the new science of immunology, Bull develops what seems like a decidedly preposterous cure, an antiserum against the patient's own tissue. After injecting it, the man develops high fevers and seems on death's door, but he survives and regains his ability to walk.

Meanwhile, the town meets to take Bull's license away because of his failure to inspect the reservoir. He says, "I can always go back to doctoring cows." Some of his neighbors defend him for having brought most of the town's children into the world and for always being there. Later, he says, "I've been a doctor long enough. I can go hunting and fishing. I've spent twenty years listening to the telephone every night. I'm going to devote the rest of my life to being a telephone-breaker." If Doc saw the party line telephone as a doctor's curse, can you imagine what he would have thought of cellular phones and beepers? After Doc's miracle cure becomes known, the front page of the local newspaper proclaims, "Medical circles are agog," and he goes off on a honeymoon with the Widow Cardmaker. The film is interesting in that it celebrates a doctor who, although relatively simple and poorly trained, is capable of extraordinary things. Yet, he not only fails to be compensated, but also is ostracized and decides to chuck it all and to enjoy himself. In short, as we will see in many films, today's doctors have no corner on the role of disillusioned dropout.

The Country Doctor (1936)

The Country Doctor, a highly romanticized portrayal of the Ontario backwoods practitioner, Doctor Allan Dafoe, who delivered the Dionne quintuplets, starred Jean Hersholt as Dr. John Luke, a kindly, selfless family practitioner. The film opens with a loud crash as a timber falls on a logger in the Canadian woods. Someone yells out, "Call the Doc." Another says, "Get some water boiling and see if you can find Nurse Kennedy." A one-legged man comments on how lucky he is to still get around. The injured man tells the Doc, "If you have to cut them off, don't let me come to. I want to die." Doc tells him to "take a deep breath, breathe through your mouth, and say 'I'll be all right,'" while he administers ether.

Next we see Doc in his office with a patient who is giving him six dollars towards his account. When Doc learns that it is all he's got, he says, "Pay me next year." The next scenes depict a diphtheria epidemic showing how perilous life was in those days and why parents had so many children. As Doc tends to a sick child, the mother says, "I know I'm saying goodbye." Doc tells her, "I brought all your chicks into the world. You think I'm going to let her go out of it already?" He tells the mother to swab the house and to "pray to God that the others don't have it, too," then takes the child through the snow to a room full of children and asks for a bed. The nurse tells him "I'm afraid we'll have one soon." A priest carrying wood tells him that he looks tired. He says "I'm OK, Father" and then mutters "If we only had a proper kind of

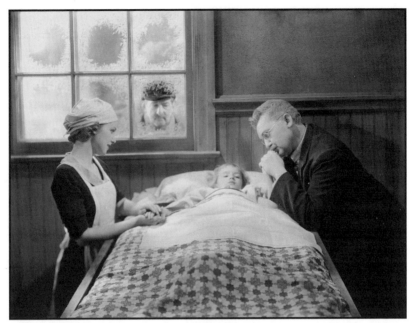

FIGURE 2. *The Country Doctor.* Dr. Luke (Jean Hersholt) comforts a child with diphtheria as a parent peers through the window.

hospital." He tells the priest to administer the Last Rites to the girl, then comforts her as a parent peers through the window (fig. 2).

A winter storm has caused the radio to go dead, cutting off the community. The man injured in the first scene, now a double amputee in a wheelchair, is trying to reach Montreal with his ham radio. Doc tells him, "As long as you were a lumberjack, you were a dum-dum. A spruce falls on your legs and you build a radio." The man succeeds in reaching Luke's brother, Paul (Frank Reicher), a wealthy surgeon in Montreal and Luke pleads for serum. Luke's handsome nephew, Tony (Michael Whalen), a doctor as well as a prizefighter (known as the "Murderous Medico"), pilots a plane through the storm to bring the needed supplies. They just don't make them like that anymore! MacKenzie (Robert Barrat), the district manager, is upset that the doctor went over his head. Doc tells him that he's "never learned to take things the way a doctor ought to be able to take them. I know these kids' mommies and daddies. I brought them into the world and to see them struggling to death..." Just then the plane arrives.

Tony proceeds to fall in love with the district manager's daughter Mary (June Lang), further jeopardizing Dr. Luke's standing. Tony tells

Mary that he's "going back to the hospital to be an intern again, learn my trade, and come back here." She tells him that "being a country doctor is like eating hash. You never know what's going to turn up next. You don't want to bury yourself in a hole like this. You want to be in a city where there are lights and excitement all the time." We 1930s film buffs just know he's going to come back. Unfortunately, before leaving, he reluctantly has to punch out his future father-in-law's lights when Dad challenges him to a fight.

After stopping the epidemic, Luke visits Montreal to plead for a hospital, but is refused by Sir Basil Crawford (Montagu Love), the pompous company owner. He visits his brother's hospital where they do tonsillectomies, plastic surgery, and have incubators with controlled temperature, humidity, and oxygen. Luke relates how, in delivering babies when it is 40° to 50° below, he has to warm their beds with a heated brick wrapped in a shawl. He must also put premature babies in the oven to keep them warm. He recounts a story of having once delivered triplets and having had only room for two in the oven. Sir Basil is unmoved.

Invited to join his brother at the medical association dinner, Luke is the only one not in evening clothes. Luke's brother introduces him, saying he knows "of no more valiant calling than a country doctor. His strength and courage in the face of a diphtheria epidemic in the North Country was an inspiration to every doctor in Canada." Luke reflects on how he could have been a specialist, maybe "the foremost authority on the earlobe," but his "patients would trade five specialists for one old-fashioned country doctor, not good at any one spot on the body, but willing to take a whack at anything." He tells of operating on kitchen tables and of getting paid in Plymouth Rock chickens. Still, he doesn't envy the city doctors' income, only their hospital.

When he returns, Sir Basil cashiers him and brings in a company doctor at two hundred dollars a month. The new doctor finds out that Dr. Luke has been practicing for thirty-five years without a license. Apparently, when he graduated from medical school, Luke didn't have the twenty dollars to pay for the license; he always meant to get one. Just as he is about to be exiled, Luke is called to the Dionne home where he delivers five babies, weighing a total of ten pounds. The survival of quintuplets, a first in the annals of medicine, earns him fame. The homestead becomes a tourist mecca and his hospital is built across the road. Luke is credited with turning away sixty thousand dollars in endorsements. He becomes the quints' surrogate father, separating them from their parents, who already have six children, ostensibly for health reasons.

The rest of the film, which is what the pre-television audience was probably waiting for, is an extended home movie of the quints taken under the supervision of Doctor Dafoe. We see them getting their teeth brushed, being bathed, fed, teething, rolling over, and pounding on their high chairs with a spoon. They call out "Dadda" to the doctor who comments that "Cecile is being naughty" and "Yvonne's always a little lady." The saddest thing is to see how happy they were and to know that the rest of their story was such an unhappy one. They were the subjects of bitter contests for custody between the family and the government of Ontario, which in the 1990s had to pay the Dionnes damages and admit profiting from them.

This real story of the tragedies in the quints' personal lives is beyond the scope of this chapter. So, let's end this account in the same way as the movie, with the Governor General of Canada awarding Luke the Order of the British Empire, calling him the "greatest of all country doctors." Luke answers, "In the name of country doctors everywhere, I accept this great honor." The audience is sent out of the theater to the sound of stirring music, with as good a feeling about doctors as from any movie ever made.

Jean Hersholt was so captivating as Dr. Luke that RKO launched a series of films featuring him as the small-town family doctor, Dr. Christian. Those films helped elevate the family doctor to mythical status. Hersholt also starred in the much-loved radio program, *Dr. Christian,* from 1937 to 1953. MacDonald Carey failed in his attempt to translate the role to television in 1956. Doctors couldn't have asked for a better standard-bearer for the noble side of the profession than the wonderfully warm and believable Hersholt, whose humanitarianism is commemorated by an annual award at the Oscar ceremonies. The Dr. Christian and Dr. Kildare films (see chapter 3) did much to enhance the image of the profession; along with Robert Young as Marcus Welby,[7] they also set impossible expectations.

Meet Dr. Christian (1939)

Like *Doctor Bull, Meet Dr. Christian*'s title is an interesting play on words. Its credits are displayed on a prescription pad with a prominent Rx. The plot line is reminiscent of *The Country Doctor.* An accident at the Hewitt Lumber Company prompts a call to Dr. C, whom the company retains for its medical services, not uncommon at the time. Dr. C, who has been up all night caring for a sick woman, is unavailable, so the boss calls another doctor and cancels Dr. C's contract, his only secure income. Most patients pay Dr. C in produce, resulting in an office full of tomatoes. His assistant tells him that "from now on we're going to send bills to your patients every month." Christian is clearly not interested in money. When a patient is cured, he says, "moments like this are worth all the hard work and sleepless nights." It seems he gave up a chance to practice in Chicago in order to remain in the small town of River's End. His main aim is to build a hospital which he fights for at the town meeting held in an old-fashioned country store/post office/soda fountain/pharmacy. This is a poignant reminder of an America before the Hill Burton Act created an explosion of hospital construction (see introduction).

Hewitt convenes the meeting to discuss replacing Dr. C (see *Doctor Bull* for a similar scene). He says: "I'm not at all sure that the methods of a country doctor are suited to running a modern municipal health department." Dr. C makes a plea for a district nurse to teach the inhabitants of Squatterstown about preventive medicine and insists that "River's End needs a hospital." "I've seen people die, seen routine operations become emergencies; just this morning, a baby died all because we need a hospital." This leads to a dialogue that could be carried on today. Hewitt, the businessman and champion of "applied efficiency," asks, "Do you have any idea how much a hospital costs?" Doc C replies, "I know how many lives it's costing not to have one." Hewitt says, "We're talking dollars and cents." Christian says, "It's a little hard to talk about medicine in dollars and cents." Hewitt counters that the town needs roads and modern highway approaches and that the government will pay most of their cost. When Dr. C says roads will cost more than a hospital, an exasperated Hewitt says: "Incompetent old fool! He should have gone out with the horse and buggy."

Though well-meaning, the story seems pretty sappy by today's standards. This is well illustrated by the denouement. Hewitt's mischievous daughter is injured in a car accident caused by his adolescent son's reckless driving. Dr. C does an x-ray without special protection and tells Hewitt that his daughter has a cerebral hemorrhage and needs an operation to save her life (fig 3). Hewitt wants to airlift her to Chicago, but Dr. C convinces him that she won't survive the trip. Hewitt then calls in a specialist, Dr. Wells, who immediately asks for spot lamps and comments that the sterilizers are ancient. Then to his amazement he learns that his assistant will be Dr. Paul Christian. The operation is a success and Hewitt tells him to name his fee. Wells replies, "Fifteen hundred is about right. Make it out to Dr. Christian, if it's all right. He performed the operation. I couldn't operate when the man who introduced the

FIGURE 3. *Meet Dr. Christian.* Dr. Christian (Jean Hersholt) showing an abnormal skull x-ray to the child's concerned father.

operation to this country was right here. You've been underestimating your local physician. No one else could have done such a delicate decompression with these facilities." PS: Dr. C gets his hospital and well he should, given that this humble general practitioner is also, in true Hollywood style, a world class medical pioneer.

Over the next two years, Hersholt made a series of Doctor Christian movies:[8] *The Courageous Dr. Christian*, in which he fights an epidemic of spinal meningitis and cleans up a slum while fighting off the advances of a spinster; *Dr. Christian Meets the Women*, in which he exposes a crooked weight loss program; *Melody for Three*, in which he helps a divorced couple reunite; and *They Meet Again*, the final installment in which Christian's common sense helps spring an innocent man from prison. Although the series outlived its ideas, as is not uncommon in sequels, Dr. Christian made an indelible mark in America's psyche.

Doctor Jim (1947)

This hokey look at the country doctor, whose theme song is "Love Thy Neighbor," is interesting primarily as a relic of a bygone sentimental era. Released in 1947, *Doctor Jim* proved to be an immediate anachronism that contrasted sharply with the gritty post World War II film noir genre. It opens with a testimonial dinner for Doctor Jim Gateros (Stu Erwin) described as the "best friend the town ever had." The townspeople reminisce about the more than thirty years "since Doctor Jim hung up his shingle." We see him carrying his wife Sally (Barbara Wood Dell) over the threshold just as the telephone rings calling him to a sick patient; he must cancel their honeymoon trip to Niagara Falls. World War I is declared and he dutifully goes to war. He is saying grace for Christmas dinner when the phone rings again. Sally automatically gets his doctor's bag saying "the phone is my only rival." He takes care of a farmer for whom he orders bed rest. Naturally, Doctor Jim, though exhausted, proceeds to milk the farmer's cows before heading home. No one can argue with the narrator when he says, "He helped people not just as a doctor but as a friend." He starts a one-man private hospital in his home and supports it out of his own funds.

The arrival of a new doctor excites the townspeople, because, as the mayor's wife says, "he's so polished and handsome too." Doctor Sylvester (William Wright) makes "regular appointments," doesn't make "country calls" (only urban ones), and "refills sedatives." When Doc discovers an epidemic of brucellosis (Bang's disease), he lets his rival take the credit because Doc doesn't want to ruin the reputation of the dairy farmer whose new stock started it. When the truth comes out, Doc is kept on as chief of the new hospital, with Sylvester as his assistant. Doc and his wife (whom he calls "the biggest reason for his success") are given new luggage and tickets to Niagara Falls, ending the movie in a warm glow.

Welcome Stranger (1947)

Also released in 1947, *Welcome Stranger* continues the "country doctor as saint" genre in a more entertaining and less saccharine way. Starring Bing Crosby and Barry Fitzgerald, it represents a replay of the Oscar-winning *Going My Way*, but this time Fitzgerald is not an old cantankerous Irish priest, but an old cantankerous Irish doctor (Dr. Joseph McRory) who is taking his first vacation in thirty-five years. Crosby plays Dr. Jim Pearson, a handsome, peripatetic, crooning doctor who takes *locum tenens* positions and moves on. The night before McRory is to leave, the townspeople hold a party for him for "giving Fallsbridge thirty-five years of good health." He is described as the first thing most of the assembled saw when they opened their eyes and the last those who died saw on departing this earth. The town is celebrating a brand new hospital ("every dime is paid for"). Caught up in the expansiveness of the moment, Doc cancels all outstanding bills and leads the first square dance. Bing sings "That's Country Style."

Doc is not too enamored of what he considers to be "an incompetent, arrogant vaudeville singer," saying, "One hundred and eighty thousand doctors in the United States and I have to get you." McRory delays his vacation until the agency sends a replacement. Meanwhile, the two fashion a "Going My Way" working relationship. The frequent use of placebos at the time is illustrated when old Doc administers "sugar pills." The most interesting plot twist involves Doc getting severe abdominal pain. Pearson does a "WBC and Diff." The white blood cell count turns out to be "16,000 with 89 percent polys" and his "pulse rate is 108." He advises an operation, but Doc refuses, saying "I'd just as soon call in Sweeney the butcher. You operate on me against my will, you'll go to prison for manslaughter" (that would be battery unless he kills him.)[9] Pearson replies, "Even with a good surgeon, 10 percent of peritonitis cases are lost." Doc finally agrees, but insists, "No ether, I want a local." Pearson tells him that he would give him a spinal if he had someone to monitor his blood pressure. Doc says, "You'll be glad for my supervision." A mirror is set up to allow Doc to see the operative field (see *Society Doctor* for the same set-up) (fig. 4). He tells Pearson what sutures to use and as expected everything turns out well. The screenwriter inserts one of a number of inside movie jokes that used to pepper the Hope/Crosby *Road* films when Doc scoffs at the accomplishment saying that "Appendectomies are often performed by pharmacists." Is that so?" replies Pearson. Doc responds, "On shipboard and in the movies." (An allusion to *Destination Tokyo*. See appendix A.)

By now, Doc is taken with his young friend and tries to recruit him to stay on "as assistant director and chief surgeon of the most modern hospital in Maine." Even the charms of the lovely schoolteacher, played by Joan Caulfield, are not enough to sway Pearson who sings of his wanderlust in "My Heart is a Hobo." Just then a hotshot new doctor (Larry Young) puts up his shingle, "Dr. Jenks, Physician and Surgeon," and immediately diagnoses a rare cause of hypertension, pheochromocytoma. A special meeting of the hospital board is convened to replace old Doc. He is forced to take a written examination conducted by the medical society. Jenks finishes quickly, but Doc, despite coaching by Pearson, draws a blank and sweats profusely as he struggles to finish. Just as the practical exam is about to begin, two very sick boys are brought in and the young doctor diagnoses "equine encephalitis," saying that more than 50 percent of patients die." He starts a panic about "brain fever."

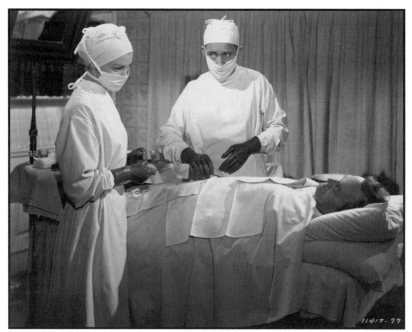

FIGURE 4. *Welcome Stranger.* Dr. McRory (Barry Fitzgerald) uses a mirror to direct his appendectomy in his living room while Dr. Pearson (Bing Crosby) and schoolteacher Trudy Mason (Joan Caulfield) assist.

Fortunately, old Doc ferrets out the facts and declares that the boys' symptoms are due to smoking cigars. This confirms an earlier line about doctors that represents the take-home message of this film: "No one has discovered a substitute for skill, for wisdom, for practical experience or for goodness of heart." If this wasn't enough for me to like this movie, the use of the term "blatherskate" warmed the cockles of this wordsmith's heart.

People Will Talk (1951)

This quirky film, based on the Broadway play *Dr. Praetorius*, though muddled and rather farfetched, occupies an important position in the doctor genre. It stars Cary Grant in the first of his two turns as a doctor. In the 1952 *Crisis*, he played a kidnapped surgeon who is forced to operate on a South American dictator played by Jose Ferrer. In *People Will Talk*, he plays an offbeat "gynecologist" who is more representative of a holistic family doctor *cum* medical school teacher. This illustrates that the recent wave of enthusiasm for holistic medicine has been building for decades. The film's prologue signals a shift in medical films by setting the tone for what turns out to be a severe indictment of the medical establishment, once one cuts through the decorative and gooey icing:

> This is the partial story of Dr. Noah Praetorius. There may be some who will claim to have identified Doctor Praetorius once. There may be some who will reject the possibility that such a doctor lived or could have lived. And there may be some who will hope that if he hasn't or doesn't, he most certainly should.
>
> Our story is also—always with high regard—about Medicine and the Medical Profession. Respectfully, therefore, with humble gratitude, this film is dedicated to one who has inspired man's unending battle against Death—and without whom that battle is never won...the patient.

The film opens with Dr. Praetorius's faculty colleague, Prof. Elwell (Hume Cronyn) trying to collect damaging evidence against him from his former housekeeper played by Margaret Hamilton, the wicked Witch of the West in *The Wizard of Oz* (fig. 5). We learn

FIGURE 5. *People Will Talk*. Miss Pickett (Margaret Hamilton) gives the malevolent Professor Elwell (Hume Cronyn) ammunition in his attempt to disbar her former employer, Dr. Praetorius (Cary Grant).

that "Doc Praetorius cured them all. He would jes' sit and talk about a patient's miseries and talk them into getting well. My aunt's 108; four times she settled down to die and four times he talked her back to health." "Was he a doctor?" she is asked. "Do you mean school doctor out of books? Wouldn't be caught dead with one of them." Elwell says, "Tell me about this healer, this miracle worker." She responds, "You're a professor. It's hard to make you understand anything that's not in a book. Most things in life are not in a book." "Spare me your philosophy," he says as he poses the most damaging questions. We are kept in the dark as to her answers when the housekeeper, who had refused to be in the room alone with Elwell with the door closed for fear of being raped, proceeds to shut the door.

Elwell is late for anatomy class and Dr. P begins it much to the delight of the students. He tells them, "A cadaver in a classroom is not a dead human being. The human body is not necessarily a human being. You won't dissect love or hate, despair or anxieties that motivated her existence. They ceased to exist when she ceased to exist. You will dissect organs." At this, a student Annabel Higgins (Jeanne Crain) faints. After she revives, Dr. P has her admitted to the hospital and continues his lecture.

When Elwell arrives to take over the class, Dr. P asks him for the diagnosis on a pathology specimen. He enthusiastically responds, "Malignant dysgerminoma." To which Dr. P says, "Elwell, you're the only one I know who can say 'malignant', the way other people say 'Bingo'." He then goes off to the clinic where we see him practicing common sense medicine, made out in this film to be some revelation. When told that a Mrs. Bixby wants to take home her gallstone which has been discarded, he says, "Give her another one, she won't know the difference." He tells the nurses that he doesn't want the patients awakened from a healthful sleep "to satisfy the culinary union that wants all patients fed at the same time." He also doesn't want people awakened for their vital signs.

He goes on rounds and charms each patient. One tells him that "The doctors gave me up for lost." He responds, "The nerve of some people giving up other people for lost, as if they had found them in the first place." To a dying patient, he recounts a near-death experience that he says was the greatest feeling he ever had in life (fig. 6). The patient responds: "you certainly make dying a pleasure." He then retreats to his office where he sits and looks out the window until his nurse interrupts his reverie. "Just my usual twilight sadness," he says. Then he adds, "Did it ever strike you that days die pretty much the way people

FIGURE 6. *People Will Talk*. Holistic Doctor Praetorius (Cary Grant) brings comfort to a dying patient.

do—fighting for every last minute of light before they give up to the dark?"

When he next sees Higgins, he thinks she'll be happy to learn that she is pregnant, only to find out that in typical pre-1960s Hollywood style, she had sex only once with a medical reservist who then abandoned her. He explains why she should be happy and she calls him a "pompous know-it-all." He admits to being "pompous, but not a know-it-all." "Are you afraid of what people will say?" he asks. She's most concerned about what her father will think. After she leaves, the nurse says, "She's old enough to take what's coming to her." To which Dr. P angrily replies: "Never let me hear you say that again. For one thing you're a nurse and for another you're a woman. I'm ashamed of both of you." Higgins goes out and shoots herself; fortunately, it's a flesh wound and Dr. P saves her. He then goes back to the medical school to conduct the student symphony.

After the rehearsal, he returns to the clinic and tells Higgins that it was someone else's frog and that she's not pregnant. This starts her crying again because now he knows the worst about her. This precipitates the following repartee: Higgins: "You know everything about

women." Dr. P: "Not enough." Higgins: "I don't mean as a doctor."
Dr. P: "Not even as a doctor." Higgins: "Are all your patients women?"
When he answers in the affirmative, she says, "I guess they all fall in love
with you." "Not all of them," he replies. "Just most of them," she says.
"Not even most of them," he answers. Since Cary Grant is at his hand-
some best, neither she nor the audience believes any of this balderdash.

Dr. P has dinner with his friend and colleague Professor Barker
(Walter Slezak), who lights up a cigarette and asks him why he lied to
Higgins. "To get her a good night's sleep and so she doesn't try it again."
Barker says, "A doctor's job is to diagnose physical ailments and to treat
them." Dr. P says, "It's to make sick people well. There's a vast difference between healing physical ailments and making sick people well."
Barker responds, "You country doctors lead romantic lives. Just think it
might be quintuplets" (a reference to *The Country Doctor*). He warns
him about an upcoming faculty hearing that will focus on Dr. P's methods and on the relationship with his mysterious constant companion,
Shunderson (Finlay Currie), called "the Bat."

Dr. P unexpectedly visits Higgins, who is recuperating at the home
of her father (Sidney Blackmer), who tells him, "You're an unusual man
of science, Dr. Praetorius." Annabel adds, "Dr. Praetorius has a way of
knowing people very well, very quickly." Meanwhile, the family's angry
and vicious dog is being calmed by "the Bat," who reports that "the dog
is merely frightened and unhappy." Dr. P says: "He has that in common
with most of humanity." This is followed by an interesting exchange
when Dr. P is asked by the father's brother, a large-scale farmer, if he
makes a lot of money. "I make a lot of money as a doctor. I am one of
the fortunate ones. We have one who works day and night and doesn't
make a red cent. Teachers make less. We're not like farmers and oil-
men; they don't pay us for patients we don't see and students we don't
teach." The farmer responds, "Oh, you mean the money we get for not
planting any crops." "Yes, and the depreciation and oil depletion allow-
ances. Teachers and writers rely on talent and creativity; they can't
depreciate them." This dialogue reflects not only a sympathy for hard-
working doctors and teachers but also the screenwriters' fight to get
appropriately compensated.

The next scene involves doctor and patient acknowledging their
love for one another. He insists on a quick marriage in New York where
he is scheduled to appear at a medical convention. Later when Dr. P, his
father-in-law, and Barker are playing with the electric trains his bride
bought him (and beauties they are), Elwell stops by to tell him that he is

being brought before the medical faculty board. Annabel breaks down and as Dr. P reassures her, she comments on her labile disposition. He tells her it's common in pregnant women. She wonders how that could be since they have been married only two weeks. After first telling her it's possible, he admits that she is almost three months pregnant. This leads her to say, "I've heard of doctors being noble and self-sacrificing, but you are more." He convinces her that he married her for love and not to save her good name, and they go off to the hearing. This stupidity about being pregnant is the weakest part of an already hard-to-believe story. Then come some more whoppers, only made acceptable by one of the most prescient and articulate assessments of medicine.

Elwell begins the hearing by saying that he is airing the charges against Praetorius, because "performance of duty is essential in a profession based on honor and dignity." Elwell takes the committee back to 1936 when Dr. P was a "highly successful quack and miracle worker in a remote little village in the southern part of the state named Goose Creek." Dr. P says, "I had a degree but I did not display my M.D. on the door." Elwell says, "In fact, you opened a butcher shop." P admits, "I sold meat at cost." "How did you make your money?" Elwell asks. "I made sick people well," he responds. Elwell shoots back, "In other words, you took advantage of the ignorance of its backwards inhabitants. Do you deny that they thought that you were a butcher rather than a doctor?" P gives a classic rejoinder, "Do you prefer the impression given by so many of our colleagues that they are doctors and not butchers." To which his friend Barker shouts, "Bravo."

Dr. P goes on to say, "Despite your definition of a quack as someone who doesn't practice medicine according to your rules, a quack is an unqualified practitioner who pretends to be a doctor. As for relying on faith and possibly miracles too, I consider faith properly injected into a patient as effective in maintaining life as adrenaline, and belief in miracles has been the difference between living and dying, as often as a surgeon's scalpel. The challenge to the profession is whether it will become more intimately involved with the human beings it treats or whether it is to go on in its present ways of becoming more and more a thing of serum, pills, knives, and eventually we shall evolve an electronic doctor." Elwell counters, "All this folderol has nothing to do with the ethics and honor of our profession." Barker disagrees, "It has everything to do with a genius for healing the sick. Call him a psychiatrist, high priest, voodoo medicine man, witch doctor, anything you like." We then learn that his accuser, the housekeeper, whom P was in the process of dismissing for embezzling funds, found P's diploma at the bottom of a drawer. After she let the people know they ran P out of town for not being a miracle-working butcher—but a doctor, a rather curious twist.

The only thing left to explain is Shunderson whose story is, if anything, more far-fetched than Dr. P's. The gist is that he was framed for murder and served fifteen years because there was no *corpus delicti*. After he left prison, Shunderson saw the "dead" person in a cafeteria and unintentionally killed him during a fight. He was sentenced to death for killing someone already dead (a clear case of double jeopardy). Shunderson was left for dead after being hanged. The cadaver was given to medical student P by the hangman's daughter and, after being resuscitated by P, stayed on as his faithful companion. You can understand why this film requires an enormous willingness to suspend disbelief.

Shunderson has the last word as Dr. P is acquitted and goes off to conduct the student orchestra in as histrionic a performance of Brahms *Academic Festival Overture* as one is likely to see. He tells Elwell, "You are a little man. It's not that you are short. You're little in the mind and in the heart. Tonight you tried to make a man little whose boots you couldn't touch if you stood on tiptoe on top of the highest mountain in the world. And, as it turned out, you are even littler than you were before." If hypoxia makes one so poetic, sign me up!

The Last Angry Man (1959)

This last of the unabashedly laudatory films about general practitioners will appear dated to many viewers. As my wife and daughter exited one-quarter of the way through the film, they turned one of my favorite lines on me. "That's why they don't make films the way they used to. And thank God, they don't!" Clearly, the film is a product of its time. It begins when two "Negroes" literally drop a young woman at the neighborhood doctor's doorstep. The Black all-star cast includes Billy Dee Williams, Godfrey Cambridge, Cicely Tyson, and Claudia McNeil. Unfortunately, they are relegated to one-dimensional characters. The Whites are paternalistic; the Blacks cower, with only a slight hint of the pent-up anger that will explode less than a decade later. There's also a "cool dude" with a "why should I work" persona. Still, the movie accurately captures a time and place, namely, Brooklyn just after the Dodgers left town. It was a time when Whites were moving to the suburbs and medicine was changing in ways that, after Medicare and Medicaid, would make it unrecognizable. In short, it is a morality play about the enormous transitions that set the scene for the turbulent 1960s and for the public's current discontent with the health care system.

FIGURE 7. *The Last Angry Man*. Old-time general practitioner Dr. Sam Abelman (Paul Muni) takes his battered medical bag on yet another house call.

Paul Muni received an Academy Award nomination in this, his last role, as Dr. Sam Abelman who had devoted himself to the care of patients in the Brownsville section of Brooklyn from 1912 to 1957 (fig. 7). He laments that the poor must go to clinics while those "with a few bucks" go to specialists. He tells his classmate, affluent specialist Dr. Max Vogel (Luther Adler), that the poor "too deserve to live." Vogel replies that "those people suck your blood" and he chides his friend, "You're sixty-eight years old and you're still trying to make people love you....You climb the stairs for a two dollar fee. They don't want to love you, they want to be impressed." Vogel then rolls out his diathermy machine and points to the light on top. "Do you know what that blinking red light is for?" he asks. "Nothing! It's only there to keep the customers happy." My wife remembers how in her lower middle class neighborhood in Rhode Island, the poorly educated were impressed by the technology in the doctor's office. But so are the highly educated, as demonstrated by baseball pitcher Jim Palmer's 1990s ad for user-friendly, nonclaustrophobic MRIs. The ads make you want to have one, just like the ballplayers do.

Two stories are interwoven through the film. The first involves the young Black troublemaker Josh Quincy (Williams) who has a new-onset seizure diagnosed as Hughlings Jackson syndrome by Abelman. His suspicion of a brain tumor is confirmed and Vogel agrees to operate only because of his long friendship with Abelman. The boy, with his head still swathed in bandages, checks out of the hospital and refuses Abelman's plea that he return. Vogel asks Abelman why he continues to care for Quincy. The reply is, "Because he's my patient." Meanwhile, Abelman's nephew writes a human interest piece about him for a New York newspaper. Seeing the article, a television producer Woodrow Wilson Thrasher (David Wayne) visits Abelman to convince him to appear on his show that glorifies "real people." Abelman tells him about his immigrant parents who sacrificed and made sure he succeeded in America by exposing him to Whittier, Thoreau, and Longfellow. Parenthetically, my immigrant grandmother bought a set of Dickens for her children and my wife's father did the same. Abelman rails against "the drug companies, the dishonest doctors, the quacks who scare people into remedies and tests they don't need." Abelman agrees to consider being on the show, although he is against it. To him, the television producer "belongs to a new age, the age of galoots, the age of the fast buck, the something-for-nothing crowd." How's that for forecasting the decades to come!

Indeed, Thrasher, whose drug of choice is dexedrine rather than cocaine, admits to using people to get ahead. What matters most are ratings and paying for his house in suburbia. He and the network try to buy the house Abelman has always wanted, in order to entice him to appear on the show. When he learns about it, Abelman refuses to be bought. Then, Thrasher asks Abelman's nephew, "Do you think we can get him on the show if we promise him no compensation at all. The answer is, "Of course we can; that's the kind of doctor Dr. Abelman is." As the television program is set to air, Abelman gets a call that Quincy is in jail and in bad shape after an attempted robbery. Abelman rushes up two flights of stairs to reach him, and as he does, he collapses of a heart attack. He insists on being taken home where, despite anticoagulants, a portable electrocardiograph and an oxygen tent, the good doctor slips away. Vogel, distraught at his friend's death, writes on the death certificate as the cause of death: "Coronary Occlusion" and "Fighting Other People's Battles."

So, yes they don't make films like this anymore, but maybe they should. Despite its flaws, the film is special because its message transcends time and place, namely, that a single individual can, without fanfare or desire for gain, make a difference in people's lives. This image of a kindly selfless solo practitioner was fixed in the minds of the public and of idealistic entrants into the profession for decades after the myth had lost any semblance of reality. In the next chapter, we will explore other images of institutional medicine and the surgeons and diagnosticians who replaced the "country doctor." Before doing so, we'll conclude with a recent glitzy attempt to resurrect the image of the solo doctor.

Doc Hollywood (1991)

Doc Hollywood, a lightweight film blessed with a thoroughly engaging cast and an offbeat love story, is a 1990s attempt to resurrect the small-town doctor. It opens in the emergency room of "Washington Presbyterian" (really Columbia Presbyterian in New York). Cocksure fourth-year medical student Ben Stone (Michael J. Fox) is suturing someone and counting the days, "Beverly Hills, plastic surgery, the most beautiful women in the world, what do these three things have in common? Answer: "me in one week." A colleague pegs him as a friendless, arrogant "schmuck," but also "a good doctor," telling him, "I thought you'd go into real medicine." "Am I making a mistake?" Stone asks. The response is "cosmetic surgery is clean, you make tons of money, nobody dies, what's wrong with that?"

Stone tools off to Los Angeles in his red Porsche convertible, but unfortunately he missed geography class, because he ends up running off the road in Grady, South Carolina, and winds up destroying the local judge's fence and smashing up his car. Touted as "the Squash Capital of the World," the town is "in acute need of medical care"; so he is sentenced to sixteen hours of community service at Memorial Hospital. It's now close to midnight and he asks to see the town doctor. The nurse on duty (Edye Byrde) shows him the doctor's sign, "When to call me: You've been stabbed, shot, poisoned, separated from an appendage, knocked or beaten unconscious, been run over by a tractor, or generally about to bleed to death (fig. 8). Otherwise, leave me alone." Shades of Doctor Bull!

Old Doctor Hogue (Barnard Hughes) may be a piece of work, but he proves to be as sharp as his screen predecessors. When a boy who is choking and turning blue is brought to the hospital, Stone diagnoses a

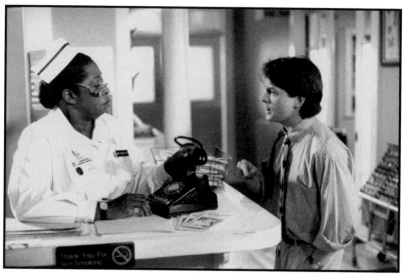

FIGURE 8. *Doc Hollywood.* Arrogant Dr. Ben Stone (Michael J. Fox), derailed on his way to his plastic surgery residency in Los Angeles, doesn't impress Nurse Packer (Edye Byrde) who warns him not to wake up the small-town general practitioner.

leaky mitral valve and arranges to send the boy by helicopter to the nearest medical center for emergency surgery. Hogue appears in the nick of time and tells Stone that the blue color is from "bismuth subnitrate, a homegrown antacid," a treatment for diarrhea. He correctly surmises that the boy is choking because he sampled his father's chewing tobacco (see *Welcome Stranger* for a similar scene). He calls Stone, "Doc Hollywood" and tells him he "doesn't know crap from Crisco." The battle of old gunfighter and new kid on the block intensifies when he asks Stone what's new in medical school. Stone responds sarcastically, "So much has changed in the forty years since you went to medical school that I wouldn't know where to begin."

Stone falls for single mother Lou (Julie Warner) who makes a striking film debut as a "vision" bathing in the local lake. We later learn that this feisty charmer was pregnant at nineteen and that she and her boy friend, Wayne, left for New York to attend college. However, after Wayne abandoned her to become a Chippendale dancer, she finished school and returned to Grady to raise their child, drive the local ambulance, and study for the bar. A committed vegetarian and environmentalist, she is content to live the small-town life with current boy friend Hank, an insurance agent, played by Woody Harrelson with a warmth he has not shown since his *Cheers* role. The screenwriter alludes to that television show by referring to its star, Ted Danson, near the end of the film.

Stone and Lou begin to bond during their rural house calls. When she says it's her favorite part of the job, he responds, "House calls used to be an essential part of every doctor's practice. It's the only way to get to know your patient." Stone pulls a toy car out of a child's ear and reads a long letter to an illiterate expectant couple. In a pretty crude conclusion to this paean to house calls, they end up running around dribbling urine (which repels deer) in a field where hunters have set up a blind. The twosome is called back to town because Hogue is having a heart attack. Hogue tries to stop Stone from administering lidocaine, saying "I'm the senior sawbones here" and then has a cardiac arrest. After being resuscitated, Hogue holds court for his friends, as they are all being shooed out by Stone. Hogue tells them, "Don't mind Doc Hollywood, he doesn't know what it means to be beloved."

At the evening soiree for the annual Squash Festival, the mayor, wonderfully played by David Ogden Stiers, tries to convince Stone to stay. He and Lou dance romantically to Patsy Cline's rendition of "Crazy For Loving You" and then row out on the lake during the fireworks. Lou, who had refused to be a "one night stand," now welcomes a night of sex, but it's Stone's turn to refuse on principle. That evening, he barrels out of town, only to be flagged down by the illiterate expectant father to help his wife who is in their truck during the last stages of labor. Stone reluctantly stops and finds that the baby is "sideways" and that he has to turn her for a breech delivery on the truck's tailgate, using his Armani shirt as a swaddling cloth. While the delivery is in progress, his car gets totaled again.

Hogue later asks him if it was his first breech. Stone responds, "It's the first baby I ever delivered by myself" Wow! Hogue then opens a cabinet filled with pictures and says, "Over seven hundred babies I delivered in this town. I helped them through every sneeze and sniffle and in some cases walked them to the gravesite." Later, the baby's mother tells Stone they named the baby Benjamina after him (see *Miss Susie Slagle's* for a similar scene) and the father who can't afford to pay him gives him a corncob pipe and a chit to take the fee out in trade. The townsfolk chip in for a plane ticket to Los Angeles and Lou refuses Stone's plea to go with him saying that she's decided to marry Hank.

In Los Angeles, he meets Dr. Halberstrom, the program chief at the luxurious clinic. Aptly played by George Hamilton (as tanned as ever), he tells Stone that it wasn't because they were from the same small Indiana town or because he knew his father that he was chosen above the hundreds of applicants. It was because of a call from Doc Hogue recommending him. He goes on to say that "the secret to medicine is building up a good case load. No one wants to admit it, but medicine is a volume business. Ninety-nine percent of cosmetic surgery is boilerplate. One percent is meaningful, like cleft palate." He asks him to check if the "patient in 434 is preop" so they can fit in one more surgery before their golf game. Predictably, despite the elegant digs and the big bucks, Stone turns his back on Hollywood and returns to Grady. All's well that ends well. Wouldn't it be great if solving the problems of maldistribution of physicians and medical care in rural America and the inner cities were so easy!

NOTES

1. Questions for Sidney Lumet. New York Times Magazine Section, November 23, 1997, p 31.
2. Dostoyevsky F. The Brothers Karamazov. New York: Modern Library, 1950, as quoted in Ann Intern Med 1996; 124: 249.
3. Steadman. The profession as viewed by the public. Boston Med Surg J 1895; 133: 177–182.
4. Spears J. The Doctors on Screen. In: Spears J., Hollywood: The Golden Era. Cranbury, New Jersey: A.S. Barnes & Co, 1971
5. Cozzens JG. The Last Adam. New York: Harcourt, Brace, and Co., 1933.
6. Herrick JB. Relation between the specialist and the practitioner: Essentials of the specialist. JAMA 1921; 76: 975–976.
7. Weiner E. Remembering Robert Young: Model dad, dream doctor. TV Guide, August 8-14, 1997, p 41–44.
8. Shortland M. Medicine and Film: A Checklist, Survey and Research Resource. Oxford: Wellcome Unit for the History of Medicine, 1989.
9. Faden RR and Beauchamp TL. A History and Theory of Informed Consent. New York: Oxford University Press, 1986.

3

Benevolent Institutions:
The Rise of the Hospital,
Internship, and Specialization

The shift from solo practice to institutional medicine resulted from the emerging dominance of the hospital in physician training and health care.[1] This chapter will look at the integral role of the hospital in the training of surgeons and internists. It may be hard to believe, but few doctors before 1900 had any supervised patient contact. That gives the term "practicing medicine" a whole new meaning. It wasn't until about 1925 that serving an internship became a common practice.[2] On completing internship, as shown in the 1933 film, *Mary Stevens, M.D.*, the fledgling doctors went out, hung up their shingles, and hoped to make ends meet. Residencies became the norm in the 1940s, when more doctors stayed on in hospitals to be trained as surgeons and internists or, as they were then called, "diagnosticians." The term intern (or interne) literally means to be confined, and so they were, within the hospital. The terms "house officer" and "residents" also implied that these doctors lived on the premises, which they did until the 1950s. They received initially only room, board, uniforms, laundry, and spending money. Hence the wonderful title of the first Dr. Kildare movie, *Internes Can't Take Money*, in which Kildare receives a whopping ten dollars a month. In *Miss Susie Slagle's*, the genial upperclassman Mead played by Billy De Wolfe, tells the griping medical students, "You guys think you work hard. Wait till you start living at the hospital."

A major restriction on house officers was their inability to marry. In *Miss Susie Slagle's*, when Mead learns that he is one of the few successful applicants for a house-staff position at Hopkins, he calls his girl friend to tell her that they can get married in a few years. Alas, she has already married someone "with a real job, in a bank." He vows "to be the best gosh-darndest diagnostician she ever saw!" Well into the 1950s, doctors were discouraged from marrying until they finished their training, in line with the advice of Hopkins' most noted doctor, Sir William

Osler, that young doctors put their affections in cold storage.[3] After World War II, the influx of returning veterans and older students into medical schools led to the abolition of such strictures. House officers were permitted to live off site in adjacent compounds and then in apartments of their own choosing. The stipend for interns rose, although slowly and never to the level of the service rendered. What is interesting in the early films is that their low pay and internment made the doctors the object of sympathy by other hospital personnel. This changed in the 1970s. Let's start with the training of surgeons and one of the more well-known films about internship, *Men in White*.

SURGEONS AS THE GOLDEN BOYS OF MEDICINE

For reasons discussed in the introduction, surgeons replaced the general practitioner in the 1930s as the predominant image of the medical profession. The excitement that they created is illustrated in the promotional trailer for *Men in White*, an adaptation of Sidney Kingsley's play.[4] It's almost better than the film. With appropriate fanfare, the narrator trumpets, "Doctor Ferguson (Clark Gable) is a heart specialist taking temperatures sky-high. It's the story of a mighty surgeon in the operating room, but just a man in the arms of a beautiful woman. He can mend broken bodies, but he can't mend broken hearts." Meanwhile, the clips show surgical film standbys (the slapping of the scalpel into the surgeon's palm and the wiping of the surgeon's brow in particularly tense moments).

Men in White (1934)

Men in White opens with a welder falling off a scaffold and sustaining "a compound fracture of both legs and possible internal injuries." He is picked up by the St. George Hospital ambulance manned by two scatter-brained interns. Clearly, this is no job for a mere intern, but for George Ferguson, the super-intern, who is busy ordering insulin for a little girl (insulin had only been discovered nine years before). Unfortunately, an over-the-hill attending physician changes his orders from 20 to 40 units, almost killing the girl and sending the parents into hysteria. But our hero saves the day. When the doctor wants to give her more insulin, Ferguson wrestles away the syringe or "hypo," as it is referred to throughout, and administers glucose (fig. 1). The attending physician threatens, "I'll have you brought before the medical board." Fortunately, that's the extent of his interference. This illustrates how long the battle between some house officers and attending physicians has gone on. Even

FIGURE 1. *Men in White*. Super-intern (Clark Gable) overrides the order of an over-the-hill attending physician and saves a child from an insulin overdose.

during my residency thirty-five years ago, there were some attending physicians who were not comfortable with procedural or hands-on acute care; they were content to let the residents handle the cases and to take the credit for any success, as this one later does.

Hungry interns grouse at their treatment in a hospital that looks like an art deco hotel with a well-stocked library and grand staircases. When one asks for a chocolate bar, he is told that there are "slops at 12:30." Another says, "There is nothing in the Hippocratic oath about what they feed us or how hard we work or what they pay us." This prompts an old-timer to declaim, " We've come so far since I was a boy. You youngsters take all that for granted. You don't know the men who have sweated to give us anesthesia, sterilization, surgery, x-ray. Pasteur, Jenner, Virchow, Metchnikoff, Sir Charles Bell. All greats. We have greats today like Doctor Hochberg."

In the next scene, we are introduced to Hochberg, played by Jean Hersholt, who completes a surgical consult by saying: "No rush to operate there; try to treat her medically first." "Fine surgeon you are, advising not to operate," another tells him. Ferguson, as the best intern, will be given the coveted opportunity to stay on and work with Hochberg, which means "16- to 18-hour days at twenty dollars a week for five years." This is crucial to whether "he'll become an important man." It involves working in Vienna with Van Heiselberg for a year before returning to join Hochberg, who later ups the ante to ten years of indentured service. "In my day," he says, "students spent all day working with only an occasional beer for relaxation." This prospect is decidedly unappealing to Laura Hudson, Ferguson's rich girl friend, played by Myrna Loy. She and George meet for a little smooching on the sunroof and she tries to convince him to open an office after internship, to specialize, and to work regular hours. He is reluctant, saying, "all my life, I've wanted to be a fine doctor." Later, he meets Doctor Levine (Otto Kruger), who got married and threw away a chance to work with Hochberg. Now he's reduced to borrowing twenty dollars because his practice is nonexistent. Levine asks Ferguson, "Medicine, why do we kill ourselves for it?" Ferguson responds, "I often wonder about it myself."

There's a scene that shows how precarious hospital budgets were before hospitalization insurance. The hospital board is told of a 163 thousand dollar deficit despite the fact that "we've cut to the bone. Interns are allowed only two outside calls a month." A board member asks, "Couldn't we reduce the laboratories?" Hochberg replies: "THEY ARE the hospital; pathology, x-ray, chemistry." The board members then express the hope that Ferguson's rich future father-in-law will underwrite the debt if they appoint him to the staff. Hochberg is sure that "he won't sacrifice his career for an easy practice."

No hospital movie would be complete without sex. A nurse walks down the hospital corridor like Mae West. The two scatterbrains argue over the "redhead" and invite Ferguson to a "party with lab alcohol and an x-ray tech who wears her dress close to her skin." When Ferguson refuses and instead agrees to start a difficult transfusion on a patient with "thrombosed superficial veins," one says, "Being in love is killing your sex life." The big subplot involves a student nurse Barbara (Elizabeth Allan), awed by Ferguson, who visits the intern quarters, ostensibly to get his materia medica notes (strictly against nursing policies). He sends her on her way and goes to see a patient, but she remains in his room until he returns.

Later, Ferguson goes to his wedding rehearsal and things start to unravel when Barbara, calling for Ferguson, gets admitted after a botched back alley abortion. As in many 1930s films, one night of passion leads to a pregnancy. Fiancée Laura gets to scrub in and faints after hearing Barbara tell Ferguson she loves him, before going under anesthesia. After the operation, Ferguson tells Hochberg he's going to marry Barbara and go into practice. Hochberg reminds him that Levine gave up a fellowship to marry and is now starving. Ferguson asks, "What good is a profession that can't give you bread and butter after you've wasted ten years of your life on it." Hochberg summons Laura who won't return Ferguson's calls and tells her that the girl is dying. "A blood clot and we're helpless. Forty years in medicine and I can't help her." Parenthetically, pulmonary embolus is an example of a once uniformly fatal condition that is now treatable with anticoagulants. Barbara, who knows she is dying, asks to see Laura and exonerates Ferguson. She says, "He had had an awful day. Six long operations. He had lost a patient. He's going to make a great doctor. He needs you." She sends for Ferguson, asks him to hold her hand, and dies. Ferguson closes her staring eyes. In the background, the shadow of the window frame suggests a cross.

Hochberg and Ferguson have another heavy dialogue about the state of medicine, "We don't know anything. We are only groping, but we're making progress. Our guesses today are closer than they were twenty years ago, and twenty years from now they'll be even closer." Hochberg tells Laura: "My father was a surgeon, a good one. I remember when I was a boy, about thirteen, he came to my room and apologized to me because he was going to die. His heart had gone bad on him. He could have lived twenty years longer if he had taken it easier and quit work, but he wouldn't quit. He used to say 'above all else is humanity.' That's a pretty big thought. Alongside of it, you and I don't really matter very much." The lines seem to foreshadow the ending of *Casablanca*. Laura meets with Ferguson and tells him that she's sailing for Europe. "Work, work with Doctor Hochberg. It's bigger than any of us—Humanity! When you're in Vienna I'd like to see you. I know you'll be frightfully busy, but there will be moments. I want to be with you then." Ferguson answers a page and the curtain comes down on another stirring doctor movie that touches all the bases.

Society Doctor (1935)

Even more explicit than *Men in White* in showcasing the conflict of the younger, better-trained doctors and their superiors is this unpretentious marriage of the gangster and doctor genres. *Society Doctor* is a little gem not because of its cinematic values but because of the preposterous scenes and classic dialogue. It also illustrates the difficulty its protagonist, an ethical paragon, has in achieving medicine's nobility as well as the flawed nature of many of its practitioners. Despite the passage of only sixty years, the dialogue, the uniforms, the pervasive smoking, and the nature of patient care make the viewer feel like an archeologist exploring medicine in a simpler time, centuries ago.

Set in Metropolitan Hospital, the film starts with the obligatory ambulance run, culminating in the patient being brought to the operating room. The scene then shifts to the office of the hospital superintendent, Dr. Waverly (Raymond Walburn) who is showing a rich couple his brand new hospital. The woman comments, "The interns look nice all dressed in white." Waverly says "Yes, yes, they're very high-tech." The husband then adds, "The nurses look nice all dressed in white," and the wife says that "it would almost be a pleasure to get sick." The wife wonders aloud, "After holding a man's life in their hands, what do they talk about?" Waverly says, "It's very technical." Cutting to the doctors, we find that their conversation is fairly mundane as one asks the other for ten bucks for a date. The hero Dr. Morgan (Chester Morris) tells assistant intern Tommy Ellis (Robert Taylor) that "young doctors can't afford to get soft on dames. To get ahead in the profession, you have to travel alone and light." Ellis tells Morgan that the millionairess Mrs. Crane (Billie Burke), who was admitted a month ago with a bruised knee, really likes him. Those were the days when nobody worried about length of stay for those who could pay.

In the next scene, a young well-dressed man is brought in complaining of a bellyache. Ellis advises an immediate operation for a perforating appendix. The patient's father says, "You're just an intern" and says he will wait for his physician Dr. Harvey (Henry Kolker). Ellis replies that he will call his superior, "Dr. Morgan is head intern and an excellent surgeon." The young man tells Morgan that his pain has ceased. Morgan notes that this is the most serious sign of a ruptured appendix and, along with the fever of 104 and the white count of 13,000, means that he must operate. The father refuses permission and Morgan calls him "stubborn." When the man asks Morgan if he knows to whom he is speaking, he replies, "You're Harris Snowden. You have a million dollars and enough pull to get me canned. But you don't have enough pull to drag this kid back to life when gangrene sets in." Then a woman arrives who turns out to have been secretly married to the son for six months. Morgan tells her that she takes precedence over the father and obtains consent to proceed. The father runs to Waverly's office to get the operation stopped, but Morgan tells the nurse to cut off the phone line. The operation is a grand success.

During a post-operative smoke, the crackerjack surgical nurse Madge (Virginia Bruce) tells Morgan that "the operation will go into the record book as a masterpiece of the surgical art," but that there will be repercussions because Harris and Harvey have complained about his behavior. He tells her that Dr. Harvey's patients are "a bunch of rich old women with vivid imaginations." She pleads with him to be respectful to Dr. Waverly, whom he calls an "old fogey," reminding him that Waverly is "your superior." Called to Waverly's office, he confronts Harvey who tells him that "there was a point of ethics involved." Morgan accuses him of being upset at "losing a fat fee" and calls him a "perfumed quack." Waverly dismisses him from the staff.

Morgan blames himself for his plight saying, "When I was a medical student, I believed in the ethics of my profession. I was a hero-worshipper. I revered men like Walter Reed, Murphy, Banting, and the others. I thought all doctors were like that. Giants serving humanity. I wanted to be like them. Then I came here to work under you. What did I find? A bunch of pygmies, little men with little knowledge bumping their heads at the feet of politicians and millionaires. Have you read Steiglitz's new theories on abdominal surgery? It's the most revolutionary medical advance in generations. I've read it. Dr. Ellis has read it. Have you read it? No. What do you read? The *Social Register*, *Bradstreet Reports*, and the financial columns. Whatever new ideas there are here are in the heads of the new doctors. There was a time long ago when you both hoped and planned to become doctors. Now look at you. Two little men with big bellies, empty heads, and craven hearts." How's that for laying out your superiors!

He walks out and tells Ellis that he "was canned." Ellis replies, "The operation was a success, but the doctor died." Madge comes to console him and it's clear that she loves him and he loves her, too. She asks why he never made a pass at her. He says, "Because any young idiot who's sap enough to become a doctor has to face one thing. There can only be two types of women in his life: meal-tickets and 'good-time Gerties.' You weren't a meal-ticket." She responds, "So you mercifully spared me the chance to be a 'good-time Gertie.'" The conversation is curtailed when Mrs. Crane, the rich socialite, calls Morgan to examine her knee. Harvey comes to the room and sends Morgan away, but not before Mrs. Crane learns that Morgan has been dismissed. Crane reminds Harvey that she has referred him a lot of rich patients and that he must tell Waverly to reinstate Morgan.

Cut to two reporters smoking in front of the "No Smoking" sign. They are joined by Ellis, Madge, and Morgan. When a reporter learns that Morgan plans to go into private practice, he says, "Private practice is pretty tough for a young sawbones. Some of these birds are yanking tonsils for a can of tomatoes." Morgan sends Madge and Ellis up to do a tonsillectomy. During a pre-op smoke, Madge says, "There's nothing like a cigarette before a tonsillectomy or after one for that matter." Ellis proposes to Madge, but she gently refuses. Meanwhile, Morgan, who has been told that he has been reinstated, goes up to see Mrs. Crane. He thinks it's because they realize how good he is, but she tells him it's because she ordered it (fig. 2). He comments, "That dull thud you heard was a few principles hitting the floor. I used to think I couldn't get along without them, but I know better now. Crane offers to set him up in practice. At first, he refuses saying that not all doctors are alike. "Some are pretty dumb. They have a sense of duty. They stick to working in hospitals where they can learn and perform a service. They don't get much money. They can't afford cars, good clothes, or to get married when they're young." When Crane asks why he shouldn't have a nice car and good clothes, he gives in. He explains to Madge, "I'm tired of being broke. I abandoned my conscience along the way." Madge is shocked. She tells him of Ellis's proposal. Morgan asks what Ellis can offer her. She tells him "his love." Morgan asks, "Is it love when all you have is four bucks and a trunk full of white pants?"

Madge leaves to assist Ellis. Afterwards, Ellis bites his lip and tells her, "I'm a doctor now, Madge....I had my diploma and have been working at my profession, but I didn't understand what it meant to be a doctor....There under my hands a human being was dying and I kept control of myself. I saved his life." He then goes to the patients' private larder to fashion a post-op celebration, but the nurses have gotten there ahead of him. He laughingly scolds them, "Filching food from a poor dame who's down to her last million?" and takes chicken, olives, and champagne. Returning to Madge, he toasts her, "Here in this house of pain, I toast the most valuable thing in the world, to your health, Lady." The disgusted Madge tells him of Morgan's decision and when Ellis again proposes, she accepts.

There are numerous subplots, including a crooked insurance agent and a gangster who shoots an Irish policeman named Harrigan. The handcuffed gangster visits his mother who was admitted to the hospital, but did not allow the house staff to examine her while waiting for her

FIGURE 2. *Society Doctor*. Rich patient (Billie Burke) gets handsome head intern (Chester Morris) reinstated and promises to build him a new operating room in pastel colors.

private doctor. Seems that Momma is a crafty one; she has a gun under her pillow for Sonny Boy. The gangster's escape is foiled by Morgan whom he shoots even after being reminded of how Morgan once cut a bullet out of him. Then, the policeman's wife kills the hoodlum.

Morgan's in dire straits. Waverly and Harvey offer him no hope. On learning that the bullet penetrated the gastrointestinal tract and the mesentery, he bypasses his superiors and tells Ellis, "You must do the Steiglitz procedure, you sap. He had only animals to experiment with. We've got me. Here's a chance to try it out." Sweating profusely, he says, "Give me a spinal; I want to know what's going on. Arrange a mirror, so that I can see it. Hurry up. If I collapse before you're through, don't forget a drain. No telling how much infectious material the bullet dragged through me." Morgan tells Madge that he turned down the money and Mrs. Crane, too. As the operation proceeds, he tells Ellis, "Better cut right through there. Now just a little bit more. Careful!" Looking up at the observation tower, he adds smilingly, "You've got a full house. Better take a look at the transverse colon. It looks pretty bad." Ellis says, "Yes, I can see it." Morgan says "You'll have to cut it out." When Ellis is reluctant, Morgan asks "Who's running this show? I said, 'Cut.'" Ellis says, "OK, you're the doctor" and Morgan passes out.

A reporter asks Waverly, "You mean to say he's directing his own operation?" When told that he is, he says, "What a man!" Later, a reporter calls in the story, saying "He was a good guy." As headlines report Morgan's death, we see him regaining consciousness. Waverly tells Ellis to record his notes, "Medical journals are sure to be interested in the advanced work we're doing here." Of course, Madge decides to marry Morgan instead of Ellis. The movie ends with Morgan uttering a classic line, "Bring on that hypo; I want to sleep." He's directing his care right to the end with panache and jargon. Like *Men in White*, this film left the impression that super-doctors strode a land crowded with pygmies.

Internes Can't Take Money (1937)

The first and one of the best of the Kildare movies, *Internes Can't Take Money* was produced at Paramount before it lost the rights to Max Brand's Kildare stories to MGM.[5] Like *Society Doctor*, it's part of the gangster/doctor movie genre, featuring such characters as "Stooly" Martin, Wipey, Weaselpuss and assorted "mugs." The 1997 film, *Playing Doctor*, is an homage to this film (see chapter 7). As the film opens, the camera pans on the Mountview General Hospital clinic where the sign reads "Clinic Hours 12 to 3 daily; Women and Men; Take a number." An intern uses a head mirror to diagnose "strep throat" and when he is told that the temperature is 101°, he says: "Better admit her and take a blood culture." This reminds us that pneumonia was a common complication of severe strep infections before antibiotics. A not-so-suave intern is asked by an obese patient (called "Stout Woman" in the credits) what she can do to lose weight. His answer is, "Try to exercise by pushing yourself away from the table three times a day."

The interns are convened by the hospital superintendent who is dismissing one of them at the request of the surgical committee for doing "wholly experimental surgery" by sewing the rectus muscle into the liver instead of using mattress sutures in a patient who would have died anyway. Like many of his successors in the 1990s, the administrator doesn't want "the hospital exposed to legal risk." He warns them: "This is a hospital, not an experimental laboratory. You worked your way through high school, college, and medical school. Don't spoil it with too much theory." Later, Kildare will challenge that edict.

A fellow intern (all are men) says, "Secretaries get $27.50 a week and there goes a possible Semmelweiss, a potential Pasteur, and we pay him ten dollars a month. If he were a truck driver or a shoe salesman, he could go out and get another job. Ten wasted years of study behind him and nothing ahead of him. Sitting up all night, standing up all day." This harks back to the Depression when medicine did not always guarantee an income and some doctors drove taxicabs.

The most interesting medical events involve impromptu surgery. The first operation is performed by Kildare (Joel McCrea) on a gangster in the back of a bar. "Get me boiling water quick," he shouts. Pulling off a violin string for suture material, he asks for "best-in-the-house four-teen-year-old rum" to sterilize the field, a pair of scissors, and a needle. An impressed bystander says: "The kid's got eyes in his fingers." Later, the bartender hands Kildare an envelope containing one thousand dollars. When he dates one of his patients, Janet Haley, an ex-con played by Barbara Stanwyck (fig. 3), he tells her that he has to give it back because "internes can't take money while they're serving at a hospital."

FIGURE 3. *Internes Can't Take Money*. The original Dr. Kildare (Joel McCrea) helps single mother and ex-con (Barbara Stanwyck) locate her daughter.

He reckons that it would take a long time for him to make that kind of money in that "two bucks a visit is all I'd rate." She replies, "You earned it; it isn't like you asked for it." But he's adamant, "I'm not allowed to take money. Internes can't do that while they're serving time at a hospital. If we took money, then the patients who couldn't pay wouldn't get the same care." What a refreshing dose of ethics! At first, the gangster Hanlon (Lloyd Nolan) is offended that Kildare won't take his money, but the bartender tells him, "You don't want to get the kid in a fix. They got rules." So Hanlon extends a carte blanche IOU anytime he can help him.

Kildare soon cashes in the IOU for Haley, a widow who is trying to locate her lost child and is being coerced into providing sexual favors by Stooly (Barry Macollum), another gangster, unless she comes up with one thousand dollars. When Stooly gets "plugged," Kildare performs emergency surgery in a betting parlor. He sews the rectus abdominis muscle into the liver, even though he risks getting cashiered from the hospital. His assistant says, "Too bad this can't go on record, you'd be famous overnight." The man survives and tells Haley that her child is in the St. James orphanage where the movie ends in a profusion of Catholic imagery. Kildare is on hand to see the good fruits of his labor.

THE DIAGNOSTICIAN

Metro-Goldwyn-Mayer's *Kildare* series that followed *Internes* was probably most responsible for sustaining a favorable impression of doctors for decades and also for attracting people to the field. For example, renowned pediatrician Mary Ellen Avery, the first woman to hold a major clinical chair at Harvard Medical School, credited the Kildare movies, along with her neighbor, a woman doctor, as well as her pediatrician, as influencing her career choice. As she recalls it, "I was about twelve when the Kildare movies appeared, an age when I was growing up and trying to decide what I was going to do with my life. The medicine excited me. Kildare could cure almost any disease in the course of a two-hour movie" (personal communication, November 11, 1997).

The best summary and analysis of the series was written by Philip and Beatrice Kalisch.[6] As they point out, the pictures were formulaic with a fairly stable group of ensemble players consisting of doctors, nurses, and administrators, as well as a stereotypic Black valet, a dotty switchboard operator who knew all the hospital gossip, and her loyal, but dumb, ambulance driver boyfriend. The central character was not Kildare, but Dr. Leonard Gillespie (Lionel Barrymore), the chief of service who, as the Kalisches note, "gave a new meaning to the public image of an authoritative medical diagnostician still wholly devoted to the high ideals of medicine."[6] Gruff and short-tempered even with patients, Gillespie did not tolerate fools or slipshod medicine. However, regular viewers of the series knew that he had the proverbial "heart of gold" and so were not put off by his gruffness.

Jimmy Kildare is "the one Gillespie has 'waited years for'—the one who has that genius for diagnosis which cannot be taught or picked up from books."[6] However, Gillespie shows him that making a brilliant diagnosis like Q fever isn't enough. The patient doesn't get better until Gillespie lends him money to pay off the remaining eight payments on his piano, something that has been weighing on his mind. This leads to Gillespie's lesson *du jour,* namely, that a diagnostician must listen to his patient and look "into the patient's mind, heart, and soul." In some respects, the patients these diagnosticians saw were more representative of those seen in office practice than in most hospital-based residency programs even well into the 1990s. Many were the "worried well" with family and personal problems, nutritional deficits, and sometimes imagined illnesses or important mental health problems and not simply exotic diseases. The following brief synopses will suffice to give a flavor of this series.

Young Dr. Kildare (1938)

This film introduces the new Kildare, played by Lew Ayres. He's fresh out of medical school and is returning home to practice with his Dad in a town described as "just like New York City with two ten-cent stores, two banks, and two doctors." Visits cost three dollars on credit or two dollars if you pay cash. Jimmy's girl friend gives him a shingle with his name on it and his folks turn the front parlor into an office. His father tells him, "If you don't starve before your first patient comes along, you'll be a success," and gives him an inscribed fountain pen and a pocket thermometer. He also passes on some advice, "Whenever you're in doubt about what ails a patient, give him bicarbonate of soda and see what develops in the morning and don't expect to get too much sleep."

Kildare describes his reluctance to hang out his shingle to his childhood sweetheart. "Alice, there are two ways of being a doctor. One is for the living you can make out of it. Now, I could marry you, settle down, and count on taking over my father's practice." "Why don't you?" she asks. "Because being a doctor is bigger than three meals a day. Ehrlich was that kind of doctor. So was Lister. I'm certainly no Lister.

But I know somehow that I have to find out where I belong in medicine. And there's no way to do it in Dartford."

That Jimmy is indeed destined for higher things is evident when he gets a call from New York telling him that he had "figured out what's wrong with a patient who had been sick for a month" and he agrees to be an intern at the cavernous Blair General Hospital. After sending him to the appropriate office, the receptionist comments: "When I get unhappy about my job, I think about what interns have to go through for twenty bucks a month." Parenthetically, the stipend doubled in one year since the last movie. As the interns talk about their future, one dreams about the day "when I'm taking out Park Avenue appendixes at ten thousand dollars each." Another thinks about getting five thousand dollars a baby. A third plans to be a "Derm doctor, the patients never get better and never get sick" (see *Not As a Stranger* for similar dialogue). Kildare says, "I'm going to be a diagnostician."

We next meet the crotchety Dr. Gillespie played by Lionel Barrymore who was mainly seen in a wheelchair because of the stage of his rheumatoid arthritis (which is evident in closeups of his gnarled hands). Gillespie is lecturing a patient, "You'll live four months with whiskey and six months without. It's a coronary and it's too late." As the patient leaves, he turns to Kildare and says, "The fools have thrown away the gift God gave them." Then, he adds, "You wouldn't talk to them like that. You'd baby them with soft talk. You're going to save the human race." He then challenges Kildare to make a diagnosis of a lesion on his hand. Kildare wants to feel above the elbow for an epitrochlear node because he thinks it's a melanoma that may have metastasized (fig. 4). Gillespie impatiently asks him, "Death? How soon?" And Kildare responds: "With luck, you have one year." Later we learn that the snap diagnosis is correct. However, amnesia for this scene developed in the course of the fourteen sequels with Gillespie even continuing on without Kildare when Lew Ayres was dropped from the series for declaring himself a conscientious objector during World War II. Van Johnson and Keye Luke, who is best remembered as Charley Chan's number one son, came on as assistants to squirm under Gillespie. Neither achieved the same chemistry or public appeal in the role that Ayres did.

Gillespie articulates his philosophy of medicine, "to treat people is one thing, but to study them and find out what's wrong with them, that's another—a diagnostician checking and rechecking." He asks the interns, "Who's going to be in charge of my ambulance?" and adds derisively,

FIGURE 4. *Young Dr. Kildare.* After making the diagnosis of melanoma, intern Kildare (Lew Ayres) proceeds to check Dr. Gillespie (Lionel Barrymore) for epitrochlear nodes.

"Every ambulance has three pairs of hands but only one set of brains." Kildare is selected, and on his first ambulance run, he administers artificial respiration to a rich socialite who has attempted suicide in a cheap apartment. As he does so, he asks the attendant "to hold a mirror to her lips and tell me when it clouds up." She survives and is transported to the hospital where he tells the nurse, "She's not a mental case, so just put a screen around her and let her sleep." Parenthetically, as a resident at Presbyterian Hospital in New York in 1963, I helped take care of an elderly hospital volunteer who had a cardiac arrest while changing at her locker. After she was resuscitated, the attending physician ordered that the curtains be drawn to see if she would come back to a sentient state before he decided to do anything else. Everyone was surprised when, within an hour, she cheerfully called out for a cup of tea.

Despite Kildare's excellent work, the rich father pressures the hospital director to call in a specialist. The director explains to Kildare why he must do so, "Hospitals have needs that can be met only through the generosity of wealthy men." He calls in a pompous, eminent psychiatrist who tells the family that the girl has "schizophrenia" and is insane.

Our intern hero finds out the real truth. She had had a mixed-up relationship with a gambler and had attempted suicide. This breakthrough leads to her cure. Nonetheless, Kildare gets discharged from the hospital for meddling in the case and the psychiatrist gets the credit for the woman's recovery.

Kildare visits Gillespie to say goodbye and is surprised that Gillespie knows that he cracked the case. Gillespie tells him, "I know everything that goes on in this hospital. That nurse Molly has been my stooge for fifteen years." Then he takes Kildare to task, calling him a "whippersnapper" and says, "You can take a thousand doctors and give all of them the same training, the same advantages and only one will have that mysterious something that makes him become a real diagnostician. It's something that God puts there for his own purposes. You have it, Kildare. I knew it the first day I saw you. I had to find out if you had the brains to use it and the courage to back it up. The last thing I wanted to know was if you thought the important thing was curing the patient or listening to the applause. And I found that out today."

He then offers Kildare the coveted position as his assistant and tells him he was right about the melanoma, so he has little time to teach him. When Kildare comments on the unfairness of it all, Gillespie (or is it Barrymore) says something that resonated with audiences who had first-hand experience with serious disease: "Disease is never fair. There is no earthly reason why we shouldn't be born healthy and live to be ninety years without even losing a tooth. We've got to work for that day. Sooner or later with all of us putting in our nickels that day will come." How's that for setting seemingly impossible expectations!

Dr. Kildare's Crisis (1940)

The *Kildare* sequels are not at the same level as their predecessors, but Dr. Gillespie and company were like family whose visits distracted Americans during a difficult time. They also had a number of redeeming moments. For example, *Dr. Kildare's Crisis* shows the terror of epilepsy as late as the early 1940s. When Kildare asks Gillespie about a condition that could cause someone to hear things besides "being nutty," his crusty mentor replies, "So you want to diagnose the case the easy way by asking me. Go to the library." Kildare finds epilepsy described as "a hereditary and seemingly incurable disease. Unless recognized and controlled, the outcome is insanity and eventual death." This one line shows how much medical knowledge has advanced in the past fifty years.

Much of the film focuses on not telling the patient or his sister (Kildare's fiancée, Mary Lamont, played by Laraine Day) (fig. 5) about the diagnosis. Gillespie advises Kildare, "It doesn't do a man any good to tell him he has an incurable disease." "What about telling his family?" Kildare asks. "It depends on their courage and character and their ability to handle the truth, unless it's hereditary and they could be affected." Parenthetically, withholding the truth about serious illness, especially cancer, was very common until the 1970s.[7]

The patient, who acts like a manic-depressive, says: "I thought epileptics fall down and foam at the mouth." Kildare gives a dissertation on "epileptic equivalents," saying, "Your kind only perverts the brain. Whiskey, meat, salt, coffee, and shock bring it on." Later, they are all thrilled when Gillespie takes a careful history and learns that the man had suffered a head injury. Gillespie, who seemed to be just an internist, does brain surgery to remove "a piece of bone that was pressing on the brain." When Kildare apologizes for missing the diagnosis, Gillespie says, "So you can see why no doctors want to have their own loved ones for patients."

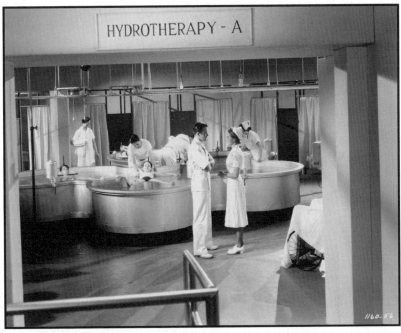

FIGURE 5. *Dr. Kildare's Crisis.* Kildare (Lew Ayres) and his fiancée, nurse Mary Lamont (Laraine Day), have a heart-to-heart in the hydrotherapy suite as polio patients receive therapy.

There are other noteworthy scenes. The nearby cafeteria's sign proclaims, "The doctors eat here. It must be good." After Kildare is up all night, Gillespie says he can have an hour for lunch, but shortens it to a half-hour when he learns that Kildare had slept a half-hour. Gillespie cautions a forty-year-old against trying to run five miles three times a week and playing baseball with his sixteen-year-old because he'll end up in the grave. The nursing superintendent, who is pictured as really running the hospital, scraps good-naturedly with Gillespie. Both are given a wide berth by the titular hospital director, an administrator.

Dr. Kildare's Wedding Day (1941)

The quintessential "Medicine Is a Jealous Mistress" movie, *Dr. Kildare's Wedding Day*, is so ludicrous that it is my series favorite. It has very little medicine and principally served to dispose of Jimmy's fiancée, nurse Mary Lamont, because Laraine Day wanted out of the series. Red Skelton adds some comic relief to cushion the blow for the audience. The film opens with Mary preparing for their impending marriage. As she tries on the dress, she wonders aloud, "Wouldn't it be terrible if getting married ruined his career?" Later, Gillespie will tell her: "A doctor's a doctor for twenty-four hours a day. The rest of the time, he can be a husband." Then he adds, "When he takes the oath, a doctor swears away all his rights as a human being. He doesn't belong to himself or his wife. He belongs to medicine." When Gillespie later realizes that he is being displaced as Kildare's second love, he petulantly tells her, "Marriage or no marriage, Jimmy Kildare's first love is medicine."

The conflict is resolved when Mary is hit by a truck on her way to catch a train for the wedding. She had been distracted by a billboard advertising, "Happiness. Nothing Down. $1 a week. Crown Furniture Co." She had had to go alone because Jimmy had an emergency call. As she lies dying, she asks, "Do I have to die?" Then she comforts Kildare, "Poor Jimmy, this is going to be much easier for me than it is for you. Poor sweet Jimmy," and she dies. This ranks as one of the sappiest lines in movie history.

Afterwards, a shaken Jimmy (fig. 6) runs away to Baltimore. Gillespie convinces him to meet him at his family's house. There he shows Kildare the microscope that "Walter Reed, who discovered the cure for yellow fever," gave him. He also tells him about his long-lost love who also died tragically, and says, "You must keep your grief in

FIGURE 6. *Dr. Kildare's Wedding Day.* A distraught Kildare (Lew Ayres) is comforted by an orderly (Jesse Green) after his fiancée's accident.

your heart. Let it temper with time, but your hands and your heart belong to medicine."

In the medical scenes, Gillespie mercilessly rebukes a woman who is despondent at not being able to have children. After telling her how he had warned her that drink was poisoning her brain, he says, "You had your warning five years ago." After the nurse removes the sobbing patient, Gillespie proclaims his inability to understand how a "woman can destroy the God-given generation that could make her life complete." Gillespie's cancer, which we remember from many movies ago, is to be evaluated by a "cancer specialist" at his sanitorium. Balking at going, Gillespie says, "Doctor's oath, you know. Patients come first." He must see a renowned symphony conductor, Labardi, who is going deaf. In a classic charting maneuver, Gillespie tells the nurse, "Put down in the case history, "a severe case of athlete's foot." This practice of writing down false diagnoses to preserve confidentiality or for insurance purposes continues today. Later, Kildare cites Goldberger's discovery of vitamin B_1 deficiency and on learning that Labardi eats a lot of spaghetti, he gives him a shot of vitamin B_1 which cures him. The picture ends with Labardi conducting a symphony written by Gillespie in memory of his lost love. These movies seem laughable today, but it's worth remembering the amazing hold they had on the public and the good will they generated for the profession.

THE TWILIGHT OF THE GOLDEN AGE OF MEDICAL MOVIES

After the Kildare series ended in 1947, the movies began to take a less reverential stance towards doctors and hospitals. *Not As a Stranger* was more hard-edged, and *People Will Talk* more offbeat and countercultural (see chapter 2). The best examples of transitional films that still have some good things to say about hospitals and doctors are *The Young Doctors* (1961) and *The Interns* (1962).

The Young Doctors (1961)

The Young Doctors nicely conveys the optimism and excitement of the twilight of the golden era: new tests, new treatments, scientifically trained doctors, but old values of compassion. Doctors take care of the folks, but don't get rich doing it, like those "specialists." It opens with an updated version of the Hippocratic oath that still affirms the proscription against giving a deadly draught, and the admonition to keep confidential what one sees and hears, but doesn't mention abortion. It adds respect for race, religion, and creed as well as treating other physicians as brothers. Filmed at St. Luke's Hospital in New York City and Vassar Brothers Hospital in Poughkeepsie, it had the full cooperation of the American Medical Association. Ben Gazzara plays Dr. Coleman, a new pathologist who is coming to help a kindly, but over-the-hill Dr. Pearson played by Fredric March in his last screen role (fig. 7). Trouble in paradise is signaled when a patient's husband complains about her bill and specifically that his wife stayed in the hospital a week longer because of the delay in getting a pathology report. Pearson's lab is a mess, staffed by a technician who is even more outdated than he is. However, he blames the surgeon for missing the diagnosis of pneumonia in a patient he operated on for appendicitis. He says, "A pathologist examines a surgeon's mistakes when it's too late." He performs an autopsy for first-year nursing students in front of the lab's motto "*Mortui vivos docent*" (the dead teach the living), a sentiment that was appropriate when autopsy rates averaged over 40 percent, not less than 5 percent, as they do now.[8]

FIGURE 7. *The Young Doctors.* The guard changes as Young Turk Dr. Coleman (Ben Gazzara) meets Old Turk Dr. Pearson (Fredric March).

Dick Clark plays Dr. Alexander, an intern whose wife is pregnant with their second child; the first died of bronchitis at one month of age. Because of their red blood cell incompatibility, a test is ordered to detect maternal antibodies that could destroy the fetus's red blood cells (erythroblastosis fetalis). He and Coleman are up-to-date enough to know that an indirect Coombs test should be done as a third test. Pearson and the technician overrule them and report the findings as negative. Later, the child develops erythroblastosis fetalis and the indirect Coombs test is positive at University Hospital. A delayed exchange transfusion provides the one piece of dramatic tension. The obstetrician, Dr. Dornberger (Eddie Albert), tells his friend Pearson that "if this baby dies, I'm going to take you up before the medical board and break you in two."

The film lauds hospitals with such lines as, "This hospital has one purpose, to serve the people" and "Medicine is a war, a constructive war, not everyone can be a Pasteur or a Salk. Keeping people alive. That's what we're doing in this hospital, because we believe in life." Other messages include, "the eternal problem with hospitals is the limitation of funds," and "anyone can make a mistake in medicine." The specialist–generalist conflict is played out in dialogue between Alexander and his wife (Phyllis Love) who wants him to be a small town family practitioner like her father. She tells him, "I never heard my father mention money. He only quoted one thing from the Bible; the only way to find yourself is to lose yourself." Alexander tells her, "Your father was part of a dying breed. Medicine is a business." She responds, "No matter how big or rich or important you are, I won't mind." Later on, when his baby is desperately ill, Alexander tells a policeman of his plans to be a small town practitioner. "I won't be rich," he says, and the policeman replies, "Well, even doctors have to get paid."

Another theme involves a nursing student with whom Coleman falls in love. She develops knee pain and refuses a biopsy because she doesn't want to have an amputation if it shows cancer, but then allows a woman orthopedist Dr. Grainger (Aline MacMahon) to do a 2 to 3 cm biopsy. This vignette provides the opportunity to show the uncertainty of medicine. Coleman thinks the biopsy is benign; Pearson thinks it is malignant. They send it to specialists in Boston and New York. Again the opinions are conflicting. Coleman goes with Pearson's call and convinces his girl friend to have the operation. Later, Pearson, the old-timer who is resigning because of his error on the baby, is proven right. He tells Coleman that he was like him when he started. He thought he knew more than his superiors and he was right then, just as Coleman is right now. Cautioning him to keep up-to-date, he sends him up to his girl friend's bedside, saying, "What's love if it isn't thinking about someone else more than yourself." The scroll at the film's end reads "This film is dedicated to the medical profession for its constant and devoted service to mankind."

The last film in this chapter was one I saw just after my internship and almost walked out of. What was pictured was completely alien to my experience, plus the portrayal of the relationships between men and women was offensive and primitive, with some of the worst stereotypes being fostered by the female characters. My assessment hasn't changed but on re-looking at the film in preparing for this book, I viewed it, not for entertainment, but with the dispassionate eye of a scientist. This allowed me to appreciate some of the recurring stereotypic themes and to see how far we've come in the last three decades.

The Interns (1962)

Based on a best-selling novel by Robert Friede, *The Interns* opens with a view of the new crop of interns. One is smoking, another is stepping out of a convertible; one is a woman, another an Asian-American.

The sign in front reads, "The new North Hospital dedicated to the medical staff, who give time and skill to heal, comfort, and sustain life." As the interns enter and look for their dormitory, the nurses laugh at their clumsiness and earnestness. One remarks on the "absence of air conditioning." Soon enough, their white bucks are dirty and blood-stained after duty in the busy emergency room. A mother cries out in anguish about her little girl who aspirated, "only a little piece of apple, she can't be dead." Unfortunately, it can happen! A woman with a post-partum hemorrhage who "went to a cut-rate jerk without a license who botched the delivery," has a cardiac arrest and survives closed chest massage, probably the earliest film portrayal of cardiopulmonary resuscitation, but then dies. As the intern Lew Worship (James MacArthur who later played Dano on television's long-running series, *Hawaii Five-O*) copes with the first death of a patient, the nurse says to an orderly, "The hemorrhage died."

The institution is described by the nurse orienting the incoming nursing students as, "3000 patients at night census; 1200 females, 1800 males; 3 Negroes for every 7 Caucasians; 2 on charity for every 8 who can pay." What the students should expect, she says, is "lots of bed to make." The nature of the expectations of the physicians is set by the chief of medicine Dr. Wohl (Buddy Ebsen). He lectures intern John Paul Otis (Cliff Robertson) who struck an old alcoholic for taunting Worship after the death of his patient. Wohl points out that although it's a municipal hospital whose patients may in some cases be undesirable, "We're not allowed to have the luxury of temper." They practice "the best medicine in the world" even though it's "bus-type medicine, not Cadillac medicine or even taxi medicine."

The chief surgeon Dr. Riccio (Telly Savalas) is a stereotypic opinionated male chauvinist (see chapter 5). He smokes cigars on rounds and tells one intern who suggests postponing an operation until the test results are in, "Aside from your degree from medical school, is there any reason why you should be called a doctor?" He is reprimanded by Wohl for throwing a scalpel at a resident during surgery. He proudly says, " In July, I pinked three nurses and two residents....When I'm training surgeons, I spit on everyone else." The conversation ends in an angry exchange of Christmas gifts.

The chief of obstetrics, Dr. Granchard (Gregory Morton), tells the interns, "Don't answer so quickly, especially when you don't know. Only surgeons do that." To an intern's question, "You don't think much of surgeons," he replies, "Not as much as they think of themselves."

Worship asks, "What's so special about delivering a baby? Taxi drivers can deliver babies." Naturally, he later does a forceps delivery as his first solo effort. As they light up a post-delivery cigarette, he says, "Quite a thrill." The chief remarks, "I've been at it for twenty-five years, but it never ceases to amaze me. Babies. Babies. Do you think a taxi driver could have handled it?" A nurse says, "You just gave a life, Doctor." PS: Worship opts for obstetrics.

Getting a residency is a recurring theme. Dr. Considine (Michael Callan) comments that there are "160 other interns, and only two residencies open" in his preferred psychiatry program. He's the prototypical "doctor as creep" cheating on his rich fiancée while he romances an older nurse who is a good friend of the residency program director. He subsists on dexedrine and beer as he goes back and forth between the two women and his ward duties. He finally cracks after achieving his goal. Another, Sidney (Nick Adams) announces to his fellow interns, "You like to think of medicine as consecrated and hallowed ground. Working for science and medical immortality. It's a business—the doctor business—we patch them up for money." Later, he admits to having his eye "on getting a quarter million in the bank and then finding a broad," but he falls for an Asian patient with the hereditary blood disorder Thalassemia. After she dies, he decides to go to her island which has no doctors and open a hospital. This self-sacrificing theme is echoed by Worship and Otis, his medical school classmate, who plan to build a free clinic for the Navajos in New Mexico. There's also a very minor role for a Black intern, who is invited to the parties. "We don't want the Russians to think we're prejudiced," says the party organizer.

The nurse orienting incoming nursing students says, "Never talk to the interns, they're all sex maniacs." Later, student Gloria Mead (Stefanie Powers) tells straight arrow Worship (fig. 8) that student nurses don't date interns. "Why not?" he asks, to which she replies, "You're all supposed to be sex maniacs." "Can we go up to your room?" he asks. "No," she says, "It's against house rules." "What about my room?" he asks. "It's against my rules," she says. The film is distinguished for its parties, during which everyone seems to be able to get time off (maybe because of those 160 interns). At the New Year's Eve party, an inhibited nurse gets sloshed and begins stripping and dancing wildly (fig. 9).

These antics were even more prominent in the sequel, *The New Interns*. Robin Cook, the best-selling physician/author, once said half-facetiously that these films influenced his decision to become a doctor.[9]

FIGURE 8. *The Interns.* Fellow interns and nurses try to fix up straight-arrow Lew Worship (James MacArthur) with a student nurse.

He commented that he was very disappointed to find that life at Columbia-Presbyterian Hospital in New York was nothing like the movies. Later, while stationed on a submarine, he wrote his first novel about internship as an attempt to set the record straight. After many publishers' rejections, he decided to read a lot of best-sellers to find out what made them successful. His breakthrough occurred with the screenplay for *Coma*, which he translated into a best-selling novel. And the rest, as they say, is history.

The two heavy-duty themes in the film are abortion and mercy killing. The first involves Dr. Otis who falls hard for an icy unwed society model Lisa Cardigan (Suzy Parker). She wants him to steal pitocin and ergotamine from the medicine cabinet so she can have an abortion. At first, he refuses, saying, "I may be green, but I still believe in that old oath we took." Later, he relents because, "I can't let you go to one of those back alley butchers." While he's stealing the pit and ergot, Worship confronts him. Otis says, "Will you forget about that damn code of ethics." His friend replies: "Don't let me turn you in." Otis stuffs the vials in his pocket as his friend goes to the obstetrics chief who races after Otis and tells him, "You'll never get a license to practice medicine

FIGURE 9. *The Interns.* The strait-laced nurse (Anne Helm) in the previous figure lets her hair down at the interns' party.

in this country. If I can, I'll run you right out of the profession." At the close of picture when residencies are being announced, Otis returns. He has left the profession and married Cardigan. He and Lew sit together on a bench in front of the hospital, next to a Star of David. Otis remarks, "You and your damn code of ethics. You know I respect that code. Don't ever let any quacks or leeches or bastards like me in medicine. You get them out of it, you hear?" and he walks away.

The mercy killing theme centers on a patient with spinal cord degeneration known as syringomyelia and syringobulbia. His condition is described as one that will lock his mind in the prison of an unresponsive body. When he asks for the "simple merciful act of killing," his wife says, "Don't embarrass the interns." Worship responds, "As physicians, it's our job to prolong life." The patient responds, "You are prolonging death. My savings are gone. How will my wife and children live? Is there one of you who has not yet become a complete physician? One of you who is still partly human? Is there such a concept as mercy in your doctor's ethics?" Worship answers, "What you are asking us to do is against the law."

The wife keeps suggesting possible cures she has heard of, such as "Gamma radiation in a cave in Utah." When these are rejected, she asks, "Why don't you put him out of his misery?" She is told that it is "a matter of ethics." At an ethics bull session in the local bar, one intern asks, "Who is to say what's right and wrong? You can do things in Japan that you can't do in Kansas." Another says that they must act with compassion. Surgical chief Riccio (Telly Sevalas) answers, "Medicine is an exact science. We don't deal in hope, we deal in facts." Bruckner (Haya Harareet), the woman intern, shoots back, "When it comes to the ethics of mercy killing, you're just another voice." Another comments, "Who are we to play God? Just because we have a diploma in medicine, we get to decide who will live and who will die."

Later, the patient dies of barbiturate poisoning and all interns who had been rotating on male medicine and neurology are prevented from accepting residencies until the hospital director finds out who did it. After much anxious waiting, an intern figures out that it was the wife. In admitting it, she says, "He kept saying 'if you love me,' over and over. I just couldn't watch him suffer anymore" (see *Critical Care* for the same plea). The film ends with a new crop of interns looking the same as the old bunch with the now seasoned Lew Worship responding to a question about when they will turn on the nonexistent air conditioning, "Warm? Well, doctor, you haven't begun to sweat." In short, for all its flaws, this film does manage to paint a sympathetic picture of a complex profession and to raise issues that are still the subject of contention. Later chapters will focus on films with an increasingly angrier vision of hospitals and the darker side of the medical profession.

NOTES

1   Rosenberg CE. The Care of Strangers: The Rise of America's Hospital System. Baltimore: Johns Hopkins University Press, 1987.
2. Martensen RL and Jones DS. The emergence of the hospital internship. JAMA 1997; 278: 963.
3. Bryan CS. Osler: Inspirations from a Great Physician. New York: Oxford University Press, 1997.
4. Raben EM. Men in White and Yellow Jack as mirrors of the profession. Literature and Medicine 1993; 12: 19–41.
5. Turow J. Playing Doctor: Television, Storytelling, and Medical Power. New York: Oxford University Press, 1989.

6. Kalisch PA and Kalisch BJ. When Americans called for Dr. Kildare: Images of phy-
    sicians and nurses in the Dr. Kildare and Dr. Gillespie movies, 1937-1947. Medical
    Heritage, 1985, September/October, pp 348–363.
7. Radovsky SS. Bearing the news. N Engl J Med, 1985; 313: 586–588.
8. Hasson J and Schneiderman H. Autopsy training programs: To right a wrong. Arch
    Pathol Lab Med 1995; 119: 289–291.
9. Panel Discussion, Columbia P&S Reunion, May 10, 1996.

4

The Temple of Science

After the Flexner report,[1] the training of medical students and medical practitioners became more rigorous and scientific in nature. The explosion of discoveries in such diverse fields as bacteriology, immunology, radiology, anesthesiology, and surgery held out the prospect of a future when science would conquer disease and possibly even death itself. People could easily see the fruits of that progress in their own daily lives. One by one, everyday scourges such as appendicitis, scarlet fever, diphtheria, mastoiditis, rheumatic fever, pernicious anemia, syphilis, tuberculosis, polio, and even pneumonia, the "captain of the legion of death," succumbed to the army of dedicated scientists who had "declared war" on them. Just as devastating illnesses and early death had not respected social class and served as one potential common bond between rich and poor, so did efforts at their eradication and the benefits they derived. Franklin Delano Roosevelt's oneness with the folks developed in large part due to the psychological and physical effects of his polio. His efforts on behalf of the March of Dimes did much to conquer it. Joseph Kennedy's power and riches were defenseless against his daughter's illness and the consequences of her subsequent lobotomy; however, in coping with their grief, the Kennedys expended enormous efforts on behalf of the retarded.

The movies, being a visual medium, showcased scientific breakthroughs in various ways. For the most part, it was indirect, illustrating advances in surgery, the administration of antisera, and the use of new equipment like the fluoroscope by practicing doctors. These films often depicted a conflict between the desire to be a dedicated family doctor and the glamor and excitement of making a medical breakthrough. Even the more direct approaches like *Arrowsmith* featured this conflict. After trying his hand at hanging up his shingle in South Dakota, Arrowsmith is discouraged at his inability to cure a child dying with diphtheria and ends up praying in "The Temple of Science." Like other cinematic versions of fictional works such as *Dr. Jekyll and Mr. Hyde*, and *Frankenstein*, *Arrowsmith* illustrates the price of scientific hubris. Other direct depictions of science were more positive celebratory "biopics" highlighting the work of major scientists like Pasteur, Ehrlich, and the Curies.[2] This chapter will focus on how the scientific aspect of medicine has been both lauded and maligned in film over the last six decades.

THE PRICE OF HUBRIS

Let's start with a cult favorite among aficionados of film, especially the horror genre, because of its sets, Max Factor's makeup wizardry, and the use of Technicolor imprints not generally available then. This otherwise deservedly little-known film depicts the prototypical unscrupulous medical researcher, a theme close to Hollywood screenwriters' hearts and one that resurfaced as recently as 1996 in *Extreme Measures* (see chapter 8).

Doctor X (1932)

This *Doctor X* is a rather bizarre tale of serial murders taking place in the vicinity of a medical school and at the height of a full moon. All the victims have an "impression in the sternocleidomastoid," the long muscle of the neck (evidence of "powerful strangulation"); an incision at the base of the brain (using a "special knife imported from Vienna"); and a missing deltoid or shoulder muscle (said to be "a sign of cannibalism"). Suspicion falls on the school's faculty, a greater collection of misfits is hard to imagine. They are all in their laboratories at midnight, because that's the only time they have for personal research work. As Doctor Xavier (Lionel Atwill), the medical school dean, notes, "They seldom leave; they live for their work. After all, this is a research institute." Brain grafting, keeping a heart alive, and cannibalism are only a few of the preoccupations of these stalwarts.

The dean, who believes the killer has a "neurotic fixation" caused by "a knot or a kink in the brain" sagely declares, "Locked inside each human skull is a little world all its own." Proving that they just don't make medical school deans the way they used to, he uncovers the killer, the hand-less Doctor Wells (Preston Foster), who tried to throw people off the scent by unscrewing his arm to prove that he couldn't be the killer. Wells needs human bodies in order to develop "synthetic flesh." His goal is to "live forever in the history of science" by making "a crippled world whole." What people won't do for science!

Let's move from the bizarre to the best-known film about science, one that many older doctors say influenced them to choose medicine as a career. As we will see, however, this tale of scientific hubris and monomania is hardly a rhapsodic treatment of the medical profession.

Arrowsmith (1932)

Based on Sinclair Lewis's novel and directed by John Ford, the film's overwrought introduction proclaims it to be "the story of a man who dedicated his life to service and his heart to the love of a woman." It opens with a fourteen-year-old driving a covered wagon west, refusing her father's pleas to take shelter in Cincinnati, but instead pushing on. This serves as a metaphor of the pioneering spirit her great-grandson, Martin Arrowsmith (Ronald Colman) will bring to medicine and science. The local doctor recounts the story and says, "That will make a medical man out of you if anything will. It may even make you a scientist if you live up to it." In addition to *Gray's Anatomy*, which Martin is reading, he lists the Holy Bible and Shakespeare as essential books in a physician's library and advises Arrowsmith to go to college in order to complete premedical studies in chemistry, Latin, physics, and biology to be a fine doctor.

On arrival in medical school, Martin tells his future mentor, Dr. Gottlieb (A. E. Anson), "I'm not going to be just an ordinary doctor. I want to be a research scientist like you. I'm not interested in just giving pills. I'd rather find a cure for cancer." Glad to hear that Martin is not afraid of hard work, Gottlieb, who has worked with Pasteur and Koch, says, "Now we begin to talk sensibly. To be a scientist, that is born into a man, and in very few men. It may be born in you. But first, go and be a medical student. Learn the names of the diseases. Learn to work in the dissecting laboratory without becoming sick. Learn to see blood flow without fainting." Little is shown of Martin's clinical years, save the obligatory ambulance obstetrical run to a tenement housing stereotypic Italian immigrants (see appendix A for other examples).

Martin next encounters Leora, a nursing student played by Helen Hayes, who is scrubbing the floor as punishment for having sneaked a cigarette (fig. 1). He chides her, "The first duty of a nurse is to stand when speaking to a doctor" and proceeds to tell her that he is on his way to Ward D to get a dangerous strain of bacteria. The scene ends with their agreeing to a dinner date at a restaurant that serves ham hocks and lima beans (the haute cuisine of yesteryear). Leora says being asked out by a doctor makes her "feel intelligent." Martin serves notice that

FIGURE 1. *Arrowsmith*. Martin Arrowsmith (Ronald Colman) insists that student nurse Leora (Helen Hayes) stand up when she addresses him. Note that she has been scrubbing the floor (as a penalty for being caught smoking) in her high heels.

although it's their first date, they are going to be married. She replies, "I guess you're pretty pig-headed and self-centered, but I like you so much I'd be a fool to pass you up." How's that for a characterization of a doctor, as well as a reason to marry one!

The next scene illustrates the promise that science holds for physicians frustrated at how little they know. Gottlieb, who has been called to the McGurk Institute in New York (read Rockefeller Institute), tells Arrowsmith, "I'm leaving this place where I teach students to kill their patients" and asks him to come along. Martin replies, "I can't go to New York. I'm going to be married. A man can't marry on what lab assistants make. I'm going to practice medicine after all." Gottlieb prophesies, "You'll be a bad doctor for a while and then you'll find your way back to us." After tying the knot at a justice of the peace, the painfully naive Arrowsmith asks Leora, "How does a doctor start practicing?" She takes him to Wheatsylvania, South Dakota, and convinces her family to lay out one thousand dollars after telling them that "Martin is giving up a great career as a research scientist just to be a country doctor so he can support a wife. You all ought to get down on your knees and appreciate him."

After he hangs up his shingle, Martin asks her what a country doctor does. She replies, "You've got to make the young folks get married when they ought to and stay married when they don't want to. You've got to lecture the big boys on the evil of drink, and do your own drinking when the shades are down. You've got to see that the backyards are tidy, the milk's fresh and the meat's pure—that's what being a country doctor means." Then, he receives his first call from a frantic father who says, "'my little girl has a terrible sore throat." He suspects diphtheria and says, "if this were a hospital I'd operate." He uses a trocar and stands by her bedside overnight while she dies. On returning home, he says, "Gottlieb was right. I am a rotten doctor." His wife responds, "Don't say that, Martin. You did your best." He replies, "I didn't, though. No matter what, I should have operated."

Later, Arrowsmith travels to Minneapolis to hear Dr. Sondelius (Richard Bennett), a member of the Swedish Academy of Medicine, lecture on the "Heroes of Health." Harking back to the doctors who sacrificed their lives in the conquest of yellow fever, Sondelius says, as modestly as a doctor can, "If I sound like a pretty important person, I am." "We want doctor soldiers, scientific soldiers." Arrowsmith mentions Gottlieb, occasioning the response that "Gottlieb is the greatest, the spirit of science." He later tells his wife: "I've been stagnating for two years. I'm not going to stagnate any longer." Leora says that the baby they're expecting "will tie you down more than ever." He replies, " I don't have to go to Africa to save mankind."

As predicted, his practice is hardly confined to medicine. For example, he helps a boy pull out a baby tooth using the old string tied to the tooth trick, after saying, "I wouldn't hurt him, only dentists do that." After seeing the local vet lose a herd of cattle from blackleg and demurring that "I'm only a physician," he sets up a laboratory in his house. Using different test doses for inoculation, he cooks up "cow medicine" by working through dinner and administers it to an experimental group, all of whom survive. The controls all die. When asked why he didn't give it to the others, he says, "You have to try both ways." The townspeople love him, especially after he decks the vet who throws a punch at him. Meanwhile, his wife is home having a miscarriage. On his return home, he tells her, "I'll never forgive myself for leaving you like this." She comforts him by saying, "If I can't have a baby, I'll have to bring you

up. Make you a great man that everybody will wonder at." Gottlieb
who has heard of his triumph over blackleg telegrams him to work at
the McGurk Institute. New York is portrayed as all hustle and bustle
and Leora refuses to go up in the elevator to the twenty-fifth floor because she must work her way up to that height.

Gottlieb whisks Arrowsmith away from the institute director
Dr. Tubbs (Claude King), saying, "Leave my Prodigal son to me. Let me
conduct him to his laboratory." On seeing it, Arrowsmith says, "A man
should do fine work with all this." Gottlieb responds, "This! This does
not make a scientist." Pointing to his head, he says, "His equipment is
here. Any man who can't make a laboratory out of toothpicks and a
piece of string should buy his ideas along with his fine equipment." Left
alone in his new lab, Arrowsmith intones the scientist's prayer, a seeming variant of the Prayer of St. Francis, "God give me clear eyes and
freedom from haste. God give me anger against all pretense. God keep
me looking for my own mistakes. God keep me at it until my results are
proven. God give me strength not to trust two Gods."

What follows is two years of failure; he is about to "chuck it before
they fire me," when he forsakes dinner to check his last experiment and
trudges back to the lab through the snow, with his wife trailing behind
him. He notices that one of the three experimental flasks is clear. Looking under the microscope, he exclaims, "They're dead. Bugs don't commit
suicide. Something in the clear flask killed them." Gottlieb tells him,
"You have a big thing here. A great thing. You will find out what it is
and how many bacteria it will destroy" (fig. 2). He then works day and
night to repeat the experiment. He apologizes to his wife for neglecting
her and being a rotten husband. She says rather tolerantly, "You are a
rotten husband, but I'd rather have you than all the decent ones in the
world."

Dr. Tubbs promises to promote Arrowsmith and proceeds to tell
the press that he has found the cure for all disease. The director admits
that it was "a slight overstatement to catch the public eye." This shows
that hyping medical news is not new. Arrowsmith says, "You've made
my name smell from one end of the country to another as a quack, a
fake, a racketeer." He tells him he's through with the "publicity-seeking
cheapjack institute." Enter Gottlieb who says to the director, "While
you were busy turning Martin into a megaphone, a Frenchman, d'Herelle,
at the Pasteur Institute has published a report with the same findings."
The director's only comment is, "Well, there'll be no more talk of head
of the department or a raise in salary." How quickly they turn on you!

FIGURE 2. *Arrowsmith*. Gottlieb tells the weary Arrowsmith (Ronald Colman) that he has made a great discovery, but now must begin work in earnest. His friend Terry Wicket (Russell Hopton) looks on.

The plot shifts to rats, fleas, and the Caribbean. After developing a new serum, Arrowsmith is sent to the West Indies with Sondelius to conquer bubonic plague. Gottlieb extracts a promise from him "to administer injections to only half your patients and to sternly deprive the other half. Then you will know if it works." Arrowsmith is hesitant, "I've done that sort of thing with cattle, but good God, chief, these are human beings." His colleague Terry Wicket (Russell Hopton) says, "So you're just a country doctor after all." Arrowsmith replies, "I've got the bowels of compassion in me." Gottlieb says, 'So many men are kind and neighborly. So few ever add to human knowledge. Are you going to fail me?" Martin meekly replies, "No. No, sir. I'm not going to fail you." Terry tells him, "For the old man's sake, keep the notes complete and keep them neat." Arrowsmith says, "You talk as if I'm not coming back." Leora won't be deterred from going with him despite the danger.

The White colonial doctors refuse to let Arrowsmith do the experiment. They sarcastically take him to task, "You call yourself a doctor and you want to see half your patients die." He responds that "the injected half will be fully as well taken care of as they are at present."

He urges them to see beyond these patients to the world at large. Then a Black doctor, Doctor Oliver Marchand (Clarence Brooks) of Howard University suggests he do the experiment on his remote island outpost (see chapter 6). Before leaving, Martin tells Leora, "I daren't take you along with me. It's no place for a woman." She replies, "Darn, being a woman!" He tells her to kill the "plague virus" on a set of test tubes in "some boiling water." Though viruses don't grow on bacterial slants and plague is caused by a bacillus, there is a scientific basis for this dialogue, as well as the screenwriter's desire to be on the cutting edge of science. On departing, he says, "Lee, I'm off to glory—wish me luck….If I pull this thing off on Marchand's island, I'll be a great man in science."

Marchand takes Arrowsmith to the "worst infected place in the colonies" and tells him "their voodoo is just about as effective as anything we've been able to do." Sondelius says, "The only thing to do with this place is to burn it. Get the people out." They commandeer a plantation bunkhouse for a hospital and inject serum into the experimental group using the same syringe and needle. Joyce Lanyon (Myrna Loy), the daughter of the plantation owner, drops into the picture for an injection, looking impeccably dressed and coiffed. Sondelius, who doesn't take an injection, gets sick. He says, "Of all the jokes God plays, the best ones are on the tropics. He made them so rich and beautiful and then he gave them the plague." Longing for one last drink before dying, he says, "Martin, you try to save all these poor devils. Save all of them. Let the science experiment go. I never knew before, people could hurt me so much." He dies and Arrowsmith says, "He used to troop all over the country lecturing on Heroes of Health. Now he's one of them."

While Arrowsmith is succumbing to Joyce's charms, his wife, back on the main island, infects herself after breaking one of the bacterial slants (in the book she contracts it by smoking one of Martin's cigarette butts, accidentally contaminated when a maid knocks over a test tube of plague bacillus).[3] Marchand, who also has been recalled to the mainland, calls Martin to tell him Leora is sick, but he dies in the middle of the phone call of plague he contracted on his island. As Leora begins to weaken, she retreats to a chair, lights up a cigarette and calls out, "Help me, Martin," but once again he's not there for her. Reaching out for the light, she dies. Martin returns and is shocked to find his wife dead. He says, "I thought you'd be safe. He carries her to bed and says, "I loved you. Lee, you knew that. Didn't you know I couldn't love anyone else?"

Martin gets drunk, laughs crazily, and tells the hospital workers, "Shoot them all full of serum. Kill all the rats. Burn all the villages. To hell with the experiments. To hell with science. To hell with Gottlieb."

He returns to his room and sobs as he hugs his wife's dress. All the patients given the serum survive. On his return to New York, Tubbs meets him. "Congratulations, there's never been anything like it. Stupendous. There 's a letter from the British government. You've ended plague. Oh my dear chap. I'm so sorry; in all my enthusiasm, I had forgotten. My deepest sympathy." Then the institute director poses proudly for photographers as Arrowsmith rushes off to see his friend Terry, who responds to Arrowsmith's admission that he "bungled it," with "I'm afraid you have."

Gottlieb refuses to leave his laboratory to attend the welcome home party, saying, "He'll come to me. He is my son. More than my son; even if you do make a clown of him. Out of my laboratory with your nonsense!" Arrowsmith, on arriving, says, "I'll go to him," and Tubbs says to all within earshot, "master and pupil you know." He approaches Gottlieb as he would a priest and says, "I want to confess. You gave me everything you knew of truth and when you gave me my chance I betrayed you. Oh, I had an excuse, perhaps, but I don't want to go into that, because whatever I may have accomplished I didn't add to knowledge. I did the humane thing and lost sight of science. Now say what you have to say and throw me out." The great man appropriately says, "Rubbish," and then has a stroke. Terry runs in and says, "He's gone down into the darkness believing in you." Arrowsmith says, "He never understood a word I said—not a word."

Tubbs offers to make Arrowsmith a department head at fifteen thousand dollars a year. Meanwhile, Terry, who is fed up, announces, that he's going to take Gottlieb and "clear out of this joint with all its publicity. I'm going to set up my own lab in the Vermont woods." Joyce Lanyon comes in and offers her friendship. Spurning both Lanyon and Tubbs, Arrowsmith takes his notes and his microscope and repeats his mentor's comment about a true scientist being able to make a lab out of toothpicks and string. "What are you thinking of?" Tubbs asks. "The rest of my life," he replies, and shouts after his friend; "Terry, wait. Lee and I are both coming with you."

Charles Rosenberg in his *Martin Arrowsmith: The Scientist as Hero*[3] nicely describes the evolution of Lewis's novel from which the movie sometimes diverges. Rosenberg credits Lewis with seeing Arrowsmith as a hero "who, in the austere world of pure science and in the example of Max Gottlieb, finds a system of values which guide and sanction his stumbling quest for personal integrity." By contrast, the filmmaker emphasizes that the demands of science conflict with a doctor's ability to be humane. This criticism of science's rationalism as evidenced by the negative portrayal of controlled experiments is echoed in later films. The collaboration of author Sinclair Lewis and scientist Paul de Kruif is extensively described elsewhere[3-5] and only the bare bones from these accounts will be recounted. De Kruif decided against medicine in favor of becoming a graduate student in Frederick G. Novy's bacteriology laboratory at the University of Michigan. He later worked as a postdoctoral fellow at the Rockefeller Institute where Jacques Loeb was a dominant force. Professor Gottlieb, Arrowsmith's mentor, is a composite of Novy and Loeb. De Kruif was fascinated by Felix Hubert d'Herelle's and Frederick Twort's pioneering work with bacteriophage, a virus that could infect and destroy bacteria including the diphtheria bacillus.[3-4]

In 1922, de Kruif, who harbored an extreme form of the laboratory scientist's antipathy for clinicians, wrote an anonymous series of articles titled *Our Medicine Men*, "attacking the pretensions of American medicine."[6] Interestingly, he did lionize the "dedicated and non-commercial" general practitioner.[6] When de Kruif's identity was discovered, he was dismissed from the Rockefeller Institute. Later that year Morris Fishbein, then associate editor of the *Journal of the American Medical Association*, introduced de Kruif to Sinclair Lewis. Their mutual fondness for alcohol helped them develop a closeness that led to "a two-month steamer trip to the Caribbean" with stops at hospitals, leper colonies, and bacteriology laboratories.[5] It was here that the idea for *Arrowsmith* took shape. While what is injected into the patients is referred to as serum, in reality it represented the bacteriophage that d'Herelle used to treat those infected with bubonic plague and which he added to the drinking water in India to combat cholera. In addition, Leora's contracting plague is based on a real-life incident when a student in Novy's lab was infected after smoking a cigarette accidentally contaminated with the plague bacillus. Unlike Leora, the student recovered after the administration of vaccine obtained from the Pasteur Institute. The collaboration also helped de Kruif craft a popular bestseller, *The Microbe Hunters*,[7] which has been recently updated by present-day scientists.[8]

The heartbreak that Arrowsmith brings upon himself by his pursuit of glory is nothing compared to the self-destruction of Dr. Jekyll and Dr. Frankenstein. Favorites of moviemakers, the stories have been filmed many times and have served as the model for countless films about scientists going beyond the bounds and intruding on divine territory.

Dr. Jekyll and Mr. Hyde (1932)

In this version, Dr. Jekyll (pronounced Gee-kill in the film) is played by Fredric March in an Oscar-winning role. He is a famous and kindly doctor who prefers to take care of charity patients and elects to stay and operate on an indigent patient rather than go off to a party and "leave it for the house surgeon." He loves Muriel (Rose Hobart), the daughter of a General Carew (Halliwell Hobbes), whom he tells, "I do love you seriously, so seriously that it frightens me. You opened a gate for me into another world. Before that, my work was everything. I was drawn to the mysteries of science, to the unknown; but now the unknown wears your face, looks back at me with your eyes." Alas, the General delays their marriage (fig. 3) and takes his daughter to Bath, so Dr. J follows his dream to separate man's good side from his evil side. This, he believes will allow him to make a human being perfect. He is warned, "There are bounds beyond which one should not go." He responds, "There are no bounds." Surrounded by skeletons and beakers of boiling chemicals, he prepares a potion, which he drinks after scribbling a note to his lover, "If I die, it is in the cause of science. I shall love you always, through eternity."

FIGURE 3. *Dr. Jekyll and Mr. Hyde.* General Carew (Halliwell Hobbes) refuses his daughter Muriel's (Rose Hobart) pleas to marry Dr. Jekyll (Fredric March) and takes her away to Bath.

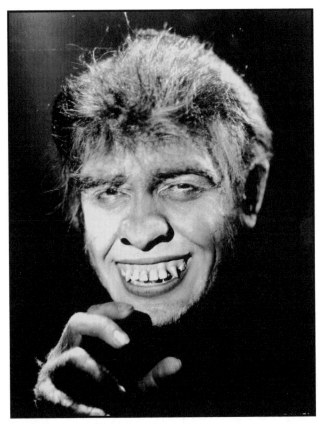

FIGURE 4. *Dr. Jekyll and Mr. Hyde.* With time on his hands, Jekyll decides to explore his evil side and becomes Mr. Hyde (Fredric March).

The film is shot in large part through his eyes. Director Mamoulian, photographer Struss, and makeup artist Westmore did a masterful job in transforming the handsome Jekyll into the hideous and sadistic Hyde (fig. 4), whose first words are, "Free, free at last. Deniers of life, if you could see me now, what would you think?" One wonders if the first part of this exclamation could have resonated in the mind of a young Martin Luther King to be put to greater use later with unmatched eloquence.

The evil Hyde takes up with Ivy Pearson (Miriam Hopkins), a cabaret singer who tried to seduce Jekyll after he saved her from a ruffian. He imprisons and mistreats her, but then has a change of heart and sends her money to leave London. When he returns to being Jekyll, he realizes that "I've played with dangerous knowledge. I've walked a terrible road." Unfortunately for Jekyll, he is once again seduced by Ivy and now no longer needs the potion to shed his kindly, handsome persona, but is transformed into Hyde without warning.

He returns to Ivy as Hyde and reveals his identity, warning her that he will have to kill her, which he does with many sexual images playing in the background. The film was produced two years before the Hays production code and ten minutes of even more explicit footage was later cut from the original version and never restored. When Hyde is unable to enter the laboratory to get the potion that would turn him back into Jekyll, he sends a message to his friend Dr. Lanyon (Holmes Herbert) asking him to bring the materials for the potion to him. His friend insists on remaining to unravel the mystery. Hyde asks him, "Do you want your eyes and your soul to be blasted by a sight that would stagger the devil himself?" When his friend persists, he says: "Remember your vows to your profession. What you are about to see is a secret you are sworn not to reveal." Then, he smiles and says, "Now, you who have sneered at the miracles of science, you who have denied the power of man to look into his own soul, you who have derided your superiors. Look! Look!" He drinks the potion and is transformed into Jekyll. His friend, Dr. Lanyon, refuses his plea for help, saying to the penitent Jekyll, "You have committed the supreme blasphemy." Lanyon leaves him, and Jekyll, with his hand on the Bible, says, "Oh God, this I did not intend. I saw a light and I could not see where it was leading. I have trespassed on your domain. I've gone further than man should go. Forgive me! Help me!" He runs to Muriel to release her from their engagement, but once again turns into Hyde and begins to ravish her. A furious battle and chase scene ensues and he is killed. So much for scientific meddling; if only Jekyll had stuck to taking care of the folks.

The other quintessential story of scientific hubris is Mary Shelley's novel, *Frankenstein*.[9] It has spawned thirty films, the most famous of which made Boris Karloff a household name. It also is the rare instance where the sequel is held in higher regard than the original. *The Bride of Frankenstein* with Elsa Lanchester ranked eightieth on a list of the world's hundred best films according to eighty-one critics from twenty-two countries.[10] The novel had its beginnings on a dark and stormy night in 1816 in lodgings overlooking Lake Geneva. Mary Wollstonecraft Godwin, her married lover Percy Bysshe Shelley, Mary's stepsister, Lord Byron, and Byron's physician, John Polidori, were entertaining one another by reading ghost stories. Believing that they could do better, Byron proposed that each write a story. Days later, the seed for the novel was planted in Mary's mind by a conversation between Byron and Shelley about the possibility of reviving a corpse using galvanism, then a scientific craze. Published in 1818, the book has never been out of print. Interestingly enough, Byron's challenge also led Polidori to write *The Vampyre*,[11] considered to be the inspiration for Bram Stoker's *Dracula*.[12]

Rather than discuss the 1930s films, I've chosen to highlight the latest remake directed by Kenneth Branagh. Though plagued by overacting and too many special effects, the film is worth a passing mention.

Mary Shelley's Frankenstein (1994)

A confession at the outset! I'm one of those people who thought Frankenstein was "the monster." I've never been much for the horror genre, believing that there are enough scary things in this world without manufacturing fright. My biases disclosed, you are free to read on. *Mary Shelley's Frankenstein* opens with an Arctic explorer (Aidan Quinn) driving his crew mercilessly to reach the North Pole when he encounters Victor Frankenstein (Kenneth Branagh). Wearily pursuing his Creature (as the nameless creation is also referred to in the book), Frankenstein accepts an invitation to rest and proceeds to recount a cautionary tale about the price of scientific hubris.

The scene shifts to his happy childhood with his beloved mother, his father ("the best doctor in Geneva"), and an orphan girl, Elizabeth, whose parents died during a scarlet fever epidemic. The idyllic existence is shattered when Dr. Frankenstein must perform a Caesarean section on his wife. She dies and Victor's life is changed forever. Vowing to stop death, he experiments with lightning and the film becomes a series of lightning flashes. Victor is destined to study medicine in Germany, but would rather stay home and marry Elizabeth (Helena Bonham Carter). A good call as it turns out. But his father tells him, "You must go and do the great things you must do," and gives him a book inscribed by his mother, "the journal of Victor Frankenstein to be filled in with the deeds of a noble life."

On arriving at medical school, Victor is greeted by warning words over the portal, "Knowledge is Power only through God." Victor's beliefs about the possibility of reanimation run counter to the Geheimrat professor's contention, "The biggest mistake students make is thinking they can ever have an original thought. You are not here to think for yourselves, but for your patients." Noting that "hair and fingernails grow after what we call death" and that "the heart continues to beat after the brain has died," Victor postulates that the best way to cheat death is to create life. He gathers the "raw materials" starting with his dead mentor's brain and creates one of the hammiest and articulate Creatures in

FIGURE 5. *Mary Shelley's Frankenstein.* Dr. Frankenstein (Kenneth Branagh) mixes bits and pieces of dead murderers and thieves with his mentor's brain to produce "The Creature."

history (fig. 5). Played by Robert De Niro, who had to tolerate four to ten hours of makeup preparation daily, the Creature gets to mouth such lines as, "Bits of thieves, bits of murderers stitched together. Evil will have its revenge. Don't you think I'll be grateful! God help your loved ones"; and "Where is my soul? Did you leave it in? Who are these people of whom I'm comprised?"; and "For the sympathy of one living being, I would make peace with all. I have love in me the likes of which you can hardly imagine. I have rage the likes of which you can scarcely believe."

The Creature asks for a woman companion but the regretful Frankenstein refuses. Uttering the chastened scientist's plaint, "What have I done?" Frankenstein futilely attempts to kill the Creature who escapes to embark on a life of rage. It's hard to keep a straight face with all the overacting. Poor Elizabeth is sacrificed and in the final scene, the Creature immolates himself and Dr. F, saying, "He who increaseth knowledge, increaseth sorrow. God will bring everything to judgment whether it be for good or for evil." In other words, take heed you scientists out there.

In Mel Brooks' spoof *Young Frankenstein*, at least the laughs are planned. Dr. Frankenstein's descendant, played hilariously by Gene Wilder, is an American neurologist who is summoned to Transylvania to claim the family castle. There he discovers his ancestor's scientific notebooks and proceeds to "hurl the gauntlet of science into the face of death itself." When his "creation" (Peter Boyle) turns into a public menace, one of the townspeople says, "These scientists are all alike. They say they're working for us, but all they want to do is rule the world." On that note, let's shift gears and discuss some films where scientists are favorably portrayed.

The Glory of Science: Pasteur, Ehrlich, and the Curies

Some have derided the next few films as hagiography, but one should not underestimate their importance in teaching a relatively unschooled public about science. These films dramatically show the intricacies of the scientific method, the importance of experimental controls, the arduous work that precedes the "Eureka!" and the difficulty in translating scientific breakthroughs into practical public good. They also depict the infighting and defamation of innovators by openly hostile scientific colleagues.

The Story of Louis Pasteur (1936)

The opening credits, illustrated with a steaming chemical flask and a microscope, are followed by a shot of a doctor's office in Paris in 1860. A doctor, readying himself to go on a delivery call, drops an instrument on the floor, picks it up, and throws it in his bag. A man steps from behind the curtain and proceeds to shoot him dead. Now that's an attention-grabber, especially for doctors. Cut to the trial where the accused says, "He killed my wife with his dirty hands. He gave her childbirth fever." When challenged as to his evidence, he brandishes a flyer that proclaims, "Wash your hands. Boil your instruments. Microbes cause disease and death to your patients. Louis Pasteur." The doctor lobby, in this case the Academy of Medicine, is led by a Doctor Charbonnet, who says, "If Pasteur continues, he will make it impossible for doctors to practice. He is not even a doctor, only a mere chemist." This is the crackling start to a superb, admittedly schmaltzy, "great man of science" movie.

Despite a recent revisionist biography,[13] if one had to choose one scientist who changed the world, it was Pasteur.[14, 15] By 1860, Pasteur had turned from chemistry to helping establish the field of microbiology and his work was credited with saving the wine, beer, and silk industries of France and Europe. Challenging the theory of spontaneous generation subscribed to by Charbonnet and other physicians, Pasteur supported the contentions of Oliver Wendell Holmes and Semmelweiss that childbed fever, which killed three in ten new mothers in Paris at the time, was spread from victim to victim by doctors and midwives.

Pasteur further infuriates the doctor by saying, "I don't practice medicine, but I try to prevent the negligence of those who do." The doctors convince the emperor, who has set Pasteur up in a laboratory because of his tremendous contributions to France, to silence him by banishing him to the provinces. Here, he embarks on his next great triumph, the conquest of anthrax, which is devastating cattle and sheep (fig. 6). The explanation of how the anthrax spore progresses to the bacterial phase and the description of the various scientific experiments are easy to follow and would probably be of interest to today's public now that Saddam Hussein has brought anthrax to the world's attention. Furthermore, it could be enlightening for other reasons in that too many in our society have only a rudimentary grasp of the scientific method.

The film conveys a very positive view of scientists as dedicated and tireless. Working at home keeps Pasteur connected with his family, but the same isn't as true for his laboratory workers. When Pasteur proves that a vaccine using a weakened or attenuated strain of anthrax can protect sheep, he earns the praise of Sir Joseph Lister, the father of antisepsis, and Roux, the discoverer of diphtheria antitoxin. Credited with enabling

FIGURE 6. *The Story of Louis Pasteur.* Pasteur (Paul Muni) saves sheep by developing a vaccine using an attenuated strain of anthrax.

France to pay off her debt to Germany after losing the Franco-Prussian war of 1870, Pasteur shrugs off the acclaim, saying to his wife, "The benefits of science are not for the scientists, Marie, they're for humanity." This stands in marked contrast to today's view of science as an opportunity to reap millions through entrepreneurial business partnerships.

The film moves on to probably Pasteur's greatest achievement, the prevention and treatment of rabies. At first, he has setbacks and must endure the ridicule of Charbonnet, who defiantly injects himself with a rabies inoculum and is apparently unaffected. Refusing to confront his detractors, Pasteur says, "Humility is a virtue, not only in those who suffer, but those who hope to heal." Comparing the progress of science to a toddler's attempt to walk, he says it "takes a step, then another, and then stops to reflect. Just as one assumes that the toddler will get the hang of it, one must have faith in science." That faith is rewarded by his successful production of a vaccine that uses progressively stronger strains of the virus to develop antibodies that are both protective and therapeutic. He also wins over his archenemy, Charbonnet, who is asked to deliver Pasteur's grandchild only after using antiseptic techniques. Charbonnet becomes a believer when he contracts a delayed case of rabies and is cured by Pasteur's vaccine.

The film concludes at the French National Academy of Medicine tribute to Pasteur, which is led by Lister, and which actually did represent his last public appearance. However, the insertion of a special tribute by Tsar Nicholas II is inaccurate in that he did not ascend the throne until two years later.[16] Also, because Pasteur had suffered a stroke and was quite frail, his son delivered the speech. The movie version both praises science and anticipates World War II by urging moviegoers to take heart. "You young men (sic), doctors and scientists of the future, do not let yourself be tainted by barren skepticism, nor discouraged by the sadness of certain hours that creep over nations. Don't be angry at your opponents, for no scientific theory has been accepted without opposition. Live in the serene peace of libraries and laboratories. Say to yourself first, 'What have I done for my instruction?' and, as you gradually advance, 'What am I accomplishing?' until the time comes when you have the immense happiness of thinking that you have contributed in some way to the welfare and progress of mankind." This speech, which is still rousing today, helped Muni win a well-deserved Academy Award as Best Actor.

Director William Dieterle also directed the next film and was quite explicit about its being a tribute: "This picture is dedicated to the memory of Dr. Paul Ehrlich whose dream it was to create, out of chemicals, 'Magic Bullets' with which to fight the scourges of mankind."

Dr. Ehrlich's Magic Bullet (1940)

The film opens as Dr. Paul Ehrlich (Edward G. Robinson) tries to allay the anxieties of a young man in a syphilis clinic (fig. 7), "You have a contagious disease, an infection like any other. I've seen cases where it was transmitted by an inanimate object" (this may have consoled the patient at the expense of alarming the audience). When informed of the man's imminent wedding plans, Dr. E replies, "I'm afraid marriage is out of the question." "Does anybody ever get cured?" he asks. Dr. E responds, "There have been many cures." Later he admits that he was lying. When the nurses complain that the clinic is running an hour past closing time (something that was very common in the venereal disease clinic I directed), Dr. E cancels sweat baths for a patient who must get to work. On being challenged by an officious colleague, Ehrlich says, "You know as well as I do there's no value in it." The doctor responds, "The hospital is an organization, and organizations have rules, and rules must be obeyed by everyone." Just then, the sound of a thud signals that the

FIGURE 7. *Dr. Ehrlich's Magic Bullet.* Dr. Ehrlich (Edward G. Robinson) offers some medicine, but no hope that he will ever marry, to a young syphilitic who is driven to suicide.

young man, despondent about his inability to marry, has committed suicide. As in *Pasteur*, Dieterle has gotten our attention.

The scene shifts to Ehrlich's home where he joins his wife (Ruth Gordon) and two children for lunch. He tells her of his intention to resign from the hospital because "we know so little in medicine, so very little. We are groping in the dark, bumping into things the nature of which we don't know." He returns to the hospital to do some experiments and meets Doctor Emil von Behring (Otto Kruger) of the Koch Institute, who drops by the laboratory to pick up a culture slant. Behring is astonished that Dr. E knows that he is trying to replicate the experiments of Pasteur's colleague, Dr. Roux, who showed the ability of diphtheria antitoxin to convey passive immunity in humans. When he learns that Dr. E is in the dermatology department, he says, "Extraordinary that you should be so well-informed"—a little slam at syphilologists. As Dr. E tells him of his work with aniline dyes that stain tissues, the idea to stain bacteria is germinated.

Meanwhile, Dr. Hans Wolfert (Sig Rumann), Ehrlich's colleague, is reporting his lack of team play to the director of the hospital, Professor Hartmann (Montagu Love). A prototypical Herr Geheimrat, he denies personal animus, but does "confess to a certain feeling against people of his [Ehrlich's] faith in our profession." This anti-Semitic theme never recurs, but it is an eerie reminder of the systematic removal of Jewish professors from medical schools in countries occupied by the Nazis during the time the picture was made. Herr Geheimrat asks if Ehrlich will obey regulations and tells him, "Any further breach of discipline on your part and your connection with the hospital will be severed." He adds, "People like you have a very difficult time in this world because they don't know how to conform. You must learn it's conform or suffer."

Dr. E is invited by von Behring to the Koch Institute to hear Dr. Robert Koch (Albert Basserman) announce that he has successfully proven that a bacterial organism causes tuberculosis. There he sees another famous scientist, Virchow, as well as the Herr Geheimrat whom he tries to avoid, because he's supposed to be on duty. Still, he can't resist speaking out about his idea to stain bacteria so that other doctors less expert than Koch can see the organism. Koch assures him, with some irony, that if he accomplishes this, his fame in science will be secured. The Herr Geheimrat fires him on the spot.

Dr. E then sets up a laboratory in his home and works constantly, refusing to turn on the heat in order to save fuel. When his wife calls him for a late meal, he leaves a slide just above the furnace which his wife had turned on. On his return, he finds the slide cooked and rails at his wife for turning on the furnace, only to find that his months of failure are ended. As Dr. E puts it, he applied fuchsin red and acid alcohol, but "it was the heat that did it," by fixing the organisms to the slide. He rewards his wife with a kiss. Behring, noting Dr. E's hacking cough, insists that he examine his own sputum, and, sure enough, he contracted tuberculosis while working with the bacillus. Ehrlich asks Behring not to tell his wife.

Behring takes Ehrlich to see Koch, who is in a meeting with the chairman of the institute's budget committee. Koch is being told about the need for budget cutbacks and utters the scientist's universal complaint, "What do members of the budget committee know about the requirements of science?" Koch reluctantly agrees to meet with Dr. E and is ecstatic when told of the breakthrough. "Little doctors everywhere will be able to diagnose tuberculosis with 100 percent accuracy." The budget chairman is sure that funding will now be authorized, and Koch invites Dr. E to join his staff. At a celebration dinner, Mrs. E tells von Behring how happy Dr. E is at the Koch Institute; he replies, "That's where he belongs. He's no medical doctor." Once again science and medicine are placed in opposition.

Ehrlich's illness becomes known and the institute pays to send him to Egypt for lots of fresh air, sunshine, rest, and milk (the mainstays of tuberculosis therapy at the time). While abroad, he tries unsuccessfully to save a boy from snakebite by applying a tourniquet and learns that the boy's father has survived four bites, each with successively less reactivity. On his return to Berlin, Koch shows him his spanking new laboratory to work on aniline dye staining of organisms. Dr. E says he wants to work on snake venom. Koch agrees, knowing he had doubted him once and was mistaken. Behring is going nowhere with his serum for diphtheria and is angry at Ehrlich for seeming to be interested only in his snake venom, not people. Dr. E redeems himself by giving a treatise on immunology explaining what happened to the boy's father, who was successively bitten by a snake. He suggests that progressively stronger doses of diphtheria toxin be injected in a horse.

The headlines blare the news of another diphtheria epidemic, just as the horse throws off the effect of the toxin. With a serum one hundred times stronger than any previous antitoxin, they do a controlled experiment as in *Pasteur* and *Arrowsmith*. Dr. E wants to give it to everyone, saying, "As long as there's a chance it will work, all should get it." The Herr Geheimrat refuses. "Only with a controlled experiment can we establish the value of your serum once and for all. So remember, twenty get the serum and twenty do without." Time passes as we watch the patients, and the turgid Max Steiner score heightens the tension. Like Arrowsmith, Dr. E can't bear to see the control patients die, so he begins to give serum to the controls. Wolfert reports him to the Herr Geheimrat who tries to stop him. When Dr. E says, "They were struggling so hard to breathe," Herr G responds, "Are you doctors or old women? Your experiment is useless. I determine what procedures will be followed in saving lives in this hospital." Herr Geheimrat relents when Dr. E says he'll tell the children's parents "that you prevented me from treating these children." He and Behring retreat to the lab and sleep on the counter to await the outcome. Behring tells him, "That man will see to it that we're both ruined in science." Later, Althoff (Donald Crisp) the health minister, reprimands Dr. E for insubordination and then reveals that all the children who got the injection were saved, including his own grandchild.

Behring leaves for a professorship in Marburg and Althoff sets Ehrlich up in a laboratory, where he vows to develop resistance to bacteria in a test tube—"a magic bullet." Fifteen years pass in which Dr. E is rewarded the Nobel Prize for his "side chain theory" and directs his own institute in Frankfurt. An ex-clinician, Dr. E laments that lab people "don't understand the principles of chemotherapy. To argue with them is like discussing color with the color blind." He also is pressured by his institute's budget committee, which is dismayed to learn that his work on arsenicals may take ten to fifteen years more. He responds, "I dare say the disease will still be with us then." When a committee member asks, "You assistants seem to be doing all the work here. What does Dr. Ehrlich do?" "He thinks," is the response (fig. 8). On seeing a Japanese assistant, Wolfert, a committee member, says, "I noted the presence of an Oriental in the laboratory" and affirms the regulation to employ only those of a "pure German blood." Dr. E replies, "What has race to do with science? Truth is science's master, not the state." The answer is, "Those are queer sentiments for someone who depends on the state for his livelihood."

The next scene highlights Schaudinn's discovery of the microbe that causes syphilis. The spirochete's motion is described as "the dance of death." Dr. E shows that the organism binds arsenic and recognizes that it is related to the trypanosomes he is working on in mice. He then articulates the theory of therapeutic/toxic potential, i.e., "aim for 100 percent effect on microbe and reduce the poisonous effect on the body to zero. Then we will have found our magic bullet." Behring visits

FIGURE 8. *Dr. Ehrlich's Magic Bullet.* Ehrlich (Edward G. Robinson), who writes chemical formulae on his shirt cuffs, knows that scientific progress comes from using one's head.

him because the budget committee is concerned about the cost of all the animals he plans to use. They toast Koch, "To the old man," and Dr. E says, "Chemistry will soon loom ever larger in medical science as time goes on. A time will come when resistance to all diseases will be manufactured in the test tube." Behring replies, "The budget committee doesn't want to give you the appropriation. Give up the dream of curing with chemicals. The idea of shooting chemicals into the veins of human beings fills me with horror." Ehrlich and Behring part in anger.

When his appropriation is cut in half, his wife suggests that Dr. E seek out a rich widow, Frau Speyer (Maria Ouspenskaya). Dr. E says, "People like Frau Speyer don't like to give away money. That's why they have money." Still, she invites him to an opulent dinner where he mentions syphilis; after a hush, he adds, "People may get it in very innocent ways, from a public drinking cup, from a table utensil." Then, at Frau Speyer's urging, he proceeds to write a diagram of his theory on the tablecloth. He and his future patron remain engrossed well after the other guests have left, and he gets his money. The months pass as he tests arsenical after arsenical until the 606th compound works in a chimp without causing side effects. He tells the staff to proceed in utmost secrecy. "Should the unexpected occur in the first human experiment, I want you to promise me that the outside world will never know. Take the afternoon off." One of his assistants says, "The old man intends to inject himself" and proceeds to beat him to it. Parenthetically, the history of self-experimentation in medicine is fascinating in its own right.[17-19] After the experiment succeeds, Dr. E injects volunteers and cures a man with syphilitic blindness.

Urged to release the drug, he wants to wait a year and test the drug on people with other conditions. He says, "I understand your desire to help someone personally known to you, but a scientist must close his heart to all such considerations and must view the problem from the broadest aspects. If we allow ourselves to become involved with our emotions, we shall be lost." Reminded of his willingness to use the diphtheria serum on all comers, he is chided, "I recall some seventeen years ago, there was a diphtheria epidemic, and a young doctor, then quite unknown, transcended the scientific attitude in order to relieve some suffering children. Working in a laboratory some years with rats and guinea pigs, that doctor may have gotten out of touch with human suffering. To us medical practitioners, human beings are not statistics. If you have a cure, in the name of humanity, you must release it." "All right," he says, after being assured that "Rhine Chemical Industries" will keep up the quality of the product despite mass production. Ehrlich has a recurrence of tuberculosis and books passage on the German-Egyptian Line ostensibly as a vacation. Before he can board, news of deaths from 606 surface. His old nemesis Wolfert libels him and Ehrlich is persuaded to stay in Germany and sue him.

It looks bleak when Ehrlich agrees that the people died of arsenic poisoning and when von Behring takes the stand. However, Behring delivers a spirited defense that carries the day, saying, "606 stops infectiousness and the individuals treated for it cannot pass it on. True, thirty-eight people died from 606. Those dead should be thought of as sacrifices, martyrs, if you will, to the public good. If ten or one hundred times that many had fallen, I would still say it was all for the best. For through it and only through 606 can the fight against this dread disease be won." Ehrlich is vindicated and Wolfert is sentenced to one year in prison for libel.

Ehrlich collapses and calls his trainees together and requests his wife to play the piano while he delivers the closing speech again with overtones of a world on the verge of wholesale war, "606 works, we know. The magic bullet will cure thousands. The principle upon which it works will serve against other diseases, many others, I think. But there can be no final victory against diseases of the body unless diseases of the soul are also overcome. They feed upon each other, diseases of the body, diseases of the soul. In days to come, there will be epidemics of greed, hate, ignorance. We must fight them in life as we fought syphilis in the laboratory. Fight. Fight. You must never stop fighting." And he dies. The film's postscript says, "And the temples to his memory are the bodies of human beings purified and made whole."

This is an excellent portrayal of the scientific method. Though reverential throughout, this picture does portray the scientist as an often unfeeling rationalist—someone who doesn't care as much about the people he sees in front of him as those who will live after. A recent article discusses the role of the Public Health Service in the making of the film.[20]

Madame Curie (1943)

The 1943 film, *Madame Curie* is an even more sympathetic portrayal of scientists. It is also a great film to inspire young women to consider pursuing a career in science. Like Pasteur, Marie Curie was not a physician, and, like him, she left a mark on medical science unsurpassed by any students of medicine. Facing determined hostility, she overcame it with grace, superior ideas, and perseverance. Indeed, she is one of a very few to have won two Nobel Prizes, the first in 1903 for physics, with her husband, Pierre, and Henri Becquerel; in 1911, she won a second in chemistry. During World War I, Curie took a portable x-ray machine to the front and worked alongside her daughter, Irene, who acted as a nurse. After the war, Irene worked as an assistant in Marie's laboratory and, in 1935, also won a Nobel Prize in chemistry with her husband, Frederic Joliot. The remarkable nature of the Curies' accomplishments is underscored by the fact that only ten women have been awarded the Nobel Prize for science and only four individuals have won two Nobels. Both Marie Curie and Irene Joliot-Curie died of leukemia, undoubtedly due to their exposure to radium. I have been surprised that the women's movement has not made more of these women who managed to balance brilliant science with their family obligations, thereby countering the mythology promulgated by the Kay Francis films (see chapter 5). Unlike too many modern women celebrities, these women deserve to be lionized. Einstein is reputed to have said of Madame Curie at her death on July 4, 1934, "She was, of all the celebrated persons, the only one whom fame has not corrupted."[21]

Although Aldous Huxley wrote the original screenplay for this film based on Eve Curie's biography of her mother,[22] the script underwent numerous changes[23] (see appendix B for later screenwriters). The film opens with a fictional account of how Marie Sklodowska (Greer Garson), an impoverished daughter of a Polish physicist, and Pierre Curie met. Marie, whose brilliance has earned admission to the famed Sorbonne, passes out during a lecture. On learning that she is barely able to pay for rent and food, her professor sets her up in the lab of Pierre Curie, played as mega-science nerd and prototypical absent-minded professor by Walter Pidgeon.

Lamenting that he had agreed to the arrangement before learning she was a woman, Pierre tells his assistant David LeGros (Robert Walker), "It's always a continual struggle against women." LeGros responds, "Women and science are particularly unattractive." Curie answers, "Women and science are incompatible. No true scientist can have anything to do with a woman. Women of genius are rare." Later, Pierre is stunned at Marie's ability to converse in mathematical equations as he escorts her home in the rain, saying, "Your conversation is very scintillating." Without realizing it, he falls hopelessly in love and is devastated to hear that she will be returning to Poland after graduating first in her class. His marriage proposal is worthy of a Massachusetts Institute of Technology graduate as he tells her that they would be like sodium and chloride. He does admit that, "For the scientist, there is no time for love," but "in their case, there is no place for generalizations." True to both their natures, they bicycle off on their honeymoon with a bunch of science books.

The film nicely illustrates that scientific breakthroughs require doggedness and incremental insights, by focusing on their struggles to isolate radium from pitchblende (uranium ore) after their colleague Becquerel shows that the ore can expose a photographic plate. It takes four years, hundreds of experiments, and exactly 5,677 crystallizations before they succeed. Their work is carried out under arduous and spare laboratory conditions (fig 9). Marie manages to maintain a household and have a child while working in the laboratory. After sustaining radium burns of her hand, she refuses her doctor's advice to abandon the

FIGURE 9. *Madame Curie.* Marie and Pierre Curie (Greer Garson and Walter Pidgeon) isolate radium under very adverse laboratory conditions.

experiment believing that if radium can kill healthy tissue, it may do the same to unhealthy tissue.

The film also conveys another important lesson about the ends of science, that seems to have been forgotten in this era of scientist/entrepreneurs. After the announcement of their Nobel Prize, a *London Times* reporter insists on interviewing the couple. He says to Marie's father-in-law, "We have heard that they have refused to take money for their radium, but that they are giving it to the world." As Marie Curie later wrote, the Curies always refused to "draw from our discovery any material profit."[21] Imagine anyone in today's "show me the money" world giving away a discovery of this magnitude. In fact, they did not attend the Nobel Prize ceremonies because of Marie's ill health and their teaching obligations. Pierre accepted the award on a separate lecture visit to Stockholm.[22] It's true that in those early days of the prize, it did not have the same cachet that it has today, but it is a reflection of how publicity-shy and modest the Curies were.

The other thing I liked about the picture was the fact that this was a couple who truly loved one another. Their deeds, as remarkable as they were, did not overshadow their human relationships. As Marie tells Pierre: "You're a very great man, Pierre, not in the way the world means; just you, your kindness, your gentleness, your wisdom. I love you, Pierre." Devastated after Pierre is killed in a street accident in 1906, Marie retreats into herself. However, her mentor reminds her of that first lecture when he told the class how Newton and Galileo had reached so high as "to catch a star in their fingertips." He tells her that she had done so and that there are more stars in the heavens. Marie is finally given a professorship at the Sorbonne and she assumes her husband's chair.

The movie concludes with Curie delivering a rousing affirmation of science to the students and faculty on her twenty-fifth anniversary at the Sorbonne. "Science," she says, "has great beauty and with its great spiritual strength will in time cleanse the world of its evil, its ignorance, its poverty, diseases, wars, and heartaches." She urges the assemblage "to look for the clear light of truth and to take the torch of knowledge and behold the palace of the future."

There is no denying that the film is slower-moving and more reverential than today's movies, which are more likely to treat good people cynically, while extolling the sleazy. Pauline Kael called the film "hokey," but she also denigrated the much beloved films of Frank Capra as "Capracorn." Indeed, Eve Curie's biography and the film have been called hagiography and criticized for their failure to deal with the widow Curie's affair with colleague Paul Langevin four years after Pierre was struck by a horse-drawn carriage while crossing a Paris street.[23, 24] In my opinion, the affair does not take away from the devastation and loneliness she felt after the premature death of what everyone admits was a beloved husband. It may in fact have flowed from it. While filling in more about Marie as a flesh and blood human being, it adds little to the understanding of the scientific discoveries during the time covered by the film. Indeed, Marie paid a heavy price for the affair, being vilified in France and elsewhere as a home-breaker of a man with a wife and four children. For me, *Madame Curie* remains both a wonderful love story and one of the most lucid presentations of science ever filmed. Call it schmaltz if you will, but I much prefer it to the celebration of the violent, the dysfunctional, and the kinky.

MEDICAL SCIENCE IN POSTWAR FILMS

Hollywood's love affair with science ended after World War II as the adverse consequences of scientific advances, such as the atomic bomb, became evident. Science fiction films became the rage and scientists often were portrayed as loonies, absent-minded professors, or downright evil. *Doctor Strangelove,* who isn't a physician, came to symbolize the latter-day version of the mad and power-hungry scientist. Movies about science in the last decade have been for the most part negative and, in the case of the next film, embarrassingly bad.

Medicine Man (1992)

"Tarzan meets Arrowsmith" in *Medicine Man*, a badly-acted, politically correct travesty where "the cure for cancer" (called "the plague of this century") is found and lost. Sean Connery plays Dr. Robert Campbell, a dedicated scientist sent to the Amazon by a foundation patterned on the Rockefeller. Scientists will envy his chutzpah in being able to continue to get money for years without sending any progress reports. Finally, after requesting a technician and some equipment, Dr. Rae Crane (Lorraine Bracco) is sent to locate him (fig. 10). You know it's going to be a long movie when she gets out of the pirogue and says, "I'm tired! I'm hungry! And I've been in these clothes for more than one dance."

Campbell is an arrogant, pony-tailed, male chauvinist gone native. A father figure to a tribe of "noble savages," he leads them in their nightly revels of drinking, dancing, and singing while wearing a medicine man mask and weird get-up. Crane, whose Brooklyn accent you can cut with a knife (so she's naturally called "Bronx" by Campbell), spends most of

FIGURE 10. *Medicine Man.* Sean Connery and Lorraine Bracco made a scientific odd couple in an absurd picture in which the "cure for cancer" is found and lost.

her time whining and dreaming up witless, snappy retorts. Campbell manages to look bored even when he admits that he has found "the cure for cancer" as if there is only one type. Crane says, "You've found the cure for cancer and all you can say is 'I know,'" before he confesses that he has lost the lab book describing how the serum was produced. "Haven't you ever lost a notebook?" he asks Crane petulantly. Later, he and Crane get to swing through the trees in their search for the plant that yielded the cure. Wouldn't you know it but those evil despoilers of the rainforest destroy the source of the cure, thereby impoverishing mankind! The final straw is the tension around the decision as to whether he should save the last remnant of the serum to take to the United States for analysis so that the cure can be replicated or give it to a child to save her life. You guess what he does.

By contrast, the belief that traditional scientists don't really care about individual patients and must be rigorously monitored even to the point of concerned parents helping them with their research is the subject of the next film. Unfortunately, as we shall see, the filmmakers appear to have seriously distorted the story. Directed by George Miller, who practiced medicine briefly at St. Vincent's Hospital in Australia, *Lorenzo's Oil* is nonetheless permeated with an anti-doctor tone. While Miller achieved more accuracy in the medical and scientific details than most contemporary directors, according to many of the participants, he went beyond artistic license in telling this story.

Lorenzo's Oil (1992)

Lorenzo's Oil focuses on the brief life of Lorenzo Michael Murphy Odone (Zack O'Malley Greenburg). Lorenzo is pictured as carefree and happy when we meet him on the Camoros Islands, as kites soar magically against the sky. Three months later, after his father, Augusto (Nick Nolte), an economist with the World Bank, is reassigned to Washington, D.C., Lorenzo starts throwing things, "out of the blue." Teachers begin to wonder about possible trouble at home. A child who once spoke three languages, now must be moved to a special education class. A battery of tests, including electroencephalogram, skull x-ray, and computerized tomography scans, is normal. Four months later (Easter 1984), he is diagnosed as having adrenoleukodystrophy (ALD), a rare, progressive, demyelinating disease.

Patients with ALD cannot break down very-long-chain fatty acids, which subsequently build up, especially in the brain and adrenal gland. The doctor at Washington Children's Hospital tells the parents it affects boys, usually between ages five and ten, and is "relentless and incurable." He very clearly explains what happens to the myelin sheath, but he cannot offer hope and says the boy will die in two years. A National Institutes of Health expert, Dr. Gus Nikolais (Peter Ustinov), has developed a diet to reduce consumption of these fatty acids and offers it to the Odones with the admonition, "We cannot reverse the disease. But if it is any consolation, you will be helping us understand the progression of this heartless disease."

Genetic counseling gets much emphasis in that ALD is a sex-linked recessive disease, characterized as the "cruelest form of genetic lottery, where the mother is likely to blame herself." In this case, the mother, Michaela (Susan Sarandon), a linguist, develops a profound depression. This is their only child, a beloved son, and she sees herself as the vehicle of his misfortune. She lashes out at her family and becomes obsessed with the care of the child. A devout Roman Catholic, she stops going to church. Even so, a friend of mine who was a parishioner at a Yonkers, New York, church where the grandmother attended, said that they always prayed for the child but never knew who he was until the film came out.

When the child gets worse on the experimental diet, the Odones are told that the protocol must run its course, and they accede to some very high-risk therapies. Finally, at an ALD parents' support group meeting, their rage erupts. They decide to start their own search for a cure. Indeed, while the story is interesting, it becomes somewhat overwrought at this point. The Odones accuse the support group of existing simply to manage grief, salvage marriages, handle nasogastric tubes, and raise money for the doctors. The Odones say they won't consign their children blindly into the doctors' hands. "Let's not do what the doctors did," they say, "doing something without knowing why." The reference is to their recommended diet. The parent leader of the support group asks, "Where do you get off to think you know more than the doctors? You can't give credence to every jerk who comes along with an apricot pit for a cure." The battle lines are drawn. The Odones wish to push "these guys" (the doctors). "They're so powerful, but they're not gods." In a later scene, we see Sir Luke Fildes' famous portrait of a physician sitting next to the bed of a dying child (see introduction); the contrast between the caring doctor of yesteryear and today's technician is meant to be stark.

In later scenes, the parents' group leaders are further demeaned, about which the real-life models expressed great resentment.[25] There are also other potshots at scientists; for example, one scientist says, "We scientists are a very competitive lot. We won't collaborate to help find a cure for a disease, but we will come together to make an atom bomb." Dr. Nikolais says, "It's the solemn responsibility of doctors to assure that evidence is not anecdotal. The only way is to use a protocol with a statistical sample derived in clinical trials." The Odones answer, "Our children seem to be at the service of medical science. We thought medical science was the servant of suffering children." In short, they assert the same sense of urgency that AIDS patients and their supporters did. The researchers' time-lines are portrayed as out of synch with those of the patients and their families. As you will note below, the model for Dr. Nikolais, Dr. Hugh Moser, a professor of pediatrics and neurology at Johns Hopkins, disputes this characterization. He remains Lorenzo's doctor for emergencies and has much praise for the Odones and, to some extent, for the movie. He noted, however, "To put me as a person who sits around diddling with statistics instead of helping people is incorrect."[25]

Michaela nurses her child at home in a makeshift ICU with around-the-clock nursing and proceeds to alienate the nurses and members of her family who don't share her monomaniacal devotion to Lorenzo. When she dismisses the last of her nurses, she asks an African friend of Lorenzo's to come and nurse him. Miller takes this opportunity for a gratuitous insult to the United States. When Michaela proposes the idea to her husband, he says, "We cannot bring an African into this racist country."

Augusto begins poring over books in the National Library of Medicine (fig. 11). We see close-up views of *Neurology*, the *New England Journal of Medicine*, *Journal of the American Medical Association*, and assorted bibliographies. The first relevant paper he supposedly finds is in an obscure Polish journal; it describes a similar disease in rats. The Odones organize an international conference to bring people together to pool information. This gathering leads to an identification of the potential value of rapeseed oil and its component, erucic acid. Finally a combination of erucic acid and oleic acid is made to form Lorenzo's Oil. The picture portrays this preparation as being effective in arresting and possibly reversing Lorenzo's disorder. Later on, the Odones work with University of Wisconsin scientists, using their animal model of the disease (dogs who naturally develop a demyelinating disease) to study the effect of implanting brain cells. This situation could have been taken as a great opportunity to support animal research, but we don't get the

FIGURE 11. *Lorenzo's Oil.* The Odones (Susan Sarandon and Nick Nolte) pore over medical journals and texts to find a cure for adrenoleukodystrophy, a rare degenerative disease affecting their son.

same preachy lines that we get against researchers, presumably because supporting animal experimentation is not currently politically correct. The issue of self-experimentation[17-19] is again raised when the sister volunteers to start on the new drug in place of Michaela, who is anxious to test the oil on herself.

The most important question is never confronted, namely: Whose life is it, anyway? Since the child is incompetent, the parents are clearly appropriate surrogates for the child's best interests. But, is Michaela, the key decision maker, doing all this for her son? Is she doing it to assuage her guilt? These are very difficult questions. Nonetheless, we are left with the fact that nine years later, at fourteen, Lorenzo is alive, although severely neurologically disabled. The parents are holding out hope that something will be found to cause the myelin sheath to be regenerated. In this respect, there is a great line in the film. "If someone can't move, can't speak, can't see, how do we know what is in his soul?"

Nolte's Italian accent is abominable and distracting, but he is a good counterbalance to Sarandon, who gives an excellent, brutally honest portrayal. Her intensity and indomitable pursuit of a cure engenders both awe and feelings of antipathy. One can understand her behavior, and if what is portrayed is true, who is to say she is wrong? Unfortunately, it isn't. The film ends with a plug for the Odones' version of the Manhattan Project, titled the Myelin Project: the telephone number for those who wish to contribute is shown on the screen. Also, we see a montage of pictures of children who are said to have benefited from Lorenzo's Oil. Although overlong and overdone, the film raises important issues by portraying attitudes of lay people that physicians and researchers ignore at their peril.

The latter is especially true after discussing the film with Dr. Moser. He is a gracious and kindly man with an uncanny resemblance to Peter Ustinov, by whose portrayal he feels honored, although he never met him. His three major concerns with the film were (1) the effectiveness of the oil is grossly overstated; (2) it invents a conflict between the doctors and the patients' families; and (3) it is mean-spirited and unfair to the advocacy group. His comments about the science and the film are thoroughly covered elsewhere,[26-28] so I shall highlight only a few. First, although there were excellent scientific reasons why the diet might work, he and his colleagues concluded in 1982, two years before he saw the Odones, that it was ineffective; so, Lorenzo never got it. Second, the Polish article is pure fabrication. The idea for glycerol trioleate, the first oil used, was proposed by Dr. William Rizzo of Virginia Commonwealth University because of its effect on the synthesis of C_{26} fatty acids in fibroblasts. The 1984 conference, funded by the Odones, was held at the John F. Kennedy Institute (now the Kennedy-Krieger Institute) in Baltimore, which Dr. Moser than directed. He invited thirty-five people from all over the world on two weeks' notice, and all attended—one of many facts arguing against scientific dithering.

He noted that the Odones deserve credit for convincing an Ohio manufacturer to produce the glycerol trioleate, for overcoming skepticism about the hazard of using erucic acid, and for testing it in the sister. The occurrence of serious side effects in patients receiving the oil, when combined with the disappointing results of the open unrandomized trial to date, however, trouble him. He is also dismayed that Miller, a physician, knew about the trial but never contacted him. Ironically, the United Leukodystrophy Foundation, which is vilified in the film, tried to assure that no one was denied access to Lorenzo's Oil, despite its high cost. He believes, however, that the net effect of the film has been positive. He drew an analogy to *Amadeus*, which he said was a similar distortion but served to publicize Salieri and even Mozart. The attention to the disease has enabled investigators to pursue some very promising genetic and immunologic research.

In a follow-up interview with Dr. Moser in July, 1998, he said that experience has shown that the oil is not helpful in patients who already have neurologic disease, but seems to reduce the incidence of progression in asymptomatic children. A few survivors of bone marrow transplant, a much riskier and costly procedure have had their disease arrested. He held out greater hope from the discovery by a Johns Hopkins researcher of a gene on chromosome 12 that has an eighty percent relationship to the defective gene and has been shown to restore the metabolic function to affected cells in culture.[29] Most exciting of all is the discovery that compounds such as phenylbutyrate that has helped sickle cell patients and lovastatin that lowers cholesterol may improve the defective gene's function[29, 30] and make Lorenzo's oil unnecessary. As for Lorenzo, he lives in intensive care at home through what Moser described as the Herculean efforts of Mrs. Odone. However, he added that a patient in Texas who got sick at the same time as Lorenzo and never took the oil is in virtually the same condition. It seemed only fair to set the record straight.

In his book *How Superstition Won and Science Lost*,[31] the historian John Burnham carefully chronicles how society's views of science have changed in this century from awe to suspicion to fear and finally to a contemptuous disdain. As we have seen, this has been mirrored in Hollywood films. The 1997 film *Extreme Measures* distills all these into its scientist villain (see chapter 8). Doctor Luthan, who has presumably received a Nobel Prize, is a far cry from the Curies and real Nobelists. Rather than evincing a selfless pursuit of truth, he displays a disregard of the rights and welfare of individuals combined with a pursuit of fame, power, and wealth. There is not even a passing attempt at a kindly portrayal. This trend is disturbing, as is the failure to tap the rich potential of well-done films for educating a public that seems indifferent, unschooled, and sometimes overtly hostile to science. The popularity of health news suggests that the market is there, but the messages are often so confusing, contradictory, and self-serving that the disorganized cacophony of press releases may be doing more harm than good.[32] Whatever the case, medical scientists would do well not to ignore Hollywood under the assumption that it represents a lowbrow cultural voice. In an era that has fulfilled Marshall McLuhan's prophecy about the media being the message, Hollywood often represents *vox populi* where perception is reality.

NOTES

1. Ludmerer KM. Time to Heal: American Medical Education from the Turn of the Century to the Era of Managed Care. New York: Oxford University Press, 1999.
2. Robinson D. Scientists of the silver screen: Stolid starry-eyed humanitarians or dangerous demented doctors? Film-makers have always been of two minds about scientists. New Scientist 1976; 72: 732–734.
3. Rosenberg CE. Martin Arrowsmith: The Scientist As Hero. In: No Other Gods: On Science and American Social Thought. Baltimore: Johns Hopkins University Press, 1976.
4. Gest H. Dr. Martin Arrowsmith: Scientist and medical hero. Perspectives in Biology and Medicine 1991; 35: 116–124.
5. Summers W. On the origin of the science in Arrowsmith: Paul de Kruif, Felix d'Herelle, and phage. J History of Medicine and Allied Sciences 1991; 46: 315–332.
6. de Kruif P (anonymously). Our medicine men. Century Illustrated Monthly Magazine 1922; 104: 501–508.
7. de Kruif P. Microbe Hunters. New York: Pocket Books, 1926.
8. Koprowski H and Oldstone MBA, eds. Microbe Hunters: Then and Now. Bloomington, IL: Medi–Ed Press, 1996.
9. Shelley MW. Frankenstein or the Modern Prometheus. New York: New American Library, 1983.
10. Kobal J, ed. John Kobal Presents the Top 100 Movies. New York: New American Library, 1988.
11. Polidori JW. The Vampyre: A Tale. London: printed for Sherwood, Neely, and Jones, 1819.
12. Stoker B. Dracula. New York: Modern Library, 1897.
13. Geison GL. The Private Science of Louis Pasteur. Princeton: Princeton University Press, 1995.
14. Dubos RJ. Louis Pasteur. New York: Little, Brown & Co, 1950.
15. Perutz MF. The Pioneer Defended. The New York Review of Books, December 21, 1995, p 54.
16. Shortland M. Medicine and Film: A Checklist, Survey and Research Resource. Oxford: Wellcome Unit for the History of Medicine, 1989.
17. Hendricks M. Do unto yourself what you would do unto others. Johns Hopkins Magazine, April, 1996, pp 14–19.
18. Nuland SB. Five doctors who advanced medicine by experimenting on themselves. Medical Economics, March 25, 1996, pp 161–167.
19. Altman LK. Who Goes First? : The Story of Human Experimentation in Medicine. Berkeley: University of California Press, 1998.
20. Lederer SE and Parascandola J. Screening syphilis: *Dr. Ehrlich's Magic Bullet* meets the Public Health Service. J Hist Med, 1998, 53: 370-405
21. Editorial. Marie Curie and a century of radiation. New York Times, Monday, November 23, 1998, p A22.
22. Curie E. Madame Curie. New York: Doubleday, 1937.
23. Elena A. Skirts in the lab: Madame Curie and the image of the woman scientist in the feature film. Public Understanding Sci 1997; 6: 269–278.
24. Quinn S. Marie Curie: A Life. New York: Simon & Schuster, 1995.
25. Marbella J. Troubled waters for Lorenzo's Oil. Baltimore Sun, January 26, 1993, pp. 1D, 3D.
26. Moser HW. Lorenzo's Oil, film review. Lancet 1993; 341: 544.
27. Moser HW. Lorenzo oil therapy for adrenoleukodystrophy: A prematurely amplified hope. Ann Neurol 1993; 34: 121–122.
28. Moser HW. Suspended judgment: Reactions to the motion picture Lorenzo's Oil. Controlled Clin Trials 1994; 15: 161–164.

29. Kemp S, Wei H-M, Lu J-F, et al. Gene redundancy and pharmacological gene therapy: Implications for x-linked adrenoleukodystrophy. Nature Medicine 1998; 4: 1261–1267.
30. Singh I, Khan M, Key L, and Pai S. Lovastatin for x-linked adrenoleukodystrophy. N Engl J Med 1998; 339: 702–703.
31. Burnham J. Popularizing Science and Health in the United States. How Superstition Won and Science Lost. New Brunswick: Rutgers University Press, 1987.
32. Shell ER. The Hippocratic wars: The feisty Journal of the American Medical Association and New England Journal of Medicine are battling for physician-readers through an unwitting ally: The media. Sunday New York Times Magazine Section, June 28, 1998, p 34-38.

5

"Where Are All the Women Doctors?"

Asked to name a male movie doctor, you might rattle off Dr. Kildare, Dr. Christian, or a television version like Marcus Welby. Chances are, though, unless you're a film buff, you probably couldn't name a woman movie doctor. I couldn't before writing this book. Mirroring the society's prevailing beliefs, moviemakers have considered women to be great patients (Bette Davis in *Dark Victory*), outstanding nurses (Rosalind Russell as Sister Kenny), and devoted girl friends or spouses. Walsh documents in her book, *Doctors Wanted: No Women Need Apply*,[1] a title derived from a 1946 full-page women's protest advertisement in the *New York Herald Tribune*, that women were almost uniformly discriminated against in medical school admission. She credits Bostonian Harriot K. Hunt, who, with her sister Sarah, completed a medical apprenticeship in 1835 as the first woman doctor to practice successfully in the United States. In 1850, Harvard, after first accepting Hunt, blocked her from receiving formal medical lectures when her fellow students claimed that it was necessary "to preserve the dignity of our school and its self-respect."[1] That pristine state persisted until 1945 when Harvard medical school admitted its first woman.[1]

In 1847, the faculty of Geneva Medical School, a predecessor of the State University of New York at Syracuse, had wanted to bar Elizabeth Blackwell, generally acknowledged to be the first woman graduate of a U.S. medical school. They passed the buck to her prospective classmates, who refused to blackball her. In 1864, Dr. Rebecca Lee became the first Black woman U.S. graduate.[1] By 1870, the United States Census recorded that only 525 of 62,383 "physicians and surgeons" were women. Over the next few decades, progress was made, in that the representation of women in medical school rose to 4 percent and they accounted for 18.2 percent of practicing doctors in Boston in 1900.

As it did for Blacks, medical education for women became harder after the closure of marginal schools following the Flexner report.[2] Despite some increase in admissions during World War I and II, the percentage of women medical school graduates overall hovered around 5 percent into the 1960s. Most had difficulty gaining entrance to postgraduate training or hospital staffs. Except for New England Hospital, a woman's hospital, only six American hospitals accepted women as interns in 1890.[1] As we will see, the film *The Girl in White* documents Emily Dunning Barringer's fight to obtain an internship in 1902. During World War I, Mary Wright, who had already interned at the Peter Bent Brigham (the last woman intern there for the next thirty years) was accepted at the Massachusetts General Hospital in pediatrics, after a man resigned to enter the service. The choice was said to be between "two undesirable male Hebrews and a woman."[1]

The percent of approved internships admitting women rose from about 10 percent in 1921 to 23 percent in 1938 and the number of women physicians to about seven thousand. As in World War I, there was an influx of women into medical schools during World War II, but at its conclusion, the numbers receded. In 1971, a prominent woman physician in a *New England Journal of Medicine* letter noted ironically that excellent internship programs were still reluctant to accept women, despite the fact that "the 5 to 20 percent quota of women in medical schools is usually chosen with caution"[3] and "had to be superior to begin with."[4] This has changed dramatically. In 1997, women physicians in the United States numbered 150 thousand, almost a quarter of licensed physicians. About 43 percent of entering medical students and 36 percent of residents were women.[5] Almost two-thirds of house staff in pediatrics and obstetrics/gynecology were women, although they comprised only 21 percent of surgical trainees and an even lower proportion in surgical subspecialties.[5] Given the move towards parity at the undergraduate and postgraduate levels, attention has now been shifted to equity in pay and promotion, as well as flexibility in career paths.[5,6]

Because women were generally excluded from leadership positions in medicine (for an exception see note about Dr. Mary Ellen Avery in chapter 2), one might conclude that there were no great women doctors whose exploits deserved chronicling. And one would be wrong. In addition to those already mentioned, consider Mary Edwards Walker, who graduated from Syracuse Medical College and served as a surgeon during the Civil War. Captured by the Confederates, she was exchanged for a Confederate surgeon and in 1865 became the only woman to be awarded the Congressional Medal of Honor.[7] In 1917, the Army asked her to return the medal which they said was meant to honor men carrying arms in combat. She refused and died in obscurity and dire straits. In 1977, the award was belatedly reinstated.

Florence Sabin, whose research at the Rockefeller Institute laid the groundwork for the discovery of anti-tuberculous therapy, was the first woman elected to the National Academy of Sciences.[4] She is one of the few women memorialized in Statuary Hall in the United States Capitol. Mary Putnam Jacobi made outstanding contributions to public health and constituted a formidable team with her husband, Abraham Jacobi, a pioneer in pediatrics. Mary Pierson Eddy was the first woman doctor allowed to enter the Turkish empire in the nineteenth century. Virginia Apgar's scoring system to rate the health status of newborns at the time of delivery is universally used. Doctor Helen Taussig was instrumental in developing the procedure that Doctor Alfred Blalock used to correct the congenital malformations of "blue babies." And on a less famous, but personally important note, my first pediatrician in 1937 New York was a woman. I still have her detailed instructions on feeding and nap time, if I ever need them.

As we shall see, there were women doctors in 1930s films, but they were not played by strong, self-possessed actresses like Bette Davis, Joan Crawford, or Barbara Stanwyck. Instead, directors cast Kay Francis, who played long-suffering, unappreciated, and conflicted heroines in films designed principally for so-called women's matinees. These pictures deserve to be revisited, although readers, especially women, should be forewarned. Seen from the perspective of the 1990s, they are likely to set your teeth on edge. They did mine. Though the women are infinitely more accomplished than any of their male counterparts, they must swallow some bitter pills to advance in the profession and to combat the prevailing societal belief that women had no business being doctors. Their place in entering classes was begrudged under the presumption that they would drop out of the profession to marry and have children, thus "wasting their education." Men, it was assumed, would continue to work the long hours medicine required. This misogynistic stance is best captured in the 1962 film, *The Interns* (see below and chapter 3). Unfortunately, this macho attitude has hurt not only women, but also men, who, in trying to live up to it, have too often neglected their families and themselves. This is alluded to by the divorced male service chief in *The Girl in White*. We'll start our tour of Hollywood's women doctors with one of the most accomplished women doctors in screen history.

Mary Stevens, M.D. (1933)

The film opens with Dr. Mary Stevens (Kay Francis) on an emergency ambulance run to a tenement housing stereotypic Italian immigrants (fig. 1). On seeing her, the father screams, "Woman doctor no good. I need a man doctor." He chases after her with a butcher's knife, and as he is being restrained, he yells "If the bambino dies, I kill you." After which, he proceeds to drink red wine and to curse the woman doctor. The attendant slips out the fire escape to call the police who, along with the firemen, arrive just as the father is carving a hole through the locked bedroom door. Dr. Stevens opens it and shows him a set of twins and the he-man faints.

Cut to the Hippocratic oath scrolling on the screen and the internship director giving his charges a rousing send-off into practice. As Stevens and her classmate, childhood friend Don Andrews (Lyle Talbot), hang up their shingle, she says, "You said a woman couldn't do it." He replies: "A woman couldn't do it, but you're a superwoman." She says, "I don't know whether to take a bow or to be insulted." Sadly, this perception that women doctors must be superwomen is still all too prevalent. They laugh about needing a patient to pay the rent. Ten months later, Andrews is shown lighting up a cigarette and saying to their nurse Glenda (Glenda Farrell), "Two more months and we'll be able to pay off the furniture." She responds, "We had five patients today, all charity." He asks Glenda if she's sorry she followed them into practice. She answers, "I'd rather be here with you two than back in the hospital saying 'No' to all the interns."

When Andrews oversleeps after a night of carousing, Stevens covers for him. A woman patient sees her and says: "A woman doctor, no thanks." A man says, "You're Dr. Stevens. I'll be back later, maybe." Stevens rousts Andrews out of bed and he tells her that he's tired of working for nothing. He decides to leave the practice to marry a politician's daughter, saying, "He can finagle me a position on the city's medical compensation board." Crushed, Stevens says, "Some people work for their money; others marry into it."

Stevens busily delivers babies of all colors and social strata while Andrews drives a Duesenberg. "How is a doctor on a six thousand dollar salary able to drive an eighteen thousand dollar car?" she asks. "I overcharge the city on the compensation claims. If I don't do it, someone else will." After a four-martini lunch, he remembers he has to operate on a charity case. She tries to stop him, but he says: "Simple laparotomy. I can do it blindfolded." She assists and takes over when he gets dizzy.

FIGURE 1. *Mary Stevens, M.D.* Intern Stevens (Kay Francis) arrives at a tenement apartment to deliver a baby, only to discover that the woman is having twins.

Later, she scolds him, "You're the head of the biggest medical department in this country." He replies, "What did it get for Barnett over at the institute? A swell reputation and nothing in the bank to bury him after he was dead." She says: "You're no benefactor to mankind. You're nothing but a cheap politician." Then she stops herself, "Nothing's guaranteed to break up a friendship like giving advice." The hospital superintendent issues Andrews a lame reprimand, "A hospital's reputation can be ruined if a surgeon shows up drunk to perform an operation." No one says anything about the poor patient!

Later, Glenda tells a dead-tired Stevens, "I bet women have babies just so they can take them to the famous Dr. Stevens." Stevens is adding an article about Andrews becoming chief surgeon to her scrapbook. Why she loves this creep becomes even less comprehensible as the film progresses. Glenda asks, "How long are you going to keep this up? Clinic in the morning, office hours all afternoon, hospital half the night." Stevens agrees to close the office and go to the Greenbrier Hotel where she just happens to meet Andrews who is running away from a possible Grand Jury indictment. He takes her up to his room and gives her the "my wife and I have drifted apart" line to which she should respond, "Buzz off, loser, I'm leaving to burn your scrapbook." Instead, she says, "You're married just the same. I'm getting out before we do something both of us will regret." Fade to black and they do it anyway.

As devotees of 1930s films know, one night of passion invariably leads to a baby. Andrews, whose father-in-law has quashed the indictment, promises to get a divorce and marry Stevens. She says, "It will be done, O Lord and Master." If you haven't gotten sick to this point, that line should do it, since he can't hold a candle to her either in character or as a physician. Andrews' wife, who also has a lover, is just as happy to go to Reno, Nevada (the divorce capital at the time), but is ordered by her father to tell Andrews she's pregnant. Over an after-dinner cigarette, Andrews tells Stevens of the new wrinkle and promises to marry her in a year. She goes along but doesn't tell him that she is really having their baby. He says patronizingly: "You're still a champion. Just a little girl who always understands." Yuk!

When Stevens decides to go to Paris to have the baby, Glenda says, "There will be a terrible scandal. Eminent baby doctor goes off to Europe and has a baby without benefit of clergy." Stevens replies, "Yesterday, I advised a young woman to be a good sport and go through with it. I can't do less." After the delivery, the ecstatic Stevens arranges to adopt her son as if he were someone else's baby. Andrews telephones her to say that his wife was lying about being pregnant and he asks her to come home. She still doesn't tell him about their baby. On board ship, Stevens is called to steerage to see a baby with infantile paralysis (polio). Stevens sends an SOS for convalescent antiserum. Meanwhile, the sick child's sister opens Stevens' purse and sucks on her fountain pen. OK, you 1930s film buffs know what's coming. The sister comes down with the disease; Stevens's son sucks the fountain pen and he, too, comes down with polio. The serum arrives just as Stevens's son dies and she says, "Give the serum to the other children; my baby won't need it."

Stevens returns home and becomes a recluse, living on black coffee and cigarettes. Glenda tells her, "Thousands of children need your knowledge, your skill." She replies, "What good was all my experience, all the good I did for other people. I couldn't help my own baby. I'll never practice again." Glenda and Andrews take away her medical bag thinking she might try to kill herself, although it's not clear with what. Instead, Stevens runs to the window ledge, and just as she is about to jump, the doorman bangs on the door, shouting that his son swallowed a safety pin and is turning blue. Glenda says, "Here's your chance to come back." On learning that her medical bag is missing, Stevens gets a cosmetics mirror and a spoon to use as a tongue depressor. She still needs something to extricate the pin and, while the child's mother bites her knuckle, Stevens runs her hand through her hair and in a flash of brilliance, takes off her bobby pin. After Stevens successfully removes the safety pin, Glenda says, "You said you couldn't do it." As Stevens leans against the mantel, she smilingly utters the film's best lines, "They say medicine is a man's game. I wonder what a man would have done in a case like this." Too bad the film didn't end there. Instead, the director cuts to the office where the reunited doctor couple are locked in an embrace. Another patient stereotype, a twelve-year-old Jewish boy, Sanford Nussbaum, comes to see Dr. Stevens because he is "worried to death about the country's going off the gold standard." Glenda tells him and his mother that Dr. Stevens is busy "working on a man."

Dr. Monica (1934)

As demeaning as *Mary Stevens, M.D.* is to women doctors, it never plumbs the depths reached by *Dr. Monica*, Kay Francis's 1934 follow-up. The old-style opening credits show Doctor Monica Braden smoking. The phone rings off the hook as the camera pans on a tray of martinis at a posh party. The hostess Anna (Vernee Teasdale) plaintively asks, "Why do all these babies attempt to struggle into this world at cocktail time?" Dr. M, who is just arriving, takes the call (fig. 2) and tells the nurse, "I know the case. On Ward B. Oh, she doesn't want to spoil her perfect 32. Well, her 32 is less important than the welfare of that baby." Ah yes, a time when a 32 bust was considered perfection and not worth ruining in order to nurse a child! Dr. M joins her husband John, a writer (Warren William), who has been discussing Dr. M's plans for a lying-in hospital. The hostess sets up the movie saying, "The only way to get you two lovebirds together is for Monica to give up delivering babies or John, his writing." John says, I'm willing, but how do we decide which?" Anna, the hostess, replies, "Discover which is the greater nuisance to society." Forced laughs all around. Dr. M is besotted with John, whose scarf she fixes as he leaves to "keep an appointment." He says, "Yes, mother." Dr. M responds, "I should be your mother."

The exchange is made even more ridiculous because Warren William looks twenty-five years older than Kay Francis. Furthermore, it turns out that John is fooling around with Mary (I'm not making this up), a cute young thing who has "a pilot's license but no profession." In the next scene, we see the oblivious Dr. M helping John pack for a European trip, apparently to break off the affair with Mary. Dr. M is staying behind to enter a hospital to have an infertility workup. She says, "After all the babies I've delivered, I should be able to bring one into this world."

FIGURE 2. *Dr. Monica*. The chic Dr. Monica (Kay Francis), a sought-after "baby doctor," answers a page.

Mary (Jean Muir) collapses when she hears that her paramour is leaving; she doesn't keep their last date, but rides around town in a taxi. He later comes to her beautiful art deco apartment and confesses that he's decided it's Monica he loves. Yet, at the dock, he evenhandedly waves to both. Monica, oblivious to the affair, comforts the distraught Mary over drinks at a friend's apartment. Her friend says, "I can't see why a woman in your position with your great responsibility would want with a baby." Dr. M replies, "It would make John happier. Having a child would give him a deeper sense of responsibility and maybe he'd write better, too" (a great reason to have a baby).

Mary and Monica go off to an estate where Mary drinks, rides horse wildly, and finally confronts the fact that she is pregnant with John's baby (of which there is no evidence even as the due date approaches). Dr. M arranges for Mary to go to a rest home where she is cared for by an ex-nurse from the hospital. Meanwhile, Dr. M learns that she can never get pregnant. After two months, John returns bearing a gift of a diamond bracelet as well as a renewed commitment to Dr. M. As Mary is about to deliver, Dr. M urges her to call the father and overhears her call "Mr. Braden" and then speak to "John." Voilá, a serious ethical dilemma! Will she or won't she deliver the child? Dr. M tells Anna, who has come to assist with the delivery, "The man is John," and then tells the nurse, "Get another doctor." Anna answers, "Her life and reputation are in your hands." Dr. M replies "Do you think I'd touch her? I'd kill her. I have every right to." "You lie," her friend says. "That woman upstairs is your patient. You're a doctor under oath. Go upstairs and deliver her child." Dr. M gets hysterical and Anna slaps her. Dr. M says, "Thanks" (latter-day viewers might add "I needed that!"). Dr. M delivers the child and high-tails it, telling Anna, "Don't let me see the baby when I come to see the mother." Mary, who can't understand the change in Dr. M asks, "Why don't you kiss me?" Dr. M answers, "I'm a doctor now. I'm a machine." At first Mary refuses to nurse the baby, who looks pretty robust to be two days old and starving. Dr. M says, "What this child needs is a mother" and convinces Mary to nurse her. She then hatches a plan to have a two-week second honeymoon with John, who doesn't know she knows. Then, she plans to go to Vienna to study for a year before directing her new hospital, She intends to mail an already-written and well-deserved "Dear John" letter.

Everything is hunky-dory until Anna tells Mary of Dr. M's plan on the day of her departure for Vienna. Mary writes Dr. M a note and leaves her the baby. She flies to Paris on two hours worth of gasoline (you do the math). Dr. M blissfully takes the baby to her apartment and cancels her trip. After learning of Mary's death, she has a few moments of sadness and then goes to show the baby to John. She smiles and tells him that she's adopted it and that it comes from fine parents. He says, "You'll be so happy." She asks, "Will you?" He responds, "Your happiness is mine, old girl." She tells him, "Let's see you pick it up. Hold her, John. She's yours." As the film fades with the lovebirds wreathed in smiles, the audience is left to ponder these ironic last lines. She knows, we know, but he doesn't.

What about her research fellowship in Vienna and her hospital, you ask. They seem to have been lost in her new-found motherhood and marital bliss. Again, when one considers her accomplishments, the tawdry private life she trades for it is incomprehensible. One is left to wonder how she could put up with such an insensitive cad, who looks like a corpse, to boot. The screenwriter's message seems to be "a woman's place is in the home, no matter how accomplished she is or how creepy her spouse."

Woman Doctor (1939)

Woman Doctor has to be the worst film I saw in researching this book and also the most expensive to obtain. Produced by Republic Studios, it has not been released in video. Given the leaden performances and the poor cinematic values, this is perfectly understandable. In all fairness, it's important to note that about twenty minutes were cut from the version I saw to adapt it for television. This includes the visit by a doctor from the Moscow Medical Center to see what Dr. Randall is doing in the field of spinal surgery and the treatment for osteomyelitis of the hip. The choppiness of the amateurish cuts further detracts from the film.

However, *Woman Doctor* has an important place in the portrayal of women doctors on screen. First, because of its title. Second, it takes an interesting twist on the career versus marriage conundrum (fig. 3). Based on a story by two women writers (see appendix B), the film concerns Dr. Judith Randall (Frieda Inescort), an accomplished woman surgeon, who is so caught up in her professional responsibilities that, in Hollywood theatrical trailer parlance, she "drives her husband into the arms of another."

Dr. Randall also alienates her daughter Elsa by leaving her in the care of an austere nanny. The child is played by an actress (Sybil Jason) who had seen too many Shirley Temple films, but lacked her talent. Elsa acts bratty so that the nanny will call her mother to tuck her into bed. She tells her mother, "Daddy says you would rather cut people than eat." She later expresses hatred for her mother when Dr. R refuses to operate on her dog who was run over by a car, because "hospital rules forbid it" and because she is being paged to take care of an emergency patient. Parenthetically, emergency operations on children's dogs were a Hollywood screenwriter's staple (see *The Babe Ruth Story* and *Miss Susie Slagle's*).

Dr. Randall is a rather cold automaton who never hugs or kisses her child. She arrives home late and is constantly being called back to the hospital. Tired of dinners alone, her husband (Henry Wilcoxon), a daredevil pilot named Allan Graeme (called Mr. Randall by the hospital staff), becomes captivated by a rich beautiful pilot, Gail (Claire Dodd) (see *Dr. Monica* for the same triangle). When he asks Dr. Randall for a

FIGURE 3. *Woman Doctor*. Dr. Judith Randall's (Frieda Inescort) successful surgical career leaves little time for her husband and child.

divorce and threatens to take their daughter, she is galvanized into action. This occasions one of the film's few good exchanges. After Allan says he wants a wife, not a doctor, Randall responds, "I was a doctor when you married me. You were proud of my work. You were willing to put up with it because you loved me. I guess you stopped loving me." When Elsa balks at staying with her, she says "It's my fault. It takes time to be a good mother."

Dr. Randall decides to resign from the hospital saying, "I've decided to give up medicine altogether." The hospital director sits her down on one of those white stools and says, "Now, young lady, what's all this I hear about?" Dr. R responds, "Purely a personal problem, Dr. Matthews." "Personal! A doctor doesn't allow his personal problems to interfere with his work." Randall answers, "Unfortunately, I'm not just a doctor. I'm also a mother. I thought I could have a career and a family too." The hospital director responds, "You are one of the finest surgeons, at the peak of your career. It took fifteen years of hard work to get where you are. Are you going to throw it all out the window?" He prevails on her to stay for two more weeks, saying, "They can say what they want about the maternal instinct. I think it's a menace to society."

Then comes the climactic series of scenes. Dr. R is served with divorce papers. Allan takes Elsa away from the mean nanny to a Rhode Island estate that he shares with Gail. Elsa is ecstatic, but Gail isn't. Dr. Randall arrives by car and when Elsa sees her, she bolts away on a horse, is thrown to the ground after a long chase, and suffers chest injuries. Randall calls her hospital in New York and Allan revs up his single engine plane. Fog delays their landing and Elsa begins to get short of breath from "a punctured lung." Dr. R asks Gail if she has a percolator. Gail wonders if she wants some coffee. Randall responds, "No, Gail, some water. I have to operate," which she proceeds to do in mid-air. Allan tries to keep the plane steady, while looking back and saying, "Good girl, Judy." He escapes a mid-air collision with a commercial airliner, prompting Randall to say, "Good boy, Allan," and lands the plane safely in "zero visibility." The child survives. The marriage is saved. Randall remains a surgeon and Allan reaffirms his pride in her. All's well that ends well, although the dysfunctional nature of the principals does not augur well. One might suggest the need for psychiatric counselling and the next movie has just the woman for the job.

Spellbound (1945)

Ingrid Bergman starred as psychiatrist Dr. Constance Peterson (fig. 4) in *Spellbound*, an Alfred Hitchcock classic. This film was the product of Hitchcock's teamwork with screenwriter Ben Hecht, artist Salvador Dali (who designed the colorized dream sequence), and composer Miklos Rozsa (who wrote the haunting musical score). We first meet Dr. Peterson smoking at her desk in a psychiatric sanitorium. Despite her apparent common sense, she gets involved in trying to cure the new institute director, J. B. Ballantine, played by Gregory Peck, who turns out to be an amnesiac and not who he seems to be. Ironically, although Hollywood is more likely to have women psychiatrists fall in love with their patients[8] (see *The Prince of Tides*), male psychiatrists report having sex with their patients much more often.[9] Her male colleagues spend a lot of time trying to hit on Dr. P. When she rebuffs their advances, they accuse her of being frigid (something that she hardly is with J.B.). Though we do see Dr. P interacting with a patient in one scene, the film mainly focuses on their love affair.

Mixed up in all this is an operation performed by psychiatrists (fig. 5), a murder of the former institute director, an escape through Grand Central Station, an eerie scene where Ballantine seems to confirm that he is the murderer, and most frightening of all, Dr. P's confrontation with the

FIGURE 4. *Spellbound*. Psychiatrist Dr. Constance Peterson (Ingrid Bergman) looks up from her desk to greet the new hospital director J. B. Ballantine (Gregory Peck, not shown).

real killer. In short, it's more of a murder mystery/romance showcasing two luminous actors (Bergman and Peck) than a story about a doctor. Oh yes, Hitchcock appears as the man with the cello.

By contrast with the previous films, the next one, despite its somewhat demeaning title, is a positive portrayal of a real-life woman physician.

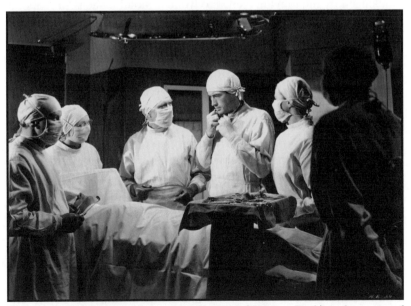

FIGURE 5. *Spellbound*. An amnesiac internist (Gregory Peck) and a group of psychiatrists scrub in for a neurosurgical procedure.

The Girl in White (1952)

Given the 1934 film, *Men in White*, one can question why this film wasn't called *Woman in White*. The only plausible reason, other than sexism, is the potential for confusion with the 1948 thriller based on Wilkie Collins mystery of the same name and starring Eleanor Parker and Sydney Greenstreet. Faithful to Doctor Emily Dunning Barringer's autobiography, *Bowery to Bellevue*[10] on which it was based, the film appears quite authentic and is certainly sympathetic to doctors. Still, the excellent critic Leonard Maltin called it "humdrum."[11] This may be because film portrayals satisfying to physicians as being realistic or uplifting may lack the dramatic tension or touch of the outlandish that are usually necessary for commercial and critical success.

The scrolling introduction reads, "A pioneer is one who goes before to prepare the way for others. Emily Dunning, who lived at the turn of the century, was a pioneer. This is her story." We meet Dunning (June Allyson) as an adolescent helping her pregnant mother move into a new house. When her mother collapses, Dunning searches for a doctor and is referred by a druggist to a Dr. Yeomans, whose office is empty. She knocks on the inner door and mistakes Dr. Yeomans (Mildred Dunnock) for a receptionist. All of this is meant to signal the low status of woman doctors. On arriving at the house, Yeoman's credentials are challenged by the moving men who wonder aloud if she is "a real doctor." After reviving Emily's mother, Yeomans slaps Dunning out of her fright and into assisting with the delivery.

Years later, during a physical exam, Emily tells Yeomans that she wants to be just like her and is entering a premedical program at Cornell University. Yeomans attempts to discourage her, "I'm not sure I would be a doctor if I had to start all over again. You go through college, through medical school. The others become interns. You don't. You don't get that training because city hospitals won't take a woman intern. To the medical profession and the public, you're nothing but a glorified midwife. You're privileged to write M.D. after your name." Dunning interrupts and says, "Look what you've done." Yeomans responds, "Yes, I set up a practice here. I ran into bigotry and prejudice. You forget the first time you came into this office. You almost ran when you saw me. You were no exception. See these books. I wrote four of them. Doctors consult them. Professors teach from them. I'm an authority. I'm also a woman. Emily, medicine is a man's world!" Emily replies, "Dr. Yeomans, I don't believe it's a man's world and I don't think you do either." Yeomans laughs and says she'll help her get into Cornell and "if they don't take you, I'll burn the place down."

At Cornell, Dunning overcomes the hazing to graduate second in her class. Her classmate and sweetheart Ben Barringer (Arthur Kennedy), who is off to Harvard Medical School, proposes to her. She asks, "You don't think a woman should be a doctor?" He answers, "No, I don't. You can't break down barriers." She refuses him and is accepted, according to the movie, at "Cornell University City of New York College of Medicine." Actually, despite her record at Cornell, Dunning had access to only two women's medical schools apart from a homeopathic college. So she entered the Medical College of the New York Infirmary for Women and Children, which had been founded by "Elizabeth and Emily Blackwell and that extraordinary group of pioneer medical women which included Mary Putnam Jacobi."[7] When Cornell University opened its medical school at the end of her sophomore year, Emily Blackwell and the Board of the New York Infirmary elected to close the school, but they kept the infirmary open to provide care for women and opportunity for postgraduate training. Dunning then transferred to Cornell.

This medical school period of the movie has two interesting sequences. The first involves Emily's detecting Yeomans's mitral stenosis and the second, the recitation of the beginning of the Hippocratic oath at graduation. Despite scoring at the top of the list of internship candidates, Emily is turned down at every New York municipal hospital. Doctor Seth Pawling (Gary Merrill), the director at Gouverneur Hospital tells her, "For three thousand years, as far as medicine is concerned, women have been restricted to midwifery. Did you ever stop to think 'why?'" Dunning answers, "Fear of competition?" Pawling responds, "Sheer biology. Special considerations that have to be allowed for. Medicine is a profession that's based on science. Women have a tendency to confuse emotions with fact. Our hospital happens to be dependent on public funds and the patients aren't likely to be pioneering or progressive. They just want to get well." He adds, "I know it's considered unethical for doctors to indulge in personalities, but you're far too attractive to follow a profession." Dunning cuts him off and says, "And I think you're far too intolerant and bigoted to be a judge of that."

Yeomans visits the city health commissioner who tells her that he is concerned that Dunning "would be working with men at all hours of the night." But, he relents when Yeomans suggests that she will leak to the press that Dunning scored third out of 286 in the qualifying test. As Dunning enters Gouverneur Hospital, "dedicated to the service of the poor," newsboys shout out the headline, "Skirt to ride ambulance." There, she is accommodated in sleeping quarters among the men and joins them for "dinner at five" (fig. 6). A petition signed by her fellow house staff to have her ousted is quashed by the director because of the potential bad publicity.

It turns out that Dunning's former classmate Barringer is also interning at the hospital (he signed the blackball petition). He is also doing research to see if radium can cure cancer in rats. Showing Dunning how radium fluoresces glass, he tells her, "I know what kind of a doctor I want to be—not a general practitioner. I want to do research. The possibilities are so tremendous if we can only control radium's energy to destroy disease tissue like cancer." He later sustains a radium burn, which he discounts (just as Marie Curie does—see chapter 4). Not surprisingly, he obtains a fellowship to study at the University of Paris with Madame Curie.

Dunning is hazed and given extra ambulance duty by the supervising physician Dr. Graham (Gar Moore). She successfully reduces a dislocated shoulder on a towering longshoreman played by a young James Arness (complete with a tall ship tattoo on his chest) (fig. 7). She then resuscitates a victim of chloral hydrate intoxication (who was "slipped a

FIGURE 6. *The Girl in White.* Emily Dunning (June Allyson), the first woman intern in a New York City municipal hospital, upsets fellow house staff when joining their regular 5 PM dinner.

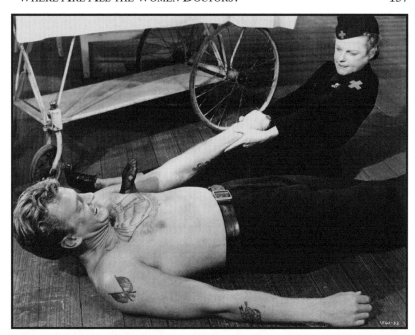

FIGURE 7. *The Girl in White.* Dr. Dunning (June Allyson) surprises and disappoints her male colleagues by single-handedly repairing a shoulder dislocation in a muscular longshoreman (James Arness).

mickey"), after the patient is given up for dead by Graham. The press gets wind of the feat and as her picture is being snapped Pawling arrives and asks for an explanation. Dunning tells him, "I'm sick and tired of being constantly called on the carpet and treated like a child in kindergarten. Do you think I like doing triple duty for men who would give their right arms to get me out of here? Do you think it's pleasant to be yelled at every time I act on my own initiative? I'm fed up with the whole thing, especially you with your delusions of grandeur." She's on the verge of quitting, when Barringer dissuades her. He tells her that he's ashamed of having been in on the conspiracy and that she should challenge them. Called to Pawling's office, she learns that a nurse had called the press because of the great work Dunning's doing despite the unfair treatment. Pawling congratulates her on having saved a life and then takes Graham "to the woodshed." Later Pawling will tell her, "You have one quality most doctors would give their right arm for. It has nothing to do with the study of medicine. You can't acquire it. You make people feel good."

This very medical film (the advisor was Harold O. Cooperman, M.D.) ends with a typhoid epidemic that forces the hospital to convert its recreation area into a ward and to recruit more doctors, one of whom is Yeomans. After Pawling meets her, he says, "I read her books. I never knew she was a woman." Yeomans joins Dunning in her quarters and says, "I always imagined what it was like to be assigned to a hospital. I expect it's more comfortable in Sing Sing; but I rather like it." When Dunning tells her that Barringer has proposed again, she says, "A wise old doctor once told me if you run into a problem and don't know what to do, do nothing, just wait. You'll be surprised at how well it works and when the time comes you'll know." But for heaven's sake, if you're sure he's the right man, don't let anything stop you. Don't wait and turn into a spinster like me, Dr. Emily Dunning." Later, Yeomans's overwork triggers a fatal arrhythmia. Dunning tells Pawling, "All that skill and knowledge that was wasted." Pawling tells her that Yeomans's skill lives on in her and that "it showed me how stupid I've been about women being doctors." Reflecting on his commitment to work that led to divorce and loneliness, he tells her, "Without an awareness of people, the work is nothing." She answers, "Being a doctor is the most important thing in my life, but it isn't the only thing." This is a cue for her to tell Barringer she'll be waiting when he returns from Paris.

The Girl in White is probably the most sympathetic portrayal of women physicians and what doctors do. It is fairly true to the book, which is a good read, but events and names have been altered. For example, Dr. Yeomans is very loosely based on one of Dunning's mentors, Dr. Mary Putnam Jacobi, who, far from discouraging her from pursuing a career in medicine, helped her map it out.[10] Also, the introduction of Marie Curie, radium, and graduate study in Paris all connect back with Metro-Goldwyn-Mayer's successful film, *Madame Curie*.

In 1960s films, women doctors are largely relegated to secondary roles. For example, in *The Young Doctors*, there's a woman orthopedist who does a biopsy and an amputation on a student nurse. There's a much more significant series of scenes, however, in *The Interns* (see chapter 3) involving the chief surgeon Dr. Riccio, played by Telly Savalas and a female intern, Dr. Mado Bruckner (Haya Harareet), who disagrees with him on rounds. To one of his questions, she begins her answer, "In my judgment…." Riccio interrupts her and says, "It will be a long time before you're entitled to so weighty a thing as a judgment. Your errors are due to intuition: excusable in a woman but not in a doctor." Undaunted, she goes on to bolster her position by quoting the literature, which he dismisses as "theory."

Later, Bruckner asks Riccio, "Why do you hate women so much?" He answers, "I like them as wives, nurses, and patients. I just don't like them as doctors. It's not a prejudice, but a studied conclusion. You take up space in medical school, drain us of our energy, and then prefer a hot stove, wet diapers, and to retire into marriage." When they next meet, she is with her three-year-old daughter. He says, "I didn't know you were married." Bruckner says, "I was, but I didn't see myself as the elected champion of women." She had left practice because she wanted to become a surgeon and thought that training under him would bring out the best in her. She tells him that she would have stuck with it if he had given her only one word of encouragement, but now she has decided to go back into "general practice in Vienna." In one of the closing scenes, she runs to thank him for selecting her as a resident on his service. He gives her the chart of "an abdomen" and tells the nurse to refer all questions to his colleague. The flustered nurse says that he's never had a woman surgeon on his service before; he replies, "Don't be so prejudiced against your own sex. They'll be damn good surgeons." So much for Hollywood's two-hour problem solving.

Probably the meatiest and hardest-edge portrayal of women physicians in film was sketched by ophthalmologist, Robin Cook, in his screenplay for *Coma*. After repeated rejections of his novels, the film's success allowed him to turn the screenplay into a best-selling book.[12]

Coma (1978)

Directed by Harvard Medical School graduate, Michael Crichton, this farfetched but entertaining thriller makes up technologically for what it lacks in humanity and passion. Genevieve Bujold plays Dr. Susan Wheeler, a surgical resident intent on uncovering the reason for the high rate of unexplained post-operative coma in relatively healthy young people undergoing elective surgery. Wheeler is nothing like Mary Stevens, M.D., as she parks her red convertible in front of Boston Memorial Hospital and runs to rounds. She has a mind of her own and is making it in a man's specialty on the basis of talent, hard work, and guts.

The men don't seem to have changed, though. Even her surgical resident boy friend, Dr. Mark Bellows (Michael Douglas), patronizes her. Bellows, who is angling for the chief residency in surgery, is caught up in hospital politics. When they return to their apartment, she refuses to get him a beer and to make his dinner. "Get your own beer," she says, as she proceeds to take the first shower. Bellows mutters, "That's what I get for becoming involved with a Goddamned doctor. I should have fallen in love with a nurse. Dorothy on the 8th floor liked me." When he starts whining about not getting respect, Wheeler tells him, "You don't want a lover. You want a Goddamned wife," and walks out of the apartment. The next day at aerobic dancing, she trades confidences with her best friend, pregnant from an extramarital affair and scheduled for a first trimester "therapeutic abortion" listed as a routine dilatation and curettage (D&C).

As they prepare for the operation, the doctors talk about journal articles and the stock market; the nurses discuss their plans for the weekend and other personal matters. There is an excellent sequence involving a Dr. George (Rip Torn) instructing medical students as well as the audience on routine general anesthesia (assuming any procedure is routine). As he says, "Anesthesia is the easiest thing in the world until something goes wrong. It's 99 percent boredom and 1 percent scared-shitless panic." His worst fears are realized when the patient's heart rhythm becomes irregular; despite Wheeler's friend appearing pink and well-oxygenated, her blood pressure falls. She seems to come around, but never wakes up; her pupils are fixed and dilated. As one doctor sensitively describes her to Wheeler, "She's got complete squash rot—a total gomer. She's brain dead. EEG completely flat." Still, George cheerily says that "we can maintain her vital signs for one, two, or three years."

Wheeler is crushed and tries to find an answer. She learns that a preoperative specimen had been sent for tissue typing (usually done only for transplant donors or recipients), but there is no doctor's name on the requisition. On gaining unauthorized access to the hospital information system, she learns that there have been 240 postoperative comas that year, 10 in healthy adults. Bellows explains it away by citing the law of averages in a hospital that does thirty thousand operations a year (more than at Johns Hopkins Hospital). Wheeler attempts to gain access to the charts of the young victims to see if there is a common thread, but is denied.

Unlike most of the coma victims, her friend dies, and during the autopsy, Wheeler learns that if carbon monoxide is delivered for a few minutes rather than oxygen, the brain suffers, but the tissue remains nice and cherry pink. Her snooping reveals that only one operating room has been involved in all the unexpected comas, a fact which strangely no one else has discovered. She is treated by everyone as a hysterical woman, earning her two visits to the office of Dr. Harris, the hospital director and chief of surgery, played with just the right mix of paternalism and menace by Richard Widmark. He spends a lot of time talking to the Governor, a United States senator, the president, and the secretary of the Department of Health, Education, and Welfare (now Health and Human Services). Harris tells Wheeler to cool it, saying, "I can protect you because you're good and, frankly, because you're a woman." After she leaves, he says, "Women! Christ!"

Bellows is instructed to take her away for a weekend on Cape Cod to get her under control. After the requisite lovemaking, they head back to Boston, but she can't resist visiting the Jefferson Institute where the coma patients are sent after discharge from the acute hospital. Bellows inexplicably stays in the car as she enters this forbidding place. Of course if he had gone in, the movie would have been a lot shorter. There, Wheeler learns that the bodies are in suspended animation, monitored by a computer attached to various lines. Adjustments in vital signs, feeding, and handling of excretion are done automatically; so the staff is lean (one nurse, one doctor on call, two computer technicians, and a lot of security). The staffing is an administrator's dream. The plan is to house one thousand patients a day, achieving economies of scale that permit charging sixty dollars a day. Visitors are only permitted on Tuesday when physicians are able to tour the facility (fig. 8). Wheeler overhears a doctor's name and some auction bidding. A heart is going to San Francisco for seventy-five thousand dollars. Bidding starts at forty-five thousand dollars for a two-hour-old kidney that can be delivered to Zurich with a twenty-three-hour elapsed time (fig. 9).

Figure 8. *Coma.* Doctors tour the experimental institute where comatose patients are kept in suspended animation until their organs are ready for harvesting.

On her return to Boston Memorial, the maintenance man tells her to meet him in the basement that evening because he knows how the comas are being induced. Any moviegoer worth her salt will know that this is the "kiss of death" for the poor guy. Sure enough, he is electrocuted in a simulated accident by a hitman who has also been stalking Wheeler. Through some pretty energetic detective work, she follows the line from a carbon monoxide tank in the basement to the operating room. The most exciting part of the picture involves her being pursued by the hitman through the hospital amphitheater, the pathology lab, the autopsy suite, and finally into the refrigerator where the dead bodies are stored. Hanging herself with the others, she manages to bury the blackguard under a ton of corpses. OK, you say, all she has to do is bring her boy friend up to see the buried hitman, but no, she goes out to the Jefferson Institute for the tour and gets into "another fine mess." Still, James Bond has nothing on her, and she doesn't need violence or high-tech gimmicks to outsmart her myriad of pursuers.

Just when you think she is the smartest person alive, she goes unescorted to the hospital director's office. There we see his Alpha Omega Alpha honor medical society certificate and she makes the

FIGURE 9. *Coma.* Dr. Susan Wheeler (Genevieve Bujold) discovers shipments of human organs and solves the mystery of a rash of comas in patients undergoing elective surgery.

connection with the name she overheard. Oh! Oh! And she took that drink he offered! Turns out it was laced with a drug that simulates peritonitis. Before he has her wheeled to OR 8, he gives an impassioned speech: "When you're older, you'll learn that everything is complicated. There is no black and white—only gray. Our society faces monumental decisions about the right to die, abortion, terminal illness, prolonged coma, transplantation decisions. Society isn't deciding. Congress isn't deciding. The courts aren't deciding. Religion isn't deciding. They're leaving it up to us, the experts, the doctors. America spends 175 billion dollars on medical care. These great hospital complexes are the cathedrals of our age. Billions of dollars; thousands of beds; a whole nation of sick people turning to us. They're children. They trust us. We can't tell them everything. Our job is to make things easier for them, because medicine is now a great social force. The individual is too small." Mercifully, Wheeler passes out, ending this megalomaniacal diatribe.

Everyone, even Bellows, is impressed that the chief himself is going to perform the appendectomy. He says, "House staff deserve the very best care in their own hospital." Finally, when Harris insists on using OR 8, Bellows becomes a believer. Still, he insists on tracking the carbon monoxide line himself. In real life, Wheeler would have been a goner, since she develops an irregular heartbeat and should go the way of her friend. In the end, though, she wakes up and Harris is carted off to the hoosegow. Don't ask how one man could orchestrate this whole enterprise. Just suspend disbelief and make sure you don't decide to watch this film before elective surgery, or any other surgery for that matter.

The remaining films, *The Prince of Tides* and *Beyond Rangoon*, feature relatively weak characterizations of two women physicians each. The former, which should have been titled *The Princess of Analysis*, is based on Pat Conroy's partly autobiographical novel.[13]

The Prince of Tides (1991)

The Prince of Tides is narrated by Tom Wingo (Nick Nolte), who sets the stage for this saga of a dysfunctional family by saying, "I don't know when the war between my parents began, but all I know is the only prisoners they took were the children." Tom, in the midst of a three-year-long mid-life crisis, has quit his job as a high school coach to keep house for his physician wife Sallie (Blythe Danner) and three children. He distances his apparently loving wife as well as his overbearing mother Lila (Kate Nelligan) with wisecracks. The action begins when he leaves the Tidewater for New York City to serve as the memory for his uncommunicative sister, Savannah, who has attempted suicide for the third time. Dr. Susan Lowenstein (Barbra Streisand) greets him at her posh office (sans receptionist) by offering to rustle him up some coffee. She convinces him to begin a series of analytic sessions in which her behavior ranges from snappy one-liners to familiarity bordering on seductiveness to angry shouting matches to "pop psychology."

Women psychiatrists have raised questions about her wardrobe, which consists mainly of short skirts, high heels, and long artificial nails.[14] In one scene, Tom lies on the couch with his eyes focused on her hemline or something a little higher up. The frequent sessions with Tom are supposed to be helping the unseen Savannah. Instead, Tom helps Dr. Lowenstein cope with her messy personal life. She is separated from an arrogant musician and has a rude, bratty son, played by Jason Gould, Streisand's son by former husband, Elliott Gould. Tom's physician wife is also a confused nebbish. We never get a clear idea of what kind of a doctor she is. In one hard-to-believe scene, Tom appears to be looking forward to going home for a short stay, but she rejects him over the telephone. Instead, she blathers incoherently about having an affair with a cardiac surgeon. When Tom asks if she loves this Dr. Levy, she says, "I'm not sure; I might be doing this just to hurt you. I can't think of anything else." The viewer can only pity her poor patients and the children.

Meanwhile, Dr. Lowenstein's professional behavior is deteriorating rapidly. During one of the sessions, Tom breaks down and, naturally, she takes him into her arms (fig. 10). She confesses that she is neurotic and needs a lot of reassurance as she takes him into her bed, her meadow, her chair, etc. This raises the issue of sex with patients,[15] which reputable physicians schooled in the Hippocratic oath believe to be a major ethical breach. In one study, up to ten percent of male psychotherapists admitted to sex with patients, three times higher than woman therapists.[15] The rate may not be much lower for other specialties.[16] Those few who believe it to be ethical to have consensual sex with patients would be quick to point out that Lowenstein's therapy seems to save Tom. Strangely, though, once healed, Tom turns his back on his lover/therapist and returns to his wife and to teaching school. Her parting words are, "One of the things I love about you is you're the kind of guy who goes back to his family." As the movie ends, we see him driving alone somewhere in Carolina calling out "Lowenstein, Lowenstein." Rather than try to understand this, you might just want to reach for a Lowenbrau instead and turn to a more substantive film.

FIGURE 10. *Prince of Tides.* Psychiatrist Dr. Susan Lowenstein (Barbra Streisand) takes her patient's brother (Nick Nolte) into her arms.

Beyond Rangoon (1996)

Beyond Rangoon opens with flashbacks to a scene where the central character, Doctor Laura Bowman (Patricia Arquette), remembers returning home to find her husband and son murdered in their apartment. Bowman has been convinced by her sister Andy (Frances McDormand), also a physician, to embark on a trip to Asia to try to forget the tragedy (fig. 11). However, on arriving in Burma, now Myanmar, she concludes that this "touch of the exotic East" reminds her of "the moment when my life ended." She no longer can stand the sight of blood and retreats when a young tourist falls from a boulder, letting her sister take care of him. The tour guide, played by Spalding Gray, points to a group of meditating Buddhists and explains that the "attainment of perfect detachment is the highest human condition." However, Bowman cannot detach herself from her past and keeps thinking that she "shouldn't have worked" as a physician. "I could have spent more time with Nick and our boy," she guiltily reflects, even to the point of thinking that the massacre would have never happened if she had

FIGURE 11. *Beyond Rangoon.* Dr. Louise Bowman (Patricia Arquette), trying to escape the memory of the death of her husband and child, asks Burmese guide Aung Ko to take her beyond Rangoon into the country's forbidden interior.

done so. Her sister reminds her, "They were so proud of you, especially Nick. They wanted so much for you to be a doctor."

The film has little medical content, indeed, we never find out what kind of a doctor Bowman is. Bowman merely serves as a device to tell Westerners the little-known story of Aung San Suu Kyi, winner of the 1991 Nobel Peace Prize for her resistance to the repressive military regime that has ruled Burma since 1962. We have to accept that Bowman, an unaccompanied American woman, breaks curfew (not trivial in such countries), wades through crowds of Burmese people and armed soldiers, loses her passport in the process, and watches close-up as Kyi makes an impassioned plea for democracy. While waiting for another passport, Bowman meets Aung Ko, a wise old revolutionary, and convinces him to take her beyond Rangoon, where only official tour guides can go. Even they are forbidden to do so during this period of martial law. Woven through the film is the thread of a healing philosophy. Bowman tells Ko, "I was brought up to believe that if I was good and if I worked hard, everything would turn out all right." He responds, "We (Burmese) are taught that suffering is the only promise that life keeps, and that if we have happiness we must treasure it because it is ours for only a brief time."

The majority of the film involves their flight through the Burmese countryside from a rather ruthless bunch of soldiers. The only real comic relief occurs early in their flight when Bowman reacts with surprise at Ko's statement that "men and women are completely equal in Burma." He responds, "Oh, yes, a woman can even become a Buddha," and then he pauses, smiles, and adds, "But for that she must first come back as man." Bowman answers, "Ah, there's always a catch." The ending is strong. As they flee to Thailand, Bowman, referring to her husband and children, says, "All I wanted to do was die to be with them and here I am fighting to live." Ko replies: "Life is too strong; it has a purpose for you. You are a healer." As she reaches the makeshift hospital in the refugee camp, a doctor asks, "Who the hell are you?" Bowman, who has resumed the practice of medicine by ministering to the injured Ko, says, "I am a doctor...do you need any help?" The doctor responds, "Are you kidding? How long can you stay?" "As long as it takes," Bowman answers.

As we have seen, the number of women doctors in films has been even less than their representation in medical school. Even those who have been portrayed have been, for the most part, generally weak or inordinately submissive. The good news for budding filmmakers is that the great American woman doctor film has yet to be made.

NOTES

1. Walsh MR. "Doctors Wanted: No Women Need Apply": Sexual Barriers in the Medical Profession, 1835-1975. New Haven: Yale University Press, 1977.
2. Ludmerer KM. Time to Heal: American Medical Education from the Turn of the Century to the Era of Managed Care. New York: Oxford University Press, 1999.
3. Lowenstein LM. Who wants lady interns? N Engl J Med 1971; 284: 735.
4. Chaff SL, Haimbach R, Fenichel C, Woodside NB. Women in Medicine: A Bibliography of the Literature on Women Physicians. Metuchen NJ: Scarecrow Press, 1977, p. 449. This is an excellent annotated bibliographic source for writings on Dr. Sabin and other women physicians cited as well as the general subject.
5. Bickel J, Croft K, Johnson D, Marshall R. Women in U.S. Academic Medicine Statistics 1998. Washington, D.C.: Association of American Medical Colleges, 1998.
6. Kirchstein RL. Women physicians—good news and bad news. N Engl J Med 1996; 334: 982–983.
7. Garza H. Women in Medicine. New York: Franklin Watts, 1994.
8. Schneider I. Images of the mind: Psychiatry in the commercial film. Am J Psychiatry 1977; 134: 613–620.
9. Gartell N, Herman J, Olarte S, et al. Psychiatrist–patient sexual contact: Results of a national survey. I: Prevalence. Am J Psychiatry 1986; 143: 1126–1131.
10. Barringer ED. Bowery to Bellevue: The Story of New York's First Woman Ambulance Surgeon. New York: W.W. Norton & Co, 1950.
11. Maltin L. Review in Cinemania 96. Microsoft CD-ROM, 1995.
12. Cook R. Coma. New York: Penguin Books, 1977.
13. Conroy P. The Prince of Tides. Boston: Houghton Mifflin, 1986.
14. McDonagh M. Psychiatrists analyze Dr. Lowenstein. New York Times, January 19, 1992, Section 2, p. 24.

15. Gabbard GO, ed. Sexual Exploitation in Professional Relationships. Washington, D.C.: American Psychiatric Press, 1989.
16. Kardener SH, Fuller M, Mensh IN. A survey of physicians' attitudes and practices regarding erotic and nonerotic contact with patients. Am J Psychiatry 1973; 130: 1077–1081.

Other first-hand accounts by women physicians include:
Morantz RM, Pomerlau CS, Fenichel CH, eds. In Her Own Words. Westport, Conn.: Greenwood Press, 1982.
Wear D, ed. Women in Medical Education: An Anthology of Experience. Albany: State University of New York Press, 1996.
Conley FK. Walking Out on the Boys. New York: Farrar, Straus & Giroux, 1998.

6

Blacks, the Invisible Doctors

That Blacks have been virtually invisible as physicians in the movies is not surprising given the racial discrimination in almost every sector of American society until the mid-1960s. Educational barriers, low societal expectations, and an entrenched segregation led to separate, but unequal medical training and care systems.[1-8] Black (or "colored") hospitals, like Catholic, Jewish, and women's hospitals, were set up not only to care for their constituent groups, but also to provide opportunities for postgraduate training.[6-10] The National Medical Association developed in parallel to the American Medical Association and its component state and county medical associations because the latter barred entry to Blacks.[11]

While a number of ex-slaves, most prominently Onesimus, Cesar, and James Derham, practiced the healing arts in early America, James McCune Smith is the first Black American credited with earning a medical degree after training in Scotland.[5, 12] In 1847, David Jones Peck became the first Black to graduate from a recognized United States medical school (Rush Medical College in Chicago) after completing two eight-week sessions.[13] Martin Robinson Delaney, a cupper and leecher, enrolled at Harvard Medical School in 1850, but was dismissed after one term by a vote of his classmates.[13] Delaney, Daniel Laing, and Isaac Snowden, who were to leave for Liberia after completing their medical studies, were accused by the same students who blackballed Harriot Hunt of being "socially repulsive" and detrimental to the value of their diploma.[14] Rebecca Lee was the first Black woman graduate in the United States (from New England Female Medical College in 1864).[14, 15] The two schools predominantly responsible for educating Black doctors until the late 1960s, Howard University and Meharry College (originally part of Central Tennessee State College) opened in 1868 and 1876, respectively.

By 1900, there were 160 medical colleges, 7 of them predominantly Black. After the medical school reforms, only 70 medical schools remained, including Howard and Meharry.[4] The few other medical schools that admitted Blacks did so with rigid quotas. From 1920 to 1964, 2 to 3 percent of students were Black.[4] In the 1940s, only ten to twenty Blacks graduated each year from schools other than Howard and Meharry and twenty-six of seventy-eight medical schools (all in southern and border states) were closed to Blacks. The differential in gender and race barriers is neatly shown by the University of Pennsylvania's graduating its first Black man in 1882, its first White woman in 1918, and its first Black woman in 1964.[16]

To illustrate the difficulty Black women had, Margaret Morgan (Lawrence), in the 1930s, was refused admission to Cornell Medical College because she was told "twenty-five years ago there was a Negro admitted...and it didn't work out....He got tuberculosis."[17] Columbia University's College of Physicians and Surgeons admitted her, after she agreed in her interview that she would ask for another patient if a White patient were to turn her away. She was denied an internship at Babies' Hospital because no Black could stay in the nurses' residence where women interns were housed.[17] After training in pediatrics at Harlem Hospital, she became the first Black trainee at Columbia's Psychoanalytic Institute.

As Dr. Morgan's experience shows, she had two strikes against her,[15] because internships and residencies were scarce for Blacks generally, let alone for Black women.[7, 8, 14] Bellevue Hospital took its first Black intern in 1918. Cleveland Municipal Hospital did the same in 1931. Black nursing students and interns were housed in separate accommodations and the races did not socialize. Johns Hopkins, which admitted two Black students in 1963, didn't take its first Black house officer until 1970.

Until well into the 1940s, segregation in many of the nation's theaters led to the production of "Negro films," many of which are lost, making it difficult to reconstruct their history.[18, 19] Still, there is little evidence that doctors were any more in evidence in Black productions than they were in mainstream Hollywood films. *Racket Doctor*, a film in the gangster-doctor genre,[19] was the only so-called "race film" with a medical twist whose existence I could verify, but it was unavailable for viewing. The remainder of this chapter will focus on the few Hollywood films that portrayed Black physicians as well as the messages they conveyed.

Probably one of the most praiseworthy Black movie doctors is also one of the easiest to miss. In the classic 1931 film *Arrowsmith* (see chapter 4), Martin Arrowsmith's request to do a controlled experiment of his plague vaccine is rebuffed by the White colonial doctors in the West Indies. Afterwards, a Black doctor approaches the dejected Arrowsmith and says, "I'm Doctor Marchand from Howard University. May I offer you an alternative? It will be a privilege to assist you, and if you succeed, it will be a privilege for my people to have served the world." Arrowsmith calls Marchand, "My savior! And a man after my own heart." Marchand takes him to the "worst infected place in the colonies" and tells him that "their voodoo is just about as effective as anything we have been able to do." Marchand assists Arrowsmith and later contracts plague himself.

This series of scenes is noteworthy for many different reasons. First, it harks back to *The Story of Louis Pasteur* and *Dr. Ehrlich's Magic Bullet* (see chapter 4) in teaching the audience about the scientific method and the need for controlled experiments even in humans. Second, it resonates with today's arguments about the unfairness of testing AIDS therapies in a third-world setting, where therapies used in the developed countries are not generally available. In this case, *Arrowsmith* is on safer ground in that plague was epidemic in the West Indies, but no longer in the United States, so there wasn't any disparity in how the disease was being treated in the two locales. More important, no known therapy, incomplete or not, was available. Third, it allows the screenwriters to add a note about how Blacks can "serve the world" in a mainstream film aimed predominantly at a White audience. Finally, it identifies the White hero as a brother to the Black doctor, who becomes a hero in his own right by dying to help mankind. Unfortunately, Clarence Brooks's appearance in *Arrowsmith*, which amounted to little more than a cameo role, did not help further his career.[20]

The first important film about a Black in medicine, is 1949's *Lost Boundaries*, based on *The Document of a New Hampshire Family* by William White, described in the movie credits as "a drama of real life from *Reader's Digest*." The film tells the story of Doctor Scott Carter, a light-skinned Negro who "passed for White." Donald Bogle, in his book, *Toms, Coons, Mulattoes, Mammies, and Bucks,*[21] acknowledges the film's critical acclaim, even in the South, except for Atlanta where it was banned. However, he criticizes the film, as do others,[22, 23] because Mel Ferrer, a White actor, was cast as Carter, just as he criticizes another 1949 film *Pinky* starring Jeanne Crain as a woman passing for White.

He also would have preferred that the films focus on the discrimination towards the vast majority of Blacks, or Negroes (in the parlance of the day). Still, it is one of the few pictures to expose the institutionalized racism that prevailed in American medicine and in hospitals for much of this century.

Lost Boundaries (1949)

Lost Boundaries opens in 1922 at Chase Medical School "just outside of Chicago" on graduation day. An honorary degree is being conferred on Charles Frederick Howard, a respected Black physician from Boston. The student body is a mixture of Blacks, Whites, and Asian-Americans. Scott Carter (Mel Ferrer) is about to graduate and three hours later he will marry Marcia Mitchell (Beatrice Pearson). Marcia's father refuses to attend the ceremony because he won't admit to being Negro. At the reception, Dr. Carter learns that Dr. Howard has secured him an internship at Garrison Memorial, a Negro hospital in Georgia. His best man, Dr. Jesse Pridham (Rai Saunders), has not received an internship offer. He says, "You know how few Negro hospitals there are, and the White hospitals...." He is interrupted, "But with your record." "That's not what keeps me out of the White hospitals. But I'm not worried. Until something comes along, there's always George Pullman." Dr. Howard promises to take him off Mr. Pullman's hands shortly.

Meanwhile, Carter is ecstatic; he tells Marcia that he has, in Doctor Howard's words, the two best things a good doctor should have, a fine medical education and a good wife. Unfortunately, his happiness is short-lived. When he arrives to start his internship, he is told the position is filled, ironically because he looks too White. The internship director, Dr. Cashman (Maurice Ellis) tells him, "You shouldn't have any trouble getting into a Northern hospital." Marcia suggests they go to Boston to stay with her family. He jokes that there are five railroad stations in Boston. "It's a good place for a Red Cap and if a passenger faints, my medical education will be invaluable."

He and his wife send out numerous letters and answer ads in the *Journal of the American Medical Association* for internships at various hospitals. All respond that they have no openings for Negro doctors. At dinner, Mr. Mitchell (Wendell Holmes) says that "Marcia has never been identified as colored. There's no need for you to be either. Being turned down by that colored hospital was the best thing that could have happened to you." Carter tells him that Marcia and he are going to live as Negroes and that they have been invited to Dr. Howard's house. Mitchell answers by recounting how he came from poverty in the South and adding, "Now I have a White man's job. We live in a White neighbor-hood. Our friends are White. We don't know any Negroes. My own sister hasn't set foot in this house. Are you going to risk all that by being seen with Negroes?" They go anyway and there is a long discussion about whether he should pass for White. Someone says, "There's an old saying in the South, 'If you're White, you're all right; If you're Brown, you can hang around; if you're Black, stand back.'"

Carter continues his quest for a position as a Negro doctor while working as a shoemaker. He finally gets an internship offer through a White classmate at Portsmouth Hospital. With a baby on the way, he decides "to be White for one year of my life." He is sent out as an intern on a call to Maine's "Isle of Shoals" and has to perform an emergency operation for a penetrating and bleeding duodenal ulcer on the island's only doctor. The grateful doctor suggests that Carter take over the prac-tice of his father, Dr. Burkitt, in Keenham, New Hampshire. When Carter says he can't because he's a Negro, he is told that, "If you looked col-ored, I never would have made you the offer." Carter agrees to think about it. Meanwhile, Marcia's father tells them not to have their baby at Boston Lying-In Hospital, because the baby may appear Negro and their cover will be blown. Scott and Marcia insist on doing so anyway, and it turns out that their son, named Howard after his mentor, as well as their next child can also pass for White. After the birth of his son, Carter decides to take the offer and becomes a highly respected citizen in Keenham, slowly earning the admiration once accorded to Dr. Burkitt for his excellent medical care and community service. This includes sav-ing someone who falls through the ice (reminiscent of a scene in *It's a Wonderful Life*), and also joining his wife and neighbors in fighting a forest fire.

Carter is also practicing one day a week in Boston as a Negro doc-tor in the Charles Howard Clinic that he helped found with his old classmate, Jesse Pridham. Its motto is, "Clinic for the treatment and care of all races and creeds." Eighteen years pass and in 1942 his wife is made head of the local Red Cross chapter. When a nurse drops a bottle of blood taken from a Negro rather than mix it with others, it angers Carter who says some soldier will die because of this (see later discus-sion of Dr. Charles Drew). Carter's son, Howard (Richard Hylton), a student at the University of New Hampshire and a budding songwriter, calls to get permission to bring a classmate home. His sister Shelley (Susan Douglas) is at first excited, but on learning he's a Negro, Arthur Cooper (William Greaves), she says, "With all the boys at college, my brother has to bring home a 'coon.'" This precipitates an angry outburst from her father. Howard and his father talk about joining the Navy. Cooper says he's trying out for the Air Force where the opportunity may be greater, because, "If you're colored, the Navy makes you a steward's mate." He also comments on how at ease he is in their home, in that he is treated normally rather than exaggeratedly as he usually is by Whites.

The doctor's patriotism turns out to be his undoing when Navy Intelligence learns that he was a member of a Negro fraternity at Chase Medical School. Investigators visit him the night before he is to leave for duty and strip him of his commission. Dressed in his brand new uniform, he decides to go along with the town's going-away party, where he is told that, "Remember, we're only loaning you to our country; when your service is over, we want you back with us." Afterwards, the revelation that they are Negroes leaves the children dazed, confused, and angry at their father for not telling them (fig. 1). Howard runs away to Lenox Avenue and 135th Street to find out what it means to be a Negro and gets involved in a melodrama that is the only weak part of the film. Its only bright side is the appearance of Canada Lee as a Harlem police

FIGURE 1. *Lost Boundaries*. Dr. Scott Carter (Mel Ferrer) and his wife Marcia (Beatrice Pearson) break the news to their son Howard (Richard Hylton) that they are "Negroes."

lieutenant. Shelley becomes estranged from her White friends and the town turns against the doctor who is discharged from the Navy "for physical reasons."

Carter leaves for Boston where he lives and works at the clinic. Ultimately, the Episcopal rector rallies the town behind him and he is welcomed back to Keenham. The rector notes the announcement that "commissions as officers in the United States Navy will be extended to all qualified citizens regardless of race or color." Again, Bogle censured the film for not hammering at the hypocrisy of the White townspeople who turn on their dedicated doctor.[20] My reaction was that the hypocrisy and unfair rejection by his White neighbors was easily visible to anyone with a modicum of good will, and no righteous anger was necessary to dramatize it or to make others get it.

Those who thought *Lost Boundaries* to be too gentle would be hard put to say the same about *No Way Out*, (not to be confused with the 1989 Kevin Costner spy movie of the same name). Filled with racial slurs, bigotry, hatred and counter-hatred, it not only is a graphic depiction of racism, but Hollywood's most powerful portrayal of a Black doctor. Starring Sidney Poitier in his feature film debut and directed by Joseph Mankiewicz, it remains one of the most daring and important Hollywood movies, despite its flawed medical premise.

No Way Out (1950)

Like many of its hospital-based predecessors, *No Way Out* opens with a harried switchboard operator directing ambulances in a county hospital. When we first meet Dr. Luther Brooks (Sidney Poitier), the first Black intern at County Hospital, he has just taken the state medical board examination and is agonizing about whether he should go into practice or stay on at the hospital. He meets Dr. Wharton (Stephen McNally), the "chief resident" and they discuss the Boards. "The boards can't be too tough—that's what all doctors agree on after they have passed. They want it to be tougher on the next group." Dr. Wharton tells him that he can stay on another year and the happy Brooks proceeds to the prison ward to admit two shooting victims. On the elevator, Lefty (Dotts Johnson), the black elevator operator tells him, "The boys are saying that the test is just for colored doctors" and that "they probably want to make it harder on you." Brooks responds that it is no harder for him than for other doctors.

The film's voltage is about to go sky-high with the entry of Ray Biddle, played by Richard Widmark with the same maniacal viciousness that he brought to *Kiss of Death* in which he shoved an old lady in a wheelchair down a flight of stairs. As Brooks begins to examine him, Ray spits at him and recalls the many times he and his White hooligan friends from the equally impoverished "Beaver Canal, went over to clean up Niggertown." Lefty reminds him, "You're talking to a doctor," prompting Ray to say, "I don't want him; I want a White doctor." The policeman says, "We'll turn the lights out, so you won't know the difference."

The next sequence sets up the dramatic tension that will carry the film, but does so at the expense of medical accuracy. Brooks learns that Johnny and Ray were caught robbing a gas station. When Johnny ran away, he appeared confused, and ran into the gas pump. On observing the young man, he appears to have abnormal breathing and a lack of sensation when a lighted cigarette burns down to his fingertips. Then using an ophthalmoscope, Brooks detects papilledema (swelling of the nerve to the eye), a characteristic finding when the pressure in the brain is increased. That it has nothing to do with the gunshot wounds is only a minor distraction. The main problem is what Brooks does next, that is, prepare to do a spinal tap (fig. 2). This is something we were taught not to do if one suspected increased pressure and a brain tumor, because the brain might herniate causing pressure on the brainstem that could be immediately fatal. Furthermore, he's all by himself and doesn't call for an attending physician back-up, reasoning that this is an emergency. This contention is hard to fathom, given that Johnny only came in because he got shot and must have been walking around like this for a while. Anyway, Brooks goes down the hall to ask the orderly for a procedure set. The orderly says, "I don't recall anyone using that thing before." Brooks does the tap and the boy suddenly dies. Ray screams out, "He took it out on Johnny. He wanted it to be me. I'll get you for that, you Black rat."

Ray's "deaf and dumb" brother, George (Harry Bellaver), visits, and the policeman says, "Get the dummy out." This insensitive line is as important as the depiction of raw racism in exposing the fallacy of another uneducated belief that needed exposure. It turns out that George "can read lips a block away." He has deciphered that Brooks wants an autopsy to prove the man had a brain tumor. Ray taunts Brooks, saying "Beaver Canal is full of Johnny's pals. Wait till they find out how he got killed and by what. I'd sure hate to be living in Niggertown." Ray then tells Brooks that George told him everything and that there won't be an autopsy.

The hospital director, Sam Moreland, M.D. (Stanley Ridges), calls Wharton into his office and tells him of a brief article on the back page

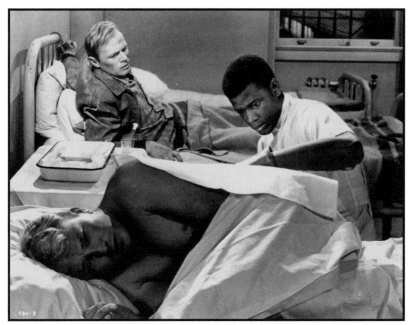

FIGURE 2. *No Way Out.* Dr. Luther Brooks (Sidney Poitier) does a spinal tap on Johnny Biddle (Dick Paxton) while racist brother Ray (Richard Widmark) curses and threatens him.

of the newspaper, saying that "one of the brothers suffering from a superficial wound in his leg, died shortly after admission to the hospital. Cause of death was not revealed." He's scared to death that the press will blow the story up and find out that the doctor was Black. He would rather let it go away and refuses to authorize an autopsy without family permission. "Don't go reading into it that I'm anti-Negro. Why if anything I'm pro-Negro," he says. Wharton replies, "I'm pro good doctor—White, Black, or polka dot." Moreland tells Wharton that getting public funds is not easy. He says that in his present position, M.D. means "something different now—Master of Doubletalk."

Wharton agrees to accompany Brooks to visit Johnny's widow, Edie (Linda Darnell), to request an autopsy. Wharton introduces Brooks as the doctor who "tried to save your husband." She says "You mean Johnny died in a colored hospital?" Wharton replied, "Doctor Brooks is on my staff at County Hospital. He couldn't have had a better doctor." It turns out that Edie hates the Biddle brothers and is divorced from Johnny. She agrees to think about visiting Ray to persuade him to agree to the autopsy.

Brooks returns home where his brother is studying for an exam to be a mailman and his mother and sister are preparing a dinner. They have invited a local physician to dinner to convince Brooks to join him in practice so that they can begin to get some money into the house. When Brooks's wife returns home from her job, he collapses on the bed and tells her that "I'm not sure of myself in so many ways. I need another year with Wharton. Clark and his big, fat practice. I'd never know when I'm a good doctor." As he drifts off to sleep, his wife comforts him saying "You've got a right to be tired. You worked so hard, harder than anybody to get where you are. Shoes you shined; dishes you washed; garbage you dumped; the food you couldn't buy because you needed books. Remember how you studied? How I asked you questions over and over? Questions I couldn't even pronounce. Coffee, coffee and more coffee. Slapping you to keep you awake and when you told me "A" was your passing mark, not for the others, just for you. You got them—all "A's.""

Edie visits Ray to convince him to grant an autopsy, but Ray tells her "You know what they do when they examine a dead body? They cut it open and chop it up into little pieces like wood." He then turns her against Brooks and goads her into helping foment a race riot by saying "That nigger doctor killed Johnny. If you had a kid, would you send him to a nigger doctor? Would you like him putting his dirty black hands on your body?" As she weakens, Rays flashes a malevolent smile and sends her to visit Rocky and his buddies at the pool hall in Beaver Creek where they lay plans to meet at Boot Hill to surprise the Blacks.

When Brooks returns to the hospital, Lefty tells Brooks "There's trouble coming over from Beaver Canal and we're going to be ready for them." Brooks responds, "If you do, you'll be no better than them." Lefty points to the long scar on his face that he got from a broken bottle and says "Isn't that asking a lot of us to be better than them when we get killed proving we're just as good?" Meanwhile at Boot Hill, Rocky and his friends are practicing breaking up bottles, brandishing whips and chains, and shouting out racial epithets. Suddenly, the Blacks descend on Boot Hill in four separate groups and surprise the Whites. When casualties begin to pour into the hospital, Ray smilingly asks "Anything left in Niggertown?" He's told, "It's the other way around. The boogies lowered the boom on Beaver Canal."

As Brooks takes care of the riot victims, a woman says, "Keep your black hands off my 'boy,'" and spits in his face. Brooks takes off his stethoscope and leaves the emergency department. The next day, his wife visits Wharton's house to tell him that Brooks walked the streets all night and when he got home, he said he hated everybody. Wharton responds, "Everybody white." She says, "Yes, even you." Then he became calm and decided to give himself up for the murder of John Biddle. Wharton reasons correctly that this was to force the coroner to do an autopsy. At the end of a suspense-filled afternoon, the coroner announces to Brooks, "You made a good diagnosis. Glioma, large area of hemorrhage." Then turning to Ray, Wharton says, "Your brother died of a brain tumor, just as Dr. Brooks said." Ray snarls, "You guys stick together, Black and White, like some kind of a mob." Wharton answers, "Maybe some future autopsy will show us how you got to be that way."

Ray escapes and in the process aggravates his injured leg. He goes after Edie, ties her up, and forces her to call Brooks to tell him to come to Wharton's deserted house. There he surprises Brooks and taunts him at gunpoint, singing "Little Black Sambo." Just when it looks like Brooks is a goner, Edie, who has escaped and joined them, distracts Ray, and in the ensuing struggle, Brooks is shot in the shoulder and Ray falls backwards, grabbing his leg and crying out in a frightened, pathetic manner, "It's bleeding hard." Edie says "Let him bleed: tear it some more, let him bleed fast." Brooks says, "I can't kill a man just because he hates me. Take your scarf and put it around his thigh. Tie a knot, not too tight." He turns to Ray and says "Don't cry, White boy. You're gonna live." Fade to black.

Of the many remarkable things in this film is the consistent performance of Widmark as a hate-filled racist. The interplay with Poitier is electric and, indeed, Widmark apologized to Poitier for being so bitter and menacing as well as for the racist language he spewed. We also get a feeling of the deprivation in Ray Biddle's background that gives insight into, without in any way excusing, his anger and hatred. This balance between "in your face" dialogue and subtlety is what elevates the film from being merely a soap opera to the level of a classic. Also ringing true are the family scenes that document the sacrifices for Luther Brooks to get where he is, as well as his struggle to overcome racism as he tries to minister to patients. The side commentary involving the supporting cast is also interesting, such as Brooks's brother studying for a difficult postal examination or Ray's impaired brother who is far from "a dummy." There's also an excellent scene where Wharton's Black maid asserts that no one can take away her pride in what she does for a living—an attitude I heard from my immigrant grandmother who also worked as a maid and cleaning woman until her retirement at age sixty-five. Then, there is the smoldering resentment of Black men who, after fighting for their country, weren't being accorded respect. In short, the film provides enough material for a whole course in sociology.

As Cripps and others point out,[21-23] these films were part of an era of Hollywood message films that culminated in the 1967 film *Guess Who's Coming To Dinner*, a film that seems to have emerged from a time capsule. It was an era when the dialogue on race combined controlled confrontation and passive nonviolence with a gentle plea for tolerance and goodwill by numerous religious groups. The first half of the 1960s, with its folk music and clean-cut dress, as exemplified by all the characters in this film, was one of general optimism. In a strange way, even the assassination of John F. Kennedy, which was a great blow to the country, set the scene for a spate of remarkable legislation. This included the Civil Rights Act, Medicare, and other long-overdue remedies to help the poor, the disadvantaged, and those discriminated against in receiving public services. Following on the heels of the 1954 Supreme Court decision on *Brown v. The Board of Education of Topeka*, constructive resolution of "the race problem" seemed possible. The dream was shattered by Johnson's escalation of the poorly conceived Vietnam War, the assassinations of Martin Luther King and Robert F. Kennedy, the urban riots, and the angry anti-war protests of the last half of the 1960s. So, by the time the film appeared in theaters, it was already an anachronism.

Guess Who's Coming to Dinner (1967)

The film stars Sidney Poitier as Doctor John Prentice, a renowned tropical medicine specialist whose dream is to go to an African country and get the twenty brightest kids and train them to be medical specialists. With Johns Hopkins, Yale, and the World Health Organization on his resumé, it's hard for his White prospective bride's family to argue with her decision to marry him on anything but racial grounds (fig. 3). Her newspaper editor father Matt Drayton (Spencer Tracy) must confront whether behind his "liberal facade, a reactionary bigot is fighting to come out." His daughter Joey (Katharine Houghton) makes it clear that she wouldn't let Prentice go, even if her father "were the governor of Alabama" (a reference to George Wallace). Their longtime Black maid Tillie (Isabel Sanford who later starred in the television show *The Jeffersons*) is outraged "at a member of my race going above hisself," saying, "Civil rights is one thing, this here is something else." She accuses Prentice of being "one of those smooth smart-ass niggers just out for anything you can get with your Black power and other troublemaking nonsense."

FIGURE 3. *Guess Who's Coming to Dinner.* Joey Drayton (Katharine Houghton) introduces her fiancé Dr. John Prentice (Sidney Poitier) to her mother (Katharine Hepburn).

His father, a retired mailman, is adamantly opposed to the union, provoking an angry response from his loving son, "You think of yourself as a colored man: I think of myself as a man." The wives, played by Katharine Hepburn (who won an Oscar) and Beah Richards, overcome their initial shock, to give the couple their blessing. Monsignor Ryan (Cecil Kellaway), one of the last of the entirely sympathetic portrayals of Catholic priests in the movies, tries to persuade his old friend to sanction the marriage. Finally, after outlining the many reasons they shouldn't marry, including the fact that interracial marriages were illegal in sixteen states, Drayton capitulates and love wins out. The film is probably most remembered now for the fact that while it was being filmed, Spencer Tracy was dying of cancer as well as for the interplay between him and Hepburn, his longtime companion. The tears in her eyes engendered by Tracy's final soliloquy were touching and real, a case where a film's symbolism was overwhelmed by what was going on in real life.

Another movie that signaled the optimism that existed before the disastrous year of 1968 with regard to solving America's race problems is *The Heart Is a Lonely Hunter.* It features excellent performances and a very sympathetic look at an older Black general practitioner who is coping with the long-standing scars of prejudice and failed family expectations.

The Heart Is a Lonely Hunter (1968)

A sad but heartwarming film, *The Heart Is a Lonely Hunter* is based on a novel by Carson McCullers.[24] It tells the story of John Singer, a deaf-mute, played brilliantly by Alan Arkin, who helps those like him who live on society's margin but get little in return. A jeweler, he leaves his steady job when the retarded deaf-mute he befriends is committed to a state hospital. Moving to a distant town to be able to visit him, Singer rents an apartment in a house where the father is wheelchair-bound because of a job injury and the family is going through difficult times. He reaches out to the adolescent daughter Mick (Sondra Locke in her film debut), whose rejection by her peers has made her feel like an ugly duckling. He also befriends an unstable drifter named Blount (Stacy Keach in his film debut), who injures himself in a fit of rage. Singer stops a Black doctor Dr. Copeland (Percy Rodriguez) who is passing by. At first, Copeland refuses to treat Blount saying, "He's a White man. I only treat my own." When he realizes Singer can't understand him because of his deafness, he says, "Very well, I will give him emergency treatment."

Singer visits Copeland's office in his home in an all-Black neighborhood to thank him. When he sees Singer, the doctor says, "If anybody knows of this, I'll be called uppity." He then enlists Singer's aid in helping him communicate with a Black deaf-mute patient (fig. 4). As they develop a friendship, Singer learns that Copeland is at odds with his daughter Portia (Cicely Tyson) for marrying Willie (Johnny Popwell), a gentle, but poor Black man whom Copeland has labeled an "Uncle Tom." He had hoped she would have become a doctor, rather than a maid.

On one of Singer's visits, Copeland shows him an x-ray of "the first patient I ever treated for tuberculosis when he was in school. Cured him or so I thought, but now he has a recurrence." It turns out that the doctor is the patient and that he has lung cancer. He tells Singer, "Here I am a man who has hated Whites my whole life and in the last year of my life I feel closer to you than anyone else." He goes on to say, "Please don't tell anyone. My work has been my life. I'd like to go on as long as possible. My patients might not take kindly to my being sick." Later, Copeland goes to the sheriff's office to protest Willie's unjust imprisonment for "molesting" a White woman and is left cooling his heels all day.

FIGURE 4. *The Heart Is a Lonely Hunter.* Dr. Copeland (Percy Rodriguez) enlists the help of deaf-mute John Singer (Alan Arkin) in reaching a deaf-mute patient.

Despite being a respected doctor, he is laughed at by the Whites and never gets to see the sheriff. Meanwhile, Singer shows Portia the x-ray and takes her to her Dad to effect a reconciliation.

There are other poignant scenes involving Singer and his retarded friend, as well as Mick's seeming rejection of him. Feeling completely isolated, Singer closes the door to his room and the next morning he shoots himself. Mick tells Copeland during one of their daily visits to Singer's gravesite, "We brought our troubles to him. We never felt he had troubles. I'll never forget him, never!" Copeland responds, "I think that would make him happy."

This film is admittedly disjointed as it weaves its four or five stories together and its ending is very sad. Nonetheless, it is worth seeing for the marvelous depiction of the isolation of the deaf as well as for Arkin's portrayal of sheer unadulterated goodness. Furthermore, Dr. Copeland illustrates the kindness, compassion, and dedication of the general practitioner who lives solely for his work and to serve his community, for which he pays a heavy personal price.

The Hollywood portrayal of Blacks in the 1970s changed to what was called Blaxploitation featuring macho characters called "Super-spades."[25] Another staple was the addition of a comedic touch and a wisecracking tough guy image best illustrated by Eddie Murphy.[26] As for doctors, there is a bit role in the 1970 film *M*A*S*H* (see chapter 8), in which ex-football star Fred "The Hammer" Williamson plays a Black neurosurgeon, but he's primarily in the film as a ringer for a hotly-contested football game. In the 1982 film, *The Verdict* (see chapter 8), a good-hearted but over-the-hill Black doctor appears as an emergency expert witness for the plaintiffs. He provides the filmmakers an opportunity for some offhand, rather gratuitous dialogue. When the defense team hears the doctor is Black, the senior partner tells the aggressive associate to be careful with his questioning and to have a Black attorney sit at the defense table. The plaintiff's Irish co-counsel on seeing him take the stand reflects on their putting a Black doctor on the stand, "Look at it this way. It's refreshing every time a doctor takes the stand and he's not a Jew."

The film image of Blacks changed somewhat in the late 1980s when Danny Glover joined Mel Gibson as buddies in the *Lethal Weapon* series. It softened appreciably in the 1990s with Morgan Freeman's outstanding performances in *Driving Miss Daisy* and in the outstanding film *Glory* with Academy Award winner Denzel Washington and Emmy Award winner André Braugher. Since then, there have been at least two films with Black doctors. In the first, *Outbreak*, Morgan Freeman plays a conflicted military doctor and Cuba Gooding, Jr., plays a combination scientist and crack helicopter pilot. The film has a lot going for it with its topical, scary, and important subject matter, emerging infections,[27] as well as an all-star cast. Yet, it manages to squander both.

Still, *Outbreak* is noteworthy, partly for the Black professionals and partly for conjuring up the 1950s and 1960s, the heyday of the Communicable Disease Center (CDC), whose director, Alex Langmuir, stimulated many a medical student to become Epidemic Intelligence Service officers. It was a time when Berton Roueché was firing the public's imagination by unraveling medical mysteries (infectious and non-infectious) in *New Yorker* essays, such as "Eleven Blue Men."[28] To get a flavor of the era, see the 1962 film *A Matter of WHO*, a delightfully fey comedy staring Peter Ustinov as a World Health Organization officer. The footprints in the credits are a tribute to his shoe-leather epidemiology.

Outbreak (1995)

Outbreak starts promisingly enough with a quote from Joshua Lederberg, "The single biggest threat to our continued dominance on the planet is the virus." But it takes a wrong turn in the opening scenes. People are dying of hemorrhagic fever in a village deep in the African rain forest, so physician scientists are called in to help. What do they do? In the noblest traditions of science and medicine, Doctor Billy Ford (Morgan Freeman) and his colleague McClintock (Donald Sutherland) take specimens for virus isolation, fly off, and order that the inhabitants be bombed to Kingdom Come.

OK, it is a rather novel way to control transmission, especially if you slept through your medical school epidemiology lectures. The theory is that, like Ebola virus, the fictional "Motaba" virus is not transmitted by airborne droplets, and the onset of the deadly disease is so rapid that those infected cannot travel far beyond the village. The preemptive strike is intended to eradicate the virus from the face of the earth, except for the isolate to be stored in the United States biological weapons laboratory. Unfortunately, it turns out to be both bad ethics and bad science. Man is once again "made a monkey of," as the natural simian host frolics from tree to tree in the African forest.

Time passes and we are transported to the United States Army Medical Research Institute for Infectious Diseases, with its four biosafety levels housing organisms varying from minimal hazard to Level 4 (those for which there is no known cure or vaccine, such as Ebola, Lassa, and Hantaviruses). We are next introduced to Dr. Sam Daniels (Dustin Hoffman), comically giving his Saint Bernards a bath that is interrupted by an urgent call from the commanding officer, Doctor, and now General, Ford. Hoffman flashes his trademark smile, which was apparently not enough to satisfy his ex-wife, Dr. Roberta "Robby" Keough (Rene Russo), a fellow epidemiologist on her way to head a similar laboratory at the CDC. Still, she agrees to dog-sit while Daniels is sent to investigate another "hot virus" outbreak in Africa.

A descendant of that frolicsome African monkey escapes United States customs agents, and an outbreak of hemorrhagic fever begins. In the great tradition of Walter Reed, Jesse Lazear, James Carroll, and Aristides Agramonte,[29] Daniels and his cohorts risk death to help others. They are scared and not too proud to admit it. They are also ambivalent toward "the bug." They hate it, but "have to love its simplicity: it's one-billionth our size and it's beating us." Unfortunately, our heroes are impeded by Generals McClintock and Ford. Sutherland, who used to be an excellent actor (see *Eye of the Needle* for an unheralded gem of a performance), seems to have become a prisoner of his past personas. He unaccountably overacts as a latter-day Doctor Strangelove abetted by an uncharacteristically weak-spined Morgan Freeman. Worried that Daniels's bulldog tenacity will blow their cover, they try to stop his investigation in order to protect the perfect biological weapon and their dirty little secret of years ago. At one point, Dr. Daniels tells Dr. Ford, "It's about being a doctor. It's about that sacred oath we took," presumably, the Hippocratic oath (see chapter 9) (fig. 5).

The movie's improbability begins to increase logarithmically as the Army quarantines a California town with a population of 2,618, and General McClintock convenes a panel of expert virologists to endorse his favorite mode of epidemic control, bombing the town. In a rather interesting perversion of the expression, "Think globally; act locally," he says: "Be compassionate, but be compassionate globally." McClintock urges the experts to stand shoulder to shoulder with the president when he goes on national television to explain the necessity of bombing his fellow Americans. "No sneaking off to the *Washington Post* saying you were the only dissenting voice, when the body bags start appearing."

Incongruously, the patients wear masks when their blood is drawn on admission to the hospital, but not when they are in their hospital beds—the better to see their pained expressions. Talk about pained expressions, you may well react as I did to a health care worker's worst nightmare when a vial of blood from an infected patient breaks in a lab worker's hands after it has been centrifuged. The protection of the CDC staff in space suits is in marked contrast to the lack of protection of the health care workers. For all their protection, however, the scientists are a pretty inept bunch, with Major "Casey" Schuler (Kevin Spacey) managing to violate the integrity of his space suit to become infected. When Dr. Keough stabbed herself with a needle, after drawing blood from her infected cohort, I was ready to pull all their medical licenses. Fortunately for the forces of good, there is a Black pathologist, Major Salt (Cuba Gooding, Jr.), who is an expert electron microscopist and also flies helicopters Top Gun style. He brings his helicopter so close to the Thai freighter that had transported the host African monkey to America that Daniels can jump onto the ship. He also lands on a television station, so that Daniels can alert the populace to the animal's whereabouts.

The film also gives a mini-immunology lesson. Because the town's inhabitants are infected with a virus strain whose protein has been altered, the antiserum against the original virus strain is ineffective. Never

FIGURE 5. *Outbreak.* General Billy Ford (Morgan Freeman) has to be reminded that he is first and foremost a doctor.

fear, Doctor Salt takes time from his piloting and microscopy to make liters of antisera in a trice. First, he has to capture the host. No problem. It turns out he is an expert shot, and we know he has *sangfroid*; so, he fires a tranquilizer into the host animal's bottom, just as it is scurrying back into the woods. After transporting the monkey to the lab by helicopter, Salt gets to work. What is especially amazing is that all this derring-do, including a helicopter dogfight in which Salt faces down the C-130 ordered to "bomb the town," is carried out on only three hours sleep total.

If you want to learn the true story on which the film was tenuously based, read Richard Preston's *The Hot Zone.*[29] You will get an appreciation of the veterinarians and animal handlers who take on the challenge of working with Level 4 organisms. Be forewarned, though, there are scenes that may make your skin crawl. That the virus could have spread like wildfire through the District of Columbia, its suburbs, and beyond makes the truth more compelling than the fiction. Indeed, why it did not is the real sixty-four thousand dollar question.

As we have seen, *Outbreak* features two Black doctors on the film's periphery, one exceedingly good and the other relatively weak, but who still does the right thing in the end. By contrast, the next film, *Eve's Bayou*, places the Black doctor at its center. Though sad, this episode in the life of an African-American, Creole dynasty is very life-affirming. The screenplay is totally unlike that of most of today's films that seem to be written by shallow movie junkies and populated by self-conscious actors rather than people. The characters have flesh, blood, and spirit. The players don't seem like actors at all, but a real family that has invited us in to view a small slice of their two centuries of life on the bayou. The many lush, misty vistas and the atmospheric dream sequences give it a slightly surreal quality that allows the viewer to enjoy the experience on its own terms. The excellent soundtrack helps sustain the mood.

Eve's Bayou (1997)

Appropriately, enough, the film opens at a soireé in the large plantation house of the descendants of French landowner Jean Paul Batiste and Eve, the African-American healer who saved his life and who later bore him fourteen children. Her adolescent namesake, Eve Batiste (Jurnee Smollett), our hostess for the evening, warns us that "memory is a selection of images, some elusive, others indelibly imprinted on the brain. The summer I killed my father I was ten years old." She proceeds to relate a painful memory at whose center is her father, the local doctor, Louis Batiste (Samuel L. Jackson). The doctor is a compassionate healer and pillar of the community. He has a charming exterior and an extraordinary bedside manner in the literal meaning of the term (fig. 6)

Like her fourteen-year-old sister, Eve desperately wants her father's affection and attention. Hurt when he chooses to dance with her sister and not her, she runs into the carriage house, where sleep overtakes her. Awakened by her father's surreptitious lovemaking with his favorite mistress Matty Mereaux (Lisa Nicole Carson), she cries out and her father runs to her and comforts her. On relating the evening's events to her sister Cisely (Meagan Good), she is told that it was not what it seemed and she is temporarily relieved. Still, she begins to see her father in a different light as she accompanies him on one of his house calls. A lovely young lady in a scanty negligee asks the doctor, "Can you give me something for my pain?" and the doctor asks his daughter to go out and play while he administers the usual therapy. When Eve asks him what was wrong with the lady, he replies, "some sickness is hard to put a finger on." Later, when she confronts him with her suspicions about his dalliance with Mrs. Mereaux, he asks her to "say aah!" and then tells her he sees nothing back there to produce such terrible ideas. Later, though, he says, "I'm just a small town doctor who pushes aspirin to the elderly. There are women to whom I'm a hero and I need to be a hero"—a rather

FIGURE 6. *Eve's Bayou.* Dr. Louis Batiste (Samuel L. Jackson) is a revered Louisiana family doctor whose secret life is discovered by his daughter.

plausible explanation of the ego needs of those in position of dominance who take advantage of the infatuated and those dependent on them.

One of the most charismatic characters, Uncle Julian, played by the ebullient Vondie Curtis Hall, is killed off too early. His wife, Roz (Lynn Whitfield), the doctor's sister, helps make up for his loss. Like her brother, Roz has inherited the family's gift for healing. Her realm, however, is the mystical. She clasps the hand of the person from whom she seeks the truth and performs "psychic counseling." She has an uncanny gift for visualizing what is going on at a distance and a witty way of predicting the future. But she is not infallible. In discussing the death of her three husbands, Roz says smilingly to Eve who appears to have inherited the gift, "Even before I did the counseling, I could look at people and see their whole lives. But with my husbands, I couldn't see a thing." The rival community psychic, Elzora, is played with humor and grace by Diahann Carroll. A purveyor of voodoo, she also correctly predicts two events involving death that touch the lives of the main characters. With the track record and appeal of the two psychics, it's almost enough to make one a believer.

I should mention a rather weak 1997 made-for-television film based on *The Ditchdigger's Daughters*,[30] an interesting and heartwarming book about a Black man who made sure all his daughters were educated, with one becoming a prominent obstetrician. Unfortunately, as this chapter has demonstrated, Hollywood filmmakers have a long legacy of neglect to make up for in portraying Black professionals in film and this is certainly true for the field of medicine. Sadly, when good films like *Eve's Bayou* and *Amistad* are made, they don't get the press or viewers they deserve even in the Black community. The good news is that there are plenty of Black doctors whose lives are worth celebrating.[12, 16]

If I were asked to recommend a story, my choice would be the life of Charles R. Drew, the "father of the blood bank."[12] A graduate of one of America's best Black high schools, Dunbar in Washington, D.C., he went on to Amherst and McGill Medical School. He received a doctorate in medical science from Columbia in 1939 and was the first Black surgical resident at Presbyterian Hospital in New York. His pioneering research led to his directing the Blood for Britain program in 1940–1941 for shipping liquid plasma and then to the development of a process for collecting blood and preparing dried plasma for use in American battlefield hospitals. Responsible for saving many American lives, he was called before a Congressional Committee in 1942 to defend the position that Blacks should be able to donate blood destined for White servicemen (remember that scene when the nurse deliberately drops the Black man's blood in *Lost Boundaries*). Democratic Senator John Rankin of Mississippi accused him of being a Communist and "trying to mongrelize the nation." Drew deserves to be recognized for his courage in standing up with civility to such racists and for his many contributions such as blood banking and the nurturing of a cadre of Black surgeons at Howard University School of Medicine. Furthermore, the dramatic circumstances surrounding his death[12] should provide more than enough material for a first-rate screenplay.

NOTES

1. Reitzes DC. Negroes and Medicine. Cambridge, MA: Harvard University Press, 1958.
2. Morais HM. The History of the Negro in Medicine. International Library of Negro Life and History Series. New York: Publisher's Co, 1968.

3. Ludmerer KM. Learning to Heal: The Development of Medical Education. New York: Basic Books, 1985.
4. Ludmerer KM. Time to Heal: American Medical Education from the Turn of the Century to the Era of Managed Care. New York: Oxford University Press, 1999.
5. Shea S and Fullilove MT. Entry of Black and other minority students into U.S. medical schools: Historical perspectives and recent trends. N Engl J Med 1985; 313: 933–940.
6. Starr P. The Social Transformation of American Medicine: The Rise of a Sovereign Profession and the Making of a Vast Industry. New York: Basic Books, 1982.
7. Seham M. Discrimination against Negroes in hospitals. N Engl J Med 1964; 271: 940–943.
8. Seham M. Blacks and American Medical Care. Minneapolis: The University of Minnesota Press, 1973.
9. Reynolds PP. Hospital and civil rights, 1945-1963: The case of *Simkins v Moses H. Cone Memorial Hospital*. Ann Intern Med 1997; 126: 898–906.
10. Thomson GE. Discrimination in health care. Ann Intern Med 1997; 126: 910–912.
11. Halperin EC. Desegregation of hospitals and medical societies in North Carolina. N Engl J Med 1988; 318: 58–63.
12. Hayden RC. 11 African-American Doctors. Frederick MD: Twenty-First Century Books, revised and expanded edition, 1992.
13. Harris MJ. David Jones Peck, MD: A dream denied. J Nat Med Assn 1996; 88: 600–603.
14. Walsh MR. "Doctors Wanted: No Women Need Apply": Sexual Barriers in the Medical Profession, 1835-1975. New Haven: Yale University Press, 1977.
15. Thompson LE. Two strikes: The role of black women in medicine before 1920. The Pharos, Winter 1995, 58: 12–15.
16. Epps CH Jr., Johnson DG, Vaughan AL. African-American Medical Pioneers. Baltimore: Williams and Wilkins, 1994.
17. Lightfoot SL. Balm in Gilead: Journey of a Healer. Reading MA: Addison-Wesley Publishing, 1988.
18. Jones GW. Black Cinema Treasures: Lost and Found. Denton: University of North Texas Press, 1991.
19. Kisch J and Mapp E. A Separate Cinema: Fifty Years of Black Cast Posters. New York: Noonday Press, 1992 (also see Web page www.separate cinema.com).
20. Cripps T. Slow Fade to Black: The Negro in American Film, 1900-1942. New York: Oxford University Press, 1993.
21. Bogle D. Toms, Coons, Mulattoes, Mammies, and Bucks: An Interpretive History of Blacks in American Films. New York: Continuum, 1973.
22. Cripps T. Making Movies Black: The Hollywood Message Movie from World War II to the Civil Rights Era. New York: Oxford University Press, 1993.
23. Jefferson RS. The Black experience and the film industry. J Nat Med Assn 1976; 68: 135–147.
24. McCullers C. The Heart Is a Lonely Hunter. Boston: Houghton Mifflin, 1967.
25. Leab DJ. From Sambo to Superspade: The Black Experience in Motion Pictures. Boston: Houghton Mifflin Co, 1975.
26. Winokur M. Black is White/White is Black: Passing As a Strategy of Racial Compatibility in Contemporary Hollywood Comedy. In: Unspeakable Images: Ethnicity and the American Cinema, ed. LD Friedman. Urbana: University of Illinois Press, 1991.
27. Le Guenno B. Emerging viruses. Sci Am 1995; 273: 57–64.
28. Roueché B. Eleven Blue Men: And Other Narratives of Medical Detection. Boston: Little, Brown & Co, 1953.
29. Preston R. The Hot Zone. New York: Random House, 1994.
30. Thornton Y and Coudert J. The Ditchdigger's Daughters: A Black Family's Astonishing Success Story. New York: Brick Lane Press (Carol Publishing), 1995.

7

The Dark Side of Doctors:
Greed, Arrogance, God Complexes, and Outright Villainy

The dark side of individual doctors and of the profession has never been absent from the movies. Selected films whose central themes have been arrogance, insensitivity, greed, incompetence, and even criminality will be the focus of this chapter. Some others where this is an important theme are covered elsewhere (see *Arrowsmith, Men in White, Society Doctor, Doctor X, Coma,* and *Extreme Measures*). Let's start with one of the best films on the subject, based on a novel by physician-writer, A.J. Cronin. Interestingly enough, Cronin began his writing career while convalescing from a duodenal ulcer (a long process in the days before specific drug therapy became available).[1] With his first novel, *Hatter's Castle,*[2] he became an author, an occupation he never abandoned.

A medical graduate of the University of Glasgow, Cronin had cared for Welsh miners, and in his autobiography, *Adventures in Two Worlds,*[3] he recounted some of the real-life events that served as the basis for his novel *The Citadel.*[4] That the film will be no paean to medicine is clear from the scrolling introduction, a regular feature in old films: "This motion picture is a story of individual characterizations and is in no way intended as a reflection on the great medical profession that has done so much towards beating back the alien forces of nature that retard the physical progress of the human race." In other words, "Doctors," as Bette Davis says in *All About Eve*, "Fasten your seat belts, kids, it's going to be a bumpy night."[5]

The Citadel (1938)

As *The Citadel* opens, Andrew Manson (Robert Donat), an eager, newly minted physician, is riding to Blaenelly, Wales, in a smoking car (an interesting reminder of a time when doctors smoked like chimneys). Indeed, cigarette smoking is pervasive throughout the film; the doctors are constantly asking for or lighting up another cigarette. He is assuming a post as an assistant to an invalid doctor in a company town with no hospital, x-ray, or ambulance, and where the district medical officer goes golfing and ignores his pleas for more resources. So begins his journey from idealism to cynicism and back again.

The film is a rich resource for discussing the evolution of medicine, but requires an attention span and tolerance for old-fashioned cinematics. Although it won a number of academy awards, as with *The Last Angry Man*, its flaws may be more obvious than its good points. For example, the neophyte doctor's first delivery involves a childless couple who desperately want the baby. He delivers what looks like a board. When the baby doesn't respond to three or four hefty whacks, Manson pronounces it stillborn and sets it by the fire. On returning to the mother, he finds her happily exclaiming that it's a boy. This spurs Manson to perform a rather feverish and disjointed resuscitation (fig. 1). No breaths are given for at least another minute or two, but voilà! the child is saved, and he says, "Thank God I am a doctor!"

After seeing the plight of the workers and the toll that typhoid is taking on the community, Manson learns from another doctor, an alcoholic idealist named Denny (Ralph Richardson), that the fault lies in

FIGURE 1. *The Citadel*. Dr. Manson (Robert Donat) resuscitates a seemingly stillborn baby and afterwards exclaims, "Thank God I'm a doctor!"

FIGURE 2. *The Citadel*. Dr. Manson (Robert Donat) tells his future wife Christine (Rosalind Russell) to say "aah."

the sewer overflowing into the water supply. Because the municipality won't replace it, Denny suggests that Manson join him in an enterprising public health maneuver, blowing up the sewer. At first Manson rejects this suggestion as "unethical," but later agrees to join in the caper. The nocturnal explosion forces the district to repair the sewer, which wins him favor with the local school teacher, Christine (Rosalind Russell). When she seeks care for a sore throat, we get to see him use a head mirror, once the general practitioner's insignia (fig. 2).

Discouraged at being exploited by his partner's wife, Manson seeks employment with a medical cooperative in Aberalaw, a lower-middle-class mining village. His stated reason for transferring is, "When I first arrived [in Blaenelly] I thought the practice of medicine was bound by textbooks and ethics. I've learned differently since." Single at the time, Manson is encouraged by his prospective employers to marry, because the miners like stable family men. So he pops the question, and Christine agrees.

The cooperative is a decided step up and provides "a hospital, an x-ray, and a fluoroscope." Manson learns, however, that the interests of the doctors and their miner allies on the governing council are too often detrimental to those of the miners generally. For example, a miner on the council, in order to avoid going down into the mines, has managed to get a health certificate for a spurious reason from the previous doctor. Manson refuses to renew the certificate—a politically unwise move. He also discovers an unwillingness to investigate the miners' respiratory disease and sets up a laboratory to prove the presence of tuberculosis. With his wife acting as research technologist, Manson identifies the microbes using the "Zeiss microscope" Denny gave him as a going-away gift. The other physicians and powerful council members, however, get wind of his experiments, which threaten to throw a monkey wrench into their cozy arrangement with management. They stir up the miners who, afraid of losing their jobs, release Manson's guinea pigs and destroy his laboratory.

Devastated, Manson moves to London to care for the poor, but his lack of a paying practice makes him easy prey when a rich socialite, while shopping in a fashionable store, calls for a doctor. Manson diagnoses "willful hysteria," to which the woman readily agrees; he then slaps her into sensibility and her condition improves. This "success" ushers Manson into the world of high-society medicine and starts him on the road to riches and adoration. Cronin, who had traveled a somewhat similar road, admitted to having made a lot of money diagnosing "asthenia."[6]

Rex Harrison is at his suave best as Dr. Lawford, Manson's old schoolmate, who tutors him in the proper behavior when attending the "most expensive snob nursing home in London." One "gold mine" carries the diagnosis of flatus ventrus. Manson is asked to consult on another "treasure chest," who he almost blurts out is disease-free, when he is cautioned that she owns half the gold mines in Rhodesia. Another golfing partner has just returned from a trip to Egypt with a patient who had a mild case of sunstroke. This scene reminded me of a fellow resident at New York's Harkness Pavilion in 1963, who with his wife was invited to accompany a well-heeled patient with a cardiac condition on a trip to Europe.

Soon Manson is delivering "bogus heliotherapy"[4] and has moved into the high life of fast cars and elegant digs, what Cronin called "bogus Harley Street."[6] Then comes the most delicious moment of the film when Denny reappears after a stint in India. He's been on the wagon for two years, taking care of folks with "fleas and other assorted problems." Denny tries to enlist his friend into joining forces to form a multi-disciplinary capitated group practice. Patients will pay the equivalent of two dollars a month and be taken care of "following scientific and humanitarian ideals" and emphasizing prevention. He argues that it is working in "the States." How about that! This could be a reference to the Blue Cross Insurance Plan that was developed by teachers in Texas in 1929.[7]

Manson, now a cynic/realist, declines the invitation, prompting a lecture by his disappointed wife: "Your work isn't to make money, it is to better humanity and you know it. Don't you remember the way we used to talk about that? It was an attack on the unknown, an assault uphill as though you had to take some citadel you couldn't see but you knew was there—an operation on a kitchen table, a microscope in a back room." Well, you get the idea. Manson rejects the noble sentiments; they won't pay for their lifestyle.

The rest of the film is melodramatic. Denny goes off the wagon, gets hit by a car, and ruptures his spleen; Manson takes him to a high-priced surgical colleague, Charles Every (Cecil Parker). Belatedly, Manson finds out that the fellow is incompetent (something he managed to miss with his carefully placed blinders). After Denny dies from a botched operation, Manson tells Every "That wasn't surgery. It was murder." He wanders all night through London, arriving at a bridge. In a scene that seems to prefigure *It's a Wonderful Life*, the disembodied Denny tells Manson that he is "not just one man, but part of a great profession, fighting for the benefit of health, life, and humanity." "That's a doctor's job, to keep on hoping and trying."

Manson then goes off to treat a friend's daughter who is dying from tuberculosis. With the help of an American scientist named Richard Stillman (Percy Parsons), who is pioneering pneumothorax treatment, he saves the patient. Even so, Manson is brought before the medical disciplinary board for violating his oath by working with an unlicensed practitioner. Never mind that the patient is sitting in the audience looking fit as a fiddle. Manson recalls other scientists who helped mankind—Pasteur, Ehrlich, Haffkine, and Metchnikoff. He then launches into an impassioned speech about repairing the profession and evoking the Hippocratic oath: "I am supposed to have done something infamous by assisting Stillman, an unregistered man and probably the best man in the world on this type of case. I ask you, gentlemen, is it infamous for a doctor to be directly instrumental in saving a human life? Gentlemen, it's high time we started putting our house in order. We're everlastingly saying that we'll do things and we don't. Doctors have to live, but they have a responsibility to mankind, too. If we go on trying to make out that everything's right inside the profession and everything's wrong outside, it'll be the death of scientific progress. I only ask you to remember the words of our own Hippocratic oath, 'Into whatsoever houses I shall enter, I will work for the benefit of the sick, holding aloof from all wrong and corruption.' How many of us remember that? How many of us practice that? I have made mistakes, mistakes I bitterly regret, but Stillman isn't one of them. And if by what has been called my infamous conduct I have done anything, however small, to benefit humanity, I am more than proud, gentlemen, I am profoundly grateful." At the conclusion, Manson and his wife leave the disciplinary hearings in a noble haze.

The book,[4] which has different plot twists from the movie, was even more critical of members of the medical profession. Cronin portrayed doctors merrily fee-splitting, charging exorbitant prices for sterile water injections that patients said helped them more than anything, and being propositioned by "scientific advertisers" who wanted to make every doctor, so to speak, a potential salesman" of their creams and salves.[1] The book earned a huge lay following and scathing criticism in the *Journal of the American Medical Association* for painting "not a fair picture of medicine in either Great Britain or the United States."[8] On the other hand, Dr. Hugh Cabot of the Mayo Clinic, in a letter to the American publishers, was full of praise. He said, "The book appears to be so important that I should be glad to believe that it would be at the disposal of every medical student and practitioner under thirty-five in this country....I can say at once that there is no important situation which he draws, the counterpart of which cannot be found in this country and probably more frequently."[9]

In short, although *The Citadel* lacks the polish of current films, it has what most recent films don't have—a soul. For all its seeming hokiness, its theme is uplifting. Medicine is a noble profession, even though some practitioners and the systems in which we work are often flawed.

In the next film, the doctors are either bizarre or sadistic. A budding idealistic medical student is our guide for a tour of the underbelly of "idyllic" early 1900s small-town America. The performances by the all-star cast, the musical score, and the memorable scenes raise this film above traditional soap opera.

Kings Row (1942)

Based on a novel by Henry Bellamann,[10] the film is set in 1890s America. The introduction proclaims Kings Row to be "a good clean town, a good town to live in and a good place to raise your children." Soon, we learn the terrible secrets hidden in the hearts of the town doctors. The first, Doctor Alexander Tower (Claude Rains) never seems to see a patient and his wife and daughter are prevented from socializing with the townspeople. The other, Dr. Gordon (Charles Coburn), is the town's leading doctor whose patients sometimes scream when he operates, as if they have not been given any anesthetic. The central figure is Parris Mitchell (Robert Cummings), who is being raised by Madame Von Eln, his wealthy, patrician grandmother, played with her usual consummate grace by Maria Ouspenskaya. Madame proposes to send Parris to Vienna to study medicine, and he prepares for his exams by studying with Tower, whose daughter Cassandra (Betty Field) he fancies. However, Tower forbids him to have any contact with Cassie, and they must steal their few moments together.

Tower asks Parris as he passes the statue of Hippocrates, "Do you want to be a good doctor or one of those country quacks?" Parris responds that he wants to be like "those legendary doctors one reads about in books." Tower says he's not sure whether that means "a pillpusher, a carpenter, or one who wants to save humanity." He then proceeds to tell him his approach to medicine: "It's a game in which man pits his brain against the forces of destruction and disease. At the beginning I don't expect you to participate in the game. You'll only listen and accept. You will study and take notes. You will memorize and do this only because I tell you to." Later, he will tell him, "In diagnosis, never underrate the value of unconscious observation, instinct, if you want to call it that, or, more properly, intuition. That's what makes a born physician." The old man's wisdom is lost on Parris who is snoozing and Tower gives him a day off.

When Madame becomes ill, she arranges for Parris to continue his studies in Vienna. Meanwhile, Parris asks Tower if Gordon, who is caring for his grandmother, is a good doctor, because he had heard about a man who went into shock after being operated on by Gordon and was left with permanent paralysis. Tower responds, "In your grandmother's case, he knows his business." It turns out that Madame has cancer and dies on schedule according to Gordon's prognosis. Before Parris leaves for Vienna, Tower interests him in "the new field of psychiatry." He says, "Pay attention to the twelfth and thirteenth centuries, because man was more comfortable in his world then than he is now. I'm speaking of psychic health"—a contention that's impossible to prove or refute. As he departs, Parris tells Cassie with starry-eyed wonder, "I want to be a good doctor, a great doctor, if I can."

While he is away, much transpires. We learn that Tower, whose wife had died, has murdered Cassie and killed himself. It turns out that both women had "dementia praecox" and that Tower was sparing them and the world from their condition (an eerie reminder of the fascination with the field of eugenics in the early part of this century). As weird as this is, Doctor Gordon's story tops it. This involves Ronald Reagan in what is generally considered to be his best role—in the movies, that is— and the one whose signature line became the title of his autobiography.[11] He plays Drake McHugh, Parris's "best pal." A happy-go-lucky play-boy, he runs around with the good-time girls, but has his sights set on Gordon's daughter, Louise (Nancy Coleman). The feeling is mutual, but Gordon refuses his request to marry his daughter. Despondent, he starts to date Randy Monoghan (Ann Sheridan), a woman from across the tracks. After a bout of drunken revelry, Drake abandons the rich side of the tracks, gets a job on the railroad through Randy's "Pa," and marries her. A freak accident occurs just as Drake is proving himself not to be a worthless lout. Gordon amputates both his legs and when Drake wakes up, he speaks his classic lines, "Randy, where's the rest of me?" (fig. 3). Slipping into the depth of depression, he refuses to be fitted for artificial limbs or to leave the room in a wheelchair. He an-grily rejects Randy's suggestion to enact his dream of developing a parcel of land for homesites.

Parris, who has decided to accept a prestigious position in Vienna instead of returning to Kings Row, hears the news of Drake's accident and sails back to the United States. He tells Drake that he is writing a prescription for him to "avoid a helpless invalid complex," and makes money available to him. Drake first refuses charity, but then agrees to develop the homesites. Randy, an extremely capable woman utters one of the most sexist lines in screen history, "You'll have to tell me every-thing to do. I'm only a woman."

Parris finds an exact replica of his lost love, Cassie, in an immi-grant from Vienna who has rented a house next to the meadow where he and Cassie would go, and he decides to stay in Kings Row for a while. Louise Gordon tells Parris that her father, now dead, "thought it was his duty to punish wickedness wherever he found it. He would say their hearts were too weak for chloroform" (fig. 4). She threatens to tell Drake

FIGURE 3. *Kings Row*. Drake McHugh (Ronald Reagan) awakens to learn that both his legs have been amputated and asks, "Where's the rest of me?"

that the amputations were unnecessary if Parris doesn't tell him. Her mother, played austerely by Judith Anderson, stands by her husband's memory and asks Parris to commit her daughter to an asylum. Parris seeks out the local attorney, who tells him that it's possible. "Sadistic surgeons are not unknown in medical history. They're scarce, thank heaven. One in millions." Parris then learns from Drake's brother-in-law that an eyewitness to the operation said, "I looked good at those legs and the bones in neither were broken."

Now comes the ethical dilemma: does Parris let Louise tell the truth as she seems intent on doing and possibly devastate Drake and destroy her father's reputation? Or should he fill out commitment papers for her? He tells his new girl friend Elise (Kaaren Verne), "I can silence her. She can be put in an asylum. Can I commit her to a life of unspeakable horror?" Elise asks, "Suppose they weren't people you loved or even knew?" This spurs Parris to tell Drake the truth, saying, "I'm not your friend now and you're not mine. I'm your doctor. You're my patient. It's as if I took you into the operating room and had a scalpel in my hand. I can make you or break you. My grandmother used to say, 'Some people grow up and some people just grow older.' I guess it's

FIGURE 4. *Kings Row*. Dr. Henry Gordon (Charles Coburn) exacts retribution for what he considers immoral behavior by performing surgery without anesthesia.

time to find out about us, whether I'm a doctor and you're a man." He then recites part of the poem, "Invictus," a favorite at the time.[12]

Parris tells Drake, "He was that kind of butcher. He felt he had an ordination to punish transgressors." Drake is stony-faced, then he breaks into a laugh, saying, "Where did Gordon think I lived? In my legs?" and adds with Reaganesque jauntiness, "For Pete's sake, let's give a party. I feel swell." An interesting sidebar is that the success of this film led to the proposal to pair Ronald Reagan and Ann Sheridan as the romantic leads in *Casablanca*. Fortunately, wiser heads prevailed and the leads were given to Bogart and Bergman.

While individual doctors have major character flaws in the previous film, the profession itself is pictured as noble. The next film returns to the theme in *The Citadel* of a profession that has great ideals, but is populated largely by a bunch of close-minded, self-protective, pompous asses with bad cases of credentialitis.

Sister Kenny (1946)

Based on the book *And They Shall Walk*[13] by Sister Elizabeth Kenny, this movie is one of the harshest critiques of the medical profession ever filmed. It opens with Kenny, a doctor's daughter in Queensland,

Australia, reciting the last part of the nurse's oath that she has just taken: "With loyalty will I endeavor to aid the physician in his work." The local doctor, Aeneas McDonnell (Alexander Knox), tells her, "And don't forget it." Later, he will become her staunchest supporter as she takes on the medical establishment. Actually, Kenny never went to nursing school,[14] but learned on the job and got "grandmothered" into nursing when she was accepted as a nurse in Australia's armed forces during World War I.

In the film, after three years in the bush, her grateful patients give her a horse to cover the wide territory because she won't take money. During a call to a sick child's bedside, Kenny is stumped by a set of symptoms and dispatches the father to send a telegram to McDonnell. He diagnoses infantile paralysis (poliomyelitis) and says that the only thing to do is treat the symptoms. Moist heat relieves the muscle spasm, but the child is left paralyzed. Five other children are similarly affected. She then tries to "reeducate" their muscles by manipulation and all recover.

Kenny and her fiancé, Kevin Connors (Dean Jagger), visit McDonnell to tell him that she is marrying and giving up nursing. Before she can do so, he questions her about the children and, on learning of her success, brings her to the region's leading orthopedist, Dr. Brack (Philip Merivale), to tell her story (fig. 5). Brack doesn't believe her, saying, "Medical science is about fact, not fancy....There is no treatment for the acute stage....The only thing that offers any hope is prompt and complete immobilization." Kenny, on the other hand, believes that's why eighty-eight out of one hundred polio survivors end up deformed. He tells her, "Stick to nursing and don't meddle with orthopedic medicine. It's a complicated subject that's difficult enough for those who spend a lifetime studying it." While in Calcutta in 1963, I encountered similar authoritativeness from a distinguished doctor who had seen thousands of cases of cholera. His morning rounds consisted of predicting the 25 percent who would die; on our experimental ward, none did.[15] This was a powerful lesson that experience alone isn't always the best teacher.

Connors, angered by Brack's close-mindedness, suggests that he would have little recourse if Kenny went to the newspaper. McDonnell tells him, "Medical questions are not settled in the newspaper. You'd brand yourself a fake in the eyes of every decent doctor." Connors responds, "You mean every decent doctor is a pigheaded fool?" McDonnell asks Connors, a military officer, how he would react if someone challenged the whole theory of military science. He adds, "The medical

FIGURE 5. *Sister Kenny*. (Rosalind Russell) demonstrates the basis for her treatment to the sympathetic family doctor, Dr. McDonnell (Alexander Knox) and a skeptical orthopedist Dr. Brack (Philip Merivale).

profession is society's only defense against quackery. Our degrees, our medical license, our associations are a wall to protect society against vicious men who are willing to trade on human ignorance." Because the doctors refuse to let Kenny treat acute cases, he advises her to take the doctors' many failures. She postpones her marriage and opens a clinic, where she implements her theory that she is "stimulating the subconscious neuromotor impulses by agitating proprioceptive receptors in the periphery." Brack and his colleagues scoff at her theories and write off her successes as evidence that the children did not have polio. When World War I breaks out and Connors is sent to the front, she also enlists, telling McDonnell that "the fight against polio will last longer than the war, probably "until the last doctor dies of it."

On returning to Australia after the war, Kenny finds a polio epidemic raging. She tells McDonnell that she plans to marry and give up the fight against polio. He convinces her to reopen her clinic which she does, giving up her plans for marriage. According to Victor Cohn's biography,[14] the romance is pure Hollywood; such artistic license was common in 1940s biopics, e.g., *The Cole Porter Story* starring Cary Grant.

Again, despite her success with intractable cases, Brack convinces the authorities to shut down the clinic. McDonnell explains why she is meeting so much opposition: "Big people make little people feel small and naturally they react. When the big person happens to be a nurse, well you know just as much as I do what a shock it is for a doctor to get told off by a nurse." She replies, "I've never said anything unkind about doctors. I'd just like to see a few of them in their own splints."

She confronts Brack who is demonstrating his technique for treating polio to an assemblage of orthopedists. Invited to the well of the amphitheater to engage in a debate, Kenny reminds the doctors of how medical ideas change. "Your fathers bled their patients for everything from a fever to a cold. Do you do it anymore?" Brack is appalled as Kenny invokes the memory of Harvey and Pasteur and humiliates her. Kenny leaves, telling Brack that if he needs "any more braces, steel corsets, or any other instruments of medieval torture, I can send them to you. I've taken plenty off your patients." Brack reminds her of that last paragraph of her nursing oath and says, "You have the arrogance to try to teach the doctors their profession." Kenny later tells McDonnell, "I can speak to the plain doctors. The Doctor Brackses, the specialists, they live in a fortress like Jericho....Inside the walls, they can't hear the crying of children." McDonnell tells her that her real hope to scale the Walls of Jericho lies in the people. He later tells her, "The people are more important than the system. That's true in government; they're fighting a war (World War II) to prove it and it's true in medicine. You've got that fight left, Elizabeth. It's a big fight. It won't be easy."

Kenny decides to accept an invitation to visit America. On landing in San Francisco, she is asked by a reporter, "Aren't you here to show up the doctors? Give us your honest opinion." She responds, "I'm here to help the children....My honest opinion is that it's easier to criticize a doctor than to be one." After two years, she is ready to leave, saying that "the Doctor Brackses are just as strong in America," when she gets a call from the University of Minnesota. Doctors there have shown a 55 percent recovery rate in thirty-two days using her method. She establishes the Kenny Institute in Minneapolis and, along with the medical director, holds a teaching clinic for physicians. The director quotes humorist Artemis Ward, "It ain't the things we don't know that cause all the trouble. It's the things we do know that ain't so." He adds that if "Miss Kenny had been a doctor, this controversy would not have gone on for thirty-five years." Still, a blue-ribbon American committee issues a report, severely criticizing Kenny and her supporters. Asked by a doctor if it isn't time for her to question the brains of the doctors on these committees, she responds, "I've fought doctors....They're stubborn, headstrong, cantankerous, domineering, quibbling people and they're wonderful. The very fact that they fought so bitterly for what they believed has made me respect them. If any group can give a better account of themselves when they come to meet their Maker..." She breaks down thinking of old Dr. McDonnell and turns over the session to the medical director. This rather weak sop to doctors is an unfortunate cop-out, given all that has gone before. The movie ends with her grateful patients singing "Happy Birthday."

This devastating indictment of the profession propounds a thesis that is too often true for all entrenched powerful professions, businesses, and trades, namely, a narrow-mindedness and self-serving use of their power to silence and destroy their critics, whom they perceive to be enemies. As we shall see in the next chapter, it foreshadows a broader attack on institutions that was characteristic of the late 1960s and 1970s.

Meanwhile, the picturing of individual doctors as heinous villains continued apace as in the 1965 film *Hush, Hush, Sweet Charlotte* and Richard Widmark's portrayal of a megalomaniacal medical chief of staff in the 1978 film *Coma* (see chapter 5). It reached its apogee in *Dead Ringers*, David Cronenberg's disturbing and, at times, barely watchable film, based on the book *Twins*.[16]

Dead Ringers (1988)

Set in Toronto, *Dead Ringers* opens in 1954 when two precocious twin boys perform intraovarian surgery on a cat. We next see them in their medical school anatomy lab where they are lionized as "the fabulous twins who have already brought us fabulous glory" for designing a retractor. Cut to 1988 when the twins, played with a remarkable blend of iciness, suaveness, and naiveté by Jeremy Irons, are running the premier gynecologic practice in Toronto. One, Elliott Mantle, is primarily a clinician/grant-getter; the other, Beverly, is a clinician/researcher. Genevieve Bujold plays Claire Niveau, an actress, who almost never has periods. She consults them because, "life is empty without children." The doctors are ecstatic because "she has one of the few things we haven't seen, a trifurcate cervix leading to a three-compartment uterus." This encounter leads to an affair as do many of their patient encounters, including one with their department chairman's wife, where the brothers trade roles as the woman's caregiver and lover. Beverly, the shy one, complains at the handoffs, to which the suave Eliott replies, "I'm no good with the serious ones; I'm no good with the frivolous ones. If we didn't share women, you'd still be a virgin. You don't have to get out to meet women." "It's not ethical," Beverly replies. How true, but why let such pedestrian concerns get in the way.

The rest of the movie involves kinky sex, with Niveau tied to the bedstead saying, "Doctor, you've cured me. I've never been a woman at all; I've only been a girl." Niveau then begins to detect that she's having sex with two different, albeit almost identical people (fig. 6). Beverly declares his love for her and vows to marry her. Elliott discourages the relationship, ostensibly for professional reasons, but really because together they are so much a complete being that he can't let anyone come between them. Beverly refuses to stop seeing Claire, the first outright disobedience of his "older brother" (by minutes). Niveau, who says her favorite bedtime reading is the *Physician's Desk Reference*, tells Beverly that she gets drugs from doctors who have a "high incidence of drug use" and who are very friendly with famous actresses. Parenthetically, this interesting role of physician supplier of drugs to Hollywood stars such as Elvis Presley, Marilyn Monroe, etc., is well known, but I've never seen it confronted in the medical literature. Those physicians more likely to gain attention, as I saw on Maryland's physician disciplinary board, are the ones who supply drugs in poorer neighborhoods.

There's a sidebar of research fraud thrown in as Elliott asks Beverly, "How's the paper coming, I trust you made us look good," in other words, "cooked the data." At the awards ceremony honoring their research,

FIGURE 6. *Dead Ringers*. Drs. Beverly and Elliot Mantle, the twin doctors from hell, played by Jeremy Irons, share sexual exploitation of their patients, including actress Claire Niveau (Genevieve Bujold).

Beverly, who has been experimenting with drugs and is by now a hope-
less drug addict and alcoholic, cries out that a fraud has been perpetrated,
just as Elliott is giving his acceptance speech. He then passes out. Elliott
tends to Beverly and cautions him that the whole scam could unravel
just as he's "finally been offered an associate professorship at the hospital with the next step being department chairman." "What about the
practice?" Beverly asks. Elliott responds that, "If I can fly around, teach,
and do research, you can find more time for the practice." Instead,
Beverly takes drugs and acts increasingly strange. Elliott tries to wean
him off drugs and, when he fails, decides to take drugs himself so that, as
twins, they can get off the stuff together.

   The most disturbing part of a thoroughly disturbing movie begins
with Beverly hurting a woman intentionally with a solid gold retractor
during a pelvic examination and then asking if it hurts during intercourse.
He then seeks out a sculptor to create some primitive gold instruments
that he has designed for pelvic surgery on "mutant women" (fig. 7). He
declares, "Patients are getting strange. They look all right on the outside, but their insides are deformed. Radical technology is required."
When he uses them in an operation, his associates finally get the message that this guy is way off the deep end. The movie ends in a blood
bath as the twins take drugs in sync and one cuts up the other and himself to achieve a separation never possible in life. After viewing this

FIGURE 7. *Dead Ringers*. Claire (Genevieve Bujold) inspects a weird golden
instrument her lover has invented to examine women's cervices.

film, no woman could be faulted for thinking twice before visiting her gynecologist. Sadly, there is a real-life case of an Ohio doctor who was charged with surgically mutilating many women over a twenty-year period without action being taken.[17]

Let's cleanse our minds by moving on to a much more entertaining depiction of what patients perceive as a common dark side of doctoring, namely, arrogance and insensitivity.

The Doctor (1991)

The film opens on a bloody surgical field. The stereo is blaring Frankie Valli's "Big Girls Don't Cry," followed by Jimmy Buffett's "Why Don't We Get Drunk and Screw"—a song that becomes meaningful later on. Surgeons sing; technicians dance. It's not exactly your typical operating room, but Dr. Jack (William Hurt) isn't your typical surgeon. He's a wisecracking, larger-than-life star. His technical brilliance is demonstrated by his race against the clock to repair a transected aorta in someone who jumped five stories in a suicide attempt. All the while, he makes jokes about needing to give the guy a course in suicide technique. His parting shot, as he exits after the tough part is over (in order to assist another surgeon) is, "Tell him, next time, ten floors minimum."

A quick perusal of Dr. Edward Rosenbaum's book *A Taste of My Own Medicine*,[18] on which the film was based, reveals that the author is a rheumatologist and that this is pure Hollywood. Nevertheless, there is more than a grain of truth in the film. Black humor is used in every difficult profession as a means of distancing oneself and lightening up otherwise tragic or distasteful jobs. Indeed, if you want to see a real-life incongruous radio overplay, look at *Please Let Me Die,* the videotape of Dax, the young man who sustained extensive third-degree burns in a Texas fire.[19] As Dax's burns are treated with astringent baths, the mind-numbing radio program drowns out his screams and pleas, serving as barrier for the caregivers who must carry out the treatment plan.

The problem with distancing is how and where to draw the line between self-preservation and callousness. Caregivers need an "invisible shield" (like the dental barrier GL-70 for those of you old enough to remember the Gleem® toothpaste commercial). It has to be thick enough so that we don't live and die with all of our patients, but thin enough so that we are sensitive to their hurts, needs, and feelings. It is a pretty tall order, actually, and one that none of us ever carries off 100 percent of the time, no matter how caring we are.

The Doctor is a medical counterpart of 1991's *Regarding Henry*, a film about a lawyer who becomes sensitive after his skull is bashed in;

only this film is better, since more time is taken to flesh out Dr. Jack's morbid state before the cure is applied. People (read patients) love the movie because it says something to doctors that they would like to say. Even so, many doctors are likely to consider the events to be overdrawn and Dr. Jack's Road-to-Damascus conversion hard to swallow.

Indeed, Dr. Jack is the soul of insensitivity. One patient, on the verge of tears, relays her husband's concern about whether the scar from her cracked sternum will ever heal over. "Tell him you look like a *Playboy* centerfold," says the doctor. Then, after a pause worthy of Jack Benny, he adds: "With the staples to prove it." "I know pain," Dr. Jack tells a patient. He's a doctor, after all. But being a doctor and really knowing pain are not equivalent. One young doctor told me that he used to tune out when people told him about their sciatica. Then he developed a herniated disk while helping someone move some furniture. This made pain radiating down the leg come alive for him and reminded him of those patients whose complaints he had tuned out.

On rounds, Dr. Jack cautions the residents against getting too involved with their patients. A surgeon's job is to cut—"get in, fix it, and get out." He would rather "cut straight and care less." Certainly, most patients would prefer that, too, if it were either/or. But is it? Most thoughtful surgeons would say no.[20,21] In fact, Murray (Mandy Patinkin), the ear, nose, and throat surgeon whom Dr. Jack goes to assist, is a caring type who talks soothingly to his unconscious patients—inviting ridicule from Dr. Jack and his merry band. When Dr. Jack develops hemoptysis (coughing up blood), he is dissuaded from seeing "the rabbi" as Murray is called; instead, he consults a woman surgeon who mirrors himself. Her method of informing Jack of his diagnosis of cancer has the hard edge of "truth dumping," wherein the truth is laid on the line no matter what.[22]

Dr. Jack's illness ushers him into the wonderful world of long waits for doctors, endless forms, failures of information systems to communicate with one another, mistaken preparation for laboratory tests (he receives a barium enema meant for someone else), anxiety-producing delays in receiving important laboratory results, and doctors dictating therapy (in his case radiotherapy rather than surgery). Later on, when his surgery is scheduled for the afternoon, Dr. Jack balks because the surgeon will be tired after working all morning. He knows about that from having operated when he was tired, but all of a sudden, it matters. While all of these instances ring true, it is hard to believe that Dr. Jack doesn't get the VIP treatment. He certainly wouldn't get a chart thrown at him by his surgeon when he terminates care with her. But if he got the VIP treatment, it would be a short picture. What is more believable is that he never noticed these things before they happened to him. It's easy to become inured to how everyday events affect others and just try to keep your head down and get through the day. Survival is the order of the day, especially in residency.

The movie illustrates the truth that the greatest assets of doctors in training are potentially their greatest liabilities. These are their good health and their good fortune. This applies to other professionals and business leaders as well. All are winners in the natural and social lotteries,[23] no matter how impoverished their beginnings. It's hard for "winners" to identify with "losers" unless one gets sick and becomes a "loser" oneself. The resultant hubris is nicely captured in the sentiment emblazoned on a sweatshirt in my school's bookstore: "It's hard to be humble at Hopkins." I'm sure other institutions could substitute their own names, albeit less alliteratively.

At the end, Dr. Jack does his part to inculcate humility and compassion by putting his trainees in Johnny coats, where the patient's bottom sticks out the back. While training at the Boston City Hospital in the 1960s, I used to fantasize that, had Winston Churchill had been admitted to the Peabody ward, standing there with his cigar in his mouth, a bare behind, and asking for a morning brandy, he would certainly have been taken for a "bum." Indeed, years ago a school in Australia routinely made students become patients and subjected them to everyday treatments to give them a foretaste of their own medicine.[24, 25] Since then, other schools and training programs have done the same.[26]

While the insensitivity theme is the most prominent, there are other subthemes with which some will resonate. One involves a well-portrayed patient with a brain tumor, June (Elizabeth Perkins), who catches Dr. Jack up from feeling too sorry for himself (fig. 8). She also helps him break down the barrier with which he has kept others, including his wife, at arm's length. Dr. Jack communicates by telephone with his sons and through his secretary with his wife Anne (Christine Lahti), whom he openly cheats on. One moviegoer told me he was most struck by how the man couldn't bring himself to love or to be loved and to confide in someone or to be helped, until the end. That's one by-product of building that invisible shield too thickly.

The usual clichés are there: the student talking about the "terminal in 1217," the doctored records, the lawyer jokes, the jabs at insurance companies for dictating practice. In a way, these clichés make the movie more true to life, because to become a cliché, something must be a truism. One of my favorites is Dr. Jack's "the system stinks" lecture, in

FIGURE 8. *The Doctor*. Dr. Jack McKee (William Hurt), an arrogant insensitive surgical whiz, is taught a lesson in humanity by a patient with a brain tumor (Elizabeth Perkins).

which he proclaims, "the insurance companies tell us what tests we can and cannot give." It's as if systems aren't composed of people just like Dr. Jack, oblivious to what's happening to the little people around them until they get caught up themselves. Too often those who are in a position to change the health care system spend enormous energy complaining rather than doing something about it. It's almost as if they believe that there is a *deus ex machina* manipulating our lives and for whom we must wait to solve our ills. Yes, the insurance companies are powerful, but standing up for what's best for patients is what good doctors do every day—despite the cost in time and excess paperwork. Furthermore, payors only got powerful because we in medicine let them.

William Hurt, as Dr. Jack, radiates the passionate coolness he brilliantly exhibited in *Gorky Park*. His concluding message is that patients feel "frightened, embarrassed and vulnerable. Most of all, they want to get better and they put their lives in our hands." After all is said and done, it's the right message, and one can even forgive the implausibility of Dr. Jack's transformation. As one surgeon said after seeing the movie, "If it makes one doctor a little bit more compassionate for even a few weeks, then it was worth it."

The next film is for those who believe in redemption. Complex, contrived, and studded with gratuitous bed rattling, it desperately wants to be terrible. Then, two-thirds of the way through, it is rescued by Anne Bancroft, who appears in an all too brief, but delightful, scene.

Malice (1993)

The movie opens innocently enough in a northwestern Massachusetts college town called Westerly (really Smith College in the town of Northampton). The bucolic serenity is suddenly shattered when a serial rapist strikes and a student is rushed near death to St. Agnes Hospital. Enter Alec Baldwin, who plays Dr. Jed Hill, a stereotypic Don Juan cardiothoracic surgeon with drop-dead looks. On the staff for only nine hours, he is pressed into service. When told he is losing the patient, he replies, "Don't bet the ranch on it." Supremely confident, he stanches the bleeding from a bruised liver, calls for epinephrine at the last moment, and saves the patient. Afterwards, in the dressing room, he introduces himself to his skeptical surgical associate, Dr. Matthew Robertson (David Bowe), and says: "Matthew, if you don't like my jokes, don't laugh. If you have a medical opinion, speak up loud. But if I ever hear you say we're going to lose a patient, I'll rip the fucking lungs out of your chest." Then, he reverts to being Dr. Charming.

When Hill is congratulated by an adoring nurse, he tells her to come to the midnight show, where he will levitate the next of kin. A hard drinker and smoker, he challenges a barroom buddy's statement about why he went into medicine and then smirkingly agrees when told that "it was to make a lot of money and to see a lot of naked women." In another particularly offensive barroom scene, after a student has been murdered, he reassures the person who found the body that he will get over it, by recounting his tasteless reaction to his cadaver in anatomy class.

The circumstances of the malpractice suit are somewhat hard to accept. These involve a ruptured ovarian cyst (which should have been diagnosed earlier), torsion of the other ovary, and Dr. Hill's abrupt departure during the delicate operation for an unrealistic and rather ludicrous presentation of options to the patient's spouse, ostensibly to obtain informed consent for a second oophorectomy. Just before exiting the operating room, he calls for a frozen section because the surface of the ovary is necrotic, presumably due to accidental torsion, but the pathologist on call is not on site. This absence surprised me and proves to be crucial to the story. I later learned, however, that I had missed the most egregious error. The coauthor of a gynecologic pathology text[27] told me that the request for a frozen section made no sense, because torsion would cause necrosis extending from inside out. If the ovary were necrotic on the surface, it would be necrotic throughout.

Another surprising development occurs during Hill's ex-chief's pretrial deposition. Dr. Hill, who has until then evinced remarkable control, answers a question against advice of counsel and acknowledges

that he not only believes he's God, but knows he's God. His chief
Dr. Kessler, played by George C. Scott, is left to defend his protegé,
saying that "the power to heal can be an enormous thing. It can be like
a drug." What a reversal from Scott's role as Dr. Bock in *The Hospital*
(chapter 8), where he was fed up with the system and everyone in it.
Bock would have had Jed Hill for lunch.

There are times when one's patience with the film is sorely tested.
For example, Bill Pullman plays Professor Andy Safian—a dean of students who is incredibly naive and dense (fig. 9). Either parents of
college-aged children should be scared that they will be counseled by
such incompetents or the dean's association should lodge a protest.
Another such point involves a bedroom scene showing Dr. Hill and one
of his many admirers. After three hours of sexual acrobatics, he lies on
the bed supine and exhausted. His bedmate says, "Hold on. I'm not
through with you yet." My wife and I wanted to say, "But we are."

Then, what did keep us in the theater besides the thirteen dollars
sunk capital? It was the excellent cinematography, the lovely musical
score, and a desire to see how the parallel story lines would be recon-
ciled. Though hard to believe at times, *Malice* effectively uses the "red
herring" technique of good mystery writers, such as Dorothy Sayers.[28]

FIGURE 9. *Malice*. Hotshot surgeon Dr. Jed Hill (Alec Baldwin) has a God
complex and college professor Andy Safian (Bill Pullman) is clearly overmatched,
or so it seems.

One is kept guessing, until at least halfway through, as to which of the stories is the distractor, what Hitchcock called the "MacGuffin."[29] There are also some funny lines involving a bartender's pain in the shoulder, the Boston Red Sox, and that scene stolen by Anne Bancroft. And one remaining issue—for those who haven't seen the movie and intend to, stop reading here!

Would a doctor conspire with a plaintiff to destroy his career, defraud his insurance company, and take the money and run? Anything is possible in this world, so I asked some members of the bar who specialize in malpractice law both in Maryland and North Carolina. Even the most flamboyant and successful practitioner with a thirty-year record encompassing some very celebrated cases had not heard of such a case. So, if it has happened, it was the perfect crime.

The next film portrays a good doctor gone bad, but who tries to go straight again. It's a 1990s version of the gangster/doctor genre (see appendix A).

Playing God (1997)

Playing God centers on Dr. Eugene Sands (David Duchovny) a junkie surgeon who, after being disbarred, is given an opportunity to be a doctor again, by working for a gangster as his staff surgeon (fig. 10). If you see it, check your sensibilities at the door. The film is a cartoonish knockoff of *Pulp Fiction*, written by a devotee of the Quentin Tarantino school of screenwritng. There's lots of hip, dispassionate dialogue; weird hitmen who engage in dumb, irrelevant conversations as they go about their business; and gallons of fake blood, with few people dying. It's also an homage to film noir with Duchovny's voice-over narration. As Spinal Tap band member, David St. Hubbins (Christopher Guest) says in *This is Spinal Tap*, "There's a fine line between clever and stupid, isn't there?" This film teeters on that line, falling periodically to one side or the other.

Duchovny, a Yale graduate and star of *X Files*, plays the anti-hero in a cerebral and downright philosophical mode ("pop" though it may be). Sands opens by telling us that, "You have to trust your instincts, what the Greeks called 'character.'" Actually, to the Greeks, "character" meant the distinctive qualities incised in us. Later, as he recounts the events leading from his glory days as a hotshot surgeon to his denouement, he says, "When a doctor sees a man, he doesn't see good or evil, only sick or healthy. I didn't pray to God for someone with exotic diseases, only something I hadn't seen before." It's him against the world, like "flying an F-14." So, Sands starts taking drugs to feel normal. He's

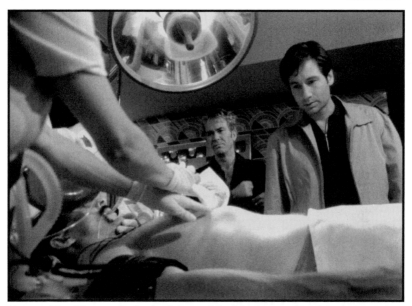

FIGURE 10. *Playing God*. A disbarred junkie doctor (David Duchovny) is recruited by a gangster to be his house surgeon.

"a doctor, not a drug addict," he tells himself. He can handle it. Then, he takes a few snorts before performing a laparotomy and, while in a drug-induced haze, he cuts the portal vein and a patient dies. Barred from his only true love, medicine, he lives the "high life" in a seedy apartment. While making a connection in a local bar, he is an innocent bystander to a mob hit. The ensuing scene is an homage to *Internes Can't Take Money* (chapter 3). Sands's doctor instincts kick in and, after a brief hesitation, he calls for hot water, clean towels, plastic (to fashion a makeshift drain), wire, tape, and a knife. After stabilizing the patient, he returns to his apartment and settles into his daily drug trip to Nirvana.

The victim's boss Raymond (Timothy Hutton) is so impressed by Sands's skill and resourcefulness that he sends his minions to give him five thousand dollars and to make him an offer he can't refuse. He can practice his trade again, make big bucks, and at the same time "discover his criminal side." It reminded me of a Sid Caesar skit on the 1950s television series, *Your Show of Shows*, in which he played a subway gum machine that started out wanting to serve mankind, but discovered a taste for larceny. At first, it simply takes the customer's penny without giving any gum, but later it gleefully sticks its tongue out at him as well. This brings the machine to the attention of Las Vegas gamblers, always on the lookout for new talent. The machine forsakes petty crime for grand theft and rises meteorically to be the top-grossing slot machine. Alas, it ends up in a broken heap of rubble after a police raid. Don't look for the same moralistic outcome here. That was then and this is now.

Hutton's portrayal of a sociopath has its moments, but is overwhelmed by overacting and a weak story line. He is also a philosophical sort as he spouts his version of the chaos theory, "A butterfly beats its wings in Tibet and a car loses a tire in Toronto" [Tibet's big in 1990s Hollywood]. There's the usual unscrupulous FBI man, who tries to recruit Sands to be an informer by offering to keep him supplied with drugs. On seeing Sands' apartment, he says, "This is squalor. You did go to med school, didn't you?" Sands replies, "What? Are you going to lock me up for not living up to my potential?" On learning that Raymond's moll, Claire (Angelina Jolie) is an FBI plant, he reluctantly agrees to cooperate. At one point, Claire and he escape to his opulent childhood home, where we learn that Sands' mother was a doctor and that "when you come from a long line of doctors, it's not being a doctor that counts, but being THE DOCTOR." At his parents' home, he goes "cold turkey," which reminds us that there is a serious problem being trivialized, namely, alcohol and substance abuse, which is estimated to affect about 10 percent of doctors.

Finally, it is the series of ludicrous surgeries that may be the most interesting aspect of this film. In one scene in a biker bar, Sands arranges a makeshift operation on a pool table. A biker takes forceps out of boiling water and hands Sands a stethoscope and a scalpel. As Sands proceeds to take a bullet out of a man's chest, he asks another biker to keep time with his foot in synchrony with the heartbeat. Sands becomes alarmed when the foot-tapping stops, only to learn that the man's heart is still beating, but that it was just time for another beer.

This portrayal of a flawed doctor is much less offensive than *Dead Ringers*; furthermore, he tries to redeem himself by helping people. In addition, the filmmaker has a healthy, rather than a sick, sense of humor. Those who want to learn more about physician criminals in the annals of medicine can consult Eckert's article[30] and for the most brutal of them all, Lifton's book, *The Nazi Doctors*.[31] We'll move on to films where institutions were no longer benign, but evil—or at the very least inept—and impersonal enemies of the forces of good.

NOTES

1. Salwak D. A.J. Cronin. Boston: Twayne Publishers, 1985.
2. Cronin AJ. Hatter's Castle. Boston: Little, Brown & Co, 1931.
3. Cronin AJ. Adventures in Two Worlds. New York: McGraw-Hill, 1952.
4. Cronin AJ. The Citadel. Boston: Little, Brown and Co, 1937.
5. Nowlan RA, Nowlan GW, eds. "We'll Always Have Paris": The Definitive Guide to Great Lines from the Movies. New York: Harper Collins, 1995.
6. Dr. A. J. Cronin on Doctors. London Times, November 10, 1937, p 11, as cited in D. Salwak. A.J. Cronin. Boston: Twayne Publishers, 1985, p 64.
7. Cunningham R III, Cunningham R Jr. The Blues: A History of the Blue Cross and Blue Shield System. De Kalb, IL: Northern Illinois Press, 1997.
8. Editorial. The Citadel. JAMA 1937; 109: 956–957.
9. Book Chatter. Jacksonville (Fla.) Times-Union. September 26, 1937, p. 3, as cited in D. Salwak. A.J. Cronin. Boston: Twayne Publishers, 1985, p. 66.
10. Bellamann H. Kings Row. New York: Simon & Schuster, 1944.
11. Reagan R with Hubler RG. Where's the Rest of Me?: The Autobiography of Ronald Reagan. New York: Karz Publishers, 1981.
12. Henley WE. Invictus. In: The Pocket Book of Verse: Great English and American poems, ed. ME Speare. New York: Washington Square Press, 1940, p 278–279.
13. Kenny E with Ostenso M. And They Shall Walk: The Life Story of Sister Elizabeth Kenny. London: R. Hale, 1951.
14. Cohn V. Sister Kenny: The Woman Who Challenged Doctors. Minneapolis: University of Minnesota Press, 1975.
15. Carpenter CCJ, Mondal A, Sack RB, Mitra PP, Dans PE, Wells SA, Hinman EJ, Chaudhuri RN. Clinical studies in Asiatic cholera, II, III, and IV. Bull Johns Hopkins Hosp 1966; 118: 174–229.
16. Wood B and Geasland J. Twins. New York: Signet New American Library, 1977.
17. Hopkins E. Doctor of Love. Health; Nov/Dec, 1990.
18. Rosenbaum EE. A Taste of My Own Medicine: When the Doctor Is the Patient. New York: Random House, 1988.
19. White RB. "Please Let Me Die": The Wish of a Blind, Severely Maimed Patient, videotape. University of Texas Medical Branch at Galveston, 1974.
20. Selzer R. Mortal lessons: Notes on the Art of Surgery. New York: Simon & Schuster, 1976.
21. Carson BS and Murphy CB. Gifted Hands. Grand Rapids, Michigan: Zondervan Books, 1990.
22. Cousins N. A layman looks at truth telling in medicine. JAMA 1980; 244: 1929–1930.
23. Beauchamp TL and Childress JF. The Principle of Justice. In: Principles of Biomedical Ethics, 3rd ed, New York: Oxford University Press, 1989; pp 272–275.
24. Editorial. Students as patients. Lancet 1974; 2, 1433.
25. Magarey C, Cox K, Hunt D, et al. Learning by experience: A student residential workshop in hospital. Med J Aust 1975; 2: 516–518.
26. Franklin D and Griffin K. Doctors as patients: How does it feel? Health 1991; 5(6):14.
27. Gompel C and Silverberg, SG. Pathology in Gynecology and Obstetrics, 4th ed. Philadelphia: J.B. Lippincott Co, 1994.
28. Sayers D. The Five Red Herrings (1931). New York: Harper, Perennial, 1993.
29. Truffaut F and Scott HG. Hitchcock. New York: Simon and Schuster, 1985, p. 138.
30. Eckert WG. Physician crimes and criminals. Am J Forensic Med and Path 1982; 3: 221–230.
31. Lifton RJ. The Nazi Doctors: Medical Killing and the Psychology of Genocide. New York: Basic Books, 1986.

8

The Institutions Turn Evil

Numerous medical films have pictured the individual in an often lonely battle with powerful societal forces. At first, the enemy was represented by the entrenched forces within the profession such as medical societies; from the 1960s on, institutions of all types became the villains. Whereas earlier films such as *The Citadel* and *Sister Kenny* (covered in the previous chapter) conveyed some sense that the nobility of individuals might carry the day, these later films are filled with a cynicism and despair that mirrors their times. Let's start with *M*A*S*H*, one of the most savage indictments of institutions whose "good guys" make no pretense that they can make a difference. Director Robert Altman used novel cinematographic techniques that have been widely emulated in film and television. They included overlapping dialogue, jump-cutting scenes, eschewing straight ahead narrative flow, and a cool detachment that conveyed a sense of cynicism and ennui in the midst of chaos and senselessness. *M*A*S*H*'s ability to capture the era's mood made it one of the most influential films of all time; yet, as I will discuss, it's an example of why it is good to remeasure a film after a generation or two has passed.

M*A*S*H (1970)

The title stands for Mobile Army Surgical Hospital, but this anti-institutional, black comedy has very little to do with medicine. Although set in Korea two decades earlier, it is really an angry anti-Vietnam war parody. Its main targets are the military, the government, and organized religion, especially Christianity (see chapter 9). Its central characters' main preoccupations, when not tending to mangled bodies, are sex and alcohol. The lyrics from its catchy theme song, ("Suicide is Painless, it brings on many changes and I can take or leave it if I please") are rather morbid and confusing. The Oscar Award-winning screenplay by

Ring Lardner, Jr., was based on a novel by Richard Hooker (a doctor's pseudonym).[1] The film opens with a helicopter bringing in a bloodied soldier. Interspersed throughout are operating room scenes full of blood, gore, and sawed-off limbs. We never get any sense of the patients as persons, nor are they ever followed out of the operating room, except to die. They are simply raw meat and that's the point: to convey the horrors of war and the stupidity of the military at a time when many of us were protesting at being misled by our leaders about a major American catastrophe. It is meant to be cruel and angry, emotions that are perfectly conveyed by those masters of cinematic cynicism, Donald Sutherland and Elliott Gould. The outlandish scenes of sex and practical jokes were unfamiliar to audiences used to movies made before the jettisoning of the Hays production code in 1967.[2] The tenor of the times made it a sensation. Interestingly enough, the Oscar was won by *Patton*, a more conventional war movie that, unlike *M*A*S*H*, has retained its power because it more closely approximates the tenor and times it purports to represent, as well as having an outstanding performance by George C. Scott.

Hawkeye Pierce (Sutherland) is an unremitting cynic and skirtchaser whose philosophy is that vows of fidelity are what you make "when you're with someone, not when you're seven thousand miles away." Major Frank Burns (Duvall) is a thoroughgoing, self-righteous Christian Pharisaic fraud, without any redeeming attributes. Trapper John McIntyre (Gould) is interested only in cutting, sex, alcohol, and winning the bet on a football game, although he does have one moment when he expresses humanity for an aide who is devastated by Burns's callousness. Captain Duke Forrest (Tom Skerritt) is a stereotypic redneck surgeon who expresses concern when a Black neurosurgeon, Oliver Harmon Jones (Spearchucker), played by Fred "The Hammer" Williamson, an ex-NFL star, is recruited to help them win a football game. The priest, "Dago Red," is a simple-minded pious ninny. His revelation of a confessional secret leads Hawkeye to set up a "Last Supper" scene, followed by the wild night of sex for the temporarily impotent dentist called "Painless." He is also referred to as the "Polish penis," because he is reputed to have "the biggest equipment in the U. S. Army" which other men ogle as does a nurse, Lieutenant Hot Dish (Jo Ann Pflug) who also has the hots for Hawkeye. The commanding officer, Colonel Blake, is married but is carrying on an affair with a nurse. They are in bed when the nursing director, Major Houlihan (Sally Kellerman), runs in to complain that the merry pranksters, Hawkeye and Trapper, have pulled the shower tent down around her. Later, her bout of sex with Frank, who professes to be happily married, is broadcast to the whole camp and leads to Frank being taken away in a straitjacket.

Trapper and Hawkeye take their golf clubs to Japan where, as the reigning surgical hotshots, they are called to operate on a Congressman's son. They look slovenly, bulldoze their way arrogantly into the hospital, and treat every regular Army nurse and doctor as incompetents. They finish their successful operation by teetime with plenty to spare for some recreational sex and alcohol. All the while, there are clever little throw-away lines that belittle evangelists who send hymnals to the front and movie programmers who show World War II anti-venereal disease films. During a particularly bloody scene, we are told that "the AMA has just declared marijuana a dangerous drug despite claims by other doctors that it is no more dangerous than alcohol." Later we see the football players dragging on weed. Hawkeye distributes some of his stash of stolen amphetamines to his Korean aide so that he can fail his army induction physical, but the Korean examining doctor is wise to the trick. One doctor moonlights at a "New Era" hospital and whorehouse, the proceeds of which presumably help pay for the care of the poor. After a vicious and relatively stupid football game featuring other ex-National Football Leaguers like Fran Tarkenton, the film closes with the hypo-critical Frank Burns joining Hawkeye to return to the States to his "loving wife and family" and leaving his mistress, Hot Lips Houlihan, behind. The movie's closing words are: "Follow the zany antics of our combat surgeons as they stitch their way along the front lines, operating, as bombs and bullets are bursting around them, snatching laughs and love between amputations and penicillin."

A favorite of mine at the time, the film, when viewed twenty-five years later, seems a distillate of angry and sadistic humor. The nation probably needed the film as a lightning rod to vent our frustrations and to channel the rage and iconoclasm that was inspired not just by the duplicity of our leaders who were waging the Vietnam War, but by the assassinations and the long overdue civil rights movement. Without that context and with the general understanding of the price our society paid for the "sex, drugs, and rock and roll" culture that prevailed at the time, the film seems to be as bereft of a port as *The Flying Dutchman*.

It's interesting to contrast *M*A*S*H* with its antithesis, *The Story of Dr. Wassell*, a film also made at the height of a war. Similarly out-dated, this jingoistic 1944 film is extravagantly introduced by Cecil B. De Mille himself and stars Gary Cooper. Based on a book[3] by

James Hilton of *Goodbye Mr. Chips*[4] and *Lost Horizon*[5] fame, it is also difficult to watch without the war raging around us. However, it may deserve more of our attention and respect than *M*A*S*H*, in that it details actual heroism. When the Japanese invaded Java, Doctor Croydon Wassell refused to get on the last boat out. Instead, he stayed to care for the seriously wounded men who could not be transported and then was able to evacuate nine men successfully to Australia.

Interestingly, the *MASH* television series started out more faithful to the movie. If it had retained the film's acerbic tenor and celebration of promiscuity,[6] it probably would have never survived year two. Writer Larry Gelbart and the cast transformed, softened, and humanized the approach, dropping its anti-religious message, while retaining its anti-war and anti-military theme. More importantly, the patients and even the staff became human beings with life stories, not simply vehicles for message deliveries. Alan Alda's sensitive Hawkeye remained a Lothario, but his humor became gentler and sometimes even self-directed, making him a far cry from Donald Sutherland's more savage, know-it-all portrayal. Alda's portrayal of a doctor was so convincing that a Columbia Medical School class asked him to be their commencement speaker.

The original television Trapper John and Colonel Blake, womanizers like their counterparts in the movie, left the show for greener pastures that did not materialize. They were replaced by two class actors, Mike Farrell and Harry Morgan, who portrayed officers who were more thoughtful and even faithful to their wives. Father Mulcahy was transformed from a pious jerk to a lovable and wise, though still simple, character. Frank Burns remained a hypocrite and a jerk, but he, not his religiosity, became the foil for humor. Burns was later replaced by another surgeon played by David Ogden Stiers in a much less one-dimensional manner. Klinger's role was expanded from a walk-on in one scene to a hilarious ensemble character. Interestingly, Radar O'Reilly (Gary Burghoff), the only carry-over actor from the movie, retained the same persona. He was sympathetic in both, but a much more important character in the television version. Finally, the greatest testimonial to that series is not just that it lasted twelve seasons or that an estimated 125 million Americans tuned in to the final episode, but that, through syndication, it is continuously being shown somewhere in the world.

Let's turn to one of the best of the anti-institutional films, *The Hospital*. It stars George C. Scott as a battered, seedy Quixote who is trying to take care of patients and train residents against all odds in an inner-city hospital meant to represent Bellevue Hospital in New York.

The Hospital (1971)

The Hospital is appropriately called the blackest of black comedies. Paddy Chayefsky, who won a well-deserved Oscar for the screenplay, fires his cannonades across the political spectrum and takes no prisoners. It starts with a patient named Guernsey being admitted from a nursing home to Manhattan Medical Center, an inner city hospital, with a diagnosis of angina pectoris. The narrator notes that "it's axiomatic that nursing home doctors are always wrong. The intern accepted the diagnosis and administered morphine." Unfortunately, the diagnosis was emphysema and when the patient developed shortness of breath, he was treated for pulmonary edema, given digitalis, developed CO_2 narcosis and died." The narrator goes on to say, "I mention this to tell you how a bed in Room 806 became available." The intern, Doctor Schaefer (Lenny Baker), "who has a good thing going with a hematology technician," seizes on the empty bed for their tryst, which has usually taken place in wheelchairs, in the morgue, or in the pantry. The next morning, the floor nurse finds Schaefer dead, with an intravenous drip hooked up. She reports his death to the other nurse who is unbelieving, but is assured that the dead man is not Guernsey, but "our Doctor Schaefer who is always grabbing everybody's ass."

The nursing director calls medical director Dr. Herbert Bock (George C. Scott), who has passed out in a drab hotel room, in front of a television with a rolling picture, with a bottle of vodka beside him. Answering the phone sluggishly, he lights up a cigarette and says, "Schaefer, the stud with the glasses who fancies all the nurses." He returns to the hospital which is being picketed by people carrying a sign saying, "People Si, Doctors No." As he approaches the hospital, Bock meets the hospital administrator, John Sunstrom (Stephen Elliott), who expresses concern that Bock sounds suicidal and has been sloughing off on his rounds. Bock replies that he just left his wife after twenty-four years and has moved to a hotel.

When Bock learns about the circumstances surrounding Schaefer's death, he comments sarcastically that the snafu has a "certain splendor." It turns out that the per diem nurse, thinking the passed-out Schaefer was Guernsey, plugged in an intravenous drip and then the night nurse gave him sparine which sedated him but shouldn't have killed him. Mrs. Christie, the nursing director played by the underrated Nancy Marchand (see 1995 *Sabrina*), says, "No one knew what Guernsey looked like." Bock says, "We have an excessive use of float nurses. You can't find the same nurse on a floor two days in a row," and adds, "Where did you train your nurses, Mrs. Christie? Dachau?"

The hospital is in chaos: three microscopes have been stolen; lab slips are late; and ambulance cases are overloading the emergency room. Bock seeks out the chief psychiatrist and confides that he is thinking about committing suicide. He recounts how he was the pride and joy of his middle-class parents. "'My son, the, doctor,' you know. Top of my class, scholarship to Harvard. Brilliant, eccentric. I was terrified of women, clumsy at sports....I left my wife twelve times....She left me a dozen times. We stuck together—obvious sadomasochistic dependency. My home was hell. We've got a twenty-three-year-old boy. I threw him out of the house last year. Shaggy-haired Maoist! I don't know where he is—presumably building bombs in basements as an expression of his universal brotherhood. We've got a seventeen-year-old daughter who's had two abortions in two years. Got arrested last week at a rock festival for pushing drugs. They let her go. A typical affluent American family. I don't mean to be facile about this. I blame myself for those two useless young people. I never exercised parental authority. I'm no good at that." He confesses that he doesn't want his death to appear to be a suicide because his family will lose the insurance money, and he leaves.

Cut to the street where protesters are carrying signs reading "This hospital is an accredited member of the American Murder Association." It should be the Joint Commission on Accreditation of Hospitals, but the line does show the American Medical Association's low public esteem. The scene shifts to someone bludgeoning a laboratory pathologist. He is brought to the emergency room and left to wait for hours. Finally, an officious clerk, concerned about getting the doctor's insurance information for billing purposes, chastises the one who filled out the emergency room intake form, saying, "I can't make out these scribbles; I have to bill these people." She goes to interview the patient and discovers that the pathologist is dead.

Meanwhile, Bock is on rounds discussing a patient with fever of unknown origin that turns out to be tuberculosis of the liver which he says is "reportable" (fig. 1). When a student answers his questions correctly, he tells him to make an appointment to discuss interning there. At the next bedside, Mr. Drummond's (Barnard Hughes), he is told, "This is Dr. Biegelman's case." He responds, "Never mind the professional ethics," and the resident recounts the hospital course: "He's a fifty-six-year-old man admitted in good health for a check-up. Because of protein in the urine, a post-grad fellow conned the patient for a biopsy for a research protocol. He nicked a vessel and the patient went

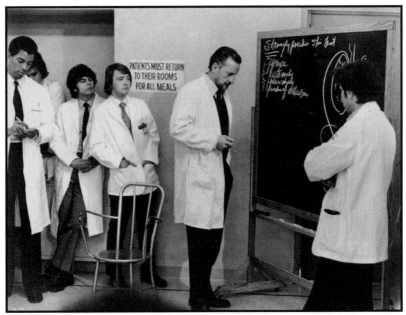

FIGURE 1. *The Hospital.* Dr. Bock (George C. Scott), conducting chief-of-service rounds, lists the major findings in a patient with fever of unknown origin.

into shock. He was referred to Dr. Welbeck (Richard Dysart)." "That barber?" Bock asks. The resident goes on, "Welbeck turned up half-stoned and ordered an IVP. He didn't check him for allergies and the patient developed tubular necrosis, renal shutdown, had a kidney removed, underwent dialysis, and lapsed into coma." Bock summarizes the case, "A patient comes in in perfect health and we manage in one week to chop out one kidney, damage another, reduce him to coma, and damn near kill him."

He confides his despair to a colleague who tells him, "You're a doctor. You're a healer. You're a chief of medicine at one of the great hospitals of the world. You're a necessary person. Your life is meaningful." He replies, "The entire machinery of modern medicine conspired to destroy one lousy patient. How can I sustain my feeling of meaningfulness in the face of it." He calls the chief of surgery: "I thought you were going to cut off all privileges to that assassin Welbeck." Later that evening with a storm raging, Bock is called to Drummond's bedside where a special "Apache ceremony" is being performed.

There Bock meets Drummond's daughter Barbara (Diana Rigg), who tells him that the shaman gets his power from the thunder and that it is imperative that he finish while the storm is raging. Bock asks her,

"You don't really believe all that mumbo-jumbo is going to cure him?
She says, "On the other hand, it won't kill him." She goes on to tell him,
"My father was a very successful doctor in Boston. Member of the
Harvard medical faculty. He was a widower. I was his only child. Not
an especially religious man. A sober Methodist. One evening about
seven years ago, he attended a Pentecostal service in the Harvard common room and began speaking in tongues. I was at the time twenty
years old, having my obligatory affair with a minority, in this case, a
Hopi Indian, a postgraduate fellow at Harvard doing his doctorate in
aboriginal languages....He recognized that father was speaking an obscure Apache dialect....Father closed his Beacon Hill practice and set
out for Mexico. I entered nursing school. I was hitting the acid pretty
regularly. I masturbated a great deal. One day, I walked to work naked,
shouting obscenities. Before they locked me up, I joined him in the
Sierra Madre mountains. I watch over father who is as mad as a hatter."
She then comes on to him, confessing that she has a thing for middle-
aged men.

Bock responds: "Your generation is more hung up on sex than the
Victorians. My son preached universal love and despised everyone. He
had a blanket contempt for the middle class....He didn't attend my
mother's funeral. He felt the chapel service was a hypocrisy. His generation didn't live with lies. Everybody lives with lies. So I grabbed him
by the neck and threw him out...He shrieked at me: 'You old fink; you
can't even get it up any more. That was it, you see. It wasn't racism, the
oppressed poor, the war in Vietnam. No, the ultimate societal sickness
was a limp dingus." He goes on to tell her that he lusts for something
more permanent than an erection ("That's what medicine was to me")
and how at thirty-four, he presented a paper that pioneered the whole
field of immunology, but he's lost his desire for work, "my reason for
being, a more primal passion than sex...the only thing I ever truly loved."
He concludes by decrying the conflict between technologic advances
and prevention, "We can do transplants, manufacture genes, produce
births ectogenetically, practically clone people like carrots, and half the
kids in this ghetto haven't been inoculated against polio. We have established the most enormous medical entity ever conceived and people are
sicker than ever. We cure nothing." In his despair, he chases her away
and prepares to inject himself with 40 milliequivalents of potassium.
Barbara returns, stops him, and they have sex. In the morning she tells
him he ravished her three times, screaming about his renewed power.
She tells him that he gets his power from the bears and that she wants
him to come to Mexico, where he can be a healer again and "because I

love you and I want children." He answers, "I raped you in a suicidal rage. How did we get to love and children? You're certifiable." Still, he asks her to stay, saying, "I do a lot of healing right here in Manhattan. I don't have to go to Mexico. I'm a teacher. I send out eighty doctors a year into the world." Barbara, who has decided to sign her father out of the hospital, gives Bock an hour to decide if he will go or stay.

Cut to the street where the protesters are taking over the Drug Rehabilitation Center, because the Hospital didn't find housing for four hundred people as it had promised. Sunstrom remarks, "the cockamamie activists are showboating for the TV cameras," and agrees to meet with the protesters in the board room. There, they accuse the medical board of "racism," "genocide by abortion and birth control," and "imperialistic extension of the medical establishment."

Meanwhile, a nurse is knocked out by the unseen avenger and given another patient's bracelet. Cut to the operating room where a patient in for a routine hysterectomy loses pressure and pulse. As they do unsuccessful resuscitation, the nurse says to the surgeon, "I don't think this is your patient." It turns out to be the nurse. The surgeon screams, "I've been chopping out three uteruses a day for twenty years. Is it too much to ask for you people to bring me the right goddamned uterus? I've already got one malpractice suit pending and I'm not taking the rap for this."

Bock learns that Drummond is not in coma; indeed, he was actually responsible for the deaths of the two doctors and the nurse as retribution for their involvement in the death of Guernsey who was "relentlessly subjected to the wonders of modern medicine and died." Drummond says, "They all died by their own hands—ritual deaths of their own institution. The hospital was to do all the killing for me. All I need do was arrange for the doctors to become patients in their own hospital. Prompt treatment would have saved the doctor in the ER, but he was forgotten to death. Mislaid like the chest pains, scalp lacerations, etc...the whole wounded madhouse of our times."

After Drummond switched the patient's identification bracelet, the nurse's sedated body was left lying around in the x-ray department for five hours where "it wouldn't seem unusual." "She was to die of the great American plague, vestigial identity." He adds facetiously, "I went to bed and rang for my nurse to assure one hour of uninterrupted privacy." Bock tells Barbara, "Let's get out of here before the police put us all in Rockland State" (a psychiatric hospital north of New York City). Still, he takes some time to ream out Welbeck, the surgeon who has just finished lecturing the residents on the benefits of incorporating, "Eight days ago you showed up half-stoned for a simple nephrectomy, botched it, put the patient in failure, and damned near killed him. Then, pausing only to send in your bill, you flew off on the wings of man to the sun in Montego Bay. This is the third time we've had to patch up one of your patients. The other two died. You're greedy, unfeeling, inept, indifferent, self-inflating, and unconscionably profitable. Besides that, I've got nothing against you; I'm sure you play a hell of a game of golf." Welbeck responds that he talks big "for a guy who makes a lousy forty or fifty grand a year."

Later, Welbeck learns that his partner, an eminent orthopedic surgeon, is "a miserable thief" who has wiped him out. He has a cardiac arrest and Bock begins cardiopulmonary resuscitation and then walks out in the middle of the chaos that follows (fig. 2). As he leaves, we see protesters storming the hospital and one asking "where's the TV camera?" A sign says, "Cure poverty. Heal the Poor." A protester confronts Sunstrom, saying, "I indict this hospital for the criminal neglect of the neighborhood in which it is situated." He replies, "Take it over. I'm finished. I quit. You run it. You pay the bills. You fight the city. You

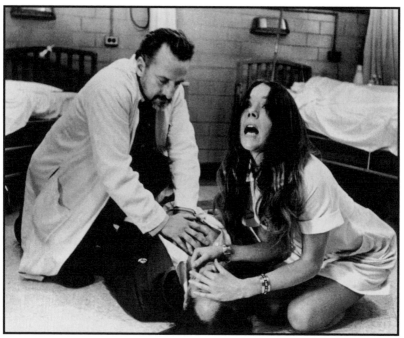

FIGURE 2. *The Hospital.* Incompetent surgeon Dr. Welbeck (Richard Dysart) has a heart attack after learning that the Securities Exchange Commission has suspended trading on his stock. Dr. Bock (George C. Scott) and his girl friend Barbara Drummond (Diana Rigg) attempt cardiopulmonary resuscitation.

fight the state. You fight the unions. You fight the community. I quit."
Bock sends Barbara and her father to the airport. His reasoning is that
"if I married anything, it's this hospital. It's been my whole life. I'm
middle class and for us love doesn't triumph over all, responsibility does."
He joins the administrator and says, "The hospital's coming apart. I
can't walk out on it. Someone's got to be responsible." As they go back
in, Sunstrom says, "It's like pissing in the wind. Right, huh?"

This is an example of a film that was good in its time and has gotten better with age. Along with *The Citadel*, *No Way Out*, *Not As a
Stranger*, *The Last Angry Man*, and *The Doctor*, it can serve as an excellent way to teach medical history and sociology. Chayefsky, a keen social
observer, captures the late 1960s and early 1970s without any "baby-
boomer" romance. He depicts the verbal opportunists who often came
from advantaged backgrounds that allowed them to go to college and to
have considerable leisure time. For them, protests were a form of theater and they made sure the television cameras were present before they
demonstrated. Also satirized in Tom Wolfe's *Radical Chic & Mau-
Mauing the Flak-Catchers*,[7] they stood in marked contrast to leaders such
as Cesar Chavez and Martin Luther King whose protests came from
their hearts and souls; they had paid their dues and peacefully and powerfully had made their points, often with considerable risk to themselves.
I got to see some of them in action while helping to establish a migrant
health clinic in Colorado.[8] I also saw the fascination with Native American rituals and mind-altering drugs whose celebration made Carlos
Castaneda a 1970s cult icon.[9] Despite his claims that what he had set
down was reality, Castaneda's invention and reinvention of himself has
led many to believe that it was phantasmagorical fiction.

The Hospital is especially rich in what it tells us about medical care;
but sadly, the medical profession missed its underlying truths when we
physicians had a chance to recapture the moral high ground. Chayefsky,
who savaged the media for the way it manipulated stories for ratings
and profits in *Network*, shows somewhat exaggeratedly what was happening during the marked technologic transformation that led to the
overburdening and understaffing of urban hospitals dedicated to serving the poor. It's all there: the long waits (that we will see again in
Veterans Administration hospitals in *Article 99*); the incorrect lab results; the short staffing; the hiring of less well-trained nurses; the
incompetent and greedy attending physician who drops in for a few
surgeries, but has his mind elsewhere; the chasing of reimbursement;
and the delayed involvement in strengthening the changing communities surrounding the medical centers. The hero is a depressed, burned-out

alcoholic ex-superstar academic with a broken marriage and messed-up kids. Taking care of the poor and training good doctors were for him better than sex. They were what he lived for and now everything is collapsing around him. This scenario is quite relevant today when the understaffing and financial woes that plagued inner city municipal hospitals have spread to academic medical centers generally.[10] In some respects, so is the message to medical directors and hospital administrators. Bock and his administrative counterpart are both inclined to cut and run, but decide to overcome the alien forces or go down fighting. In short, in a rather perverse way, this black comedy is uplifting.

One Flew Over the Cuckoo's Nest (1975)

Again, in contrast to *M*A*S*H*, this brilliant anti-institutional classic, based on Ken Kesey's novel, *One Flew Over the Cuckoo's Nest*,[11] retains the power and relevance that made it the first film since *It Happened One Night* in 1934 to win all five major Oscars for Best Picture, Actor, Actress, Director, and Screenplay. Jack Nicholson is outstanding as R. P. McMurphy, a maverick who refuses to accept society's constraints or to play by the rules (fig. 3). Behind him are five arrests for assault and a conviction for statutory rape with a "fifteen-year-old going on thirty-two." He is sent from the prison work farm to a mental institution for evaluation because of belligerence, laziness, and "talking when unauthorized." The chief psychiatrist, a rather pleasant nebbish, realizes that

FIGURE 3. *One Flew Over the Cuckoo's Nest.* Randle McMurphy (Jack Nicholson) is committed to a mental hospital for being a troublemaker.

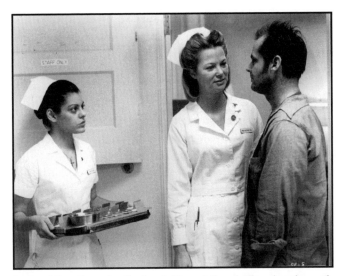

FIGURE 4. *One Flew Over the Cuckoo's Nest*. After challenging the authority of Nurse Ratched (Louise Fletcher), the effervescent McMurphy is turned into a complete zombie.

McMurphy is not mentally ill, but doesn't have the gumption to buck the system and send him back to the prison farm. Instead, McMurphy remains on a ward where the inmates are cowed by a controlling, sadistic nurse. Louise Fletcher gives one of the screen's quintessential performances as Nurse Ratched, an unusual cinematic example of a nurse as villain.

McMurphy and Ratched engage in a battle of wills that turns out to be an unfair fight because Ratched has the power of the institution behind her and he is "too clever by half." McMurphy inspires the inmates to challenge authority and stand up for their rights. He tells one that he's "no crazier than the average asshole walking around on the street." He is stunned to learn that most of the patients are "voluntary" and could walk out anytime, but choose not to do so. McMurphy manages to win a few Pyrrhic victories, such as when he leads an escape from the institution for a fishing trip and when he smuggles women and booze onto the ward.

Nurse Ratched argues against discharging him, realizing that this subversive is "dangerous but not crazy." After all, one can't challenge "The Rules" and get away with it. The ending, in which Ratched manages to gain control over the lobotomized McMurphy, seems foreordained (fig. 4). Unlike *The Hospital*, we get no sense that the individual has even a ghost of a chance against the system. Nonetheless, one

Native American patient manages to survive by fleeing to Canada, another reminder of the sense of futility and the attractiveness of Canada as a destination for escape during the Vietnam war. In the 1920s, it would have been Paris.

The Verdict (1982)

The Verdict is especially outstanding because of Paul Newman's performance as Frank Galvin, a down-and-out alcoholic lawyer who spends his mornings drinking beer and playing pinball. He begins his afternoons by swallowing an egg in his beer and freshening his breath before going to his secretary-less office where he continues to drink while waiting for nothing to happen. Still, he will be this film's Don Quixote, thanks to his former Boston College law school teacher Mickey Morrissey (played with great humanity by Jack Warden) who has thrown a great case his way.

Galvin's adversaries are the Archdiocese of Boston, St. Catherine Labouré Hospital and two well-known doctors, including Dr. Towler (Wesley Addy), the author of the standard anesthesia text. Morrissey says, "all these guys are God; they walk on water." The case involves a young healthy woman who goes into a hospital to deliver her third child, is given a general anesthetic, vomits, arrests, and suffers irreversible brain damage due to delayed resuscitation. Her baby dies and her husband leaves town with their two children. The incident occurred four years before and Galvin has had the case for a year and a half, but he has not contacted the plaintiffs, the woman's sister and brother-in-law. They have to seek him out when they learn from the Archdiocese that the case is going to trial in a week. Their pastor has told them, "It was God's will" and they are ready to settle because they want to pay the fifty thousand dollars required to get perpetual care for their sister before they leave Boston and its bad memories.

Frank is finally "Galvinized" into action. He contacts his medical expert Doctor Gruber, who tells him that it was the doctors' fault and that he is ready to testify to keep the "bozos out of medicine" and "to do the right thing." Galvin, who was unjustly accused of jury-tampering and whose career and marriage were destroyed, is clearly overmatched. He has lost his only four cases in the past year and a half. Arrayed against him is the slickest law firm this side of Philadelphia, led by Ed Concannon played with just the right unctuousness and malice by James Mason. After visiting the patient to take Polaroids in order to position the case for a settlement, her pathetic appearance convinces

FIGURE 5. *The Verdict*. Down-and-out lawyer Frank Galvin (Paul Newman) questions his expert witness Dr. Thompson (Joe Seneca) during a malpractice case.

Galvin to go to trial. Buoyed by the doctor's statement, he turns down 210 thousand dollars (of which he would get a third) without consulting the plaintiffs.

Things start to go south as Concannon orchestrates a public relations campaign about the greatness of the hospital and moves to sabotage Galvin's defense. Dr. Gruber, Galvin's expert witness, mysteriously leaves for a Caribbean vacation. The Judge refuses a continuance until he returns and the insurance company refuses the distraught Galvin's request to reinstate its settlement offer. On short notice, Galvin calls on his backup medical expert Dr. Thompson (Joe Seneca), a seventy-four-year-old non-board certified Black doctor who testifies regularly in malpractice cases and does not know the meaning of "code blue" (fig. 5).

The key to the case turns out to be the missing admitting nurse who took the history about when the patient had last eaten. It makes a big difference whether it was one hour before general anesthesia, as the plaintiffs maintain, or nine hours before, as the chart reads). Galvin tells his partner, "Call the AMA. Tell them you're a doctor and need to find a nurse." I'm inclined to think that calling the ANA, the American Nursing Association, would make more sense, but the AMA is clearly the organization on screenwriters' minds. He then uses a more clever though illegal method, tampering with the U.S. mail, to find her.

She agrees to testify and brings a copy of the original form and says, "Doctor Towler told me he had had five difficult deliveries in a row and that he had never looked at the admittance form. He told me to change the one to a nine or he'd have me fired. I would never work again as a nurse. Who were these men? All I wanted to be was a nurse." The judge, who has consistently sided with the defense, strikes the testimony and the Xeroxed copy of the original admission form from the trial record. It looks bleak that truth and justice will prevail. Then, Galvin summons his last ounce of genius in his summation. He reasserts the theme that the jury is the last defense against powerful institutions and speaks of the failure of justice to be won by the powerless and the poor, saying, "We doubt ourselves. We doubt our beliefs. We doubt our institutions. Today you are the law." See the film for an excellent performance by Charlotte Rampling, for the ending, and also for a young Bruce Willis among the courtroom spectators. Later in this chapter, we will visit director Sidney Lumet's even more scathing indictment of medicine and institutions.

Article 99 (1992)

Article 99 opens with the typical bureaucratic absurdity for which the Veterans Administration (VA) has become famous. A VA hospital intake clerk tells a wheelchair-bound veteran, "Without certification, we have no proof that you're disabled." "You want proof?" he screams and takes off his leg prosthesis and pounds the counter. Meanwhile, a bewildered vet with coronary artery disease tries futilely to get admitted for an indicated coronary artery bypass. Luther Jerome (Keith David), the resident sage, a savvy veteran in a wheelchair, recites some passages from the Gospel according to Luther: "The enemy is behind the desk." "Whatever you need, you're not going to get. Whatever you get, ain't worth shit." "You need a bypass?" he asks the hapless vet. "Be sure, they'll bypass you." He adds that veterans can't sue for benefits during what he calls "Congress's creeping cutbacks."

Clearly, this is a film where the good guys and the bad guys are quickly established. There are no subtleties. Doctors and veterans are good. Administrators and Washington bureaucrats are bad. Still, it's a fairly enjoyable movie. The lines are sharp, the acting generally good, and the pace is so fast that you're swept along and don't have much time to reflect. It's a film that anyone who works or has worked at a VA hospital should see, if only to determine if subsequent reforms have made these concerns obsolete.

Indeed, released at the beginning of America's health care reform debate of 1992-1993, the film was a timely commentary on the ways medical care was being rationed in contemporary America. Unnecessary and duplicative care stood cheek by jowl with denial or unavailability of needed services. A Darwinian competition for the insured among providers of "product lines," a seemingly endless ability to create billable services, and a patchwork payment system with multiple rules resulted in a fragmented system that resisted all attempts to rein it in. Matching patients with necessary services takes a health care system with a brain and a heart, but too often what we had was one with a ravenous bovine stomach, with multiple compartments—the better to digest all available (and potentially available) dollars.

What was not apparent during the debate was the fact that the VA was in a good position to be part of the solution, since it is the only freestanding integrated national health care system.[12] It has primary, secondary, and tertiary care facilities, skilled nursing and domiciliary institutions, and the strongest nationwide commitment to geriatrics research and treatment—just what our increasingly aging population needs.[13] Clearly, the VA has lagged in the care of women as well as outpatient care, and it has no pediatric facilities. Nonetheless, it could have provided a skeletal template for a desperately needed integrated system.

OK, I know what you're thinking. Yes, I've worked in VA hospitals and have seen how dreary they can be. They have suffered from years of political infighting among the central office staff, the local administrators, and the veteran's lobby. Once, that lobby was as powerful as the American Association of Retired Persons (AARP). Any cutback would be greeted by orchestrated outrage. No more. Gone are the days when hospitals spent down their budgets at the end of the year to assure that the base for next year's budget held steady. Gone are the days of inflating the inpatient census with marginal admissions. The affiliations with academic centers, largely beneficial, but not above being exploited in academe, are getting closer scrutiny. At one time, there was talk of dismantling the system and paying for the care of eligible veterans at local community hospitals. This idea was worth testing in many parts of the country, but seems to have been abandoned. Meanwhile, the sharp limiting of services to those conditions that are service-connected leaves the system in a potential never-never land. Despite its faults, the VA still deserves to be a bigger player in future discussions of health care reform.[12,13]

Regrettably, though overdone, much of what is portrayed in the film has a basis in fact. Patients are "turfed around the system"; some supplies are short; doctors and administrators are measured by different yardsticks and all too often have conflicting agendas. The veterans feel cheated when care is deemed necessary, but is denied if it is not service connected. The film is a *M*A*S*H* clone with a generational connection through Kiefer Sutherland. As Dr. Peter Morgan, a green intern, he plays a more reluctant and gentle revolutionary than his father, Donald Sutherland, played in *M*A*S*H*. Ray Liotta plays the hero, Dr. Richard Sturgess, the "best surgeon in the whole system" with the same self-righteousness but more vulnerability and sympathy for the folks. As with Hawkeye Pierce in *M*A*S*H*, he is joined by a small loyal band of physician co-conspirators fighting the system.

The forces of evil are led by an ambitious administrator Dr. Henry Dreyfoos (John Mahoney) who has his eye on Washington and is said to be only interested in "saving a buck." He is played with just the right touch of sneer and sleaze. While we have all encountered administrators who resemble this fellow, he is less believable because he actually sets foot on the wards. In my experience, such administrators have only been able to maintain the invincible ignorance necessary to be so cocksure about their bottom-line projections either by never visiting patient-care settings (the splendid isolation approach) or by making sure that any such visits were carefully scripted (the head of state approach). This fellow actually exposes himself to reality. There is also a stereotypic out-to-lunch psychiatrist Dr. Robin Van Dorn (Lea Thompson), who is won over to the conspirators' side and who turns out not to be the mousy lightweight our hero thinks she is. The cast is completed by a group of nurses whose hard-boiled portrayal should offend nurses everywhere. While there are a few sadistic nurses in this world, the abusive head nurse—who welcomes intern Morgan with "for the next thirty-six hours, Tern, your buns belong to me" and remains unrelievedly obnoxious—defies belief.

There is abundant black humor, such as the response to a death with the line that Doctor X is "approaching the most kills by a doctor in a major hospital." One woman doctor pegs Morgan as a budding surgeon who will spend a "few years practicing on a group of rundown bastards who can't sue" and then go out and set up a practice taking care of rich folks. He spends much of the film living down his initial honest assent to her characterization. Indeed, there's a great scene involving the wonderful character actor Eli Wallach, who plays Sam Abrams, one of the homeless vets who cooperate in being "turfed" around the hospital to avoid being discharged. Morgan looks through a photo album as Abrams reminisces about D-Day, when he won a silver star for bravery, and about the Frenchwoman with whom he shared a happy marriage (fig. 6). Later, when the man tires of the games and, faced with being discharged, commits suicide, Morgan tells the orderly who comes to retrieve the body not to call him a "gomer." "He was a person," he says.

This reminded me of an anecdote that Dr. Hacib Aoun recounted in his eloquent reflections on being a doctor, which turned out to be a poignant envoi.[14] Aoun tells how, while a house officer, he was feeling tired, sorry for himself, and resentful at having to work up yet another patient, a rather pathetic, terminally ill, middle-aged man. Later, when a visitor brought in a picture, taken a few months before, showing a vigorous, self-assured person now replaced by the shell before him, he was caught up by the realization that, like Yorick, here was once a vibrant, happy man.

In the end, the inmates and their keepers take over the asylum. The administrator, with help from Washington, lays siege to the institution. A security guard recites a great line when he is asked to oust the armed veterans. I won't give it away.

Just when you think they're going to give you a happy ending, they add a nice twist. *Plus ça change; plus la même chose*, as the French say. It isn't a documentary after all, so it may not satisfy those who care about

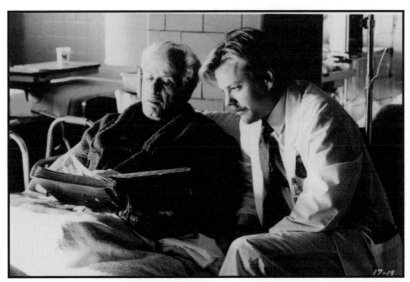

FIGURE 6. *Article 99.* Dr. Peter Morgan (Kiefer Sutherland) listens as Veterans Administration patient Sam Abrams (Eli Wallach) flips through a scrapbook of his life.

the issues it portrays. It also may be too "inside" for those who haven't experienced the VA firsthand. Even so, art need not be great to instruct and certainly to entertain.

THE NEW VILLAINS: HMOS AND INSURERS

The late 1990s have seen the ascendancy of health insurance companies and managed care organizations as the principal villains. In the next three films, the doctors are either invisible or are portrayed in various ways, from good guys to incompetent bunglers to greedy, sex-crazed ne'er-do-wells.

As Good As It Gets (1997)

Billed as a "comedy from the heart that goes for the throat," *As Good As It Gets* turns political correctness on its head. Yet, its beginning is such as to cast doubt that it can retrieve itself. Imagine a hard-boiled cynic who writes sensitive, best-selling Harlequin romances. Played by Jack Nicholson, Melvin Udall's personal life is anything but sensitive. He is a homophobic, anti-Semitic, animal-hating, obsessive-compulsive recluse who spews venom at anyone and everyone. Like Bill Murray in the classic *What About Bob?* (see chapter 10), Melvin is afraid of "germs," doesn't step on cracks, and has three locks on his door. He's the gentle Bob's evil twin.

However, instead of being pigeon-holed by the usual Hollywood faux-liberalism, his character begins little by little to reveal some redeeming qualities as his tormentees begin to take him on and to crack the tough-talking veneer that encases his soft interior. Screenwriter Mark Andrus and director James Brooks are not interested in creating dueling stereotypes, scoring points, achieving polarization, and leaving the field. Rather, their goal is seriocomic engagement between alienated groups and an attempt at reconciliation. So, when the gay artist, Simon Bishop (Greg Kinnear), is victimized by a gay hustler, it's the homophobe who helps, not his gay friends. The Black gallery-owner, Frank Sachs (Cuba Gooding, Jr.), when provoked by Melvin, is dissuaded from punching out his lights and walking away. Instead, he uses the threat of violence as well as clever nonviolent tactics to deflate the bully.

Helen Hunt plays Carol Connelly, a single mother of a severely asthmatic child, who works as a waitress at Café 24 Heures. She manages to tolerate serving Melvin the Misfit's daily atherogenic brunch of bacon, sausage, and eggs, which he eats with his own plastic utensil set. For all his brutishness, Melvin processes what goes on around him in the eatery and comes to understand Carol's difficult struggle as a working mother to care her son and make ends meet. In his obsession to help himself, he contrives to help her enormously.

The medical content of the film revolves around a few scenes relating to Carol's son's asthma. Carol tells Melvin that she goes "to the emergency room five or six times a month where I get whatever nine-year-old they just made a doctor." On another occasion, she says that her son "had a full-blown attack and just for fun they gave him the wrong antibiotic." One has to ignore the fact that the son never looks as sick as he is described. After Melvin helps take the boy, who looks surprisingly fit, to the emergency room, he gets his publisher to promise to have her doctor-husband examine the child. An older, experienced doctor, he visits the house and ascertains that the care has been solely in the emergency room. Parenthetically, it is extremely unlikely for a managed care program to authorize such care; if anything, they try to keep patients out of emergency rooms; but why quibble with facts when you're trying to cast villains. He also learns that skin testing was not done because the "plan didn't cover it and they said he didn't need it." This prompts the following lines that led to universal audience applause and Senator Ted Kennedy's invitation for Helen Hunt to appear before his subcommittee when the patients' rights bill was being considered: "Fucking HMO bastards, pieces of shit!" When she realizes the crudity of her outburst, she apologizes to the doctor, who says, "That's OK. I think that's their technical name." He then proceeds to give her his home number, to assign a nurse to make the house allergen-free, and to arrange for allergy testing. He says, "There are still a lot of tests I need to do. Whatever we do, I promise that your son is going to feel a whole lot better." Carol hugs him and rues the fact that he's already married. In this respect, the film is a throwback to the days when doctors were heroes and helped patients navigate through institutions.

In short, the film seems to be a return to some honest dialogue after two decades of political correctness. While thoroughly entertaining, it also represents an acting clinic, for which Nicholson and Hunt won well-deserved Oscars. Turning in his best performance in a long time, Nicholson doesn't preen, but looks and acts his age. He evinces a vulnerability that is endearing even to those he repels. To their credit, the filmmakers don't try to transform him into a fully healed person in two and a half hours. He's still got a lot of the jerk left in him at film's end.

Helen Hunt is nothing short of magical. She can convey more with her eyebrows than some actors can with their whole bodies.

FIGURE 7. *As Good As It Gets*. Obsessive compulsive Melvin Udall (Jack Nicholson) tries to show his neighbor Simon Nye (Greg Kinnear) how to win back the affections of his dog Verdell (Jill).

Greg Kinnear is excellent as Simon the artist, with whom Melvin develops a symbiotic relationship through Simon's dog, Verdell (fig. 7), whom Melvin at first mistreats, but then comes to love. Verdell was played by a veritable dog conglomerate, but the principal actress was Jill, a Brussels Griffon. A worthy successor to Asta of the *Thin Man* movies, Jill is outstanding as she uses her soulful eyes to great advantage and imitates Melvin's avoidance of stepping on the cracks. Finally, any film that states in the closing credits that "the actors in this film were in no way mistreated" has its tongue so firmly planted in its cheek that it deserves all the acclaim it receives.

The Rainmaker (1998)

Following on the anti-insurance company theme, but with a neophyte lawyer playing the role of good guy is the 1998 film, *The Rainmaker*, based on a John Grisham novel.[15] This weakly-plotted film is saved by its appealing cast. We are supposed to believe that Rudy Baylor (Matt Damon), an accomplished Memphis State Law School graduate who has drop-dead looks and a great personality, can't find a job and is reduced to joining a sleazebag law firm run by Bruiser Stone played by Mickey Rourke. He also brings along with him three cases from his law school clinic. Just as the FBI is set to close Bruiser down, Rudy and Dick Schifflet, a paralegal played by Danny De Vito, open their own firm. The young do-gooder gets involved with a woman who is regularly beaten up by her husband, who later dies at Rudy's hands under very questionable circumstances. Rudy also helps out Miss Birdie, a rich widow, beautifully played by Teresa Wright.

The most interesting and pertinent story involves his third case, a young man with acute myelocytic leukemia. When the insurance company declines to authorize a bone marrow transplant, the doctors discharge him from the hospital. After a very convincing epistaxis (nosebleed), the boy authorizes going forward with the case. At the pre-trial hearing, there is no doctor in sight to support him; the only testimony is from the family doctor who says a transplant wouldn't help his form of leukemia. The boy's mother doesn't believe him because he's not a specialist. The young lawyer is arrayed against experienced lawyers headed by a smoothie similar to Concannon in *The Verdict* and played with proper oily rottenness by Jon Voight. The first judge, played by Dean Stockwell, is a defendant's judge and the case seems doomed. Then, Grisham employs a *deus ex machina* trick and the judge dies. He is replaced by a plaintiff's judge (played by Danny Glover) who expedites the deposition of the terminally ill boy's testimony.

The paralegal sidekick locates the senior claims analyst (she also was pressured by the bad guys to quit her job, like the star witness in *The Verdict*). She testifies that the company insured poor people, using insurance salesmen who went door-to-door and collected premiums monthly, as was common in poor neighborhoods. All claims were initially denied. If re-filed they were sent to the underwriters with instructions not to pay until told to do so. The company was playing the odds that the claimants wouldn't resubmit the claim or consult a lawyer. Of 11,462 claims, 9,141 were denied (fig. 8). As the analyst says, "Subtracting all quick out-of-court settlements, it leaves a pot of gold at the end of the year."

The sidebar is that the claims analyst is a single mother with an alcohol problem. As long as she had sex with the executives, she was promoted. When she stopped, she was demoted and then fired. She absconds with notes from the medical advisory board meeting where the insurance company's chief executive officer is quoted as saying that "now that bone marrow transplants have become standard procedure, we would be financially justified to invest in a bone marrow clinic." Instead of a summation, Rudy plays the videotape of the deposition in which the boy says that when the first claim was filed, he was 160 pounds and had a 90 percent chance of survival. After all the delays, he is now

FIGURE 8. *The Rainmaker.* Lawyer Rudy Baylor (Matt Damon) reveals how many medical claims were denied by the insurance company he is suing.

110 pounds and on death's door. The jury awards costs and more punitive damages than asked for. Rudy decides not to practice law; he doesn't want to become a sellout and he has nowhere to go but down after this victory. Maybe he'll teach and produce other idealists like himself. The messages are clear. Insurance companies are evil. The system stinks. If you work within the system, you'll become corrupted and sell out. And, by the way, don't count on your doctors to help you.

The next film reinforces this message about the nefariousness of doctors and the institutions in which they work, until the closing scenes when the young doctor has a change of heart and bucks his superiors to become the mensch he really is.

Critical Care (1997)

Based on Richard Dooling's 1992 novel,[16] this profane, unrelievedly angry, and caustic film was directed by Sidney Lumet (see chapter 1). Lumet has directed many excellent socially concerned films such as *Twelve Angry Men, The Last Angry Man, Serpico, Network,* and *The Verdict.* Seeing *Critical Care* for the first time with my family, its coarseness and outlandishness made me sorry I had rented it. On revisiting it in the process of writing this book, I realized it's just the kind of film that physicians should watch, not for entertainment, but to see the extreme boundary of public attitudes.

To the accompaniment of "Dry Bones," nurse Stella (Helen Mirren) checks patients in an austere high-tech intensive care unit (ICU). She wakes an exhausted resident Dr. Werner Ernst (James Spader), who says "twenty-two hours down, fourteen hours to go." Stella replies, "And actually one or two of them wasted on patients. What turned you into the stud you are today?" He responds, "The MD after my name. Science dweeb in high school, biology nerd in college. Suddenly from a dork doofus, I was transformed into a smart, powerful, sexy, all-knowing, potentially rich bastard. Just the kind of man every girl wants to marry." Stella muses aloud, "Did you ever realize how many nasty names begin with 'D?' Dweeb, doofus, dickhead, dork, doctor." After that slam, you shouldn't be surprised that nothing's sacred, not even Hippocrates. Stella says "I worry about you, Dr. Ernst; life without sleep and prodigious sex is not healthy." "Who says?" he asks. "Hippocrates," she replies. "You know what else he said? 'When the dingus gets hard, the brain gets soft.'"

On work rounds, Stella asks why so much is being done to the patients. Ernst replies, "It's important that we say we did everything we could." Her snappy retort is, "That's doctorspeak for 'we put this patient through hell before he died.'" Later, she will ask, "Why are we wasting thousands of dollars on this intravenous drip? With what people pay us to keep them in suspended animation, you could pay for every kid in Brooklyn to have a decent education."

Another elderly patient who has been comatose for three months, has five charts, with five operations in just the first one. Ernst comments that "the insurance forms go to Medicare or Amnesty International." Wondering why the unit director Dr. Butz has made the patient a full code, Ernst adds, "Lettuce in my refrigerator has a better chance of regaining consciousness than this fellow." This patient (Mr. Potter or "Bed Five") will be the object of contention between two daughters fighting over the man's ten million dollar estate whose disposition depends on when he dies. Constance (Margo Martindale) is dumpy-looking and described as "totally bonkers, a Holy-Rolling, Bible-Belting, religious nut" who sees signs of recovery in the man's repetitive tremor and wants "everything done." Felicia (Kyra Sedgwick), a beautiful model, is seeking an injunction to prevent doing a gastrostomy. She entraps Ernst on videotape during a bout of sex in her apartment when, *in flagrante delicto*, he admits that her father is in a persistent vegetative state and that the proposed gastrostomy is useless. Recognizing Ernst's naiveté, but not knowing about his indiscreet admission, the hospital lawyer mutters, "Geez, I wish they would teach more about litigation in medical school."

A Black patient with Goodpasture's syndrome, known as Bed Two (Jeffrey Wright), has rejected two kidneys. He tells Stella that he doesn't want "to go back on the fucking ventilator and fucking dialysis. Tell those fucking doctors to turn the fucking machines off." Stella says that his parents love him and have requested a full code. He is the subject of a number of bizarre scenes that break the narrative flow. One involves Stella showing him her mastectomy scar and telling him what she went through to live. Then, Wallace Shawn (*My Dinner with André* and *Princess Bride*), playing Furnaceman, the devil's assistant, lectures him on how little time he spent comforting the dying when he was healthy. Now he's just like them. All he has to offer the world is his health insurance! Later, when Bed Two develops a Torsade de Pointe arrhythmia and is just about to die, Furnaceman tells him why he won't get to heaven. Finally, Stella, intent on letting him die rather than have his arrhythmia reversed, disconnects the monitor and hooks it up to herself so that the alarm won't go off. She disconnects the ventilator and tells "Bed Two" she loves him. We then see him remove his tubes, walk into the light, and ascend to heaven.

The other subtheme involves Ernst being chosen to be the next fellow on the team of the head researcher, Dr. Hofstader, played with arrogant smarminess by Philip Bosco. Ernst is assured that the fellowship will make him "medical royalty" and that he'll be "set for life." The lab gets "up-to-the-minute data from sixty hospitals in fifteen states and eleven foreign countries. When other medical staffs are stumped, they call us. We analyze the data. Dr. Hofstader diagnoses and treats the patient from right here." Hofstader appears and says, "Look at the future of medicine. Seeing patients is a waste of a doctor's time. We try to correct that problem. We like to think of patients as information that can be digitized. Then, we can build computer models for surgeons to practice on that are identical with any patient. We can bioengineer a device to roam the body and automatically notify us of any abnormality. We can diagnose and treat the problem before the patient knows anything is wrong."

Ernst is introduced to Poindexter, an intensive care nurse and a genius with computers. The current fellow tells him, "Rumor has it that Poindexter has never had a patient die on him." Poindexter says that "There's no longer any condition that is truly terminal, just patients we choose not to maintain." When Ernst excitedly tells Stella that he will be a fellow with Hofstader, she says sarcastically, "So, you're going with Robodoctor to practice medicine in cyberspace?" Later Hofstader, maintaining conversations on two cellular phones, tells Ernst he has rescinded the offer because of the lawsuit.

The most entertaining parts of the film are three scenes with Doctor Butz, played hilariously by Albert Brooks. Butz pages people and promptly forgets about it. He tells Ernst, "I had the medical licensing board coming after me with a pack of rattlesnake lawyers; so, I was kicked upstairs to professor emeritus of intensive care medicine." He's now being accused of having Korsakoff's syndrome, which Ernst defines as "short-term memory loss while still being able to do complex tasks," obviously what Butz has. He announces proudly that he graduated *magna cum laude* from Yale and wrote the standard textbook, *Fundamentals of Intensive Care Medicine*, "thirty years ago, before I started drinking, chasing women, and having some fun."

Later, Ernst is paged again to Butz's office. After the usual confusion, Butz asks, "What's wrong with Bed Five? He's all paid up." Ernst says, "We should let him go." Butz replies, "Being a doctor is not good enough for you. Now you want to play God. Why should we proceed? Where have you been all your life? It's called REVENUE! He's got catastrophic health insurance. The works." Ernst asks, "What difference does insurance make?" Butts exasperatedly replies, "This must be the generation gap. These HMOs are confusing the issue. If the patient was part of an HMO, I'd understand your dilemma. We'd get paid not to do anything. With insurance, we get paid to do procedures. I get a cut for every procedure." The billing clerk comes in and says that for Bed Five the hospital is "getting $112,000 a month; three insurance companies are paying like clockwork."

Ernst asks, 'If you were comatose, would you want to be kept alive for months with a machine?" Butz replies, "Hell, no! I wouldn't want to be tortured in some bed. If I get sick, no doctor on this planet is going to come near me. I don't have insurance. My money is tied up in a trust. Just make sure you don't have money for health insurance." He plans to die smoking a cigar, with a big drink, on a full stomach, and lying on a beach somewhere.

The third time Butz pages Ernst, Butz remembers paging him and says, "First lawsuit? When those lawyers start crawling over you, that's when you know you're a doctor." Just then, Ernst is paged by a nurse at a Dr. Miller's direction, because the emergency room is stacked up and they have a nineteen-year-old with a severe head injury dumped by

University Hospital. Butz asks, "Does the patient have coverage, insurance, an HMO, something?" Confirming that he's "as bare as a baby's behind," Butz tells the nurse, "What a surprise! I bet University Hospital sends over all its paying patients. Tell Dr. Miller his head is full of horseshit. If he disagrees, slip him in an MRI machine and look for yourself."

Butz refuses to release Ernst to see the patient saying, "You work for me. If you work for nothing, I work for nothing. What if I asked him to cut my grass and told him that if I get any money I'll pay him?" When Ernst says that there is quite a difference between emergency care and cutting grass, Butz replies that "this is still a service economy." Meanwhile, Dr. Miller tells the nurse to call Butz and tell him that the patient they want Ernst to see is a seventy-six-year-old man who has had a stroke and has major medical insurance, catastrophic health insurance, and Medicare." Butz quickly releases Ernst but not before regaling him with the following recollections: "I was on one of the very first critical care teams in 1959. We developed most of the basic code blue techniques. In the Bible, Jesus brought Lazarus back from the dead, but he did it only once. People were amazed. We did it every day. We made miracles every single day. People treated us like Gods as opposed to overpriced auto mechanics, which is what we've become."

Ernst now faces a conflict. Felicia, who has the videotape, tells him, "Just kill my father or I'll end your medical career." He goes to disconnect the ventilator and proceeds to take the man's hand (fig. 9), when he is confronted by the spirit of a nun played by Anne Bancroft, who engages Ernst in a dialogue about eternity and the meaning of suffering. She tells him, "Suffering teaches us to love each other. When we see people suffering, we remember what it is to suffer pain and loneliness. Think of him as your father." He responds, "I feel ashamed." She says, "It's because you didn't love him. You can change. Struggle to love him and to love yourself. If you did love him, what would you do?" Stella interrupts this reverie saying, "Hands-on patient care from a doctor. I'm impressed."

Cut to boardroom where a fact-finding proceeding is being convened. The judge allows Ernst to speak. He begins, "There's a man in Bed Five whom we should all care about." He then recounts how the two daughters and their lawyers should care, but all they care about is "the ten million dollars." The doctors, the hospital, and their lawyers should care, but what they care about is "patient turnover, occupancy rates, expensive tests, overpriced drugs, and profits." There's a lawyer for the insurance company, but "no one ever believes that an insurance

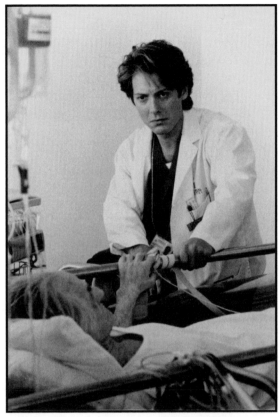

FIGURE 9. *Critical Care.* Resident Werner Ernst (James Spader) begins to empathize with dying patients in the Intensive Care Unit.

company cares about anything except collecting premiums and honoring as few claims as possible." "Then there's me, one of his doctors, who is concerned about making money, getting a new car, meeting pretty women, becoming a bigshot doctor when I should have cared about the patient, my patient. So we have the family, the doctors, the hospital, the insurance company, and the lawyers, each of us concerned only about ourselves. The only one missing is the patient. The only one without a voice. All of us together are the health care system which has collapsed, is comatose and near death like Mr. Potter in Bed Five, and we should care." Ernst proceeds to help resolve the dilemma, but not before making an impassioned speech about going against everything he believes in, that is, defeating the enemy, death, and never surrendering at any cost. Then, he turns off the ventilator.

After leaving the hospital, he goes to aid a boy who has an inline skate accident. Butz calls out from his office, "Ernst, stay away from him. You want to get sued again? Ask him if he's got proof of insurance. Haven't you learned anything from me?" The injured boy asks, "Are you a doctor?" Ernst smiles and says, "Yes, I'm a doctor," and he helps the young man. Let's end the chapter on this happy note, rather than accentuate the negative by commenting further on this picture. In the next two chapters, we will turn to some films where the better nature of physicians has been portrayed.

NOTES

1. Hooker R. MASH. New York: Morrow, 1968.
2. Morris CR. American Catholic: The Saints and Sinners Who Built America's Most Powerful Church. New York: Random House, 1997.
3. Hilton J. The Story of Dr. Wassell. Boston: Little, Brown & Co, 1943.
4. Hilton J. Goodbye Mr. Chips. Boston: Little, Brown & Co, 1934.
5. Hilton J. Lost Horizon. New York: W. Morrow, 1934.
6. Bontempi C. Adultery and TV: The early M*A*S*H. New York Times, August 24, 1997.
7. Wolfe T. Radical Chic & Mau-Mauing the Flak-Catchers. New York: Farrar, Straus and Giroux, 1970.
8. Dans PE and Johnson S. Politics in the development of a migrant health clinic: A pilgrim's progress from idealism to pragmatism. N Engl J Med 1975; 292: 890–895.
9. Castaneda C. Journey to Ixtlan: The Lessons of Don Juan. New York: Pocket Books, 1974.
10. Goldberg C. Teaching hospitals battle cutbacks in Medicare money. New York Times May 6, 1999, p A1, A22.
11. Kesey K. One Flew Over The Cuckoo's Nest. London: Pan Books, 1973.
12. Smith CB and Wolcott M. Veterans health care: Lessons for a national health care system. Ann Intern Med 1991; 115: 907–909.
13. American College of Physicians. The role of the Department of Veterans Affairs in geriatric care. Ann Intern Med 1991; 115: 896–900.
14. Aoun H. From the eye of the storm, with the eyes of a physician. Ann Intern Med 1992; 116: 335–338.
15. Grisham J. The Rainmaker. New York: Doubleday, 1995.
16. Dooling R. Critical Care. New York: Morrow, 1992.

9

*The Temple of Healing**

Once considered callings, medicine and religion have been intimately linked for over two millennia. Their practitioners are entrusted with the care of the most precious of human possessions, namely, body and soul. Egyptian, Babylonian, and ancient Greek physicians invoked deities even as they applied practical remedies. Hippocrates did much to make medicine more empiric and to distinguish it from a priesthood.[1, 2] Yet, the oath ascribed to him acknowledged the dominion of a higher power by invoking Apollo and other gods to witness promises being made in practicing the art. Jews, Christians, and Muslims incorporated many of the oath's precepts into their own moral guides. Well into the second half of this century, long after the Greek gods had any claim on their religious beliefs, graduating medical students evidenced continuity with their ancient counterparts by reciting the traditional Hippocratic oath.[3] Indeed, if you ask people to name the code that serves as the moral basis for the practice of medicine, most would cite that oath, even though few doctors in a recent survey remembered its contents.[4]

This lack of awareness is not surprising. Beginning in the 1960s, the Hippocratic oath was seen as too proscriptive and out of touch with an increasing respect for moral pluralism. Modified versions of the code proliferated. In the most extreme versions, swearing to pagan gods, references to male physicians, proclamations of fidelity to teachers, and clauses proscribing abortion, sex with patients, and the administration of a deadly draught (assisted suicide) were dropped. In their place, statements regarding patient autonomy, truth-telling, and community relationships were substituted. One can applaud some of these changes as being long overdue and still lament that, after surviving millennia, the Hippocratic oath could be so radically altered and even cast aside. If truth be told, the role of the Hippocratic oath in inspiring physician

---

*This chapter appeared in part in *Literature and Medicine* 1998; 17:114-125.

behavior was always more myth than reality. Yet, as Joseph Campbell has written, myths can serve as history's guideposts to deep inner mysteries.[5]

The association between religion and medicine, so strong in medieval times, continued well into this century. After the fall of the Roman empire, medical teaching, as with other forms of learning, survived in monasteries, such as those at Salerno.[6] Hospitals were, for the most part, staffed and directed by religious communities or had strong Christian, Jewish, and Islamic connections. Religiously affiliated medical institutions coexisted amicably with municipal and secular hospitals that burgeoned after the Hill-Burton Act.[7] All this has changed dramatically with the drop in numbers of religious staffing in hospitals, the increased costs and financial stakes of health care, and the changing attitudes towards religion in America. So much so that in the 1990s, there have been a number of bitter protests against mergers of religious and secular hospitals, because of concern about the imposition of religious beliefs, especially regarding reproductive services.

In my estimation, the uncoupling of medicine from its ancient codes and any religious associations helped change the patient-physician relationship from a sacred covenant to what seems today to be a business contract for a technical service. The purpose of this chapter, however, is not to argue this point, but to illustrate how the uncoupling of medicine from religion, as well as from the Hippocratic oath, has played out in the movies. I will begin with two little-known films in which Judaism and Protestantism provide a context for compassionate care by their physician protagonists.

Symphony of Six Million (1932)

> I dedicate these two hands in service—
> That the lame may walk, the halt may be strong—
> Lifting up the needy; comforting the dying—
> This is my oath in the Temple of Healing

This is the epigraph of a 1932 film, whose title, *The Symphony of Six Million*, eerily presages the Holocaust. Based on Fannie Hurst's screenplay, the reference is to New York City: "A city with six million human hearts, each with a dream, a hope, a goal. Each soul a vagrant melody in the eternal symphony of life." The film focuses on the Klaubers, an immigrant family living on the Lower East Side of New York. The family is nominally headed by Meyer (Gregory Ratoff), an excitable and hard-working garment cutter, who wants his sons to be educated

FIGURE 1. *Symphony of Six Million*. As "Felixsa" (Ricardo Cortez) studies late into the night, Mama (Anna Appel) gives him her nest egg to pay for his microscope and asks him not to tell Papa (Gregory Ratoff, not shown). Shortly after, Papa does the same.

and his daughter to marry well. This symphony's concertmaster (and real director) is the all-suffering mother, Hannah (Anna Appel), whose wise counsel and tireless efforts keep the family together (fig. 1). Felix (Ricardo Cortez), their eldest child, desperately wants to serve the poor by becoming a doctor. The movie's old-fashioned scrolling narrative announces his admission to medical school as if it were a Bar Mitzvah: "After years of devoted study striving towards an ideal, dream becomes reality as the boy becomes man!"

After graduating, Felix happily attends to lines of the sick poor in his home and at the Cherry Street clinic. The personification of Richard Selzer's well-known image of the surgeon as doctor-priest[8] or, in Felix's case, a doctor-rabbi, he tells his girl friend, Jessica, that "if it hadn't been

for the suffering I saw as a child, I would never have been a doctor."
Jessica (Irene Dunne), ridiculed as a "cripple," is Felix's soul-mate as
she dedicates her life to teaching Braille to the blind. His brother Magnus
(Noel Madison) is appalled that Felix "is not interested in money."
"What's the difference," his mother asks, "as long as he's a good doctor?" Magnus replies, "He ought to have a real office where people
would take pleasure in being sick. He doesn't understand that medicine
is a business—climbing three to four flights of stairs for fifty cents or a
dollar a visit!" Magnus convinces his mother to counsel Felix to move
uptown for the sake of the family. The rest of the film is devoted to
Felix's reaching Park Avenue, where he treats wealthy neurotics in an
art deco ballroom office and appears on the cover of *Vanity Fair* as "the
surgeon with the million-dollar hands." He sets his brother up in business, helps sister Birdie (Lita Chevret) to marry rich, and gives money
(but little time) to his family or the clinic.

The film becomes overtly religious as the family convenes for the
rite of the Redemption of the First-born in which Birdie's son, "who
belongs to God," is to be redeemed through a charitable donation. Because of the demands of his fancy practice, Felix arrives late. Surrounded
by his family, which has succeeded so well in America, Meyer dances
deliriously and thanks God for the fulfillment of his dreams. As he acknowledges his readiness to depart this life, Meyer collapses. A brain
tumor is diagnosed, and Felix is convinced, against his better judgment,
to operate on his father. As Meyer is being wheeled into the operating
room, he comforts his worried son, "Don't be afraid, my son, God will
guide your fingers." Then he and Felix say a prayer in Hebrew. During
the operation, Max Steiner's music, the first complete movie score by
the way, incorporates the poignant "Kol Nidra" theme from the Yom
Kippur service. Meyer dies on the operating table, and "the surgeon
with the million-dollar hands" is driven to despair. Felix's return to the
ghetto to care for the people who really need him signals the reclama-
tion of his soul, which had been lost when he abandoned his roots.

In the 1930s this film's connection between the selflessness of the
medical profession and a belief in a higher power than money could be
made without embarrassment. Yet its assertion of a conflict between
this moral basis and the view of medicine as a business shows that some
issues are timeless. If one looks beyond the primitive cinematic values—with its fake backgrounds, the miscasting (for example, of Irene
Dunne as a Jewish girl in the ghetto), and the schmaltz—one is rewarded
with a film that still speaks powerfully. Certainly, it does to me. I grew

up in the early 1940s on New York's Lower East Side, a block from Cherry Street, in a cold-water flat like the one pictured in the movie. Though my immigrant family was Italian, we had much in common with our Jewish neighbors where religion, education, hard work, and a sense of community were highly valued. Moving up and out was important, but so was keeping faith with those around us.

In 1948 our flat was leveled to build the Alfred E. Smith housing projects and we were moved to a nearby tenement that had hot water and a bathtub in the kitchen. When that building was also demolished to enlarge the project, we were again relocated to the Dyckman housing project uptown. In their realization of the American Dream, my family later rented an apartment in a two-family house, and when I graduated from medical school, we moved into a home of our own in Riverdale, a community made up principally of Jewish, Irish, and Italian, upwardly-mobile and middle-class. True, I never returned to practice on the Lower East Side as Felix did. But I did spend three months in a cholera hospital in Calcutta, helped establish a migrant health clinic in Colorado, and worked for over a decade to improve care in an inner-city hospital. My story is similar to that of many physicians for whom medicine was not seen as a pathway to riches. In short, this film is a reminder that personal beliefs extending beyond self are fundamental to realizing the much-vaunted nobility of medicine as a helping profession.

However, it's important not to get overly romantic here. For all the similarities, doctors are not clerics who profess a vow of poverty; they should be fairly compensated for their considerable efforts. Money is important to them and to their families. It's really a matter of priorities. Indeed, it may be harder for medical school graduates today than it was for me to subordinate financial concerns. An only child, I had strong family support and scholarships to cover college and medical school tuition. Today's students are burdened with a heavy debt and with what is referred to by some as an "entitlement complex."[9] This legacy of the "me generation" creates an expectation of pay commensurate with their sacrifice and on the scale of their college classmates who made it big in law and business with seemingly less effort. So, as hokey as it sounds, the film epitomizes for me the essence of the battle for the profession's soul.

In many respects, so does *The Green Light*, a second little-known film based on a story by Lloyd C. Douglas,[10] an Episcopal priest who lost his job at a California parish and turned to writing. It focuses on the conflict between the pursuit of money and the ends of medicine. It also affirms the importance of religious beliefs in helping patients not only to cope, but to heal, a power confirmed in recent studies and once again being selectively incorporated into patient care.[11] Latter-day viewers will be turned off by the over-the-top, treacly performance by Sir Cedric Hardwicke, its turgid musical score (again by Max Steiner), a wooden performance by a naively sweet Anita Louise, and the confused narrative. Still, it's worth revisiting, much like one reads *Miss Susie Slagle's*, Augusta Tucker's sentimental novel of the same era, about medical student life at Johns Hopkins.[12]

The Green Light (1937)

The movie opens with a policeman stopping traffic in downtown Chicago to speak to Dr. Newell Paige, played by Errol Flynn. After the chat, the policeman gruffly bellows, "Can't you see the green light?" as he waves on the honking motorists. On arriving at the hospital, Paige visits Mrs. Dexter, a patient whose critical surgery has been delayed because her surgeon, Dr. Endicott (Henry O'Neill), is out of town attending to his stocks. Played with her usual serenity by Spring Byington (was this actress ever young and confused?), an unworried Mrs. Dexter tells Paige that "a shorter word for confidence and courage is faith." As she speaks, she conjures up the cathedral rector Dean Harcourt (Cedric Hardwicke) giving a sermon about red lights as analogues for how God sometimes appears to stop us in our tracks. We must open our hearts, he says, to learn our destiny before the green light will signal us to move on.

While walking his dog later that day, Paige meets the dean and tells him that his "ethics" will force him to step in and operate if his old mentor doesn't show. The dean responds, "Troublesome things, ideals. They get in the way of logic." The next day, Paige performs the operation flawlessly until Endicott arrives, moves him aside, and proceeds to cut a vessel, causing the patient to bleed to death. A fellow surgeon comments that the patient would have survived if Endicott had kept out of it. Paige confronts Endicott, who tells him, "You were absolutely right. My place was with the patient, not in a broker's office watching my life savings being swept away. Interesting how greed and medicine don't mix." Paige urges him to tell the truth, expressing confidence that he will recoup his savings. "Not if I'm dismissed for the Dexter case," responds Endicott who pauses and adds, "A split second, a woman dies and a whole career dies with it. A split second against thirty years I've given to medicine." Then, the Hippocratic oath appears on the screen and the camera passes over the lines, "To reckon him who teaches me the art equally dear with my parents" and lingers on the last paragraph:

With purity and holiness, will I pass my life and practice my art and into whatsoever house I enter, I will go
for the benefit of the sick and will abstain from every
voluntary act of mischief and corruption. Whatever, in
connection with my professional practice or not in connection with it, I may see or hear, I will not divulge,
holding that all such things shall be kept as sacred secrets.

Staying true to the Hippocratic oath's admonitions of fidelity to
one's teachers and the keeping of confidences, Paige refuses to blame
his former mentor and declines to attend the medical board hearing to
defend himself. When Endicott does not take responsibility for the mis-
hap, the crackerjack surgical nurse Ogilvie (Margaret Lindsay) resolves
to tell the truth, but Paige's friend, Dr. Stafford (Walter Abel) and Dean
Harcourt dissuade her from doing so. They argue that it would under-
mine Paige's desire to be "noble." Paige's fellow surgeons also keep
silent, and he is discharged from the hospital staff. In the Episcopal
rectory, Harcourt counsels Mrs. Dexter's angry daughter Phyllis (Anita
Louise) and Ogilvie that all things will become clear when they see the
"green light."

Paige also seeks out the dean who asks, "Still troubled with ideals,
Doctor?" Paige asks how Harcourt's concept of eternal life can square
with life's unfairness, including the destruction of his career. The dean
tells him, "You have a fine religion, Doctor." Paige answers, "I don't
have any religion, as far as I know." The dean counters, "There are many
definitions of 'religion' in my dictionary, such as 'loyalty,' 'devotion,'
honor.'" Paige answers, "My dictionary defines it as a kind of opiate
used by people with hurt sensibilities to dull them into drowsiness."
"Would you say that of Mrs. Dexter?" asks the dean. "No," answers
Paige.

Harcourt then tells Paige, "You won a great victory over him
[Endicott] and over yourself and in the end, he will be left behind and
you will survive." Paige says, "Perhaps, but will it be worth it. You have
to wait too long and give up too much for moral victories." The dean,
who was left crippled by poliomyelitis, tells him, "There's hardly anyone
who hasn't been stopped by circumstances. I preferred death to wasting
my life as an impotent cripple. Then I discovered my course was up-
ward. I've been delayed. There's no telling how long, but eventually I
get the green light and I realize that once again I have commenced that
irresistible onward drive." Paige muses, "A man must have something

to live for." Harcourt responds, "Or something to die for." Paige says,
"I can't think of anything to die for. Perhaps something will turn up."
Fade to black.

As in other 1930s films (for example, *Arrowsmith* and *Dark Victory*), Paige, goes off to do research in a remote locale, in this case,
Montana, where Stafford has gone to study the wood tick, *Dermacentor
andersoni*, the principal vector of Rocky Mountain spotted fever. Having nothing else to live for, Paige decides to let a tick infect him to promote
development of an antiserum to treat patients with spotted fever. This
selfless act, which brings him close to death, causes his metaphoric "green
light" to appear. At Phyllis's urging, Endicott charters a plane and they
fly to his bedside (fig. 2). Paige recovers, and the film ends in the cathedral with Harcourt presiding at Paige's marriage to Phyllis.

Probably the most direct linking of religion and medicine in American film, *The Green Light* has much to say about having a higher purpose
in life and in one's profession. While affirming that ideals matter and
that medicine is not a business, it does not imply that everything will be
rosy if you do the right thing. Paige's selflessness costs him. Still, the
message is to avoid despair and continue to seek the "green light" by

FIGURE 2. *The Green Light.* Paige (Errol Flynn) utters his version of "It's a far,
far better thing I do," but his friend Stafford (Walter Abel) and the contrite
Endicott (Henry O'Neill, not shown) won't let him die. The once resentful but
now lovestruck Phyllis Dexter (Anita Louise) is overjoyed.

submerging self in the service of others. Though pretty corny by today's standards, it probably didn't seem so to an audience mired in the Depression.

A more accessible film adaptation of a Lloyd C. Douglas novel, *Magnificent Obsession*,[13] also features medicine, religious imagery, and a theme of redemption. The original 1935 film and the 1954 remake tell the tale of a playboy whose reckless driving causes a woman to become blind and her doctor-husband (who is never seen) to die. Remorseful, he decides to go to medical school to become a surgeon so that he can restore the woman's sight. Again, he must sacrifice everything for his life to regain its meaning.

Magnificent Obsession (1935)

This first version, starring Robert Taylor and Irene Dunne, is not available on video. The movie opens with Dr. Hudson's daughter happily conversing with her new stepmother on the way to their house on the lake. She says, "I can't get over it. When Daddy was coming into renown for performing the first head operation of its kind, you were still in the nursery." The happiness is shattered when they learn that Hudson has died during a post-work swim from an "overtaxed heart." The artificial respirator that was always kept handy for him was being used to save Bobby Merrick, a rich playboy who had an accident while showing off with his speedboat. The statement of the theme is not subtle, "To save him, a man on whom thousands depend had to die." Merrick was a star-making role for Robert Taylor, who interestingly was the son of a Nebraska family physician. We meet Merrick in a 1930s hospital where despite "a temp of 101 and a weak pulse," he seems hale and hearty, bantering with the nurse. His shiftlessness is attested to in the parlance of the times by having "gotten thrown out of a couple of colleges for getting into scrapes with chorus girls." He flees the hospital, gets drunk, has an auto accident, and seeks shelter in a stonecutter's house by a graveyard filled with statues of angels and saints.

There he learns that Dr. Hudson had changed the life of the owner, a gravedigger named Randolph, by teaching him "how to make contact with the source of infinite power, an entirely different powerhouse than the ones your father has stock in." Once Merrick makes contact with this infinite power, he will fulfill his destiny. The secret is to help people and to do so in absolute secrecy. He must also refuse repayment, because the money, once given, is all used up and cannot be returned. He learns that Hudson, who endowed the hospital and had "made several personal fortunes," had given it all away.

Later, Mrs. Hudson, played by Irene Dunne, unknowingly accepts a ride from Merrick, whom she loathes because of the circumstances surrounding her husband's death, but never has met. As luck would have it, she gets blindsided while exiting the car and suffers a "depressed fracture affecting the occipital lobe and will never see again." The now distraught Merrick visits Mrs. Hudson and tells her that he dropped out of medical school because "there were enough second-rate doctors in this world." "Why not be first-rate doctor?" she asks. "There are so few of them." Ouch!

Merrick quietly replaces Hudson's worthless stocks and bonds with blue chips and arranges to have her seen by five specialists in Paris. He is told that the "optic nerve is intact" and that an operation would be fruitless, but that "cases of concussion have recovered after many years." What is our repentant hero to do? Well, simply to go back to medical school, become a surgeon at a fancy New York hospital, establish clinics, donate a fortune to medical research, and win the Nobel Prize for a new surgical procedure. With that string of accomplishments in just five years, you would think there's nothing left, but you would be wrong. There is one more thing to do.

Randolph reappears, lauds his work and tells him that "through one all may be reached. Christ believed that he died for all humanity." Now he presents Merrick with his last test. Helen Hudson is gravely ill in a Virginia sanitarium. Merrick rushes to her side and with trembling hands, he realizes that he has been "preparing for this moment for five years." Naturally he saves her life and restores her sight (fig. 3).

Magnificent Obsession (1954)

The remake of *Magnificent Obsession* starred Rock Hudson (in his breakthrough performance) and Jane Wyman. Because it has much better cinematic values and is more appealing, this version is available on video. In this one, they tell us that Mrs. Phillips's (not Mrs. Hudson's) diagnosis is a subdural hematoma. The "resident physician" at Brightwood Hospital looks like a senior attending. Otto Kruger plays Randolph, now an artist rather than a stonecutter, who turns Merrick on to a life of service to others. He tells him to invest his life in helping others, "It will be a magnificent obsession." "Ode to Joy" and "No Other Love" are appropriate musical accompaniments. The love story is more natural and believable. Although the script was based very closely on the 1935 version, the specialists are now in Paris (fig. 4), instead of Swit-zerland. The sanitorium has also been moved from Virginia to New

FIGURE 3. *Magnificent Obsession.* In the 1935 movie, Dr. Bobby Merrick (Robert Taylor) is apprehensive when told he must be the one to operate on Helen Hudson (Irene Dunne, not shown), the woman he loves.

Mexico. Also, Merrick doesn't win a Nobel Prize, but he has the same butterflies before pulling off the miracle operation. While not as explicit in its reference to Christianity as the first film, Randolph does say that what he is advising Merrick to do is "dangerous stuff; the first man who used it died on a cross at thirty-three."

Most medical films have not been as openly religious, using instead the Hippocratic oath to make their moral statements. The oath makes an appearance in the 1933 film, *Mary Stevens, M.D.* and the 1952 biography *The Girl in White* (see chapter 5 for more on both) to signal passage from training to practice. It also appears in the 1934 classic *Men in White*, (see chapter 3). The 1938 film adaptation of physician-novelist A. J. Cronin's *The Citadel* (see chapter 5) also features the Hippocratic oath when the idealistic Dr. Andrew Manson (Robert Donat) fights to keep his license at the film's conclusion.

One of the last of the popular films to invoke the Hippocratic oath was the 1962 film, *The Interns* (see chapter 3). In that film, the interns refuse a cancer patient's plea to help him die. One of the interns

FIGURE 4. *Magnificent Obsession*. In the 1954 remake, the blind Helen Phillips (Jane Wyman) is examined by ophthalmologists in Paris.

(Cliff Robertson) tries to help a beautiful model (Suzy Parker) gain access to a drug to induce an abortion. He is turned in to the chief of obstetrics by his best friend (James MacArthur) with whom he had planned to open a free clinic for Navajos in New Mexico. Drummed out of the profession, he tells his friend at the film's end, "You and your damn code of ethics. You know, I respect that code. Don't ever let any quacks or leeches or bastards like me in medicine. You get them out of it, you hear?" It is hard to overstate the importance of such hortatory statements on earlier attitudes of patients towards physicians and medicine. Indeed, Joseph Turow begins his book on television doctors, *Playing Doctor*[14] with a recounting of how Max Brand, the creator of Dr. Kildare and author of *Destry Rides Again*,[15] helped shape the kindly image of physicians by lacing his *Kildare* films with such sentiments.

THE SEPARATION OF MEDICINE AND RELIGION

The affirmations of a moral basis for medicine were consistent with general societal beliefs about religion and institutions. Invocations to God in schools, by politicians, and during times of national crisis were common. Popular movies, especially during the Depression and World

War II, had religious themes or explicit references to God. When someone was dying in the old movies, a priest or minister was sure to appear alongside the doctor. Those dying in today's films are more likely to be surrounded by New Age symbols as in the recent film, *Phenomenon*. After dying, one enters the new vision of heaven, whatever one wants it to be. This is portrayed in the vapid, color-splashed 1998 extravaganza, *What Dreams May Come*, which terribly misused the talents of Robin Williams, Annabella Sciorra, and Cuba Gooding, Jr.

Not coincidentally, this dissociation of medicine and religion has been paralleled by a sharp change in attitude towards organized religion in the movies. Michael Medved in his book, *Hollywood vs. America*,[16] richly documents what he calls Hollywood's "war against religion." Under the headings, "Kicking the Catholics," "Bashing the Born-Agains," and "Jabbing the Jews," he cites scores of recent films that have ridiculed Catholics and Protestants and, to a lesser extent, Jews (as in Woody Allen's trashing of rabbis in *Everything You Wanted to Know About Sex* and *Radio Days*). Muslim fundamentalists haven't fared too well either; witness *True Lies, Executive Decision,* and *Siege*. The only reverential treatment Hollywood is currently bestowing on organized religion seems to be reserved for Tibetan Buddhism, as in *Kundun* and *Seven Years in Tibet*.

In the 1940s, *The Bells of St. Mary*, and *Song of Bernadette* were blockbuster hits, and *Going My Way* was credited by Pope Pius XII with increasing priestly vocations. Major films respectful of faith, such as *Keys To The Kingdom, The Ten Commandments, I Confess, The Robe, Quo Vadis, Exodus, Lilies of the Field,* and *The Sound of Music*, continued to be made into the 1960s. Interestingly, these films owed their existence in large part to the original powerful Hollywood moguls, mainly Jewish, who were very respectful of the beliefs of Catholics and other Christians who represented a large segment of their audience.[16, 17] Medved[16] suggests that the root cause of the change in the tenor of today's films is a secular orthodoxy embraced by moviemakers, one that rivals in intensity the orthodoxy of the abandoned Jewish and Christian religions of their forebears. As Yale Law Professor Stephen L. Carter chronicles in his book *The Culture of Disbelief*,[18] the societal fallout during the past twenty-five years has been a largely successful campaign to expunge God and religion from public spaces. The movies have mirrored and possibly accentuated this change in our national ethos, as filmmakers responded to being freed from the Hays Production Code in 1967.

Nothing signals this abrupt change in societal philosophy more than the 1970 film *M*A*S*H* (see chapter 8). Some of its sharpest barbs are aimed at religion. The clearest is the recreation of "The Last Supper" for the stud dentist, who is despondent over his sudden impotence (fig. 5). After the meal, he is wrapped in a shroud and assumes a death-like pose, only to have his most prized and envied possession brought back to life by a voluptuous nurse. The sole doctor who professes religion, Major Frank Burns (Robert Duvall), is an incompetent hypocrite. The priest, irreverently named Dago Red (Rene Auberjonois), is a nebbish who dithers over whether to give absolution to the Polish dentist in advance of his "suicide." In a discussion of its director Robert Altman, Paul Giles[19] provides some background on motivations that have affected his filmmaking. He quotes Jesuit-trained Altman as saying, "Catholicism to me was school. It was restrictions; it was things you had to do. It was your parents. It was Mass on Sunday and fish on Friday. And then when I got out of that I got into the army. It was the same thing—you had to have a pass to get out." Giles concludes that in *M*A*S*H* "Altman's compulsion is to lampoon religion itself as much as the U. S. Army."[19] The author contrasts Altman's attitude with the different approach of another great director John Ford, also a lapsed Catholic, who was much more sympathetic to the religion of his ancestors.[19]

In another 1971 anti-institutional classic, *The Hospital*, (see chapter 8), the killer (Barnard Hughes), who dispenses murder as divine retribution, is a countercultural, Timothy Leary-like Harvard physician-turned-Methodist-missionary, who embraces peyote and Apache rituals. But the clearest articulation of the complete disjunction between religion and medicine is spoken in ophthalmologist Robin Cook's *Coma* (see chapter 5) by a doctor who puts elective surgery patients into coma so that he can sell their organs. He tells the idealistic resident, "When you're older, you'll learn that everything is complicated. There is no black and white, only gray. Our society faces monumental decisions about the right to die, abortion, terminal illness, prolonged coma, transplantation. Society isn't deciding. Congress isn't deciding. The courts aren't deciding. Religion isn't deciding. They're leaving it to us, the experts, the doctors."

Fast forward to the 1990 film *Flatliners* (see chapter 1), a dark film full of satanic and grotesque religious imagery that follows a group of first-year medical students as they stop one another's hearts for four to five minutes in order to glimpse the after-life. Their post-resuscitation after-effects consist of "being paid back for their sins" and, as each suffers

FIGURE 5. *M*A*S*H*. The Last Supper scene.

the consequences of hubris, the smartest of the group says, "I'm sorry, Lord. We stepped on your fucking territory."

It seems doubtful that organized religion and medicine will ever again be conjoined in film or that the Hippocratic oath will reappear on screen to remind viewers of medicine's moral tradition. Indeed, one of the most recent references to Hippocrates by a resident in the 1998 film *Critical Care* is more flippant than reverential (see chapter 8). Still, at least one Hollywood writer recognizes that medicine, at bottom, is a moral enterprise. The 1996 film, *Extreme Measures*, based on the novel by the physician-writer Michael Palmer,[20] is a veritable medical ethics textbook.

Extreme Measures (1996)

Two derelicts wearing nothing but plastic sheets hobble out of a dark alley in a daring nighttime escape from a New York research laboratory. This bizarre, dramatic, opening scene is about the only time Hugh Grant is not on the screen. Grant plays Dr. Guy Luthan, the resident in charge of Gramercy Hospital's emergency room, to which one of the men is brought after standing, arms outstretched, in the middle of New York traffic. Shot partly at Bellevue Hospital, the film captures the stereotypic picture of municipal hospital emergency room chaos:

stretchers in the hallways, handcuffed prisoners, drug-seeking street people, mounds of bureaucratic paper, and caregivers with stethoscopes draped around their necks, running around and shouting.

Luthan immediately confronts an ethical dilemma as he attends to a crack addict whose blood shoots out of an artery into his eye. It's not a pretty sight, but, strangely, the possibility of HIV infection is not raised. The patient is critically injured, as is the police officer he shot. Luthan shouts for two operating rooms to be readied, but only one is available. After a second or two, Luthan says, "Take the cop," and prepares to operate on the "shooter" in the emergency room (fig. 6). Later, when both are stabilized, he is chastised by nurse Jodie Trammel (Sarah Jessica Parker): "You knew the other guy was in much worse shape. You made a moral choice, not a medical one," an interesting but spurious dichotomy. Luthan points out that he asked for two operating rooms and that one patient is a decorated police officer with a wife and children, whereas the other man, who instigated the shooting, is self-destructive and homeless. Furthermore, Luthan stayed back to care for the shooter and saved him. He does not add that police officers, firemen, and emergency medical technicians are like "family" in urban emergency rooms. It hardly seems worth all the agonizing, but Luthan trails off, "I hope I made the right choice; maybe I didn't." Chalk up another one for moral obscurantism.

Luthan is then called on to treat another homeless man who is rigid and in midseizure. He orders an arterial blood gas, a serologic test for syphilis (why this when he should have ordered an HIV test) and 10 mg of Valium. The man becomes stabilized enough to give his name and that of his friend, as well as to utter an enigmatic "Triphase," before crashing. Luthan, who has been surrounded by a host of emergency room support staff up to this point, is inexplicably alone with him when he crashes. After his death, the man's body mysteriously disappears, and Luthan begins to suspect foul play. Luthan resembles those innocent Hitchcock characters played by Jimmy Stewart and Cary Grant, as he digs deeper and deeper, all the while jeopardizing life, limb, and career. Luthan learns that both homeless men had come through the emergency room for minor ailments and had had a battery of laboratory tests. A visit to the record room reveals that their charts have disappeared. Most older physicians will identify with the service chief's lack of surprise when he tells Luthan, "I've been bitching about the record system since they first put it in." He counsels him not to bother worrying about what happened, adding, "We're a repair shop; we're not here to do research."

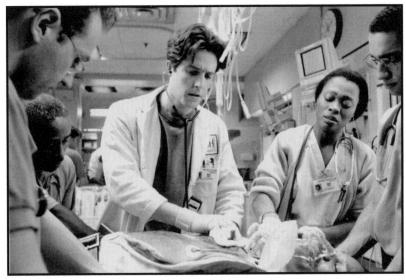

FIGURE 6. *Extreme Measures*. Resident physician Guy Luthan (Hugh Grant) works on a gunshot victim in a busy New York City emergency room.

Gene Hackman plays Dr. Lawrence Myrick, a brilliant neurosurgeon whose research on patients with transected cords has presumably garnered him a Nobel Prize. Because he feels time is running out, he shifts to experimenting on humans, soliciting the help of family members of paraplegics and quadriplegics. Both the setup of this fairly taut thriller and the view of Myrick's ward full of specimens are reminiscent of *Coma*, but the latter was a better film. There are a lot of twists and turns, some bordering on the comedic, others on the bizarre. One involving a fly lighting on a paralyzed Luthan is particularly good. The descent into the fourth circle of hell below Grand Central Station echoes the film, *Interview with a Vampire*. That such an organized subterranean city of homeless could exist is implausible, but the atmosphere and Luthan's descent and rise are chilling.

There are the inevitable health care jokes. On hearing a lady scream in another part of the emergency room, Luthan quips, "She must have just seen her bill." When Luthan comments on the missing body, Myrick says, "Your hospital is known for losing patients." As noted, the film can serve as a trigger for a number of ethics teaching sessions. For example, Luthan's father is an English doctor whose license was revoked for putting "an old friend with terminal liver cancer out of his misery." The allusion to assisted suicide is raised again when Luthan himself seems to be quadriplegic and asks to die before considering to what extreme he will go to be healed. The most obvious issue involves experimentation on the homeless without informed consent, which is held to a higher standard in such a vulnerable population.

Myrick, another of the over-the-edge scientists with whom Hollywood has been enamored (see chapter 4), makes no pretense of obtaining consent to transect their spinal cords and to repair them surgically. He asks Luthan, "If you had to kill one person to cure cancer, wouldn't you do it?" In an impassioned defense similar to Richard Widmark's speech in *Coma*, he notes that the men have "no families, no futures, and are unproductive." "These men are not victims; they are heroes. Because of them, millions will walk." This climactic scene contains some of the best dialogue, as Luthan responds, "Maybe they are heroes, but they did not choose to be. You chose for them. You can't do that, because you took an oath. You're not God."

As the eyes of Luthan and the dying Myrick meet, the director should have yelled, "It's a wrap." He unwisely chose to continue the film, adding another ethical dilemma, as Myrick's wife turns over his notebooks to Luthan in order to help future patients with spinal cord injury. The scene reminds one of the debate over whether the records of inhuman and unethical Nazi doctor experiments should be drawn upon by scientists, even if they contained some helpful scientific information, which is open to serious question.[21] Continuing the film allows Luthan to utter one more rather enigmatic line, "Good doctors do the correct thing. Great doctors do the right thing."

This presumed distinction between doing what's correct and doing what's right could be the starting point for discussion of this medical ethics primer. What does correct mean? Right by what moral theory? How do such distinctions, if they exist, apply to the myriad of questions raised by the film, such as: Who receives scarce resources? What constitutes informed consent for research on vulnerable populations? Should the fruits of immoral research be used? Does the end justify the means? The questions are all there. What's missing are the answers.

The doctor, aptly played by that consummate ditherer, Hugh Grant, is confused and given to moral obscurantism. He is probably representative of a number of students in my medical ethics classes who argue that in an age of presumed greater respect for moral pluralism, there is no real right and wrong. I say "presumed" because I have found that those who trumpet the loudest about their tolerance for diversity are often the most intolerant of beliefs that conflict with their orthodoxy, whether secular or religious. Many of us who believe that there is a right and wrong are also humble enough to know that it cannot be proven to everyone's satisfaction. The texts and rationales that underlie various moral beliefs are often irreconcilable. In the end, each of us is left with Pascal's wager[22] as to whether to believe in the existence of God and an afterlife. His quite rational answer was that believing there was and being wrong lost you little, whereas the consequences of the reverse were devastating. Whatever the case, how one answers that question can have profound effects on how one lives one's life and treats others.

In sum, medicine, like the society in which it operates, is groping to achieve a consensus on values. Having cut ourselves adrift from our age-old moral compass, we physicians are finding it difficult to assert a shared ethos to substantiate the claim that medicine is a noble profession.[23] The proliferation of medical oaths and the increasingly sharp debate on assisted suicide give witness to the ongoing struggle for medicine's soul. As we have seen, movies can provide a window into medicine's and the larger society's amoral evolution. While movies may have contributed to the current moral confusion, they didn't create it. To paraphrase Shakespeare, "The fault, dear Brutus, is not in our stars [or the movies they make], but in ourselves."[24]

NOTES

1. Richards DR. Medical priesthoods, past and present. Tr Assn Am Physicians 1962; 75: 1–10.
2. Burnham JC. The medical profession and cultural change. Pennsylvania Medicine, July, 1976, p 56–63.
3. Crawshaw R. Evolution and form and circumstance of medical oaths. West Med J 1996; 164: 452–456.
4. Wagley PF. The Hippocratic oath. Humane Medicine 1987; 3: 110–114.
5. Campbell J with Moyers B. The Power of Myth. New York: Doubleday, 1988.
6. Loudon I, ed. Western Medicine: An Illustrated History. New York: Oxford University Press, 1997.
7. Starr P. The Social Transformation of American Medicine: The Rise of a Sovereign Profession and the Making of a Vast Industry. New York: Basic Books, 1982.
8. Selzer R. The Surgeon As Priest. In: Mortal Lessons: Notes on the Art of Surgery. New York: Simon and Shuster, 1974, p 24–36.
9. Dubovsky SL. Coping with entitlement in medical education. N Engl J Med 1986; 315: 1672–1674.
10. Douglas LC. Green Light. London: Peter Davies, 1935.
11. Larson DB, Sawyers JP, McCullough ME, eds. Scientific Research on Spirituality and Health: A Consensus Report. Rockville, MD: National Institute for Healthcare Research, 1998.
12. Tucker A. Miss Susie Slagle's. New York: Grosset and Dunlap by arrangement with Harper & Brothers, 1939.
13. Douglas LC. Magnificent Obsession. Boston: Houghton Mifflin, 1929.
14. Turow J. Playing Doctor: Television, Storytelling, and Medical Power. New York: Oxford University Press, 1989, p 3–24.
15. Brand M. Destry Rides Again. New York: Dodd, Mead & Co, 1930.

16. Medved M. Hollywood vs. America: Popular Culture and the War on Traditional Values. New York: Harper Collins, 1992.
17. Gabler N. An Empire of Their Own: How the Jews Invented Hollywood. New York: Crown Books, 1988.
18. Carter SL. The Culture of Disbelief: How American Law and Politics Trivialize Religious Devotion. New York: Basic Books, 1993.
19. Giles P. The Cinema of Catholicism: John Ford and Robert Altman. In: Unspeakable Images: Ethnicity and the American Cinema, ed. LD Friedman. Urbana: University of Illinois Press, 1991, p 140–166.
20. Palmer M. Extreme Measures. New York: Bantam Books, 1991.
21. Lifton RJ. The Nazi Doctors: Medical Killing and the Psychology of Genocide. New York: Basic Books, 1986.
22. Siegler M. Pascal's wager and the hanging of the crepe. N Engl J Med 1975; 293: 853–857.
23. Churchill LR. Reviving a distinctive medical ethic. Hastings Center Report 1989; 19: 28–34.
24. Adapted from Shakespeare W. Julius Caesar Act 1 Scene 2, Line 140–141. In: The Complete Works of William Shakespeare, Volume IV, ed. D. Bevington. Toronto: Bantam Books, 1988.

10

More Good Movie Doctors
and Other Personal Favorites

This final chapter affords the opportunity for some personal reflections and to reaffirm why the book was written in the first place. As noted in the introduction, I love movies and have tried to convey that sense of enjoyment, while calling attention to the traditional values that medicine must project if it is to survive as a profession in the new millennium. To reinforce these aims, I will discuss a few of my favorite films not previously covered; the first group were chosen for pure enjoyment; the second group illustrates the important values a physician should possess, namely, kindness, self-effacement, keen observation, and persistence. They may be summed up in a trait that was said to characterize my mentor, Dr. David Seegal—"magnanimity" or the possession of a great soul.[1]

The first two favorites will never make the critics' "Top Whatever" list. They're just plain fun. This is of little consequence because compiling a Top 10 or even Top 100 list is a sure way to stir up controversy. The most obvious reason is that tastes vary so widely. That's what makes life so interesting and at times maddening. As the old Romans used to say, *de gustibus non disputandum* or there's no arguing about taste. Another reason for the controversy is that some compilers list those films that had an impact on moviemaking, even though they may be watched today only by film buffs. This type of list should really be called "the most influential" rather than "the best." Indeed, the listmakers may never have seen the films or intend to see them again, but they know that if the films are left off, they will be branded Philistines by the cognoscenti.

An alternate approach is to list those films that one saw and liked for whatever reason. Here again, listmakers risk embarrassment by including films that meant something to them at an earlier age, but no longer have the same appeal and are sure to be laughed at by snobby cinéastes. In addition, most of us who go to movies as a hobby are at a disadvantage in that, unlike the critics who review movies for a living, we don't see all the films (thank goodness). We also have preferences that may exclude whole genres from the list of favorite movies. For example, I have never been a fan of silent films or sci-fi, horror, and slasher movies. So my list would be deficient in those categories, because I am not in a position to comment intelligently on them. Even the presumed definitive list of one hundred top films compiled by the American Film Institute in 1999 was criticized for excluding foreign language films.

My preference is that people be asked to list their favorite films, those that they would want on hand if they were marooned on a desert island that just happened to have power enough to run a VCR. There would be no presumption that these were "the best films of all-time" or that the list was inclusive. Most films on my list I've seen a number of times; a few only once or twice. There are "important films" and others that might be considered "fluff." No one would put *Flamingo Kid* or *Tin Men* in the same category with others such as *Schindler's List* or *The Seventh Seal* as works of art, but the former films hit responsive chords when our four children were growing up. They are more likely to be shown on our home video at family gatherings. Indeed, one holiday, I tried showing *Bicycle Thief*, ranked eleventh in Kobal's *Top 100 Movies* as compiled from the preferences of over eighty international critics.[2] The grainy print, the uneven subtitling, and the sad poignancy of the rather simple, straight-ahead story resulted in it being stopped early. This is not a reflection on its importance in screen history or the marvelously natural performances. It was simply that watching it, like some of the old black-and-white films we have discussed, demands a certain receptivity and timing. The next two "doctor" films are among those that our family can see again and again. I'll leave the armchair psychiatrists to fathom why.

House Calls (1978)

The cast of this delightful farce includes four well-known gifted comedic actors (Walter Matthau, Art Carney, Glenda Jackson, and Richard Benjamin), an unheralded one (Candice Azzara), and Matthau's son, Charlie. Matthau plays Charley Nichols, a recently widowed surgeon, who has his pick of lovely admirers as a newly eligible bachelor. Glenda Jackson is marvelous as Ann Atkinson, a divorced mother who refuses to be a one-night stand and fall all over "the doctor." The chemistry between them is so good that they were later cast in another underrated hilarious romp, *Hopscotch*, spoofing the CIA, FBI, and KGB, and also starring Sam Waterston, and Ned Beatty.

Much of the medical story takes place in Kensington General Hospital, whose chief of staff, Dr. Amos Willoughby, played with just the right dottiness by Carney, "is senile." The hospital's chief of medicine is "ten years older" than Willoughby. Later at the annual medical staff meeting, we learn that no graduates of American medical schools applied for an internship and that the hospital recruited one from the Philippines and an acupuncturist from Formosa. Benjamin is at his wicked best as Doctor Solomon, who says of Willoughby, "Whenever he doesn't know what to do, he takes out the gall bladder." Seeing him in a scrub suit in the parking lot, Solomon asks with alarm, "Have you been operating, Dr. Willoughby?" "No, just washing my car," is the reply. Begging for another five-year term as chief of staff (fig. 1), Willoughby says: "I've got a pacemaker, ten inches of plastic aorta, a corneal transplant, a colostomy pouch, $1\frac{1}{4}$ kidneys, a hearing aid, and no prostate. I'll expire before my term will." He adds, "I'm not going to operate any more; you boys will see to it that I don't get into trouble."

Nichols first meets Atkinson when he repairs her wounded jaw after Willoughby has mishandled it. Their romance begins on a rocky

FIGURE 1. *House Calls.* Senile Dr. Amos Willoughby (Art Carney) lobbies his heir-apparent, surgeon Dr. Charley Nichols (Walter Matthau), to nominate him for another term as chief of staff.

note when they meet as panelists on a public television program titled "How Healthy Is the Medical Profession?" The moderator (Anthony Holland) intones, "Since the nineteenth century and the advances in medical science, the physician has assumed a god-like role in American society. But what has happened to the old-fashioned family doctor making house calls, going out in all weather, snow, cold?" Nichols wisecracks, "He froze to death." Then, he points out the practicality of being able to help five patients in the office for every one in the home. Atkinson chimes in, "And you can bill five times as much." She asks why all the doctors are incorporated and launches into a polemic about medicine. Finally, Nichols says, "I know there are things wrong with the medical profession. And we're trying to change them, but it must be done slowly, patiently, and tactfully." This instigates a shouting match between the two as the moderator closes the program by announcing next week's show, "Transvestism: Aberration or Alternate Life Style."

Over coffee, Nichols suggests that the out-of-work Atkinson fill in at the hospital's admitting office. "Isn't that where people are asked to sign away their homes, their insurance, and their property, real and personal?" she asks. Still, she agrees and is later seen dissuading a mother from allowing her child to undergo a tonsillectomy, citing a *Reader's Digest* article reporting that "90 percent of tonsillectomies are totally unnecessary, 50 percent of all appendectomies, and 75 percent of all hysterectomies." This is presumably based on Wennberg's small area variation analyses studies.[3] She also finds an unattended patient on the elevator and reports the "lost patient" to Willoughby, who says they found a lost patient yesterday. Told that it must be another one, he bursts out, "Patients, bunch of crybabies. Who's running this hospital, us or them?"

The spark-filled romance, which includes a great scene spoofing the Hays code requirement that lovers in bed must keep one foot on the floor, is interspersed with the case of the local baseball team owner Harry Grady who is admitted to Willoughby's service for an elective procedure. Later, Willoughby convenes a medical staff meeting to announce, "I have good news and bad news. The bad news is that Harry Grady died on the operating room table. The good news is that he left five million dollars to build a new wing for Kensington General." Reminded that the death was preventable because he forgot to tell the anesthesiologist about the patient's bronchitis, Willoughby says that they should "stonewall it." Grady's wife, Ellen (Azzara), a Brooklyn native whom he met when she was a hat-check girl at Toots Shor's Manhattan restaurant, shows she's not the "dumb blonde" they took her for. Brooking no nonsense about her husband being "a sick man," she tells the medical board, "What you people know about medicine, you can stuff in a cocktail olive." Her lawyer adds, "This is the sorriest excuse for a hospital— malpractice—malnutrition." "Mal-everything," adds Mrs. Grady. The assignment of Nichols to sweet-talk the widow produces a series of delightful scenes that end the film on a high note. In short, this is a comedy with just enough truth to cut close to the bone. Still, I wouldn't mind having Nichols or Solomon for my doctor.

What About Bob? (1991)

Of all the fields in medicine, psychiatry probably elicits the most ambivalence, for medical personnel and lay persons alike. Take the case of my medical school, where the department of psychiatry was so persuasive that our thirtieth class reunion hosted three psychiatry department chairmen and numerous other successful practitioners of the specialty. During internship, however, I learned that psychiatry did not have the same cachet at all medical schools. Medical interns graduating from Johns Hopkins called psychiatrists "spook doctors," a term that poked fun at patients and their doctors. Labeling all patients without objective findings as "crocks," they jokingly ordered "serum porcelain" levels. Such behavior seems rather incongruous, inasmuch as good internists are really closet psychiatrists. After all, the majority of problems we deal with are rooted in the psyche. The attitude of current Hopkins students has changed, and so apparently has that of the general public. Burt Dubrow, creator and executive producer of *The Sally Jessie Raphael Show* one of the 1990s show-and-tell programs, was quoted as saying: "Ten or fifteen years ago, you'd never admit you went to a psychiatrist. Now if you don't go, you're not hip."[4]

Who better to explore the thin line between normal and abnormal as well as patient and psychiatrist than Bill Murray, who as usual, plays Bill Murray. He's no crazier than ever (see the delightful *Groundhog Day*), but this time he is labeled a psychiatric patient. There are numerous instances of people acting very strangely, but having enough money or fame to function without being labeled a patient. How physicians separate diseased from non-diseased and when and why patients assume a sick role are fascinating subjects that are not given sufficient time in most medical school curricula. These issues are germane to all of medicine but especially to psychiatry. In fact, much of the ambivalence about psychiatry results from the concern that so much of it is subjective, as evidenced by the many official reworkings of their diagnostic handbook of what constitutes mental illness.

There's no doubt, however, that Bob Wiley's strangeness limits his social functioning. He begins his day in his New York City walk-up, shouting a pep talk to himself about how great he feels. He brushes his tongue as he prepares to face the day. Leaving his apartment, he says good-bye to his fish and stares at the three locks on the door, not unusual in New York City. He uses a tissue to turn the doorknob, bolts down the stairs, and on hitting the sidewalk he is immediately repelled by a blast of diesel exhaust from a passing bus. Is he neurotic or merely hypersensitive to the assaults of life in the big city?

Next we meet Dr. Leo Marvin (Richard Dreyfuss), a self-satisfied, puffed-up psychiatrist who has just written the book *Baby Steps*, that will be featured on the television program, *Good Morning America*. Wrapped up in the whole celebrity-media schtick, he telephones his wife, Fay (Julie Hagerty), to say that, like only Dr. Ruth before him, he will be interviewed by a television crew at a vacation home. A call from a colleague interrupts the conversation. Assuming that the doctor is calling to acknowledge his brilliance, Marvin takes the call. Instead, the doctor wishes to dump the phobic Wiley on him. Bob's good points are emphasized. He pays early, arrives on time, and, indeed, needs someone "brilliant." "We're a dying breed," the other psychiatrist tells him as he relates how he is quitting practice, an allusion to how much difficult patients take out of their therapists. Marvin agrees to take Bob on when he returns from his annual vacation. No sooner has he hung up the phone than Bob, who has already made an appointment, pops through the door, and their association begins (fig. 2). Marvin will later characterize Bob as "human crazy glue." Bob immediately makes for the family photo and tries to guess the doctor's children's names, which turn out to be very Freudian (Anna and Siggy). Freud's bust will later play a featured role. Marvin gives Bob a copy of his book, which details how one can overcome life's problems by simply taking one baby step at a time, and ushers the baby-stepping Bob out of his office. He dictates a note about Bob's phobic personality, catalogues the charges for the visit and the book, and leaves for their picture-perfect cottage on a New Hampshire lake.

On learning that the *Good Morning America* crew will be visiting, Siggy (Charlie Korsmo) remarks that, "We are going to have another vacation that is not a vacation." This hits close to home, since true vacations are luxuries that physicians don't usually afford themselves. They are either too short, permitting little time to unwind, or are piggy-backed on some business trip or conference. We and our families and, indeed,

FIGURE 2. *What About Bob?* Multiphobic patient Bob Wiley (Bill Murray) feigns a cardiac arrest to ward off a real one as his blasé psychiatrist Dr. Leo Marvin (Richard Dreyfuss) looks on.

our patients pay the price. There are the usual clichés about the children of analysts. Siggy has a death phobia and wears black. When asked why, he says he is "mourning his lost childhood." As Marvin reminisces about his childhood, Siggy comments that he always thought his father was "born an adult." Bob, petrified at being without the great Dr. Marvin for a month, uses various subterfuges to ferret out his location. One scheme involves impersonating a policeman calling the answering service to say that Bob, unable to reach Marvin, has committed suicide. When Marvin is called about this at two in the morning, he at first expresses shock; then he rolls over and tells his wife, "Let's not let this spoil our vacation." Would any psychiatrist react this way?

After locating Marvin, Bob barely surmounts his phobia and makes the long bus trip to Lake Winnipesaukee. Marvin orders him to return to New York, but Bob starts to win over the family. In so doing, he has a revealing conversation with Anna (Kathryn Erbe), who demurs at his statement that, "It must be wonderful sleeping in the next room to a great analyst." She points out that their family has its own problems, one of which is "analyzing things to death." Later, Bob teaches Marvin's young son how to dive, something that Marvin has been unable to do. Bob's successes with the children lead Marvin to say, "I'm a failure. Here I am going on national television posing as an expert on behavior and my children hate me." It's very true that some people who are adept at helping others may not be able to help themselves or their families. Ted Williams once recounted how his mother, a Salvation Army worker, was called "The Angel of Tijuana" because of her numerous acts of kindness to others.[5] Yet, she never was at home for him.

Whatever his failures, Marvin has unwittingly helped Bob to come out of himself. Over Marvin's objections, Bob stays overnight at their cottage because of a flash storm and sleeps in the same room as the twelve-year-old son. They have a ball, with Bob acting like the over-grown boy that he is. The next day, the *Good Morning America* crew arrives at the house as Bob is being thrown out. They think it would be great to have a patient on camera, and, as one might expect, Bob steals the show. The scene says a lot about television and how it frames issues, as well as how we all get caught up in its excitement and presumed importance. Marvin has spent considerable time trying to see how he should look and what he should say for the camera crew. Should he be next to Freud's bust or pose in front of the fireplace with his arm resting gently on the mantel? But when his fifteen minutes of fame arrive, he is tongue-tied and frozen.

The film goes out of control at the end as Dr. Marvin begins to fall apart and is hospitalized at the sanitarium to which he wanted to admit Bob. The final credits tell us that Bob went back to school to become a psychologist—a clear case of need fulfillment. In short, this is, like *House Calls*, a very entertaining film with some rather interesting messages for the profession from our patients. In the latter, it's how hospitals, the profession, and doctors of good will covered for incompetence and ignored the cost crisis, thinking that they could go about their own business and things would be corrected "slowly and tactfully." In *What About Bob?* it's about the fine line between doctor and patient, how doctors, like others, can get wrapped up in themselves, and how humanity can sometimes triumph over cold expertise.

Now on to two dramatic entertainments with tenuous medical connections. One, *The Third Man*, is an all-time favorite of mine, and the other, *Doctor Zhivago*, is a sentimental favorite of many.

The Third Man (1949)

Fifty years after it appeared, *The Third Man* retains its power, pointing up that talent and creativity trump mega-bucks anytime. Set in post-World War II Vienna, the black-and-white photography conveys the starkness and sinister nature of the time. We do not see the travel poster view of Vienna of *gemütlicheit*, but its darker side, the one that welcomed and cheered Hitler, paid a heavy price for it, and was now trying to reinvent itself. People scrape for existence, and the black market flourishes against a backdrop of bombed out buildings rather than those glittering chandeliers of the Staats Opera House. At the time, Vienna was partitioned into four sectors among the Americans, British, French, and Russians, with the center city defined by the Ring, alternately occupied by each of the former Allies and patrolled by multinational units. Instead of sprightly Strauss waltzes, Anton Karas's brilliant "Third Man Theme" conveys a haunting atmosphere that draws us inexorably into the film. The theme became an international sensation at a time when instrumentals could regularly hit the top of the popular music charts. It also introduced most of us to the zither.

The literate screenplay was written by Graham Greene (the noted author of *Confidential Agent*,[6] *The Power and the Glory*,[7] and *Our Man in Havana*[8]). He had convinced Alexander Korda and David O. Selznick to produce the film.[2] The inventive cinematography, so unerringly keyed to the story, won an Oscar for Robert Krasker. Carol Reed (later knighted) also directed *Odd Man Out* and *The Fallen Idol*, part of a remarkable post-World War II explosion of British films which continued into the late 1960s, when their film industry began to decline. He brings out the incomparable talent Orson Welles displayed in *Citizen Kane*, the stuff that led him to be labeled a young genius, rather than what in later performances seemed to be a larger-than-life caricature of himself. Indeed, if anyone's life illustrated the hazards of early celebrity and adulation, it is his. As he himself said, "I started at the top and worked my way down."

Joseph Cotten is outstanding as Holly Martins, an earnest American writer of "pulp fiction," in this case, potboiler westerns. He travels to Vienna after receiving a plane ticket and an invitation from Harry, his childhood friend, to work for him writing publicity for his "medical charity." Shortly after his arrival, he learns that Harry was hit by a car in an extraordinary series of coincidences involving Harry's close associates. Harry's driver's car had struck him just as his doctor and a good friend were passing by.

The accident is made even more inexplicable by the absence of traffic on the street in every street scene. One might explain the lack of traffic by the shortage of cars and gasoline, but the real reason is that the scenes were filmed on location at night after hosing down the street to make it look rainy and more ominous.[2] It is simply one of those practical compromises a director hopes will go unnoticed as he propels us into the story. As the mystery begins to unfold, we are treated to a true "film noir" with elaborate deceptions, conflicted loyalties, and betrayal. Holly is told by a British military officer, Major Calloway, portrayed by that actor's actor Trevor Howard, that Harry was a crook with ties to the black market. Our ingenuous American does not believe him and begins a relentless campaign to clear Harry's name.

At Harry's interment, Holly meets Anna, Harry's girl friend, played by Alida Valli, an Italian cinema star who went to Hollywood and had her name shortened to Valli. After appearing with Gregory Peck in *The Paradine Case*, she made a series of forgettable films before returning to Europe, where, under Reed's direction, she radiates an enigmatic beauty and power one usually associates with Ingrid Bergman. An unapproachable manner and impervious veneer guard Anna's past and protect her inner self—a sharp contrast with Holly, the stereotypical outgoing American who wears his heart on his sleeve. Their shared love for Harry brings them together, and Holly becomes increasingly fascinated by her. As they reminisce about Harry, we learn that he was one of those charmers who managed to play all the angles, but who had a *je ne sais quoi* quality that made him come off as merely a lovable rogue rather than a sociopath. Holly relates how, when they were children, Harry taught him how to fake a fever before an exam, create the best crib notes, and play three-card monte before he was fourteen. We are told that "Harry never grew up in a world that grew up around him." He was, as an ethicist might say, someone who got stuck in the first of Kohlberg's six stages of moral reasoning.[9]

By contrast, Holly is one of those characters who, while creating problems for those around him, manages to walk blithely through the world, unscathed. He inadvertently leads Major Calloway to Anna's apartment, which is thoroughly searched. Calloway's aide, Sergeant Paine (Bernard Lee), with whom Calloway conducts some marvelous repartee, confiscates some of Harry's love letters. When Holly objects to the invasion of privacy, Paine says: "It's all right. We're used to it, like doctors." One can only cringe when the porter of the building in front of which Harry died shouts at Holly from the window to return in the evening and he will give him some key information. Mystery lovers will suspect that it is time to order the flowers.

The subplot involves a military hospital orderly who steals scarce penicillin and sells it on the black market for use by civilian hospitals that do not have access to the drug. During his research for the film in Vienna, Greene heard of just such a ring.[2] The conspirators dilute the drug so as to stretch it, because it fetches seventy pounds a tube, but the unsuspecting health care workers administer it at the concentration stated on the vial. As Major Calloway shows Holly, the result is a trail of dead or profoundly neurologically disabled children and adults, on whom the drug was used to treat gangrene, childbed fever, and meningitis. The scene conjured up memories of stories of the early days of penicillin use related by the world-renowned Harvard physician, Dr. Maxwell Finland, with whom I had the good fortune to train as a clinical infectious disease fellow. His professional dedication helped literally millions of patients and countless fellows. By truly caring about his fellows and their families, Uncle Max engendered a loyalty and good feeling that has endured for lifetimes.

Dr. Finland used to contrast the mega-doses of penicillin we prescribed in 1967 with the small amounts available two decades before. In those early days, when bacteria were unfamiliar with the drug and consequently much more susceptible, remarkable cures were documented using very small doses, but not always. Glen Leymaster, a house officer from 1942 to 1944, recounted in the history of the Boston City Hospital the first use of penicillin on the Second Medical Service,[10] "The stuff was so valuable that it came in 5,000-unit ampules and had to be reconstituted and administered by a house officer. Unfortunately, it didn't permanently cure a disseminated staphylococcus infection, in doses of 25,000 units." The memories of H. William Harris, a fellow house officer, were happier. He noted that "penicillin was used for the first time in Dr. Finland's laboratory between January and October 1944." He recalled the excitement of seeing people who would have died the year before from "extensive pneumonia, pneumococcal meningitis, bacteremia, bacterial endocarditis" recover with daily doses of 15,000 to 100,000 units.[10] He also noted that because of penicillin's scarcity and the ignorance about the risk of adverse reactions, "only doctors and not nurses were permitted to give injections." How times have changed!

Certain films stay with you, and this is one of them for me. I was lucky to visit a totally rebuilt Vienna in 1963 on my way back from Calcutta (see *City of Joy*) and I made sure to stop at Sacher's, where one scene takes place, for their famous torte and the wonderful Staats Opera House for a performance of *Der Rosenkavalier* with Elizabeth Schwarrzkopf. Today's travelers may wish to book a place on "The Third Man tour" of the sewer system (site of a great chase scene), being conducted by Vienna's Sewer Department.[11] My most vivid memory, however, was the sight of the Prater Ferris Wheel, where the movie's climactic scene occurs (fig. 3). I could almost hear Harry's famous line

FIGURE 3. *The Third Man*. Holly Martins (Joseph Cotten) confronts Harry Lime (Orson Welles) in the climactic scene on the Prater Ferris Wheel in Vienna.

affirming the value of turmoil over peace as well as a subtle swipe at Switzerland which managed to prosper during two world wars as other countries were devastated around it: "In Italy for thirty years under the Borgias, they had warfare, terror, murder, and bloodshed. But they produced Michelangelo, Leonardo Da Vinci, and the Renaissance. In Switzerland, they had brotherly love. They had five hundred years of democracy and peace. And what did they produce? The cuckoo clock."[12] The sense of "déjà vu," as the scene played in my head, was like Proust's Madeleine in *Remembrance of Things Past*,[13] a vivid example of how our unconscious and subconscious store evocative memories not just from life but from art as well.

Doctor Zhivago (1965)

For many, *Zhivago* is their favorite doctor film. A phenomenon in its time, this film was based on a book by Russian dissident Boris Pasternak,[14] which gave it a lot of pre-release buzz in intellectual and political circles. Added to that were a lavish widescreen Vistavision treatment by acclaimed director David Lean, some top-notch acting, as well as an overture and an intermission. I must confess that it never won my

heart completely because of its length (originally 197 minutes), convo-
luted story, which Leonard Maltin described as veering towards soap
opera,[15] and its ponderous attempts at times to be "important." Still, I
must confess that it is a film that I find hard to forget and like Lean's
even better film, *Lawrence of Arabia*, must be seen on a big screen. Viewing it on television is like seeing it projected on a sardine can. My
impressions of *Zhivago* follow.

Zhivago stars a darkly handsome Omar Sharif, he of the soulful
eyes, as a doctor/poet tortured by his love for his wife and another woman,
a lovely, sensuous Julie Christie, she of the pouty lips, as Lara, the kept
woman/nurse/revolutionary who captivates Zhivago. Rounding out the
all-star cast are: an aristocratic, doll-like Geraldine Chaplin as Tonya,
Zhivago's wife who bears his children and stands by her man; a worldly-
wise, ruthless Rod Steiger, with his New York accented method acting,
as Komarovsky, a roué who keeps Lara and then "gives" her to Zhivago;
and an intense, idealistic Tom Courtenay as Pasha who puts revolution
above his love for Lara, but exacts jealous retribution on the star-crossed
pair. It also features a lush soundtrack introducing Maurice Jarre's
"Lara's Theme," which soared to the top of the musical charts, cinematography by Freddie Young that justly won an Oscar, a dazzling scene of
daffodils in bloom which alone is worth the price of admission, a train
ride across the icy Siberian landscape with ill-clothed peasants trying to
climb aboard in one memorable scene, and wanton killing of children as
idealistic revolutionaries march into the Tsar's soldiers' guns.

Where's the medicine? you ask. Although Zhivago is really a poet,
he studies medicine because "poetry is no more a vocation than good
health." Amusingly, although the film is set in Russia, we see the same
general practice-research conflict as in previously-discussed American
films. At a ball, Zhivago says that he plans to go into general practice.
His mentor replies, "Think of doing research. It's important, exciting,
and beautiful." Turning to Tonya, the mentor says, "He wants to do
general practice." And then to Zhivago, "You'll learn that pretty people
do ugly things." Zhivago then asks Tonya, "How would you like to marry
a general practitioner?" "None has asked me," she says. "Do you fancy
a professor of pathology?" "Does he write poetry?" she asks. "No."
"Then, it is out of the question."

After the engagement is announced, Zhivago and his mentor are
called away by Komarovsky to attend to Lara, who has taken poison
which they remove using a stomach pump and an emetic. The mentor
reinforces his warnings to Zhivago about "pretty people," "that's not
how poets see them. That's how G.P.s see them." Later, the love story

FIGURE 4. *Doctor Zhivago*. Assisted by Lara (Julie Christie), Doctor Zhivago (Omar Sharif) performs battlefield surgery.

begins in earnest when Zhivago meets Lara, a volunteer nurse caring for the wounded at a hospital. She has "a strange gift of healing that doctors don't believe in" (fig. 4). The epic continues among revolution, daffodils, ravenous wolves, cold-blooded murder, all the while with Christie remaining well-coiffed and beautiful. Seen as the visual equivalent of poetry, one can forgive the film's glossy extravagance. As the screenwriter says, "If people love poetry, they love poetry. And nobody loves poetry like a Russian."

Let's turn to another poetic film about star-crossed lovers. It represents the first in a concluding series of four films that capture either briefly or in depth the essence of being a doctor.

Like Water for Chocolate (1992)

(Como Agua para Chocolate)

Based on the acclaimed first novel by Laura Esquivel,[16] who also wrote the screenplay, the film begins in the dark recesses of a well of scandal and hostility and ascends subtly and gracefully into a sparkling and dazzling sunshine. The setting for *Like Water for Chocolate* is turn-of-the-century Mexico, where we meet Tita (Lumi Cavazos), whose sensitivity to onions is so great that her resulting intrauterine wailing induces her mother's premature labor, and she is brought forth on the cutting board, among the herbs and onions. She grows into a beautiful and sensual woman whose love for Pedro (Marco Leonardi), a handsome young man of means, is reciprocated. Were this made-in-heaven union allowed to take place, the film would have been a happy short subject.

Tita is, however, the youngest daughter of a patrician family and is expected to remain unmarried to take care of her mother, Mama Elena (Regina Torne). This provides the first layer of a rich cake, namely, the exploration of how societies enforce customs that do not inure to an individual's benefit but to that of other members of the community and how readily some comply despite the impact on their own lives.

The film also reminds us of how daughters have traditionally been the ones expected to care for their elderly parents (especially mothers, because women generally live longer). Many women have recently spoken of the disorienting nature of this role reversal.[17] The daughter becomes the mother and must reconcile her new feelings with childhood memories and simultaneously balance her own personal goals and responsibilities. This role reversal (which never really takes place in this film because mother is "Mami" to the end) leads to a bittersweet relationship, as Linda Bird Francke has pointed out in her poignant essay, "Loving Mother, At Last."[18]

The cake's second layer appropriately involves food, which always has had a special meaning with regard to love and sexuality. The title refers to the use by Mexicans of water rather than milk in making hot chocolate. The chocolate is added when the water is on the verge of boiling over, and the expression "like water for chocolate" connotes an intensity of emotions, as with a state of sexual arousal. Indeed, the book[16] begins each of its dozen chapters with a recipe, which is then woven through the narrative. The film uses this technique to great effect, as Tita's creations under the tutelage of the mestizo servant, Nacha (Ada Carrasco), are savored by the family but have strange physiologic and, at times, aphrodisiac effects. For example, she prepares an exquisite feast for the wedding of her lover to her sister Rosaura (Yareli Arizmendi), the firstborn daughter (whom Pedro agrees to marry because he wants to be near Tita). In doing so, Tita's tears mix into the cake batter, transmitting her emotions and passions through the food, which remains delicious to the taste but potent to the nervous system.

The result is an extraordinary scene of longing and sighing that culminates in a mass vomiting that is lyrical rather than repelling.

The film's third layer is presented by the third daughter, Gertrudis (Claudette Maille), who is angered by the treatment of her younger sister and by her older sister's acquiescence with her mother's idea that she marry Tita's lover. She bolts for a cold shower during a remarkable scene of ecstasy brought on by another of Tita's culinary creations. This ablution is followed by an updated Lady Godiva rendition (sans demureness), as she hops on the horse of a Pancho Villa-like bandido and rides away. In an amusing feminist twist, after her stint as a prostitute on the Mexican border, she rejoins her lover and becomes the revolutionary band's leader. Her name, Gertrudis, is an allusion to a storied Mexican woman revolutionary.

A final layer involves an interesting depiction of the privileged, aristocratic life of the turn-of-the-century upper classes and their paternalism towards others. In this hierarchical society, everyone plays his or her role, as does an Anglo doctor, John Brown, played with sympathy and sensitivity by Mario Iván Martinez. He learns the language and strives to fit in but is caught in a no-man's-land between the Anglo culture across the Texas border, which he has rejected, and that of the Mexican upper class, with whose members he can fraternize because of his profession but never really be part of. Dr. Brown is a skillful practitioner, sensitive to the cultural beliefs of those under his care. When necessary, he also uses folk medicines that, we learn, are based on his own shared Indian heritage.

These scenes reminded me of my experiences in the previously mentioned migrant health clinic established in Fort Lupton, Colorado, in 1970.[19] Now a thriving community health center, it was a joint effort of physicians from the University of Colorado Medical Center and the Migrant Health program along with community organizers and local Chicanos. The goal was to deliver the latest in medical care while remaining sensitive to Chicano beliefs and to the profound influence of jobs, education, housing, and nutrition on health. The greatest allies of the clinic were the consejeros or advisers, the respected people in the community to whom others turned for help. They gave us an understanding of the community's needs and allowed us to reach out with Western medicine while respecting the community's values and the role of natural caregivers. They provided links to the local folk healers, primarily the curanderas[20, 21] and even brujas (or "witches"). We were able to maintain a dialogue with them in a manner analogous to our professional relationship with community physicians. Simultaneously, a university-hospital colleague, Robert W. Putsch, was involved in investigating the blend of cultural anthropology and clinical medicine pioneered by Arthur Kleinman and others[22]—and now popularly called ethnomedicine—by drawing on his experience on the Navajo Reservation in Shiprock, New Mexico.[23, 24]

Although Dr. Brown's role in the film is minor, he receives my vote for getting it right about doctoring. In addition to his sensitivity to patients and their cultural beliefs, what struck me was the sense of kindness, honesty, and gentleness he conveys as he cares for his patients. Suspecting that Tita and Pedro are having clandestine meetings, Tita's mother, Mami, banishes Rosaura, Pedro, and their child across the border. Tita retreats into the barn and becomes catatonic after learning of the death of her nephew, with whom she had a special relationship. Refusing to send Tita to an insane asylum, Dr. Brown cares for her and helps her reestablish contact with the world. Although he loves Tita deeply, he never takes advantage of the supererogatory relationship. His aspiration to marry her sets up an interesting triangle (quadrangle, if you count Mami).

If you see the film, watch for other excellent scenes involving Tita's bedspread and an interesting wedding night custom involving a hole in a sheet. The film's blending of fantasy and realism explains why it endeared itself to many diverse audiences and stayed around in theaters for months because of word-of-mouth rather than the Hollywood megahype and orchestrated celebrity talk-show visits. It also brought to mind the passing of the marvelous Mexican star Cantinflas. Best known in the United States for his portrayal of Phileas Fogg's sidekick, Passepartout, in *Around the World in Eighty Days*, Cantinflas was so revered that upwards of a million Mexicans filed by his bier. The poor especially identified with his honest and knowing portrayal of the common Mexican, weighted down but not beaten down by a pyramidal economic structure. *Like Water for Chocolate*, full of both pyrotechnics and warmth, is a fitting though unintended tribute to someone who also could deliver profound messages in magically funny and simple ways.

My list of favorite doctor films includes one that surprises people, namely, *The Fugitive*. Let me explain why.

The Fugitive (1993)

For those who think they don't make movies like they used to, *The Fugitive* is just what the doctor ordered. The film is based on the David Janssen television series, which, in turn, was loosely based on the conviction of Dr. Sam Sheppard, a Cleveland osteopath, for the 1954 murder of his wife in their fashionable home on Lake Erie.[25] Beginning with the opening credits, you are propelled on a roller-coaster ride, hurtling from scene to scene, with only momentary pauses to allow you to catch your breath. The pace is so quick that before the credits are complete you have seen fragments of a brutal killing of the wife of Dr. Richard Kimble, a respected vascular surgeon at "Chicago Memorial Hospital"; his subsequent arrest; and his trial and conviction for first-degree murder. All of this is set against an apparently loving relationship cut short on the evening of a festive fund raiser for the Children's Research Center. As Dr. Kimble and his wife drive home, the infernal car phone rings, and he is called back to the hospital to help with a patient who has manifested an unrecognized bleeding tendency during gallbladder surgery. The patient is taking an experimental drug, RDU90, and the doctor of record doesn't answer his page. On his return home, Dr. Kimble follows his wife's love notes to their bedroom and encounters a man with a prosthetic hand, the intruder who, Kimble later says, killed his wife.

He is not believed and becomes the prime suspect. During the investigation someone asks why a surgeon would kill his wife. The response is, "For her money. She was wealthy and he stood to inherit her fortune." The stereotypical disbelieving answer is, "He's a doctor; he's already rich." This is only one of a number of snide side comments about physicians in the film. For example, as the investigation progresses, the comment is made that "the good doctor's skin was found at the scene"; "Good doctor?" is the sarcastic response. On balance though, Dr. Kimble is portrayed as a sympathetic character, and the movie has a number of medically interesting scenes.

The first involves the convincing feigning of a grand mal seizure by a convict as the felons are being transported by bus to a maximum security prison. This event triggers the escape, involving a series of spectacular visual effects that, unlike most effects in today's movies, are integral to the story. Now enters the other protagonist, Deputy U.S. Marshal Sam Gerard. Stunningly portrayed by Oscar-winning Tommy Lee Jones. Gerard combines cunning and earthiness. The relationship between the hunted and the hunter, while reminiscent of *Les Misérables*, differs in that a bond of mutual respect, and even compassion, is cumulatively forged between the fugitive and his relentless blood hound. Parenthetically, another excellent "hunter and hunted" film, *In the Line of Fire*, was released in 1993 and features brilliant portrayals by John Malkovich and Clint Eastwood.

The first of the scenes where the filmmakers get it right about what being a doctor is all about occurs when Kimble visits Cook County Hospital in order to check out who might have had a prosthesis like the intruder's (fig. 5). In trying to escape notice, Kimble poses as an orderly and is asked by a nurse to transport a child who has sustained chest trauma and whose diagnosis has been missed. He unsuccessfully mutters under his breath for the nurse and physician to check the chest x-ray in order to see the source of the problem, but the nurse orders Kimble to take the child to the observation suite. Knowing that the child needs immediate surgery, he gently comforts him while taking him instead up the elevator to the operating room, where he announces that emergency surgery was ordered. Even the hoodwinked nurse and the marshal, his declared enemy, marvel that he can't help being a doctor, no matter what the risk to himself. His doctor persona is shown again when, as he is escaping, he saves a wounded guard, not once but twice.

These scenes reminded me of another film where this hallmark of a profession, namely, the placement of another's welfare above self, is shown. In a brief scene towards the end of *The Greatest Show on Earth*, Jimmy Stewart is a doctor masquerading as Buttons the Clown to escape imprisonment for the mercy killing of his wife; yet, he reveals his true identity to save an injured circus worker.

FIGURE 5. *The Fugitive.* Dr. Richard Kimble (Harrison Ford) tries to find a prosthesis similar to the one worn by the man who killed his wife.

There are some scenes that strain the imagination, for example, when Kimble gives himself local anesthesia and sutures his own lacerated abdomen. Still, I imagine there are surgeons who could do this skillfully, especially if a layman can cut off his own trapped leg, as a Pennsylvanian recently did, and drive himself to safety. Kimble also is the beneficiary of a breakfast tray left by a nurse at the bedside of an incompetent patient whom she expects to feed himself. It's hard to believe that any nurse worth her salt would do that. Kimble also moves remarkably fast for all the trauma he has sustained and the fatigue he must be feeling. But I guess he's running on adrenaline, like the *Alive* survivors were.[26]

Having obtained a list of patients who have had a prosthesis, Kimble proceeds to call them, as if he were doing a follow-up study. Anyone who has made such return calls to patients can identify with his first call. We can't hear what is said on the other end of the line, but it sounds as if the patient had died. After a gulp, he answers compassionately and sensitively before moving on to the next call.

Another interesting sidebar is the lax security at the hospitals, a sore point in contemporary America. Hospitals, as their derivation from the Latin for "guest house" implies, were designed to be open and inviting places, based on their role as helping institutions. Turning them into armed camps can make them unwelcoming and forbidding. Still some accommodation has had to be made to the realities of today's real-world random violence and "baby-snatching." Nonetheless, it is interesting to see how Kimble's familiarity with hospitals makes it easy for him to negotiate the presumably heightened security.

The most important medical theme relates to the pharmaceutical industry and the doctors who work with them. It shows how far drug companies, doctors, and research have fallen in the public's esteem. Back in the 1930s, a symbiotic relationship existed between doctors and pharmaceutical companies, as both were seen as dedicated to helping folks. Pharmaceutical advertisements showed doctors rushing out to get a medicine to help save a child or doctors studying late at night in the library, while the city slept, in order to put their knowledge to work for mankind (fig. 6). Much of this good feeling was beneficial, not just to physicians, but to the public. It's hard to believe that only a decade ago, the chief executive officer of a pharmaceutical company was honored in *Time* magazine as having made it "America's most admired firm."[27] As drugs have become more costly, however, and "me-too" drugs have replaced others going off patent, the pharmaceutical industry has been increasingly bashed. Along with insurers and doctors, they were early

FIGURE 6. Pharmaceutical advertisement showing physicians studying late into the night in order to put their knowledge to work for the good of mankind.

targets in the Clinton health care reform publicity initiative; although some of the criticism was muted as the Administration sought allies in its effort to pass its proposed legislation. So, it is not surprising to find that the villains of this piece are the "unscrupulous" doctors doing research in collaboration with "greedy" pharmaceutical companies. As Gerard says, after being told that the drug company does 7.5 billion dollars in net sales, "That company's a monster!" Calvin Coolidge must be turning in his grave.

As the story unfolds, we learn that the results of the RDU90 study were tampered with so that adverse events like bleeding tendencies and hepatic injuries were hidden. Near the end of the picture, there's a gala dinner highlighting the International Association of Cardiologists meeting where the keynote speech is "Alternatives to Cardiac Plaque-Reducing Surgery." "They're going to be lining up for that one," says the deputy marshal sarcastically, and indeed, they are. As the physician who headed the RDU90 project launches into his address, he heaps praise on the "joint venture between academic medicine and the research industry."

Again, it is interesting to hear people outside of medicine alluding to a relationship that has caused concern within medicine and the academic community. As many leading institutions have embraced entrepreneurship and collaboration with industry, they have had to establish ethical guidelines for intellectual property.[28] Such joint ventures are valuable, but the trick is to keep an appropriate arm's length, a lid on greed, and proper safeguards about sharing data, so that discoveries do not remain solely proprietary but benefit the public at large. It's a tough struggle to retain the "nobility," not just of the profession, but also of research, in a highly cynical era that has become more bottom-line oriented.[29]

Finally, it was interesting to contrast this film with the first and last episodes of *The Fugitive*, which aired between 1963 and 1967. Shown by NBC early in the film's run, the opening episode was amateurish, and the last episode was only marginally better. Yet, the latter captured 70 percent of the viewing public, making it the most watched television program until the shooting of JR on *Dallas*. This film is light years better. The marriage of good acting, nice human touches, especially on the part of Tommy Lee Jones, a crackling story, and some interesting medical issues rate it four stethoscopes as entertaining escape.

The next film, based on the book *City of Joy* by Dominique Lapierre,[30] shows how a hedonistic, self-centered doctor discovers his better side. In so doing, he portrays another beneficial set of professional values.

City of Joy (1992)

Before this movie, my image of Patrick Swayze, best known for his role in *Dirty Dancing*, was the much ballyhooed episode of him diving in a swim suit unable to contain his most prized asset, the year after he was named the sexiest man on the planet. So, the fact that he could play a jerk, which he is called on to do early in this film, was not surprising. That he could give the sensitive portrayal called for in the last two-thirds, was. The film, however, belongs to Om Puri, who plays a noble rickshaw driver. Readers of the nonfiction book that focused not just on the rickshaw driver but on a priest and a quite different doctor may be disappointed. Regardless, the film captures the book's powerful message, "All that is not given is lost."[30]

The screenplay begins in a Houston operating room, where Dr. Max Lowe (Swayze) unsuccessfully attempts closed chest massage to restore a child's heartbeat. Surprisingly, he doesn't appear to crack the child's chest but simply walks despondently out of the operating room directly into his Indian odyssey, to "find enlightenment" following the well-worn path of *Lost Horizon*,[31] the Beatles, et cetera.

The director transports us next to rural India, where Hasari Pal (Om Puri) is readying his family for a trip to the big city, Calcutta, to find work, after droughts have ruined the crops. "Stay away from the cinema," the grandfather warns the children. This is an allusion to the fact that the movie industry, centered in Calcutta, churns out more movies than Hollywood and that the over-the-top melodramas provide a

FIGURE 7. *City of Joy.* Hasari Pal (Om Puri) and his family, having left their rural village to seek a better life in Calcutta, spend their first night in the shadow of the Howrah Bridge.

much-needed escape from the dreariness that pervades the lives of ordinary Indians. Grandfather then turns to his son and in the philosophic manner for which Indians are justly famed, says, "A man's journey to the end of his obligations is a very long one."

In Calcutta, we see views of a large mass of people crossing the Howrah Bridge (fig. 7), ceremonial bathing in the Hooghly river (a branch of the Ganges), and women bearing bundles on their heads as they walk. The scenes took me back to 1963, when a fellow Hopkins resident and I were sent to Calcutta as part of an international program for cooperation in medical research and training. Each day, we were taken from the Ramakrishna Mission—a legacy of Swami Vivekenanda's attempt to reconcile Eastern and Western religions—on a hair-raising ride through the city with horns blaring as the driver dodged pedestrians and rickshaws. Our destination was the infectious disease hospital in Ballygunge, a desolate area bordering on terrible slums called bustees. Sheds of patients with tuberculosis, smallpox, cholera, and tetanus were overseen mainly by sweepers and irregularly by nurses and doctors. Better than any public health course, the experience made us appreciate how much more important housing, food, water supply, education, and jobs were for health than sophisticated technology. Also, one couldn't help but be struck with where India was on the curve that the United States had traversed in the past century, largely by addressing socioeconomic factors.

Taking care of hypotensive cholera patients with limited technology challenged our clinical skills. Indeed, when I moved on to Presbyterian Hospital in New York later that year, I felt as if I had been let loose in an all-you-can-eat smorgasbord at a luxury hotel after being subjected to a starvation diet on a desert island. Since then, I have harbored the vague desire to achieve a seemingly unattainable middle ground between the stultifying and wasteful plate-filling mentality of having too many available technologic and consultative options with the effects of having too little to help people who truly need them. The most difficult adjustment was reconciling the zero percent death rate that we were able to achieve even in the sickest patients[32] and knowing that next door 25 percent would die because of lack of replacement fluids, electrolytes, and antibiotics. We were guests, so we couldn't impose our values, nor was our mission to transform the hospital by rebuilding and restaffing it. Talk about ethics and value clashes. *City of Joy* rekindled all these memories and more.

Once in Calcutta, Hasari is swindled by a countryman out of his entire savings of two hundred rupees, so he, his wife, and three children must go to the City of Joy, a self-help school, dispensary, and conglomeration of relatively neat hovels. Dr. Max arrives in Calcutta about the same time, apparently thinking he's on a Club Med tour. His surprise at not being able to order a cheeseburger seems unbelievable. Clearly, he had no prior understanding of Indian religious beliefs or culture and had no required readings (as we did), such as E. M. Forster's sensitive, penetrating analysis, *A Passage to India*.[33] If he had, he would have been prepared for the dal, chapati, and other dishes, including the occasional tasteless "treat" of mutton.

Max gets rolled for his money outside a bar controlled by the Indian mafia and is rescued by Hasari, who takes him to the City of Joy. After he is nursed back to health, he resists all entreaties to stay and give health care to the poor. During an exchange with Joan Bethal (Pauline Collins), the woman who runs the clinic, he tells her that he has no desire to be a saint and asks if she doesn't think it's a little bit stupid to try to drill a hole in the water? She tells him, "You have three choices: to run, to spectate, or to commit." He shoots back, "Simple-minded, but tidy." He also wonders aloud if she's a "fool or a fraud," and she answers, "Maybe the world is meant to break your heart."

Even when he successfully manages a difficult breech delivery in a leprous woman, Max is not happy. While the ecstatic short-statured parents look on, he rants about bringing "another little mouth into this cesspool of a country." Clearly, anyone caring for people in such poverty must wrestle with the incongruity that saving a patient often means sending him or her back to unbelievable squalid lean-tos without water, electricity, or any conveniences, and where life expectancy hovers around forty. Indeed, that was one of the arguments an Indian doctor raised to me about our efforts at saving more patients with cholera. While it is not for the physician to judge what is a quality life, observing such situations should energize him or her to do everything possible to obviate such poverty. Indeed, my subsequent work among the migrants[19] flowed directly from the Indian experience.

Later, Dr. Max loses his ticket home and must work at the clinic to earn money to buy another one, so he agrees to be a doctor for a while. He has a nice exchange with a mother who sells the milk intended for her baby in order to pay the rent; he arranges to make sure both are covered and sternly lectures her to feed her child. (It's not unlike what Dr. Jack Geiger described doing in a Mississippi Delta community health center he helped start—where he bent the federal rules to prescribe food and not just drugs, reasoning that food was the recognized treatment for malnutrition.)[34] There's a great scene of a well-baby exam in which an infant boy urinating like a human fountain makes a direct hit on Dr. Max. On leaving the movie, some former ethics students, turned pediatric residents, told me how easily they identified with that scene.

Meanwhile, Hasari applies to be a rickshaw driver and is brought to the Bihari extortionist/entrepreneur Ghatak, or godfather (Shyamanand Jalan), who runs the trade. When the Ghatak taunts him about wanting to become a "human horse," Hasari replies, "I do, Babu" (an Indian term of respect). He then is asked, "Can you neigh?" This episode raised another area of personal ambivalence. I remember not being able to ride a rickshaw because of the sense that it would be shameful to be pulled by another human; yet one sees that Hasari not only takes pride in this very difficult life (fig. 8), but also earns an income important to him and his family. In the book,[30] the godfather calculates that outlawing the trade from which he gets a substantial percentage would affect one hundred thousand people, the drivers and their dependents— a convenient rationalization for keeping people in their place.

On seeing the upper-class Indians use his service, one gets the sense of how the caste system, though outlawed, remains ingrained in the culture. We have analogous social systems in the United States, which have become more pronounced in the last decade. Indeed, the upper-class Indians are more like the British, from whom India took both the best

FIGURE 8. *City of Joy*. Dr. Max Lowe (Patrick Swayze), exultantly riding a rickshaw pulled by his new friend Hasari Pal (Om Puri), finds fulfillment in a Calcutta slum, the City of Joy.

and the worst of traditions. The Indian entrepreneur points out that money is the wall that separates him from the degradation outside. He lives in one of the old British villas whose walls are topped by jagged glass. The legacies include the clubs, the afternoon tea, the cricket, the Shakespeare Wallah, but also a system of justice and administration— which unfortunately is too often carried to extremes in the literal bureaucratic sense; again, read the book.[30] It is probably true that all colonies distill the best and the worst of their occupiers; we have our examples in the Philippines and Cuba.

Dr. Max, now a social convert, encourages the people in the City of Joy to abandon the protection of the godfather. This leads to a crackdown, both on the clinic and on the rickshaw drivers. Hasari loses his job for being disloyal to Ghatak—and then rails against Dr. Max for his imposition of U.S. values. Hasari notes that from the time we are born "we are shipwrecked and live in different cultures." Again, this raises another delicate and important theme: Are concepts of justice and fairness transportable from culture to culture? Despite his misgivings, Hasari emerges as the strong leader of the rickshaw drivers and successfully fights the godfather's cruel son, vindicating the clash of values.

The worth of individuals is touched on again during an exchange with the lepers of short stature, who obviously have a lot to offer. One of them notes that he has "the body of a sparrow but the eyes of an eagle." When the monsoon rains come, Dr. Max saves the short-statured man and the family he previously disparaged. Seeing him swim in Calcutta's turbid water and coming away unscathed was somewhat unbelievable. It seemed to resonate with a theme uttered in the film and not uncommonly heard in India that if your heart is pure nothing will harm you; this leads people to bathe in and drink Ganges water—heavily laden with bacteria.

Many Indians have told me, "Don't judge India by Calcutta;" nonetheless, it is dualistic in the same way India is. In this marvelous crowded land of almost one billion people, abject poverty contrasts with the extraordinary beauty of the Taj Mahal, as well as the majestic city of Darjeeling with its tea plantations and breathtaking view of Mount Kanchenjunga in the Himalayas. Calcutta is over three hundred years old, founded as a trading post by Job Charnock of the British East India Company. Built to take advantage of where the Ganges meets the sea, it was the capital of imperial India from the mid-nineteenth century to 1911. It has always been a city of contrasts. Rudyard Kipling called it the "city of the dreadful night" a century ago, and vultures can still be seen filling the trees as they await dinner. Despite its magnificent parks and its status as India's cultural capital where the great director Satyajit Ray lived and worked, Calcutta is a strong contender for being the worst city in the world. Through its graphic descriptions of rat-infested, verminous hovels, the book is much more successful in portraying the terrible hardships many of Calcutta's residents must endure.[30]

Hasari's struggles to fulfill his "journey to the end of his obligations" is nicely portrayed in his efforts to acquire a dowry for his daughter. It reminds us of how much this tradition weighs on the minds of devoted Indian fathers. The economic burden that daughters place on families helps explain the high abortion rates and the fact that more than 90 percent of aborted fetuses are females. As Hasari sells his blood to make ends meet, he becomes weaker and his tuberculosis flares up.

As the film ends, Dr. Max, who now feels free to go, also feels free to stay, prompting Hasari's assertion that "the gods have not made it easy to be a human being." All in all, this magnificent film is a ringing affirmation of the idealism that leads many to enter helping professions such as medicine. The next film marvelously reinforces this theme. Based on the superb book by neurologist Oliver Sacks,[35] it manages, in an understated way, to capture the quintessence of doctoring. For this reason, I have chosen it to conclude the book.

Awakenings (1990)

As the opening credits roll, we are transported back to the 1920s where a young boy is progressing from being a straight-A student to having difficulty writing and concentrating. Fast forward to 1969 and change the setting to Mount Carmel (really Beth Abraham), a Bronx chronic disease hospital where Dr. Malcolm Sayer (Robin Williams), a research neurologist is being interviewed for a job. When asked if he is a "Doctor Doctor," he admits to having spent the previous five years fruitlessly trying to extract a decagram of myelin from tons of earthworms. Later, we will see that this subtle form of pigeonholing (are you a clinician, researcher, administrator, etc.?) doesn't necessarily predict someone's ability to care for the folks. After being hired, Sayer enters a world of immobile patients. When he asks what they are waiting for, he is told "Nothing." "How are they going to get well?" he responds. "They aren't; that's why they call it a chronic disease hospital" is the reply. An orderly shows him a ward they call "the garden," because "all we do is water and feed them like vegetables."

As Sayer studies these so-called "vegetables," he begins to notice that, although the light appears to be out, someone is home. He throws a ball and a patient catches it. As another's eyeglasses drop, she reaches out to retrieve them. Sayer sees a patient staring at a television with a rolling picture. After he fixes it, the man averts his gaze, but returns to his viewing once the picture starts rolling again. Beginning to think like the patients allows him to see why a person with no apparent impediment stops walking; a simple correction sends the woman on her way.

The film shows how much we can learn from patients, not just about disease, but about humanity. In dealing with them as individuals, Sayer sees persons behind the masks and begins to liberate them from their prisons. Some patients respond to operatic arias; another only when a Jimi Hendrix song is played. Stimulation is important for all of us, but especially for the psychologically or neurologically impaired and those with sensory deficits. Playing the right note or making the right connection can turn unresponsiveness into animation. Woody Guthrie, the singer who died of Huntington's chorea expressed in song how much an "Oklahoma Nurse Girl" meant to a ward full of "psycho ravers."[36]

The movie also affirms the need for clinicians to have a research approach, by which I mean a restless mind unwilling to accept things as they are, but constantly asking questions. Sayer makes the diagnosis of encephalitis lethargica, von Economo's disease, a brain disease that afflicted many after the influenza pandemic of 1916-1927. The patients became less and less responsive. Many died; others retreated into themselves. Sayer seeks out the resident expert on the condition and is told that the disease did not spare the higher brain functions. "Do you know this for a fact?" he asks. "Yes," is the reply. "Why?" Sayer shoots back. "Because the alternative is unthinkable." We are about to get an object lesson about the fallibility of received wisdom, which in this case is a form of self-protection for the caregivers.

Sayer decides to experiment with L-Dopa, a drug shown to help patients with Parkinsonism (a condition that can vary in severity from mild as in the case of Michael J. Fox to more severe as in Muhammed Ali), because the combination of a locked-in mind and immobility is similar. Most of the film focuses on Leonard Lowe (Robert De Niro), the now-adult patient we saw at the outset (fig. 9). Sayer asks Leonard's

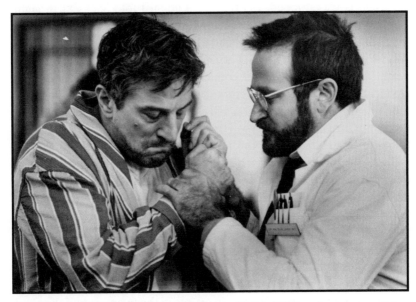

FIGURE 9. *Awakenings*. Dr. Malcolm Sayer (Robin Williams) uses compassion and observation to reach Leonard L (Robert De Niro) and other patients whose lives have been frozen in time.

devoted mother if he speaks to her. "Not in words," she replies. "Does he speak to you in other ways?" Sayer asks. Her quizzical response, "You don't have children, do you?" underlines the existence of an unspoken communication between parent and child. Reading the book gives one an understanding of why Leonard L is the film's main focus. Even before receiving L-Dopa, this remarkable man, when asked what it was like being the way he was, spelled out, "Caged. Deprived. Like Rilke's panther."[35] Sacks noted that Leonard swept his eyes around the ward and spelled out, "This is a human zoo." He was also fond of tapping out passages from Dante and T. S. Eliot. Although Leonard developed post-encephalitic disease at fifteen, he went on to Harvard where he almost obtained a Ph.D. After three years at home, he became totally immobile and was institutionalized in 1939.

On receiving L-Dopa, he is portrayed in the film as a gentle giant and resident wise man who tries to make a match between the doctor and an adoring nurse. This is pure Hollywood. The real Leonard L dreamt of being transformed from a "meek, mild, and melancholy man to a burly caveman equipped with an invincible club and an invincible phallus." He would masturbate for hours each day. Conflicts with staff finally led him to be placed in a punishment cell. He did get the tics and athetoid movements so well portrayed by De Niro, and after many trials, L-Dopa was stopped. As the real Leonard told Sacks, "I thought L-Dopa was the most wonderful thing in the world, and I blessed you for giving me the Elixir of Life. Then when everything went bad...I cursed you for giving it to me....Now, I accept the whole situation. It was wonderful, terrible, dramatic, and comic. It is finally sad....I am best left alone—no more drugs."[35] He returned to his pre L-Dopa state and spelled out: "I am what I am. I am part of the world. My disease and deformity...are beautiful in a way, like a dwarf or a toad. It's my destiny to be sort of grotesque."[35] Now that's profound!

As the other patients come out of their stupor, they marvel at such things as applying make-up and going to the bathroom unaided for the first time in years. They also act up, prompting the nurses to say that they liked it better the other way. This rings true. How much easier we caregivers have it when patients are docile and cooperative. Some may find the absence of anger in many awakening patients hard to believe. It's best illustrated by the case of Rose R, a *bon vivant* flapper admitted in 1935. Awakened in 1969, "she spoke of Gershwin and other contemporaries as if they were still alive; of events in the twenties as if they had just happened."[33] Sacks was astounded to hear her say: "I can give you the date of Pearl Harbor. I can give you the date of Kennedy's assassination. I registered it all—but none of it seems real. I know it's '69. I know I'm 64—but I feel like it's '26; I feel I'm 21. I've been a spectator for the past 43 years."[35] Again, this reflection goes into the "Wow!" file.

Another important theme is the symbiosis of the patients and their loved ones who become co-patients. Changing the conditions can disorient the caregivers. In the film, Leonard's mother refuses Sayer's advice to take a vacation now that he can care for himself. "He would die without me," she replies. This is true to the real-life intense and mutual dependence between Leonard and his mother who looked after him ten hours a day. When she changed his diapers, Sacks saw "a look of blissful babylike contentment on Mr. L's face, admixed with impotent resentment at his degraded, infantilized, and dependent state."[35] His mother similarly showed and verbalized a mixture of pleasure with her life-giving, loving, and mothering role, as well as intense resentment at her life being "'sacrificed' to her grown-up but helpless 'parasite of a son.'"[35] Once the L-Dopa took effect, she said that her son had been "taken away" and that she couldn't go on unless he were "restored" to her. She is quoted as saying, "I can't bear Len the way he is...so active and full of decision. He has pushed me away. He only thinks of himself. I need to be needed. It's the main need I have."[35] These and other reactions forced Sacks to have second thoughts about the experiment.

Penny Marshall's direction is superb, as evidenced by her ability to restrain Robin Williams, thereby taking full advantage of his genius (see *Patch Adams* for just the opposite). De Niro is particularly remarkable in managing to get inside Leonard L. During the production, Sacks observed him trying on expressions of rage and suspicion as well as mimicking the patient's deformities. De Niro said his greatest challenge was imagining the nothingness that Leonard L and the others experienced. During a rehearsal break, he quoted Beckett: "Nothing is more real than nothing."[35]

Although not one of your usual feel-good movies, the film tries to be upbeat by focusing on the fact that most patients benefited from L-Dopa, if only for a short time. In the end, it is both entertaining and filled with important lessons about what these patients have taught Sayer/ Sacks. The primary personal lesson is to be happy with work, friendship, joy, family, and to appreciate the simple things that matter in a life which can be so fragile and transient. The professional take-home messages for doctors include: not writing off patients, but rather individualizing care with affection; reemphasizing observation and perception in a technologic age where we rely more on laboratory tests than on our senses and communication skills; using a research orientation in clinical care; and attending to the needs of the caregivers.

An interesting subtlety that escaped me and many other viewers was the appearance of Lillian T, the only living actual survivor in the film. Sacks described the effect of her entry on the set as "like Caesar ... stepping out of the pages of a history book."[35] The actors knew that they could step out of their roles, but she could not. As De Niro was wheeled in and took up the frozen dystonic posture of Leonard L, Lillian T, herself frozen, cocked an alert and critical eye." Then, she gave Sacks "a wink, and a barely perceptible thumbs-up sign, meaning, 'He's okay - he's got it! He really knows what it's like."[35] The same can be said for Williams's portrayal of a doctor. *Awakenings* is Hollywood at its best, and a fitting end for our odyssey to the land of doctor movies. I hope you enjoyed the trip.

NOTES

1. Barach AL. David Seegal, the magnanimous. P&S Quarterly, Fall 1973, 18: 23-25.
2. Kobal J, ed. John Kobal Presents the Top 100 Movies. New York and Scarborough, Ontario: New American Library, 1988.
3. Wennberg JE and Gittelsohn A. Small area variation in health care delivery. Science 1973; 182:1102-1108.
4. Carey M. Show and tell: Do we need to share all our private lives? Baltimore Sun, July 18, 1991, p. B1.
5. Halberstam D. Summer of '49. New York: William Morrow, 1989, p 159.
6. Greene G. Confidential Agent. New York: Viking Press, 1939.
7. Greene G. The Power and the Glory. New York: Penguin Books, 1977.
8. Greene G. Our Man in Havana. New York: Penguin Books, 1979.
9. Rich JM and DeVitis JL. Theories of Moral Development. Springfield, IL: CC Thomas, 1985.
10. Finland M and Castle WB. The Harvard Medical Unit at Boston City Hospital, Vol. 2. Part 1: The Peabody-Minot Tradition, 1915-1950. Boston: Francis A. Countway Library of Medicine, 1983, pp 473, 501–502.
11. Barth J. Lights...camera...Europe. I: New York Times Advertising Supplement, Your Invitation to Europe. October 8, 1995, pp 16–23.
12. Nowlan RA, Nowlan GW, eds. "We'll Always Have Paris": The Definitive Guide to Great Lines from the Movies. New York: Harper Collins, 1995, p 702.
13. Proust M. Remembrance of Things Past. New York: Random House, 1981.
14. Pasternak B. Doctor Zhivago. New York: Pantheon Books, 1959.
15. Maltin L. "Doctor Zhivago" review. In: Cinemania 96 CD, Microsoft, 1995.
16. Esquivel L. Like Water for Chocolate: A Novel in Monthly Installments, with Recipes, Romances and Home Remedies. New York: Doubleday & Co, 1992.
17. House MK. Home-style nursing. JAMA 1978; 240: 2472–2474.
18. Francke LB. Loving Mother, at Last. New York Times, October 10, 1979, p 27A.
19. Dans PE and Johnson S. Politics in the development of a migrant health center. A pilgrim's progress from idealism to pragmatism. N Engl J Med 292: 890–895. Correspondence, N. Engl J Med 1975; 293: 362–363.

20. Kiev A. Curanderismo: Mexican-American Folk Psychiatry. New York: Free Press, 1968.
21. Trotter RT II and Chavira JA. Curanderismo: Mexican-American Folk Healing. Athens, Georgia: University of Georgia Press, 1981.
22. Kleinman A, Eisenberg L, Good B. Culture, illness, and care: Clinical lessons from anthropologic and cross-cultural research. Ann Intern Med 1978; 88: 251–258.
23. Putsch RW III. Cross-cultural communication: The special case of interpreters in health care. JAMA 1985; 254: 3344–3348.
24. Putsch RW III and Joyce M. Dealing with Patients from Other Cultures. In: Clinical Methods, 3rd edition, ed. HK Walker, WD Hall, and JW Hurst. Boston: Butterworths, 1990, p 1050–1065.
25. Farquhar M. Nowhere to hide. The bizarre case of Dr. Sam Sheppard will be forever linked to "The Fugitive." Even if he never ran. Washington Post, October 3, 1993, pp F1,4.
26. Read PP. Alive, the Story of the Andes Survivors. New York: Avon Books, 1974.
27. Bock G. Merck's medicine man: How Roy Vagelos turned the drugmaker into America's most admired firm. Time, February 22, 1988, p 44.
28. The Johns Hopkins School of Medicine Intellectual Property Guidelines, April 21, 1993, unpublished.
29. Moukheiber Z. Science for sale. Forbes, May 17, 1999, pp 136-144.
30. Lapierre D. The City of Joy. Transl. K. Spink. Garden City, New York: Doubleday & Co, 1985.
31. Hilton J. Lost Horizon. New York: W. Morrow, 1934.
32. Carpenter CCJ, Mondal A, Sack RB, Mitra PP, Dans PE, Wells SA, Hinman EJ, Chaudhuri RN. Clinical studies in Asiatic cholera, II, III, and IV. Bull Johns Hopkins Hosp 1966; 118: 174–229.
33. Forster EM. A Passage to India. New York: Harcourt, Brace & Co, 1924, p 83.
34. Geiger HJ. Community Health Centers: Health Care as an Instrument of Social Change. In: Reforming Medicine: Lessons of the Last Quarter Century, ed. VW Sidel and R Sidel. New York: Pantheon Books, 1984, p 11–32.
35. Sacks O. Awakenings, First Harper Perennial Edition. New York: Harper/Collins Publishers, 1990, pp 205, 207-208, 213, 218-219, 381, 385, 386.
36. Guthrie W. Pastures of Plenty—A Self-Portrait. New York: Harper/Collins Publishers, 1990.

APPENDIX A

Recurring Medical Themes and Stereotypes

What would movies be without stereotypes and clichés? Certainly, less fun. This appendix contains some of the recurring clichés and stereotypes that Hollywood transformed into the popular mythology of medicine. The films in which they appear are discussed more fully in the text.

"BOIL THE WATER!"

The cry for boiling water has been uttered in numerous films, usually as a pregnant woman is about to deliver (see *Internes Can't Take Money*, *Miss Susie Slagle's*, *Mary Stevens, M.D.*, and *Gross Anatomy*). It appears to be a recognition of the germ theory and, appropriately enough, is best illustrated in *The Story of Louis Pasteur*. Having attacked doctors for transmitting bacteria and being responsible for the deaths of many women in childbirth, Pasteur asks for water to be boiled and orders Charbonnet, the skeptical member of the French Academy of Medicine, to wash his hands and sterilize his instruments before delivering his daughter's baby. In *Arrowsmith*, Martin tells his wife to "boil water" to kill the "plague virus" in test tubes. In *The Citadel*, Dr. Manson has the townspeople boil the water to kill the typhoid bacillus.

My favorite "boil the water" scene occurs in *Woman Doctor*. As Dr. Judith Randall's husband pilots wildly to get their critically injured son from Rhode Island to a New York hospital, she asks her husband's mistress, Gail, if she has a percolator. Gail wonders if she wants coffee and Randall responds, "No, boil some water, I have to operate," which she proceeds to do in mid-air.

"JUST SAY AAH"

This request is usually spoken to a frightened, uncomfortable youngster with a throat infection by a kindly doctor wearing one of medicine's traditional symbols, the head mirror. This can be seen in *Internes Can't Take Money*, *The Citadel*, and *Miss Susie Slagle's*, where

Sonny Tufts, as a third-year student, puts on his mirror and exclaims excitedly, "She just called me 'Doctor.'" The most dramatic scenes involve doctors dealing emergently with children choking from hard material stuck in the larynx or trachea, all too common before diphtheria vaccines became widely available. For the most creative of such scenes, see *Mary Stevens, M.D.* for how she handles such an emergency without a head mirror or other equipment. Although the phrase is still used, the head mirror has been replaced by better tools for visualizing the mouth and throat.

GETTING IN

This preoccupation with getting into medical school is best captured in a cheesy 1994 movie of the same name starring Stephen Mailer, Kristy Swanson, Dave Chappelle, and Andrew McCarthy. Gabriel Higgs (Mailer) descends from a dynasty of four males who graduated from Johns Hopkins Medical School. His family is obsessed with his continuing the tradition, even though he wants to be a botanist. Higgs skips a blank on the Medical College Admission Test (MCAT) seventy-five questions from the end and, after blowing the interview, is wait-listed. A computer-geek friend (Chappelle) hacks into the Johns Hopkins computer and learns that Higgs is sixth on the list. Since "no one turns down Johns Hopkins," the distraught young man first determines to explain the circumstances to those above him and appeal to their better natures to drop off the list. His friend says, "We're talking about med students. They don't have better natures. They're mean, competitive, and greedy." He decides to propose a bribe. The first student, played by a pre-"Friends" Matthew Perry, turns out to be an arrogant extortionist. Another is a monomaniacal Princetonian (McCarthy), who is not above cleverly murdering his rivals. In short, it looks like the three screenwriters were permanently scarred by association with pre-med grinds who hoarded course reference materials to get ahead.

ANATOMY CLASS AS A RITE OF PASSAGE

This is most evident in *Gross Anatomy*. *Not As a Stranger* and *People Will Talk* also have brief scenes with reflections on the cadaver. In *Malice*, there's a particularly tasteless comment by hotshot surgeon Jed Hill (Alec Baldwin) about his cadaver. Also see *Miss Susie Slagle's*, *Doctor in the House*, and *The Girl in White* for scenes involving skeletons, another staple of medical student films.

FAINTING AT THE SIGHT OF A CADAVER OR OF BLOOD

Cadavers and blood are usually inserted into movie scenes to signify the squeamishness of beginning medical students. In *Mary Shelley's*

Frankenstein, Tom Hulce plays a first-year student who faints as the pro-sector makes the first cut in the cadaver. The same thing happens in *Not As a Stranger*. As for fainting at the sight of blood, in *Doctor in the House*, head surgeon Sir Lancelot Sprat (James Robertson Justice) warns students observing their first operation, "Fall backward if you faint and not across the patient." Of course, a student faints. The same advice is given in *Not As a Stranger*.

DOCTORS AS SEX MANIACS

Movies have usually devoted more time to portraying doctors and medical students as having easy access to sex, usually involving nurses and technicians, than to actually taking care of people. The latest example is the 1998 film, *Critical Care*. The most direct reference to this stereotype is in a scene from *The Interns* when a nursing supervisor orienting incoming nursing students tells them, "Never talk to the interns, they're all sex maniacs." The sickest and probably most literal example of doctors as sex maniacs is in *Dead Ringers*.

THE RICH DOCTOR/PLAYBOY

Besides having access to fast women, doctors are often portrayed as playboys with fast cars, predominantly concerned with making money. In *Not As a Stranger*, Frank Sinatra plays Alfred Boone, a student who becomes a surgeon, to "pull in the big bucks and drive a fancy convertible." Having accomplished his goal, he later ruefully declares that the car "owns him," rather than the reverse. In *Mary Shelley's Frankenstein*, Victor Frankenstein (Kenneth Branagh) introduces himself to his first-year classmate saying "I'm here to do research." His new friend Henry (Tom Hulce) replies "I'm here to be a mere doctor. Too bad, really, because I find sick people revolting. I plan to take care of rich patients and their daughters." The doctors in *Society Doctor* and *The Citadel* as well as Dr. Welbeck in *The Hospital* would serve as good role models for greed. In *Malice*, surgeon Jed Hill agrees with a fellow drinker at his local bar that he went into medicine "to make a lot of money and to see a lot of naked women."

DOCTORS SMOKING

From its earliest days, smoking has been used extensively in al-most every movie as a conversation enhancer or for breaks in the action.[1] Doctor pictures are no exception (see *The Citadel*, *The Young Doctors*, and *No Way Out*). In *Society Doctor*, the chief operating room nurse tells an "assistant intern" played by Robert Taylor, "There's nothing like a cigarette before a tonsillectomy or for that matter after a tonsillectomy." In *The Interns*, everybody smokes. One intern asks for "a pack of king-size Chesterfields," while a nurse buys a box of cigars for the psychiatry chief. In the old-fashioned credits for *Dr. Monica*, she is shown sitting at her office desk, wreathed in smoke.

In *Not As a Stranger*, Professor Aarons sends his charges on their way after internship, with an intriguing line: "Don't endorse any cigarettes." The line suggests that the screenwriter and director were making their little sly protest against the tobacco industry. It also is a reminder of a time when it was common to see advertisements, such as, "More doctors smoke Camels than any other cigarette" or doctors endorsing Chesterfields, which was said to be "Good for the T-Zone" (the throat).

HIPPOCRATIC OATH

Considered to be the moral basis of the profession of medicine, the Hippocratic oath is usually trooped out in films as a counterpoint to something that is deemed unethical. See chapter 9 for a full treatment of this subject in such films as *Men in White*, *The Green Light*, *The Young Doctors*, and *The Girl in White*.

HANGING UP A SHINGLE

It wasn't until 1925 that internships became common.[2] Thereafter, most doctors went directly into practice by hanging up their shingle (see *Arrowsmith* and *Mary Stevens, M.D.*, when she and her classmate go into practice after internship). My proud father, who only had a high school education, gave me a shingle when I earned my M.D., signaling his hope that I would enter private practice in a house to be built on a piece of land he had bought. Alas, I did not. In *Young Dr. Kildare*, Jimmy Kildare's girlfriend hangs up a shingle in front of the family's house in anticipation that he will join his father in practice. Jimmy decides against practicing in the small town of Dartford, in favor of studying internal medicine in the big New York hospital.

DOCTORS ON AMBULANCE RUNS

Until the 1950s, it was common for doctors to ride the ambulance. This can be seen in numerous films including *Mary Stevens, M.D.*, *Men in White*, *No Way Out*, *Not As a Stranger*, and *Miss Susie Slagle's*. In *Young Dr. Kildare*, Dr. Gillespie asks the interns, "Who's going to be in charge of my ambulance?" and adds derisively, "Every ambulance has three pairs of hands but only one set of brains." The most spectacular movie ambulance scenes are of the horse-drawn variety in *The Girl in White*. The film is based on *Bowery to Bellevue*,[3] the autobiography of Emily Dunning, the first woman intern to ride New York City's ambulances.

USING A MIRROR TO SEE IF SOMEONE IS ALIVE

In *Young Dr. Kildare*, Kildare (Lew Ayres) revives a rich socialite who has attempted suicide in a cheap apartment. As he does so, he asks the attendant to "hold a mirror to her lips and tell me when it clouds up."

NURSE/DOCTOR RELATIONSHIPS

Despite the fact that nurses are responsible for most direct patient care, especially in hospitals, Hollywood has focused most of its attention on the doctors, with the nurse playing a subsidiary role. The 1997 film *Critical Care* caustically notes the real truth when ICU nurse Helen Mirren tells a resident who is holding a comatose patient's hand, "Hands-on patient care from a doctor? I'm impressed." No one exemplifies the dedicated nurse better than Kristina Hedvigson (Olivia De Havilland) in *Not As a Stranger*. She is an operating room nurse required to stand for hours on end, in the days when surgery routinely lasted many hours. Called the "Swedish Nightingale" by her peers, she reflects on how she was drawn to the profession at the age of six when she saw a nurse in a blue cape. This illustrates the enduring power of symbols and externals.

The once rigid hierarchy of doctors and nurses is demonstrated in numerous movies. For example, when Arrowsmith stops to ask directions from a nursing student who is scrubbing the floor as punishment for having sneaked a cigarette, he chides her, "The first duty of a nurse is to stand when speaking to a doctor." In *Vigil in the Night*, nurses are in awe of the doctors. The Doctor–Nurse game,[4-6] where nurses are supposed to act in a subservient manner, even when they know more than the doctor, is nowhere more pointedly challenged than in *Sister Kenny*.

In the Kildare films, the chief of service, Doctor Gillespie (Lionel Barrymore), has a relationship with the nursing supervisor that alternates between mutual respect and a crusty expectation of subservience. In *Young Dr. Kildare*, Kildare asks how Gillespie knows that he visited a patient. Gillespie replies, "I know everything that goes on in this hospital. That nurse Molly has been my stooge for the last fifteen years." In the same film, when a nurse directs a newspaper reporter to a socialite's room, he says, "Thanks, Babe." Respect for nurses and the lack of it are shown in *Not As a Stranger*, when the chief of service wisely warns the interns, "Make friends with the nurses; they run the hospital." Naturally, the happy-go-lucky Sinatra character greets the first nurse he sees with "Hi ya, Doll."

MARRYING A DOCTOR

In *Miss Susie Slagle's*, the main roles of women are to become nurses or marry doctors. Margaretta Howe (Joan Caulfield), tells medical student Pug Prentiss (Sonny Tufts) that her mother was "a perfect doctor's wife."[7] He asks, "That's what you want to be?" When she answers "yes," he says, "Listen, lady, I'm just a poor medical student." "That's OK," she says, "that's how all doctors begin. I'm young, I'll wait." See *Of Human Bondage* and *Not As a Stranger* for other statements about what doctors' wives are supposed to be like. For a seamier depiction of medical marriages, see *Doctors Wives*.[8]

That doctors may still be considered prime marriage material, consider the following dialogue from the delightful 1994 romantic comedy *Only You*[9] when Faith, Kate, and Leslie, played by Marisa Tomei, Bonnie Hunt, and Siobhan Fallon, respectively, discuss Faith's recent marriage proposal: Kate: "What a catch!" Leslie: "Did he get down on his knee?" Faith: "Well, no, but he turned down his beeper." Kate: "He's a doctor. He's practical. He doesn't have to get down on his knees." After some discussion of Faith's decision to delay her answer and the requisite look at "the ring," Leslie says: "He's so intelligent." Kate: "Naturally. He's a doctor. What do you want?" Leslie: "And such a sense of humor!" Faith: "He's got a mild sense of humor." Kate: "He's a doctor. It's a tradeoff. He can't have a sense of humor, too. He saves lives." Faith: "He's a foot doctor." Kate: "OK, he saves feet. They're important too!"

MEDICINE IS A JEALOUS MISTRESS

The expression "medicine is a jealous mistress" is widely, but probably inaccurately, attributed to Sir William Osler, who did recommend to young doctors "to put your affections into cold storage for a few years."[10] If he was indeed the first to coin the expression, he drew heavily on Ralph Waldo Emerson who said "art is a jealous mistress."[11] Whatever the case, the expectation that doctors must be on call twenty-four hours a day, even at the expense of their families, permeates many of the older films. The best example of this occurs in *Dr. Kildare's Wedding Day* when Jimmy Kildare is poised to marry nurse Mary Lamont. His mentor Dr. Gillespie, says grumpily to Mary, "A doctor's a doctor for twenty-four hours a day. The rest of the time, he can be a husband." Note the masculine pronoun and the interesting math.

Another classic exchange takes place in *Society Doctor* between Chester Morris as a super-intern and Virginia Bruce as the operating room nurse. Though they are attracted to one another, the nurse wonders why he hasn't made a move on her. He says, "Because any

young idiot who's sap enough to become a doctor has to face one thing
before he starts—there can only be two types of women in his life: meal
tickets and 'Good-time Gerties.' You weren't a meal ticket." She responds, "So you mercifully spared me the chance to be a 'Good-time
Gertie.'"

In *Arrowsmith*, the townspeople love Dr. A, who is out taking care
of the folks while his wife is having a miscarriage. He tells her, "I'll
never forgive myself for leaving you like this." She comforts him by
saying, "If I can't have a baby, I'll have to bring you up. Make you a
great man that everyone will wonder at." When he later apologizes for
neglecting her and being a rotten husband, she says, "You are a rotten
husband, but I'd rather have you than all the decent husbands in the
world." How's that for dumb loyalty!

WORK IS MEDICINE'S MASTERWORD

In an address to medical students at The University of Toronto,
William Osler did call work the masterword of medicine.[10] In that respect, it is a variation of the "medicine is a jealous mistress" theme and
applies not only to medical students and doctors in training, but also
after they become established. In *No Way Out*, as the city hospital's
chief of the medical service, played by Stephen McNally, comes home
weary after caring for the injured in a race riot, his maid says to him,
"You can use a day off." He replies, "I had one once." As he leaves the
room, another woman sees the circles under his eyes and asks, "Why
does he do it?" The maid responds, "Doctors aren't like other people
and they shouldn't expect to live like them." Also see *Not As a Stranger*
for family doctor Luke Marsh (Robert Mitchum) passing out after seeing two hundred patients in one week. In the process, he neglects his
wife who can't even get his attention to tell him she's pregnant.

MONEY AND MEDICINE

In the 1932 film, *Symphony of Six Million*, Magnus, the doctor's
brother, is appalled that he "is not interested in money." "What's the
difference," his mother asks, "as long as he's a good doctor?" Magnus
replies, "He ought to have a real office where people would take pleasure in being sick. He doesn't understand that medicine is a business—
climbing three to four flights of stairs for fifty cents or a dollar a visit!"

Numerous films since then have echoed the same words about
medicine. In *The Young Doctors*, Dick Clark plays an intern who wants
to be a specialist. His wife wants him to be a family practitioner like her
father. She tells him, "I never heard my father mention money. He only
quoted one thing from the Bible, 'the only way to find yourself is to lose

yourself.'" The intern responds, "Your father was part of a dying breed. Medicine is a business."

See *The Green Light*, *The Hospital*, *Doc Hollywood* and *Critical Care* for films from different eras about greed and medicine as a business. See *Men in White*, *Internes Can't Take Money*, *The Last Angry Man*, *Meet Dr. Christian*, and other films in chapter 4 for doctors who put a low premium on making money.

COST OF HEALTH CARE

In *Not As a Stranger*, Luke Marsh (Robert Mitchum) decides to hang up his shingle in a small town with an old-fashioned family doctor, Dr. Runkleman (Charles Bickford). While escorting Luke and his wife Kris from the airport, Runkleman points out a patient who "nearly severed his arm with farm machinery and walked a mile to my office. First thing he asked was…" Kris completes the sentence, "How much is it going to cost?" This may seem to be hyperbole, but it's not far from the truth in the days before Medicare and Medicaid. When another patient asks if the doctor is sure the operation will help, he tells him it "will make you a new man." The patient replies, "Afterwards, send him the bill." The doctors in *Meet Dr. Christian* and *Doctor Bull* rarely get paid and have to take it out in trade such as chickens and other in-kind services (not uncommon before health insurance).

HEALTH INSURANCE

One of the first references to pre-paid health insurance is in *The Citadel* when the protagonist's friend tries to enlist him to join forces to form a multidisciplinary capitated group practice. Patients will pay the equivalent of two dollars a month and be taken care of "following scientific and humanitarian ideals" and emphasizing prevention. He argues that it is working in "the States." This is probably an allusion to a program that became known as Blue Cross, initiated in 1929 by teachers in Texas to insure themselves against catastrophic hospital bills that could reach hundreds of dollars.[12] In 1938, Kaiser organized a pre-paid group practice for its workers in California that became the model for other plans in New York and Washington state. The percentage of Americans who had some form of health insurance rose from 10 percent in 1940 to over 60 percent in the 1950s because of tax law changes and to a high water mark of over 90 percent in 1975 after the enactment of Medicare and Medicaid. The percentage of patients covered by medical insurance has since fallen.

The flip side of insurance coverage is seen in the 1997 *Critical Care*. At the bedside of a patient who has five hospital charts, with the record of five operations in just the first one, the resident asks the nurse, "Why is he full code? Lettuce in the refrigerator has a better chance of regaining consciousness than this fellow." "Insurance" is the answer.

KEEPING UP WITH PATIENTS

In *Not As a Stranger*, just out of his internship and anxious to get started, Luke Marsh lets his wife go to their new home while he accompanies country doctor Runkleman to his office. When he admires the extensive library, Runkleman tells him that he needs it to keep up, because his patients read about the latest advances in *Reader's Digest*. Ah, the days before CNN, *The New York Times*, and every media outlet including the *National Enquirer* developed ravenous appetites for the countless press releases issued by medical journals, institutions, and subspecialty societies. What would Runkleman have thought of the internet which is likely to revolutionize patient education even more?[12]

"BURYING MISTAKES"

The commonly-held dictum that doctors could hide their errors is a carry-over from the time when doctors really did know little about why people died. One reference is in the 1947 film, *Miss Susie Slagle's* when the butler pours a mint julep for himself at the invitation of the doctors he is serving. Accused of misjudging the amount of bourbon, he says, "I ain't no doctor. When I misjudge, nobody dies from it." Ironically, now that the autopsy rates in hospitals have declined in some cases to practically zero, more doctors may be unwittingly burying their mistakes.[13] In *Not As a Stranger*, medical student Luke Marsh is obsessed with stamping out error. In *The Green Light*, *Mary Stevens, M.D.*, and *Critical Care*, among other films, doctors' mistakes are covered up by their peers. In *Vigil in the Night*, Carole Lombard plays a nurse who takes responsibility for her nursing student sister's negligence that leads to the death of a young boy with laryngeal diphtheria.

AH, VIENNA!

Vienna is a favorite place for doctors to go for study (see *Men in White*, *Dr. Monica*, and *Kings Row*). In *Miss Susie Slagle's*, when a student comments on her china, Miss S proudly says, "One of my boys sent it over from Vienna." Although Paris is a distant second as an academic Mecca for postgraduate training (see *The Girl in White*), many date the modern era of clinical medicine, especially as it relates to diagnosis, to 1819 Paris when Laennec introduced the forerunner of the stethoscope. At about the same time, Pierre Louis began to apply scientific and statistical methods to patient care. As a result, Paris became a center for advanced training,[14] and a few decades later, so did Vienna and Berlin,[15] where Virchow was establishing the field of cellular pathology. The latter remained medical Meccas until the Nazi purge of Jewish physicians, a veiled reference to which occurs in *Dr. Ehrlich's Magic Bullet*. It was not until after World War II that the United States supplanted Europe as a magnet for those seeking postgraduate education.

PATIENT STEREOTYPES

There are numerous ethnic stereotypes especially in older films. Some are used repeatedly. For example, in *Mary Stevens, M.D.*, Dr. Stevens makes an emergency ambulance run to a tenement housing stereotypic Italian immigrants. This scene is noteworthy for showing her successfully dealing with a wine-drinking, knife-wielding male chauvinist, as she proceeds to deliver twins. Will Rogers as Doctor Bull also delivers a baby at a stereotypic Italian immigrant's house. This portrayal is more sympathetic in that after he delivers a baby boy, Bull drinks some red wine with the men and says, "I love to bring Italian babies into the world." There's a similar scene in *Arrowsmith*. In *Society Doctor,* an Italian woman has a knife confiscated by the hospital receptionist, who nonetheless allows her to visit her husband whose skull she fractured in a fight.

In *Mary Stevens, M.D.*, there are two scenes where a twelve-year-old Jewish boy, Sanford Nussbaum, is brought by his mother to see Dr. Stevens; the first time it's because he's worried all the time about the depression and the bank failures. The second time, his concern is about the country going off the gold standard. As for Blacks, movies have frequently pictured them as servants; in the few movies where they portray patients, they are poor and at times uncooperative (see *The Last Angry Man, The Heart Is a Lonely Hunter*).

PATIENTS AS INANIMATE OBJECTS

Patients are spoken of as inanimate objects in a number of films. For example, in *Men in White*, patients are referred to as "Bed 3" and "Room 401." In *Young Dr. Kildare*, Dr. K tells the nurse, "You can take the restraining sheet off Room 322." In *The Interns*, a nurse says, "the hemorrhage died." In *The Doctor*, there's "the terminal in 1217."

GANGSTER/DOCTOR MOVIE GENRE

See *Society Doctor* and *Internes Can't Take Money*. Another entry is *Doctor Socrates* starring Paul Muni as a brilliant surgeon whose name comes from his forever reading Plato. He has retreated from Chicago to "Big Bend, the biggest little city in Wayne County" after unsuccessfully operating on his wife. Since then, his hands have been shaking. Colleagues visit to coax him back, saying, "If you get your mind under control, your hands will be steady again. Every surgeon loses a patient once in a while. No surgeon living could have saved her after the accident." He refuses even though he doesn't have enough patients to pay his bills. He regains his skills after being coerced into serving as the house surgeon for an overacting gangster. The Black equivalent in so-called "race films" was *Racket Doctor*. For an updated version of the same plot, see the 1998 film *Playing God*.

INCOMPREHENSIBLE PRESCRIPTIONS

Obscure prescriptions are commented upon in numerous films. For example, in *Young Dr. Kildare*, Gillespie agrees with Kildare's physician father about the liberal use of bicarbonate of soda, but adds, "Don't tell the patient it's bicarbonate of soda. That's why prescriptions are written in Latin." In *Not As a Stranger*, a lawyer accuses doctors of writing prescriptions in Latin to mystify patients.

ORDERS SURE NOT TO BE FOLLOWED

In *Not As a Stranger*, as his mentor Aarons had predicted, Luke Marsh's first patient has a boil on his bottom. After the boil is lanced, his partner tells the patient not to sit down for a week. The patient laughingly replies, "I'm a bus driver." This is a variant of my wife's reason for refusing to go to the emergency room when she had four children to care for. She used to say, "The resident will tell me to stay off my feet for a week."

PLACEBOS

See *Not As a Stranger* for administration of sugar pills as Runkleman tells Luke, "If they have a pain, treat it; if they think they have a pain, treat the pain they think they have." The use of placebos is also prominent in the Kildare films. During my medical internship at Hopkins in 1961, patients were sometimes given saline injections when we had nothing else to offer and they would not be satisfied unless given something. Placebos (literally "I please") fell into disrepute as more drugs became available and they were seen as a form of deception and a sign of disrespect for the patient. Still, when all avenues of help were exhausted (and that's the most important thing), it was good to be able to help some people without harming them. Indeed, the utility of placebos is once again being championed.[16-18]

"YOU HAVE TWO MONTHS TO LIVE"

In *Not As a Stranger*, as he drives Luke and Kris from the airport, Dr. Runkleman points out a patient who doesn't talk to him anymore and says, "Thirty years ago I told her she would be dead in two months. Diagnosis is my specialty." In many Hollywood films, doctors pronounce almost to the day how much time a patient has to live. In contrast to movie doctors, most good physicians are reluctant to give such strict timetables for death.

DOING EVERYTHING

In *Critical Care*, the doctor answers the nurse's question as to why a patient in a persistent vegetative state is being maintained on every possible life support: "It's important that we say we did everything." She replies, "That's doctorspeak for we put this patient through hell before he died."

DOCTORS AS ARROGANT AND GODLIKE

Doctors acting like gods or being seen as gods is a movie staple. Invariably, they are men and, for the most part, surgeons. In *Malice*, the hotshot surgeon from the Massachusetts General Hospital doesn't just think he's God, he knows he is. In *The Interns*, the chief of obstetrics tells the interns, "Don't answer so quickly, especially when you don't know. Only surgeons do that." When an intern responds, "You don't think much of surgeons," he replies, "Not as much as they think of themselves."

In the same film, Telly Savalas plays the hard-nosed chief of surgery who laughs when he is reprimanded by the chief of medicine for throwing a scalpel at a resident during surgery. He proudly says, "In July, I pinked three nurses and two residents....When I'm training surgeons, I spit on everyone else." The central character in *The Doctor*, also a surgeon, has his arrogance and condescension knocked out of him after being diagnosed with cancer.

WHAT IT TAKES TO BE A SURGEON

In *Doctor in the House*, Harley Street surgeon Sir Lancelot Sprat (James Robertson Justice) quotes John Halle (1529-1568) who cited the following desirable attributes for a "chirurge" or surgeon: "A surgeon must have 'the eyes of a hawk, the heart of a lion, and the hands of a lady.'"[19] The saying also served as the basis for the signature quotation for the 1950s television series, *Medic*.

In *Miss Susie Slagle's*, Dr. Fletcher, the chief of surgery takes issue with this when he asks medical student Pug Prentiss, "Do you aspire to be an obstetrician? An ear, nose, and throat doctor, to prescribe pills, cough medicines or powdered dog legs as a general practitioner?" Pug responds: "No, a surgeon, but my hands are big and blunt." Fletcher counters, "Not long and thin like a fiddle player? That's a myth perpetuated by surgeons with long thin fingers." Fletcher then tells him, "You've got it, Prentiss, work hard, develop the rhythm. Look out for what you can do better. Howard Kelly [one of the "Four Doctors" in John Singer Sargent's portrait in the introduction] had blunt fingers and he was one of the greatest surgeons in the world."

PLAYING SURGERY STRAIGHT

Many early films like *Men in White, Vigil in the Night, The Girl in White* and *Not As a Stranger* recognized the cinematic values of surgery and tried to portray it honestly, if overdramatically, with the nurse wiping the surgeon's brow, slapping the scalpel and forceps in the surgeon's hand, and with hordes of spectators in the galleries or on the sidelines.

In *Not As a Stranger*, the chief of surgery, Doctor Dietrich (Whit Bissell) attempts "to remove a tumor without damaging the spinal cord." After sewing the patient up, Dietrich says, "Anatomically the operation is a success, now let's see if we helped the patient," reminiscent of the old saying, "The operation was a success, but the patient died." Dietrich rather humbly calls his job "mechanic's work" but adds that "one hundred years ago, it was the physician who was important; surgery was left to the barbers." This prophetic film forecast an era when incentives would make procedural medicine ascendant, sometimes at the expense of talking and listening to patients.

PORTRAYALS OF SURGERY THAT CAN MAKE A SURGEON CRINGE

Ludicrous portrayals of surgery have a rich tradition in "Hollywood," including Joel McCrea as the first Dr. Kildare, operating in a bar at the behest of a gangster in the wonderfully titled film, *Internes Can't Take Money*. Two other classics, *Society Doctor* and *Welcome Stranger,* portray, respectively, Chester Morris and Barry Fitzgerald as expert surgeons who, while under local anesthesia, direct their major operations through the use of mirrors.

In *Playing God*, David Duchovny as a disbarred "junkie" surgeon deftly executes a series of unorthodox surgeries. One scene played for laughs involves an operation on a pool table in a biker bar. A biker takes forceps out of boiling water and hands Doctor Sands a stethoscope and a scalpel, as he proceeds to take a bullet out of a man's chest. Another biker is told to keep time with his foot in synchrony with the heartbeat. Sands becomes alarmed when the foot-tapping stops, only to learn that the man's heart is still beating, but that it was just time for the biker to get another beer.

Sometimes in the movies, the unskilled perform surgery. One example, based on real life,[20] occurs in *Destination Tokyo*, when a pharmacist's mate is coached from a textbook as he performs an emergency appendectomy (fig.). In *Spellbound*, psychiatrists and an internist scrub in on a craniotomy. A recent example is the 1999 film *Ronin*, in

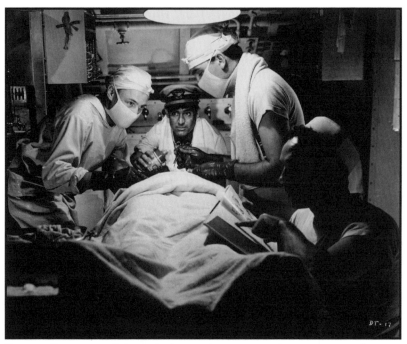

FIGURE. *Destination Tokyo*. A pharmacist's mate performs an appendectomy on board a submarine, while instructions are read from surgical text. Worried commander (Cary Grant) pours the ether.

which Robert De Niro plays a CIA operative who directs the removal of a bullet from his right side after telling his buddy that there's going to be a lot of bleeding. Once it's out, he says, "Can you stitch me up on your own. If you don't mind, I'm going to pass out."

DOCTORS AT WAR

Numerous films have depicted doctors and nurses caring for patients on the battlefield; many show the gruesome conditions and sparse supplies. Noteworthy examples include the hospital scenes in *Gone with the Wind* and *Glory* during the Civil War; *The Horse Soldiers* set during the Indian Wars; *The Story of Dr. Wassell* during World War II, and *M*A*S*H*, which although representing the Korean War, really reflected conditions during the Vietnam War.

DOCTORS AND LAWYERS

A scene in *Not As a Stranger* illustrates the long-standing and counterproductive animus between members of the legal and medical professions. Luke has an argument at the country club with a lawyer who contends that medicine is a secret society, saying, "You have every-thing but the grip and the high sign. When they (the public) get wise to how little you know, you won't be able to kill people and get away with it." Even Luke's wife accuses doctors of fee-splitting and tells an old joke that the reason why "doctors wear rubber gloves is so that they won't leave any fingerprints." The argument ends with the doctor and the lawyer trading "quack" and "shyster" insults.

PUBLIC HEALTH DOCTORS AS GOOD GUYS

See *A Matter of WHO*, *Panic in the Streets*, and *Arrowsmith*.

CONTROLLED EXPERIMENTS

See chapter 4 on scientists, especially *The Story of Louis Pasteur*, *Dr. Ehrlich's Magic Bullet*, and *Arrowsmith*.

COUNTRY DOCTORS

See chapter 2 for movies featuring these kindly saviors and *Arrowsmith* in chapter 4 for the best description of what's expected of the country doctor.

HOUSE CALLS

See *Doctor Bull*, *Meet Dr. Christian*, and *Eve's Bayou*. For a dif-ferent twist on the practice, see *House Calls*.

DISCRIMINATION

See chapters 5 and 6 on women doctors and Black doctors. Classic exchanges occur in *The Girl in White* in chapter 5 when a woman doctor played by Mildred Dunnock tries to dissuade Emily Dunning from go-ing to medical school.

In *No Way Out*, Dr. Brooks, played by Sidney Poitier, is told by his wife to persevere after yet another manifestation of discrimination, as she describes how he worked harder than everyone else and that "A" was his passing grade. There are brief allusions to anti-Semitism in *Dr. Ehrlich's Magic Bullet* and *Not As a Stranger*.

This is just a selected sampling of stereotypes and clichés found in films over the years. You are encouraged to find your own favorite ex-amples in the films covered in the text or from others in Shortland's excellent checklist for researchers interested in medicine and film.[8] I welcome readers' suggestions and comments.

NOTES

1. Carnall D. Medicine and the media: Smoking on celluloid. BMJ 1998; 316: 712.
2. Martensen RL and Jones DS. The emergence of the hospital internship. JAMA 1997; 278: 963.
3. Barringer ED. Bowery to Bellevue: The Story of New York's First Woman Ambulance Surgeon. New York: W.W. Norton & Co, 1950.
4. Stein LI. The doctor-nurse game. Arch Gen Psychiatry 1967; 16: 699-703.
5. Prescott PA and Bowen SA. Physician-nurse relationships. Ann Intern Med 1985; 103: 127-133.
6. Stein LI, Watts DT, Howell T. The doctor-nurse game revisited. N Engl J Med 1990; 322: 546-549.
7. Weiss B. Remember when doctors' wives were 'deserving mates'? Medical Economics, August 10, 1998, p 128 ff.
8. Shortland M. Medicine and Film: A Checklist, Survey and Research Resource. Oxford: Wellcome Unit for the History of Medicine, 1989.
9. Ebert R. "Only You" (review). In: Cinemania 96, Microsoft CD-ROM, 1995.
10. Bryan CS. Osler: Inspirations from a Great Physician. New York: Oxford University Press, 1997.
11. Emerson RW. Wealth, as cited in The Oxford Press Dictionary of Quotations, revised, 2nd edition. New York: Crescent Books, 1985, p 199.
12. Cunningham R III and Cunningham RM Jr. The Blues: A History of the Blue Cross and Blue Shield System. De Kalb, IL: Northern Illinois University Press, 1997.
13. Hanzlick R, Baker P, and the Autopsy Committee of the College of American Pathologists. Institutional autopsy rates. Arch Intern Med 1998; 158: 1171-1172.
14. Warner JH. Against the Spirit of the System: The French Impulse in Nineteenth-Century American Medicine. Princeton, NJ: Princeton University Press, 1998.
15. Eisenberg L. Rudolph Ludwig Karl Virchow, where are you now that we need you? Am J Med, 1984; 77: 524-532.
16. Brown WA. The placebo effect. Scientific American, January, 1998, p 90 ff.
17. Shapiro AK and Shapiro E. The Powerful Placebo: From Ancient Priest to Modern Physician. Baltimore: Johns Hopkins University Press, 1997.
18. Blakeslee S. Placebos prove so powerful even experts are surprised. New York Times, October 13, 1998, pp D1, D4.
19. Halle J. In: Familiar Medical Quotations, ed. MB Strauss, Boston: Little, Brown, & Co, 1968, p 584.
20. Herman JK. Battle Station Sick Bay: Navy Medicine in World War II. Annapolis, MD: Naval Institute Press, 1997.

APPENDIX B

Filmography

This filmography includes information on each movie given substantial coverage. It is arranged alphabetically by movie title. In addition, each listing includes the chapter number in which it is discussed. Information was adapted from Microsoft Cinemania 96 and Internet Movie Database, IMDb, along with promotional brochures.

The cast listing has been abbreviated to include only the more prominent actors in each film. The production credits include producer, director, screenwriter, cinematographer, and composer or musical director.

Samuel Goldwyn

Arrowsmith

US (1931)
100 min, No rating, Black & White,
Available on videocassette and laserdisc

See chapter 4

CAST LIST

Performer	Character
Ronald Colman	Dr.Martin Arrowsmith
Helen Hayes	Leora
A.E. Anson	Prof. Gottlieb
Richard Bennett	Sondelius
Claude King	Dr. Tubbs
Beulah Bondi	Mrs. Tozer
Myrna Loy	Joyce Lanyon
Russell Hopton	Terry Wicket
Clarence Brooks	Oliver Marchand

PRODUCTION CREDITS

Producer	Samuel Goldwyn
Director	John Ford
Screenwriter	Sidney Howard
based on the novel	
by Sinclair Lewis	
Cinematographer	Ray June
Composer	Alfred Newman

Orion Pictures

Article 99

US (1992)
99 min, Rated R, Color, Available on videocassette and laserdisc

See chapter 8

CAST LIST

Performer	Character
Ray Liotta	Dr. Richard Sturgess
Kiefer Sutherland	Dr. Peter Morgan
Forest Whitaker	Dr. Sid Handleman
Lea Thompson	Dr. Robin Van Dorn
John C. McGinley	Dr. Rudy Bobrick
John Mahoney	Dr. Henry Dreyfoos
Keith David	Luther Jerome
Kathy Baker	Dr. Diana Walton
Eli Wallach	Sam Abrams
Noble Willingham	Inspector General
Julie Bovasso	Amelia Sturdeyvant
Troy Evans	Pat Travis
Lynne Thigpen	Nurse White
Jeffrey Tambor	Dr. Leo Krutz

PRODUCTION CREDITS

Producer	Michael Gruskoff
	Michael I. Levy
Director	Howard Deutch
Screenwriter	Ron Cutler
Cinematographer	Richard Bowen
Composer	Danny Elfman

TriStar Pictures

As Good As It Gets

US (1997)

138 min, Rated R, Color, Available on videocassette and laserdisc

See chapter 8

CAST LIST

Performer	Character
Jack Nicholson	Melvin Udall
Helen Hunt	Carol Connelly
Greg Kinnear	Simon Bishop
Cuba Gooding, Jr.	Frank Sachs
Skeet Ulrich	Vincent
Shirley Knight	Beverly
Yeardley Smith	Jackie
Lupe Ontiveros	Nora
Jill	Verdell
Bibi Osterwald	Neighbor Woman
Lawrence Kasdan	Dr. Green

PRODUCTION CREDITS

Producers	Bridget Johnson
	Kristi Zea
Producer/Director	James L. Brooks
Screenwriters	Mark Andrus
	James L. Brooks
Music	Hans Zimmer
Director of Photography	John Bailey, ASC

Columbia Pictures

Awakenings

US (1990)
121 min, Rated PG-13, Color, Available on videocassette and laserdisc

See chapter 10

CAST LIST

Performer	Character
Robert De Niro	Leonard Lowe
Robin Williams	Dr. Malcolm Sayer
Julie Kavner	Eleanor Costello
Ruth Nelson	Mrs. Lowe
John Heard	Dr. Kaufman
Penelope Ann Miller	Paula
Alice Drummond	Lucy
Judith Malina	Rose
Anne Meara	Miriam
Dexter Gordon	Rolando

PRODUCTION CREDITS

Producers	Walter Parkes
	Lawrence Lasker
Director	Penny Marshall
Screenwriter	Steve Zaillian
	based on the novel
	by Oliver Sacks
Cinematographer	Miroslav Ondricek
Composer	Randy Newman

Castle Rock Entertainment

Beyond Rangoon

1995
99 min, Rated R, Color, Available on videocassette

See chapter 5

CAST LIST

Performer	Character
Patricia Arquette	Laura Bowman
U Aung Ko	U Aung Ko
Frances McDormand	Andy
Spalding Gray	Jeremy Watt
Adelle Lutz	Aung San Suu Kyi

PRODUCTION CREDITS

Producer	John Boorman
Director	John Boorman
Screenwriters	Alex Lasker
	Bill Rubenstein
Cinematography	John Seale
Music	Hans Zimmer

Metro-Goldwyn-Mayer

The Citadel
UK-US (1938)
114 min, No rating, Black & White, Available on videocassette

See chapter 7

Cast List

Performer	Character
Robert Donat	Andrew Manson
Rosalind Russell	Christine Manson
Ralph Richardson	Denny
Rex Harrison	Dr. Lawford
Emlyn Williams	Owen
Penelope Dudley-Ward	Toppy Leroy
Francis L. Sullivan	Ben Chenkin
Cecil Parker	Charles Every
Felix Aylmer	Mr. Boon
Percy Parsons	Mr. Stillman

Production Credits

Producer	Victor Saville
Director	King Vidor
Screenwriters	Ian Dalrymple
	Frank Wead
	Elizabeth Hill
	Emlyn Williams

based on the novel
by A.J. Cronin

Cinematographer	Harry Stradling
Composer	Louis Levy

TriStar Pictures

City of Joy

France-UK (1992)
134 min, Rated PG-13, Color, Available on videocassette and laserdisc

See chapter 10

CAST LIST

Performer	Character
Patrick Swayze	Max Lowe
Pauline Collins	Joan Bethal
Om Puri	Hasari Pal
Shabana Azmi	Kamla Pal
Art Malik	Ashoka
Ayesha Dharker	Amrita Pal
Shyamanand Jalan	Godfather/Ghatak

PRODUCTION CREDITS

Producers	Jake Eberts
	Roland Joffe
Director	Roland Joffe
Screenwriter	Mark Medoff

from the novel
by Dominique Lapierre

Cinematographer	Peter Biziou
Composer	Ennio Morricone

Metro-Goldwyn-Mayer

Coma

US (1978)

113 min, Rated PG, Color, Available on videocassette and laserdisc

See chapter 5

CAST LIST

Performer	Character
Genevieve Bujold	Dr. Susan Wheeler
Michael Douglas	Dr. Mark Bellows
Elizabeth Ashley	Mrs. Emerson
Rip Torn	Dr. George
Richard Widmark	Dr. Harris
Tom Selleck	Murphy

PRODUCTION CREDITS

Producer	Martin Erlichman
Director	Michael Crichton
Screenwriter	Michael Crichton
	based on the novel
	by Robin Cook
Cinematographers	Victor J. Kemper
	Gerald Hirschfeld
Composer	Jerry Goldsmith

Twentieth Century Fox

The Country Doctor

US (1936)

110 min, No rating, Black & White, Available on videocassette

See chapter 2

CAST LIST

Performer	Character
The Dionne Quintuplets	The Dionne Quintuplets
Yvonne	Yvonne
Cecile	Cecile
Marie	Marie
Annette	Annette
Emelie	Emelie
Jean Hersholt	Dr. John Luke
June Lang	Mary MacKenzie
Slim Summerville	Constable Jim Ogden
Michael Whalen	Tony Luke
Dorothy Peterson	Katherine Kennedy
Robert Barrat	MacKenzie
Jane Darwell	Mrs. Graham
John Qualen	Asa Wyatt
Frank Reicher	Dr. Paul Luke
Montagu Love	Sir Basil Crawford
David Torrence	Governor General

PRODUCTION CREDITS

Producer	Darryl F. Zanuck
Director	Henry King
Screenwriter	Sonya Levien
	based on a story idea
	by Charles E. Blake
Photography	John Seitz
	Daniel B. Clark
Musical Direction	Louis Silvers

Scenes of the Dionne Quintuplets were photographed at Callander, Ontario, under the supervision of Dr. Allan R. Dafoe.

LIVE Entertainment

Critical Care

1997
109 min, Rated R, Color, Available on videocassette

See chapter 8

CAST LIST

Performer	Character
James Spader	Dr. Werner Ernst
Kyra Sedgwick	Felicia Potter
Helen Mirren	Stella
Margo Martindale	Connie Potter
Jeffrey Wright	Bed Two
Wallace Shawn	Furnaceman
Anne Bancroft	Nun
Albert Brooks	Dr. Butz
Philip Bosco	Dr. Hofstader
Edward Herrmann	Robert Payne
Colm Feore	Wilson
James Lally	Poindexter

PRODUCTION CREDITS

Producer	Don Carmody
Director	Sidney Lumet
Screenwriters	Richard Dooling
	Steven S. Schwartz
Music	Michael Convertino
Cinematography	David Watkin

Twentieth Century Fox

Dead Ringers

Canada (1988)
115 min, Rated R, Color, Available on videocassette and laserdisc

See chapter 7

CAST LIST

Performer	Character
Jeremy Irons	Beverly Mantle/
	Elliot Mantle
Genevieve Bujold	Claire Niveau
Heidi von Palleske	Cary
Barbara Gordon	Danuta
Shirley Douglas	Laura
Stephen Lack	Anders Wolleck

PRODUCTION CREDITS

Producers	David Cronenberg
	Marc Boyman
Director	David Cronenberg
Screenwriters	David Cronenberg
	Norman Snider

based on the book *Twins*
by Bari Wood and Jack Geasland

Cinematographer	Peter Suschitzky
Composer	Howard Shore

Warner Bros.

Doc Hollywood

US (1991)
104 min, Rated PG-13, Color, Available on videocassette and laserdisc

See chapter 2

CAST LIST

Performer	Character
Michael J. Fox	Ben Stone
Julie Warner	Lou
Barnard Hughes	Doctor Hogue
Woody Harrelson	Hank
David Ogden Stiers	Nick Nicholson
Frances Sternhagen	Lillian
George Hamilton	Doctor Halberstrom
Bridget Fonda	Nancy Lee
Roberts Blossom	Judge Evans
Edye Byrde	Nurse Packer

PRODUCTION CREDITS

Producers	Susan Solt
	Deborah D. Johnson
Director	Michael Caton-Jones
Screenwriters	Jeffrey Price
	Peter S. Seaman
	Daniel Pyne

from Laurian Leggett's adaptation of the book
What?.. Dead Again? by Neil B. Shulman

Cinematographer	Michael Chapman
Composer	Carter Burwell

Touchstone Pictures

The Doctor

US (1991)
121 min, Rated PG-13, Color, Available on videocassette and laserdisc

See chapter 7

CAST LIST

Performer	Character
William Hurt	Jack McKee
Christine Lahti	Anne
Elizabeth Perkins	June
Mandy Patinkin	Murray
Adam Arkin	Eli
Charlie Korsmo	Nicky
Wendy Crewson	Leslie Abbott
Bill Macy	Al Cade

PRODUCTION CREDITS

Producer	Laura Ziskin
Director	Randa Haines
Screenwriter	Robert Caswell

from the novel *A Taste of My Own Medicine*
by Edward E. Rosenbaum

Cinematographer	John Seale
Composer	Michael Convertino

Twentieth Century Fox

Doctor Bull

(1933)
75 min, No rating, Black & White

See chapter 2

CAST LIST

Performer	Character
Will Rogers	Dr. Bull
Vera Allen	Janet Cardmaker
Andy Devine	Larry Ward
Nora Cecil	Aunt Emily
Ralph Morgan	Dr. Verney

PRODUCTION CREDITS

Director	John Ford
Screenwriter	James Gould Cozzens

based on the novel *The Last Adam*
by James Gould Cozzens

J. Arthur Rank

Doctor in the House

UK (1954)
91 min, No rating, Color, Available on videocassette

See chapter 1

Cast List

Performer	Character
Dirk Bogarde	Simon
Muriel Pavlow	Joy
Kenneth More	Grimsdyke
Kay Kendall	Isobel
James Robertson Justice	Sir Lancelot
Geoffrey Keen	Dean
Jean Taylor-Smith	Sister Virtue

Production Credits

Producer	Betty E. Box
Director	Ralph Thomas
Screenwriters	Richard Gordon,
	Ronald Wilkinson
	Nicholas Phipps

based on the novel
by Richard Gordon

Cinematographer	Ernest Steward
Composer	Bruce Montgomery
Music director	Muir Mathieson

Doctor Jim

US (1947)

48 min, No rating, Black & White, Available on videocassette

See chapter 2

CAST LISTING

Performer	Character
Stuart Erwin	Doctor James Gateros
Barbara Wood Dell	Sally Gateros
William Wright	Doctor Sylvester
Hobart Cavanaugh	Mayor
Netta Packer	Emily

PRODUCTION CREDITS

Producer	Jerry Fairbanks
Directors	Lew Landers
Original story by Lyle Robertson and Lou Lilly	
Cinematographer	Allen Siegler
Music	Edward Paul

First National Pictures — United Artists

Doctor X

US (1932)
80 min, No rating, Color, Black & White,
Available on videocassette and laserdisc

See chapter 4

CAST LIST

Performer	Character
Lionel Atwill	Doctor Xavier
Fay Wray	Joanne Xavier
Lee Tracy	Lee Taylor
Preston Foster	Dr. Wells
John Wray	Dr. Haines
Harry Beresford	Dr. Duke
Arthur Edmund Carewe	Dr. Rowitz

PRODUCTION CREDITS

Director	Michael Curtiz
Screenwriters	Earl Baldwin
	Robert Tasker

based on a play
by Howard W. Comstock and Allen C. Miller

Photography	Ray Rennahan
Music	Leo F. Forbstein
Mask Effects	Max Factor

Metro-Goldwyn-Mayer

Doctor Zhivago

US (1965)

197 min, No rating, Color, Available on videocassette and laserdisc

See chapter 10

CAST LIST

Performer	Character
Geraldine Chaplin	Tonya
Julie Christie	Lara
Tom Courtenay	Pasha/Strelnikoff
Alec Guinness	Yevgraf
Siobhan McKenna	Anna
Ralph Richardson	Alexander
Omar Sharif	Yuri
Rod Steiger	Komarovsky
Rita Tushingham	The Girl
Adrienne Corri	Amelia
Geoffrey Keen	Prof. Kurt
Jeffrey Rockland	Sasha
Lucy Westmore	Katya
Klaus Kinski	Kostoyed
Jack MacGowran	Petya

PRODUCTION CREDITS

Producer	Cario Ponti
Director	David Lean
Screenwriter	Robert Bolt

based on the novel
by Boris Pasternak

Cinematographer	Freddie Young
Composer	Maurice Jarre

Warner Bros.

Dr. Ehrlich's Magic Bullet

US (1940)
103 min, No rating, Black & White

See chapter 4

CAST LIST

Performer	Character
Edward G. Robinson	Dr. Paul Ehrlich
Ruth Gordon	Mrs. Ehrlich
Otto Kruger	Dr. Emil von Behring
Donald Crisp	Minister Althoff
Maria Ouspenskaya	Franziska Speyer
Montagu Love	Prof. Hartmann
Sig Rumann	Dr. Hans Wolfert
Donald Meek	Mittlemeyer
Henry O'Neill	Dr. Lentz
Albert Basserman	Dr. Robert Koch
Edward Norris	Dr. Morgenroth
Harry Davenport	Judge
Louis Calhern	Dr. Brockdorf
Irving Bacon	Becker
Frank Reicher	Old Doctor
Ann Todd	Marianne

PRODUCTION CREDITS

Producer	Wolfgang Reinhardt
Director	William Dieterle
Screenwriters	John Huston
	Heinz Herald
	Norman Burnstein

based on a story by Burnstein from letters
and notes owned by the Ehrlich family

Cinematographer	James Wong Howe
Composer	Max Steiner

Metro-Goldwyn-Mayer

Dr. Jekyll and Mr. Hyde

US (1932)

97 min, No rating, Black & White, Available on videocassette and laserdisc

See chapter 4

CAST LIST

Performer	Character
Fredric March	Dr. Henry Jekyll/ Mr. Hyde
Miriam Hopkins	Ivy Pearson
Rose Hobart	Muriel Carew
Holmes Herbert	Dr. Lanyon
Halliwell Hobbes	Brig-Gen. Carew

PRODUCTION CREDITS

Producer	Rouben Mamoulian
Director	Rouben Mamoulian
Screenwriters	Samuel Hoffenstein
	Percy Heath

based on the novel *The Strange Case of Dr Jekyll and Mr. Hyde* by Robert Louis Stevenson

Cinematographer	Karl Struss
Makeup	Wally Westmore

Metro-Goldwyn-Mayer

Dr. Kildare's Crisis

US (1940)
73 min, No rating, Black & White

See chapter 3

CAST LIST

Performer	Character
Lew Ayres	Dr. James Kildare
Robert Young	Douglas Lamont
Lionel Barrymore	Dr. Leonard Gillespie
Laraine Day	Mary Lamont
Emma Dunn	Mrs. Martha Kildare
Nat Pendleton	Joe Wayman
Bobs Watson	Tommy
Walter Kingsford	Dr. Walter Carew
Alma Kruger	Molly Byrd
Nell Craig	Nurse Parker
Frank Orth	Mike Ryan
Horace MacMahon	Foghorn Murphy

PRODUCTION CREDITS

Director	Harold S. Bucquet
Screenwriters	Harry Ruskin
	Willis Goldbeck

based on a story by Max Brand and Willis Goldbeck

Cinematographer	John Seitz
Composer	David Snell

Metro-Goldwyn-Mayer

Dr. Kildare's Wedding Day

US (1941)

83 min, No rating, Black & White

See chapter 3

CAST LIST

Performer	Character
Lew Ayres	Dr. James Kildare
Lionel Barrymore	Dr. Leonard Gillespie
Laraine Day	Mary Lamont
Red Skelton	Vernon Briggs
Fay Holden	Mrs. Bartlett
Walter Kingsford	Dr. Walter Carew
Alma Kruger	Molly Byrd
Samuel S. Hinds	Dr. Stephen Kildare
Emma Dunn	Mrs. Martha Kildare
Nils Asther	Constanzo Labardi
Miles Mander	Dr. Lockberg
Nell Craig	Nurse Parker
Frank Orth	Mike Ryan

PRODUCTION CREDITS

Director	Harold S. Bucquet
Screenwriters	Willis Goldbeck
	Harry Ruskin

based on a story by Ormond Ruthven, Lawrence P. Bachmann
from characters created by Max Brand

Cinematographer	George Folsey
Composer	Bronislau Kaper

Warner Bros.

Dr. Monica

US (1934)
75 min, No rating, Black & White

See chapter 5

Cast Listing

Performer	Character
Kay Francis	Dr. Monica Braden
Warren William	John Braden
Jean Muir	Mary
Vernee Teasdale	Anna
Emma Dunn	Nurse Monahan
Hale Hamilton	Dr. Brent
Louise Beavers	Mary's Maid

Production Credits

Directors	William Dieterle
	William Keighley
Screenwriter	Charles Kenyon

from a story by Laura Walker Mayer
based on a Polish play by Marja Morozowicz Szczepkowska

Cinematographer	Sol Polito
Music	Leo F. Forbstein

Trimark Pictures

Eve's Bayou

(1997)
109 min, Rated R, Color, Available on videocassette

See chapter 6

CAST LIST

Performer	Character
Jurnee Smollett	Eve Batiste
Meagan Good	Cisely Batiste
Samuel L. Jackson	Louis Batiste
Lynn Whitfield	Roz Batiste
Debbi Morgan	Mozelle Batiste Delacroix
Jake Smollett	Poe Batiste
Ethel Ayler	Gran Mére
Diahann Carroll	Elzora
Vondie Curtis Hall	Julian Grayraven
Lisa Nicole Carson	Matty Mereaux

PRODUCTION CREDITS

Producers	Caldecot Chubb
	Samuel L. Jackson
Writer & Director	Kasi Lemmons
Composer	Terence Blanchard
Director of Photography	Amy Vincent

Castle Rock Entertainment

Extreme Measures

US (1996)
117 minutes, Rated R, Color, Available on videocassette

See chapter 9

CAST LISTING

Performer	Character
Hugh Grant	Dr. Guy Luthan
Gene Hackman	Dr. Lawrence Myrick
Sarah Jessica Parker	Jodie Trammel
David Morse	Frank Hare
Bill Nunn	Det. Burke
Paul Guilfoyle	Dr. Jeffrey Manko
Debra Monk	Dr. Judith Gruszynski

PRODUCTION CREDITS

Producers	Elizabeth Hurley
	Chris Bingham
Director	Michael Apted
Screenwriters	Michael Palmer
	Tony Gilroy
Music	Danny Elfman
Cinematography	John Bailey

Columbia Pictures

Flatliners

US (1990)

105 min, Rated R, Color, Available on videocassette and laserdisc

See chapter 1

CAST LIST

Performer	Character
Kiefer Sutherland	Nelson Wright
Julia Roberts	Rachel Mannus
Kevin Bacon	David Labraccio
William Baldwin	Joe Hurley
Oliver Platt	Randy Steckle

PRODUCTION CREDITS

Producer	Michael Douglas
	Rick Bieber
Director	Joel Schumacher
Screenwriter	Peter Filardi
Cinematographer	Jan De Bont
Composer	James Newton Howard
Music director	Dick Rudolph

Warner Bros.

The Fugitive

US (1993)

127 min, Rated PG-13, Color, Available on videocassette and laserdisc

See chapter 10

CAST LIST

Performer	Character
Harrison Ford	Dr. Richard Kimble
Tommy Lee Jones	Deputy US Marshal Samuel Gerard
Sela Ward	Helen Kimble
Julianne Moore	Dr. Ann Eastman
Joe Pantoliano	Cosmo Renfro
Andreas Katsulas	Sykes— "The One Armed Man"
Jeroen Krabbé	Dr. Charles Nichols
Daniel Roebuck	Biggs
L. Scott Caldwell	Poole

PRODUCTION CREDITS

Producer	Arnold Kopelson
Director	Andrew Davis
Screenwriters	Jeb Stuart
	David Twohy

from a story
by David Twohy

Cinematographer	Michael Chapman
Composer	James Newton Howard

Metro-Goldwyn-Mayer

The Girl in White

US (1952)

93 min, No rating, Black & White

See chapter 5

CAST LIST

Performer	Character
June Allyson	Dr. Emily Dunning
Arthur Kennedy	Dr. Ben Barringer
Gary Merrill	Dr. Seth Pawling
Mildred Dunnock	Dr. Marie Yeomans
Jesse White	Alec
Marilyn Erskine	Nurse Jane Doe
Herbert Anderson	Dr. Barclay
Gar Moore	Dr. Graham
Don Keefer	Dr. Williams
Ann Tyrrell	Nurse Bigley
James Arness	Matt
Curtis Cooksey	Commissioner of Hospitals Hawley

PRODUCTION CREDITS

Producer	Armand Deutsch
Director	John Sturges
Screenwriters	Emily Dunning Barringer
	Philip Stevenson
	Allen Vincent
	Irma von Cube

based on a book

Bowery to Bellevue by Emily Dunning Barringer

Music	David Raksin
Cinematographer	Paul Vogel
Medical Consultant	Harold O. Cooperman, MD

Warner Bros.

The Green Light

US (1937)
85 min, No rating, Black & White

See chapter 9

CAST LIST

Performer	Character
Errol Flynn	Dr. Newell Paige
Anita Louise	Phyllis Dexter
Margaret Lindsay	Frances Ogilvie
Cedric Hardwicke	Dean Harcourt
Walter Abel	Dr. John Stafford
Henry O'Neill	Dr. Endicott
Spring Byington	Mrs. Dexter
Henry Kolker	Dr. Lane
Pierre Watkin	Dr. Booth
Wade Boteler	Traffic Cop
Jim Thorpe	Indian

PRODUCTION CREDITS

Producer	Henry Blanke
Director	Frank Borzage
Screenwriter	Milton Krims
based on the novel by	
Lloyd C. Douglas	
Cinematographer	Byron Haskin
Composer	Max Steiner

Touchstone Pictures

Gross Anatomy

US (1989)

109 min, Rated PG-13, Color, Available on videocassette and laserdisc

See chapter 1

CAST LIST

Performer	Character
Matthew Modine	Joe Slovak
Daphne Zuniga	Laurie Rorbach
Christine Lahti	Dr. Rachel Woodruff
Todd Field	David Schreiner
John Scott Clough	Miles Reed
Zakes Mokae	Dr. Banumbra
Max Perlich	Ethan Cleaver
Alice Carter	Kim McCauley

PRODUCTION CREDITS

Producers	Howard Rosenman
	Debra Hill
Director	Thom Eberhardt
Screenwriters	Ron Nyswaner
	Mark Spragg

based on a story
by Mark Spragg, Howard Rosenman,
Alan Jay Glueckman, Stanley Isaacs

Cinematographer	Steve Yaconelli
Composer	David Newman

Columbia Pictures

Guess Who's Coming to Dinner

US (1967)

108 min, No rating, Color, Available on videocassette and laserdisc

See chapter 6

CAST LIST

Performer	Character
Spencer Tracy	Matt Drayton
Sidney Poitier	John Prentice
Katharine Hepburn	Christina Drayton
Katharine Houghton	Joey Drayton
Cecil Kellaway	Monsignor Ryan
Roy E. Glenn, Sr.	Mr. Prentice
Beah Richards	Mrs. Prentice
Isabel Sanford	Tillie
Virginia Christine	Hilary St. George

PRODUCTION CREDITS

Producer	Stanley Kramer
Director	Stanley Kramer
Screenwriter	William Rose
Cinematographer	Sam Leavitt
Composer	Frank DeVol

Warner Bros.

The Heart Is a Lonely Hunter

US (1968)

123 min, Rated G, Color, Available on videocassette

See chapter 6

CAST LIST

Performer	Character
Alan Arkin	John Singer
Laurinda Barrett	Mrs. Kelly
Stacy Keach	Blount
Chuck McCann	Antonapoulos
Biff McGuire	Mr. Kelly
Sondra Locke	Mick Kelly
Percy Rodriguez	Dr. Copeland
Cicely Tyson	Portia

PRODUCTION CREDITS

Producers	Thomas C. Ryan
	Marc Merson
Director	Robert Ellis Miller
Screenwriter	Thomas C. Ryan
	based on the novel
	by Carson McCullers
Cinematographer	James Wong Howe
Composer	Dave Grusin

United Artists

The Hospital
US (1971)
101 min, Rated PG, Color, Available on videocassette

See chapter 8

CAST LIST

Performer	Character
George C. Scott	Dr. Herbert Bock
Diana Rigg	Barbara Drummond
Barnard Hughes	Drummond
Richard Dysart	Dr. Welbeck
Andrew Duncan	William Mead
Nancy Marchand	Mrs. Christie, Head Nurse
Stephen Elliott	Sunstrom
Donald Harron	Milton Mead
Roberts Blossom	Guernsey
Tresa Hughes	Mrs. Donovan
Lenny Baker	Dr. Schaefer
Robert Walden	Dr. Brubaker
Frances Sternhagen	Mrs. Cushing
Christopher Guest	Resident

PRODUCTION CREDITS

Producer	Howard Gottfried
Director	Arthur Hiller
Screenwriter	Paddy Chayefsky
Cinematographer	Victor J. Kemper
Composer	Morris Surdin

Universal City Studios

House Calls

US (1978)

98 min, Rated PG, Color, Available on videocassette and laserdisc

See chapter 10

CAST LIST

Performer	Character
Walter Matthau	Dr. Charley Nichols
Glenda Jackson	Ann Atkinson
Art Carney	Dr. Amos Willoughby
Richard Benjamin	Dr. Norman Solomon
Candy Azzara	Ellen Grady
Dick O'Neill	Irwin Owett
Thayer David	Pogostin
Charles Matthau	Michael Atkinson
Anthony Holland	TV Moderator

PRODUCTION CREDITS

Producers	Alex Winitsky
	Arlene Sellers
Director	Howard Zieff
Screenwriters	Max Shulman
	Julius J. Epstein
	Alan Mandel
	Charles Shyer

based on a story
by Julius J. Epstein, Shulman

Cinematographer	David M. Walsh
Composer	Henry Mancini

Paramount Pictures

Internes Can't Take Money

US (1937)
79 min, No rating, Black & White, Available on videocassette

See chapter 3

CAST LIST

Performer	Character
Barbara Stanwyck	Janet Haley
Joel McCrea	Jimmie Kildare
Lloyd Nolan	Hanlon
Stanley Ridges	Innes
Gaylord "Steve" Pendleton	Interne Jones
Lee Bowman	Interne Weeks
Irving Bacon	Jeff
Barry Macollum	"Stooly" Martin
Pierre Watkin	Dr. Fearson
Charles Lane	Grote
Fay Holden	Sister Superior

PRODUCTION CREDITS

Producer	Benjamin Glazer
Director	Alfred Santell
Screenwriters	Rian James
	Theodore Reeves

based on a magazine story
by Max Brand

Cinematographer	Theodor Sparkuhl
Music director	Boris Morros

Columbia Pictures

The Interns
US (1962)
130 min, No rating, Black & White, Available on videocassette and laserdisc

See chapter 3

CAST LIST

Performer	Character
Michael Callan	Dr. Considine
Cliff Robertson	Dr. John Paul Otis
James MacArthur	Dr. Lew Worship
Nick Adams	Dr. Sid Lackland
Suzy Parker	Lisa Cardigan
Haya Harareet	Mado
Anne Helm	Mildred
Stefanie Powers	Gloria
Buddy Ebsen	Dr. Sidney Wohl
Telly Savalas	Dr. Riccio
Katharine Bard	Nurse Flynn
Kay Stevens	Didi Loomis
Gregory Morton	Dr. Hugo Granchard
Angela Clarke	Mrs. Auer
Connie Gilchrist	Nurse Connie Dean
Charles Robinson	Dr. Dave Simon
William O. Douglas	Dr. Apschult

PRODUCTION CREDITS

Producer	Robert Cohn
Director	David Swift
Screenwriters	Walter Newman
	David Swift

based on the novel
by Richard Frede

Cinematographer	Russell Metty
Composer	Leith Stevens

Warner Bros.

Kings Row

US (1942)

126 min, No rating, Black & White, Available on videocassette and laserdisc

See chapter 7

CAST LIST

Performer	Character
Ann Sheridan	Randy Monoghan
Robert Cummings	Parris Mitchell
Ronald Reagan	Drake McHugh
Betty Field	Cassandra Tower
Charles Coburn	Dr. Henry Gordon
Claude Rains	Dr. Alexander Tower
Judith Anderson	Mrs. Harriet Gordon
Nancy Coleman	Louise Gordon
Kaaren Verne	Elise Sandor
Maria Ouspenskaya	Mme. Von Eln
Harry Davenport	Col. Skeffington
Ann Todd	Randy as a Child

PRODUCTION CREDITS

Producer	David Lewis
Director	Sam Wood
Screenwriter	Casey Robinson
	based on the novel
	by Henry Bellamann
Cinematographer	James Wong Howe
Composer	Erich Wolfgang Korngold

Columbia Pictures

The Last Angry Man

US (1959)
100 min, No rating, Black & White, Available on videocassette

See chapter 2

CAST LIST

Performer	Character
Paul Muni	Dr. Sam Abelman
David Wayne	Woodrow Wilson Thrasher
Betsy Palmer	Anne Thrasher
Luther Adler	Dr. Max Vogel
Nancy R. Pollock	Sarah Abelman
Billy Dee Williams	Josh Quincy
Claudia McNeil	Mrs. Quincy
Godfrey Cambridge	Nobody Home
Cicely Tyson	Girl Left on Porch

PRODUCTION CREDITS

Producer	Fred Kohlmar
Director	Daniel Mann
Screenwriters	Gerald Green
	Richard Murphy

based on the novel
by Gerald Green

Cinematographer	James Wong Howe
Composer	George Duning

Like Water for Chocolate
(Como Agua para Chocolate)

Mexico (1992)
113 min, No rating, Color, Available on videocassette and laserdisc
In Spanish, with English subtitles

See chapter 10

CAST LIST

Performer	Character
Marco Leonardi	Pedro Muzquiz
Lumi Cavazos	Tita de la Garza
Regina Torne	Mama Elena
Mario Iván Martinez	John Brown
Ada Carrasco	Nacha
Yareli Arizmendi	Rosaura
Claudette Maille	Gertrudis

PRODUCTION CREDITS

Producer	Alfonso Arau
Director	Alfonso Arau
Screenwriter	Laura Esquivel
from the novel	
by Laura Esquivel	
Cinematographers	Emmanuel Lubezki
	Steve Bernstein
Composer	Leo Brower

Universal Pictures

Lorenzo's Oil

US (1992)

135 min, Rated PG-13, Color, Available on videocassette and laserdisc

See chapter 4

CAST LIST

Performer	Character
Nick Nolte	Augusto Odone
Susan Sarandon	Michaela Odone
Peter Ustinov	Professor Nikolais
Kathleen Wilhoite	Deirdre Murphy
Gerry Bamman	Doctor Judalon
Margo Martindale	Wendy Gimble
James Rebhorn	Ellard Muscatine
Ann Hearn	Loretta Muscatine
Maduka Steady	Omouri
Zack O'Malley Greenburg	Lorenzo Odone

PRODUCTION CREDITS

Producers	George Miller
	Doug Mitchell
Director	George Miller
Screenwriters	George Miller
	Nick Enright
Cinematographer	John Seale

Film Classics, Inc.

Lost Boundaries

US (1949)

99 min, No rating, Black & White, Available on videocassette

See chapter 6

Cast List

Performer	Character
Beatrice Pearson	Marcia Carter
Mel Ferrer	Dr. Scott Carter
Richard Hylton	Howard Carter
Susan Douglas	Shelley Carter
Canada Lee	Lt. Thompson
Rev. Robert Dunn	Rev. John Taylor
Grace Coppin	Mrs. Mitchell
Carleton Carpenter	Andy
Wendell Holmes	Mr. Mitchell
Maurice Ellis	Dr. Cashman
Rai Saunders	Dr. Jesse Pridham
William Greaves	Arthur Cooper

Production Credits

Producer	Louis de Rochemont
Director	Alfred Werker
Screenwriters	Virginia Shaler
	Eugene Ling
	Charles Palmer
	Furland de Kay

based on an article
by William L. White

Cinematographer	William Miller
Composer	Louis Applebaum

Metro-Goldwyn-Mayer

Madame Curie

US (1943)

113 min, No rating, Black & White, Available on videocassette and laserdisc

See chapter 4

CAST LIST

Performer	Character
Greer Garson	Mme. Marie Curie
Walter Pidgeon	Pierre Curie
Robert Walker	David LeGros
Dame May Whitty	Mme. Eugene Curie
Henry Travers	Eugene Curie
C. Aubrey Smith	Lord Kelvin
Albert Basserman	Prof. Jean Perot
Reginald Owen	Dr. Henri Becquerel
Van Johnson	Reporter
James Hilton	Narrator
Ray Collins	Lecturer's Voice
Margaret O'Brien	Irene at Age Five
Gigi Perreau	Eva at Age 18 Months

PRODUCTION CREDITS

Producer	Sidney Franklin
Director	Mervyn LeRoy
Screenwriters	Paul Osborn
	Paul H. Rameau

based on the book
by Eve Curie

Cinematographer	Joseph Ruttenberg
Composer	Herbert Stothart

Universal Pictures

Magnificent Obsession

US (1935)
112 min, No rating, Black & White

See chapter 9

CAST LIST

Performer	Character
Irene Dunne	Helen Hudson
Robert Taylor	Bobby Merrick
Charles Butterworth	Tommy Masterson
Betty Furness	Joyce Hudson
Sara Haden	Nancy Ashford
Ralph Morgan	Randolph
Henry Armetta	Tony
Arthur Treacher	Horace

PRODUCTION CREDITS

Producer	John M. Stahl
Director	John M. Stahl
Screenwriters	George O'Neil
	Sarah Y. Mason
	Victor Heerman
	Finley Peter Dunne

based on a novel
by Lloyd C. Douglas

Cinematographer	John Mescall

Universal Pictures

Magnificent Obsession
US (1954)
108 min, No rating, Color, Available on videocassette

See chapter 9

CAST LIST

Performer	Character
Jane Wyman	Helen Phillips
Rock Hudson	Bob Merrick
Barbara Rush	Joyce Phillips
Agnes Moorehead	Nancy Ashford
Otto Kruger	Randolph
Gregg Palmer	Tom Masterson
Mae Clarke	Mrs. Miller

PRODUCTION CREDITS

Producer	Ross Hunter
Director	Douglas Sirk
Screenwriters	Robert Blees
	Wells Root

based on the novel
by Lloyd C. Douglas and the 1935 screenplay

Cinematographer	Russell Metty
Composer	Frank Skinner
Music director	Joseph Gershenson

Castle Rock

Malice

US (1993)

107 min, Rated R, Color, Available on videocassette and laserdisc

See chapter 7

Cast List

Performer	Character
Alec Baldwin	Dr. Jed Hill
Nicole Kidman	Tracy Safian
Bill Pullman	Andy Safian
Bebe Neuwirth	Dana Harris
George C. Scott	Dr. Kessler
Anne Bancroft	Ms. Claire Kennsinger
Peter Gallagher	Dennis Riley
Josef Sommer	Lester Adams
Tobin Bell	Earl Leemus
Debrah Farentino	Tanya
Gwyneth Paltrow	Paula Bell
David Bowe	Dr. Matthew Robertson

Production Credits

Producers	Rachel Pfeffer
	Charles Mulvehill
	Harold Becker
Director	Harold Becker
Screenwriters	Aaron Sorkin
	Scott Frank
	from the story
	by Sorkin and Jonas McCord
Cinematographer	Gordon Willis
Composer	Jerry Goldsmith

TriStar Pictures

Mary Shelley's Frankenstein
US (1994)
128 min, Rated R, Color, Available on videocassette and laserdisc

See chapter 4

CAST LIST

Performer	Character
Robert De Niro	The Creature/ Sharp Featured Man
Kenneth Branagh	Victor Frankenstein
Tom Hulce	Henry
Helena Bonham Carter	Elizabeth
Aidan Quinn	Captain Walton
Ian Holm	Victor's Father
Richard Briers	Grandfather
John Cleese	Professor Waldman
Robert Hardy	Professor Krempe

PRODUCTION CREDITS

Producers	Francis Ford Coppola
	James V. Hart
	John Veitch
Director	Kenneth Branagh
Screenwriters	Steph Lady
	Frank Darabont

based on the novel
by Mary Wollstonecraft Shelley

Cinematographer	Roger Pratt
Composer	Patrick Doyle

Warner Bros.

Mary Stevens, M.D.

US (1933)
71 min, No rating, Black & White

See chapter 5

CAST LIST

Performer	Character
Glenda Farrell	Glenda Carroll
Kay Francis	Dr. Mary Stevens
John Marston	Dr. Lane
Reginald Mason	Hospital Superintendent
Sidney Miller	Nussbaum
Harry Myers	Nervous Patient
Lyle Talbot	Don Andrews
Thelma Todd	Lois
Walter Walker	Dr. Clark

PRODUCTION CREDITS

Producer	Hal B. Wallis
Director	Lloyd Bacon
Screenwriters	Rian James
	Robert Lord
Cinematography	Sidney Hickox
Music	Leo F. Forbstein
Dialogue Director	William Keighley

Twentieth Century Fox

M*A*S*H

US (1970)

116 min, Rated PG, Color, Available on videocassette and laserdisc

See chapter 8

CAST LIST

Performer	Character
Donald Sutherland	Hawkeye Pierce
Elliott Gould	Trapper John McIntyre
Tom Skerritt	Duke Forrest
Sally Kellerman	Maj. Hot Lips Houlihan
Robert Duvall	Maj. Frank Burns
René Auberjonois	Dago Red
Roger Bowen	Col. Henry Blake
Gary Burghoff	Radar O'Reilly
Fred Williamson	Spearchucker Jones
Michael Murphy	Me Lay
John Schuck	Painless Pole
Jo Ann Pflug	Lt. Hot Dish
G. Wood	Gen. Hammond
Bud Cort	Pvt. Boone

PRODUCTION CREDITS

Producer	Ingo Preminger
Director	Robert Altman
Screenwriter	Ring Lardner, Jr.
	based on the novel
	by Richard Hooker
Cinematographer	Harold Stine
Composer	Johnny Mandel

Hollywood Pictures

Medicine Man

US (1992)

106 min, Rated PG-13, Color, Available on videocassette and laserdisc

See chapter 4

CAST LIST

Performer	Character
Sean Connery	Dr. Robert Campbell
Lorraine Bracco	Dr. Rae Crane
Jose Wilker	Dr. Miguel Ornega
Rodolfo De Alexandre	Tanaki
Francisco Tsirene Tsere Rereme	Jahausa
Elias Monteiro DaSilva	Palala
Edinei Maria Serrio Dos Santos	Kalana
Bec-Kana-Re Dos Santos Kaiapo	Imana
Angelo Barra Moreira	Medicine Man

PRODUCTION CREDITS

Producers	Andrew Vajna
	Donna Dubrow
Director	John McTiernan
Screenwriters	Tom Schulman
	Sally Robinson
from the story	
by Tom Schulman	
Cinematographer	Donald McAlpine
Composer	Jerry Goldsmith

RKO Radio Pictures

Meet Dr. Christian

US (1939)
68 min, No rating, Black & White, Available on videocassette

See chapter 2

CAST LIST

Performer	Character
Jean Hersholt	Dr. Paul Christian
Dorothy Lovett	Judy Price
Robert Baldwin	Roy Davis
Enid Bennett	Anne Hewitt
Paul Harvey	John Hewitt
Marcia Mae Jones	Marilee
Jackie Moran	Don Hewitt

PRODUCTION CREDITS

Producers	Monroe Shaff
	William Stephens
Director	Bernard Vorhaus
Screenwriters	Ian McLellan Hunter
	Ring Lardner Jr.

based on a story
by Harvey Gates

Metro-Goldwyn-Mayer

Men in White
US (1934)
80 min, No rating, Black & White

See chapter 3

CAST LIST

Performer	Character
Clark Gable	Dr. Ferguson
Myrna Loy	Laura
Jean Hersholt	Dr. Hochberg
Elizabeth Allan	Barbara
Otto Kruger	Dr. Levine
C. Henry Gordon	Dr. Cunningham
Russell Hardie	Dr. Michaelson
Henry B. Walthall	Dr. McCabe
Wallace Ford	Shorty
Samuel S. Hinds	Dr. Gordon

PRODUCTION CREDITS

Producer	Monta Bell
Director	Richard Boleslawski
Screenwriter	Waldemar Young
	based on the play
	by Sidney Kingsley
Cinematographer	George Folsey
Composer	William Axt

Paramount Pictures

Miss Susie Slagle's

US (1945)
88 min, No rating, Black & White

See chapter 1

Cast List

Performer	Character
Veronica Lake	Nan Rogers
Sonny Tufts	Pug Prentiss
Joan Caulfield	Margaretta Howe
Ray Collins	Dr. Elijah Howe
Billy De Wolfe	Ben Mead
Bill Edwards	Elijah Howe, Jr.
Pat Phelan	Elbert Riggs
Lillian Gish	Miss Susie Slagle
Morris Carnovsky	Dr. Fletcher
Lloyd Bridges	Silas Holmes
J. Louis Johnson	Hizer
Michael Sage	Irving Asrom

Production Credits

Producer	John Houseman
Director	John Berry
Screenwriters	Anne Froelick
	Hugo Butler
	Theodore Strauss
	Adrian Scott

based on the novel
by Augusta Tucker

Cinematographer	Charles Lang
Composer	Daniele Amfitheatrof

United Artists

Not As a Stranger

US (1955)

136 min, No rating, Black & White, Available on videocassette

See chapter 1

CAST LIST

Performer	Character
Olivia De Havilland	Kristina Hedvigson
Robert Mitchum	Lucas Marsh
Frank Sinatra	Alfred Boone
Gloria Grahame	Harriet Lang
Broderick Crawford	Dr. Aarons, Medical Professor
Charles Bickford	Dr. Runkleman
Myron McCormick	Dr. Snider
Lon Chaney, Jr.	Job Marsh
Jesse White	Ben Cosgrove
Harry Morgan	Oley
Lee Marvin	Brundage
Whit Bissell	Dr. Dietrich
Mae Clarke	Miss O'Dell

PRODUCTION CREDITS

Producer	Stanley Kramer
Director	Stanley Kramer
Screenwriters	Edna Anhalt
	Edward Anhalt

based on the novel
by Morton Thompson

Cinematographer	Franz Planer
Composer	George Antheil
Technical advisors	Dr. Morton Maxwell
	Dr. Josh Fields
	Marjorie Lefevre

Twentieth Century Fox

No Way Out

US (1950)

106 min, No rating, Black & White, Available on videocassette

See chapter 6

CAST LIST

Performer	Character
Richard Widmark	Ray Biddle
Linda Darnell	Edie
Stephen McNally	Dr. Wharton
Sidney Poitier	Dr. Luther Brooks
Mildred Joanne Smith	Cora
Harry Bellaver	George Biddle
Stanley Ridges	Dr. Moreland
Dotts Johnson	Lefty
Amanda Randolph	Gladys
Bill Walker	Mathew Tompkins
Ruby Dee	Connie
Ossie Davis	John

PRODUCTION CREDITS

Producer	Darryl F. Zanuck
Director	Joseph L. Mankiewicz
Screenwriter s	Joseph L. Mankiewicz
	Lesser Samuels
Cinematographer	Milton Krasner
Composer	Alfred Newman

RKO Pictures

Of Human Bondage

US (1934)

83 min, No rating, Black & White, Available on videocassette and laserdisc

See chapter 1

CAST LIST

Performer	Character
Leslie Howard	Philip Carey
Bette Davis	Mildred Rogers
Frances Dee	Sally Athelny
Reginald Owen	Thorpe Athelny
Reginald Denny	Harry Griffiths
Kay Johnson	Norah
Alan Hale	Emil Miller
Desmond Roberts	Dr. Jacobs

PRODUCTION CREDITS

Producer	Pandro S. Berman
Director	John Cromwell
Screenwriter	Lester Cohen

based on the novel
by W. Somerset Maugham

Cinematographer	Henry Gerrard
Composer	Max Steiner

Republic Pictures

One Flew Over the Cuckoo's Nest

US (1975)

129 min, Rated R, Color, Available on videocassette and laserdisc

See chapter 8

CAST LIST

Performer	Character
Jack Nicholson	Randle Patrick McMurphy
Louise Fletcher	Nurse Mildred Ratched
William Redfield	Harding
Michael Berryman	Ellis
Brad Dourif	Billy Bibbit
Peter Brocco	Col. Matterson
Dean R. Brooks	Dr. John Spivey
Scatman Crothers	Turkle
Danny De Vito	Martini
Christopher Lloyd	Taber
Louisa Moritz	Rose
Will Sampson	Chief Bromden

PRODUCTION CREDITS

Producers	Saul Zaentz
	Michael Douglas
Director	Milos Forman
Screenwriters	Lawrence Hauben
	Bo Goldman
	based on the novel by Ken Kesey
	and the play by Dale Wasserman
Cinematographers	Haskell Wexler
	William A. Fraker
	Bill Butler
Composer	Jack Nitzsche

Warner Bros.

Outbreak

US (1995)
127 min, Rated R, Color, Available on videocassette and laserdisc

See chapter 6

CAST LIST

Performer	Character
Dustin Hoffman	Col. Sam Daniels, M.D.
Rene Russo	Dr. Robby Keough
Morgan Freeman	Gen. Billy Ford
Kevin Spacey	Major "Casey" Schuler
Cuba Gooding, Jr.	Major Salt
Donald Sutherland	Gen. Donald McClintock
Patrick Dempsey	Jimbo Scott
Zakes Mokae	Dr. Benjamin Iwabi
Malick Bowens	Dr. Raswani
Susan Lee Hoffman	Dr. Lisa Aronson
Benito Martinez	Dr. Julio Ruiz
Bruce Jarchow	Dr. Mascelli

PRODUCTION CREDITS

Producers	Arnold Kopelson
	Wolfgang Petersen
	Gail Katz
Director	Wolfgang Petersen
Screenwriters	Laurence Dworet
	Robert Roy Pool
Cinematography	Michael Ballhaus
Music	James Newton Howard

Universal Pictures

Patch Adams

US (1998)

109 min, Rated R, Color, Available on videocassette

See chapter 1

Cast List

Performer	Character
Robin Williams	Patch Adams
Daniel London	Truman
Monica Potter	Carin
Philip Seymour Hoffman	Mitch
Bob Gunton	Dean Walcott
Josef Sommer	Dr. Eaton
Irma P. Hall	Joletta
Harve Presnell	Dean Anderson
Peter Coyote	Bill Davis

Production Credits

Producers	Barry Kemp
	Mike Farrell
Director	Tom Shadyac
Screenwriter	Steve Oedekerk

based on the book

Gesundheit: Good Health Is A Laughing Matter

by Hunter Doherty Adams with Maureen Mylander

Director of Photography	Phedon Papamichael
Composer	Marc Shaiman

Twentieth Century Fox

People Will Talk

US (1951)

110 min, No rating, Black & White, Available on videocassette

See chapter 2

CAST LIST

Performer	Character
Cary Grant	Dr. Noah Praetorius
Jeanne Crain	Annabel Higgins
Finlay Currie	Shunderson
Hume Cronyn	Prof. Elwell
Walter Slezak	Prof. Barker
Sidney Blackmer	Arthur Higgins
Margaret Hamilton	Miss Pickett

PRODUCTION CREDITS

Producer	Darryl F. Zanuck
Director	Joseph L. Mankiewicz
Screenwriter	Joseph L. Mankiewicz

based on the play *Dr. Praetorius*
by Curt Goetz

Cinematographer	Milton Krasner
Composers	Johannes Brahms
	Richard Wagner
Music director	Alfred Newman
Makeup	Ben Nye

Touchstone Pictures

Playing God

US (1997)
94 minutes, Rated R, Color, Available on videocassette

See chapter 7

CAST LISTING

Performer	Character
David Duchovny	Eugene Sands
Timothy Hutton	Raymond Blossom
Angelina Jolie	Claire
Michael Massee	Gage
Peter Stormare	Vladimir

PRODUCTION CREDITS

Producer	Mark Abraham
Director	Andy Wilson
Screenwriter	Mark Haskell Smith
Music	Richard Hartley
Cinematography	Anthony B. Richard

Columbia Pictures

The Prince of Tides

US (1991)

132 min, Rated R, Color, Available on videocassette and laserdisc

See chapter 5

CAST LIST

Performer	Character
Nick Nolte	Tom Wingo
Barbra Streisand	Dr. Susan Lowenstein
Blythe Danner	Sallie Wingo
Kate Nelligan	Lila Wingo Newbury
Jeroen Krabbé	Herbert Woodruff
Melinda Dillon	Savannah Wingo
George Carlin	Eddie Detreville
Jason Gould	Bemard Woodruff
Brad Sullivan	Henry Wingo

PRODUCTION CREDITS

Producers	Barbra Streisand
	Andrew Karsch
Director	Barbra Streisand
Screenwriters	Becky Johnston
	Pat Conroy
from the novel	
by Pat Conroy	
Cinematographer	Stephen Goldblatt
Composer	James Newton Howard

Paramount Pictures

The Rainmaker

US (1997)

135 min, Rated PG-13, Color, Available on videocassette

See chapter 8

CAST LIST

Performer	Character
Matt Damon	Rudy Baylor
Danny De Vito	Deck Schifflet
Claire Danes	Kelly Riker
Jon Voight	Leo F. Drummond
Mary Kay Place	Dot Black
Dean Stockwell	Judge Harvey Hale
Teresa Wright	Miss Birdie
Virginia Madsen	Jacki Lemancyzk
Mickey Rourke	Bruiser Stone
Andrew Shue	Cliff Riker
Red West	Buddy Black
Johnny Whitworth	Donny Ray Black
Danny Glover	Judge Tyrone Kipler

PRODUCTION CREDITS

Producer	Michael Douglas
Director	Frank Coppola
Writing Credits	Frank Coppola
	based on a novel
	by John Grisham
Cinematographer	John Toll
Music	Elmer Bernstein

RKO Radio Pictures

Sister Kenny

US (1946)

116 min, No rating, Black & White, Available on videocassette and laserdisc

See chapter 7

CAST LIST

Performer	Character
Rosalind Russell	Elizabeth Kenny
Alexander Knox	Dr. Aeneas McDonnell
Dean Jagger	Kevin Connors
Philip Merivale	Dr. Brack
Beulah Bondi	Mary Kenny
John Litel	Medical Director
Dorothy Peterson	Agnes
Frank Reicher	Chuter
Regis Toomey	Reporter

PRODUCTION CREDITS

Producer	Dudley Nichols
Director	Dudley Nichols
Screenwriters	Dudley Nichols
	Alexander Knox
	Mary E. McCarthy
	Milton Gunzburg

based on the book *And They Shall Walk*
by Elizabeth Kenny and Martha Ostenso

Cinematographer	George Barnes
Composer	Alexandre Tansman
Music Director	C. Bakaleinikoff

Metro-Goldwyn-Mayer

Society Doctor

US (1935)
63 min, No rating, Black & White

See chapter 3

CAST LIST

Performer	Character
Chester Morris	Dr. Morgan
Robert Taylor	Dr. Ellis
Virginia Bruce	Madge
Billie Burke	Mrs. Crane
Raymond Walburn	Dr. Waverly
Henry Kolker	Dr. Harvey
Dorothy Peterson	Mrs. Harrigan
Donald Meek	Moxley
Louise Henry	Telephone Operator
Johnny Hines	Hardy
Addison Richards	Harrigan

PRODUCTION CREDITS

Producer	Lucien Hubbard
Director	George B. Seitz
Writing Credits	Michael Fessier
	Samuel Marx
Cinematographer	Lester White
Music	Oscar Radin

United Artists

Spellbound

US (1945)

111 min, No rating, Black & White, Available on videocassette and laserdisc

See chapter 5

CAST LIST

Performer	Character
Ingrid Bergman	Dr. Constance Peterson
Gregory Peck	John "J.B." Ballantine
Jean Acker	Matron
Donald Curtis	Harry
Rhonda Fleming	Mary Carmichael
John Emery	Dr. Fleurot
Leo G. Carroll	Dr. Murchison
Paul Harvey	Dr. Hanish
Wallace Ford	Stranger in Hotel Lobby
Bill Goodwin	House Detective
Irving Bacon	Gateman
Regis Toomey	Sgt. Gillespie
Michael Chekhov	Dr. Alex Brulov
Alfred Hitchcock	Man Carrying Violin

PRODUCTION CREDITS

Producer	David O. Selznick
Director	Alfred Hitchcock
Screenwriters	Ben Hecht
	Angus MacPhail

based on the novel *The House of Dr. Edwardes*
by Francis Beeding Hilary,
St. George Saunders, John Palmer

Cinematographers	George Barnes
	Rex Wimpy
Composer	Miklos Rozsa

Warner Bros.

The Story of Louis Pasteur

US (1936)

87 min, No rating, Black & White, Available on videocassette

See chapter 4

Cast List

Performer	Character
Paul Muni	Louis Pasteur
Josephine Hutchinson	Mme. Pasteur
Anita Louise	Annette Pasteur
Donald Woods	Jean Martel
Fritz Leiber	Dr. Charbonnet
Henry O'Neill	Roux
Porter Hall	Dr. Rosignol
Akim Tamiroff	Dr. Zaranoff
Walter Kingsford	Napoleon III
Frank Reicher	Dr. Pheiffer
Halliwell Hobbes	Dr. Joseph Lister
Dickie Moore	Phillip Meister

Production Credits

Producer	Henry Blanke
Director	William Dieterle
Screenwriters	Sheridan Gibney
	Pierre Collings

based on the story
by Sheridan Gibney and Pierre Collings

Cinematographer	Tony Gaudio
Music Director	Leo F. Forbstein

RKO Radio Pictures

Symphony of Six Million

US (1932)

94 min, No rating, Black & White

See chapter 9

CAST LIST

Performer	Character
Ricardo Cortez	Dr. Felix Klauber
Irene Dunne	Jessica
Anna Appel	Hannah Klauber
Gregory Ratoff	Meyer Klauber
Lita Chevret	Birdie Klauber
Noel Madison	Magnus Klauber
Oscar Apfel	Doctor
John St. Polis	Dr. Schifflen
Lester Lee	Felix as a Boy

PRODUCTION CREDITS

Producer	Pandro S. Berman
Director	Gregory La Cava
Screenwriters	Bernard Schubert
	J. Walter Ruben
	James Seymour

based on the novel
by Fannie Hurst

Cinematographer	Leo Tover
Composer	Max Steiner

British Lion

The Third Man
UK (1949)
100 min, No rating, Black & White, Available on videocassette and laserdisc

See chapter 10

CAST LIST

Performer	Character
Joseph Cotten	Holly Martins
Orson Welles	Harry Lime
Alida Valli	Anna Schmidt
Trevor Howard	Maj. Calloway
Paul Hoerbiger	Porter
Ernst Deutsch	Baron Kurtz
Erich Ponto	Dr. Winkel
Siegfried Breuer	Popescu
Bernard Lee	Sgt. Paine
Wilfrid Hyde-White	Crabbin

PRODUCTION CREDITS

Producers	David O. Selznick
	Alexander Korda
	Carol Reed
Director	Carol Reed
Screenwriter	Graham Greene
Cinematographer	Robert Krasker
Composer	Anton Karas

Twentieth Century Fox

The Verdict
US (1982)
128 min, Rated R, Color, Available on videocassette and laserdisc

See chapter 8

CAST LIST

Performer	Character
Paul Newman	Frank Galvin
Charlotte Rampling	Laura Fischer
Jack Warden	Mickey Morrissey
James Mason	Ed Concannon
Milo O'Shea	Judge Hoyle
Lindsay Crouse	Kaitlin Costello Price
Edward Binns	Bishop Brophy
Julie Bovasso	Maureen Rooney
Roxanne Hart	Sally Doneghy
James Handy	Kevin Doneghy
Wesley Addy	Dr. Towler
Joe Seneca	Dr. Thompson
Lewis J. Stadlen	Dr. Gruber
Bruce Willis	Courtroom Observer

PRODUCTION CREDITS

Producers	Richard D. Zanuck
	David Brown
Director	Sidney Lumet
Screenwriter	David Mamet
based on the novel	
by Barry Reed	
Cinematographer	Andrzej Bartkowiak
Composer	Johnny Mandel

Paramount Pictures

Welcome Stranger

US (1947)
107 min, No rating, Black & White

See chapter 2

CAST LIST

Performer	Character
Bing Crosby	Dr. Jim Pearson
Joan Caulfield	Trudy Mason
Barry Fitzgerald	Dr. Joseph McRory
Wanda Hendrix	Emily Walters
Larry Young	Dr. Ronnie Jenks
Percy Kilbride	Nat Dorkas

PRODUCTION CREDITS

Producer	Sol C. Siegel
Director	Elliott Nugent
Screenwriters	Arthur Sheekman
	N. Richard Nash

based on a story
by Frank Butler

Cinematographer	Lionel Lindon
Composer	Robert Emmett Dolan
Costumes	Edith Head

Touchstone Pictures

What About Bob?

US (1991)
99 min, Rated PG, Color, Available on videocassette and laserdisc

See chapter 10

CAST LIST

Performer	Character
Bill Murray	Bob Wiley
Richard Dreyfuss	Doctor Leo Marvin
Julie Hagerty	Fay Marvin
Charlie Korsmo	Siggy Marvin
Kathryn Erbe	Anna Marvin
Tom Aldredge	Mr. Guttman
Susan Willis	Mrs. Guttman
Fran Brill	

PRODUCTION CREDITS

Producers	Bernard Williams
	Laura Ziskin
Director	Frank Oz
Writing Credits	Alvin Sargent
	Laura Ziskin
Cinematography	Michael Ballhaus
Music	Miles Goodman

Republic Pictures

Woman Doctor

US (1939)
65 min, No rating, Black & White

See chapter 5

CAST LISTING

Performer	Character
Frieda Inescort	Judith
Henry Wilcoxon	Allan
Claire Dodd	Gail
Sybil Jason	Elsa
Cora Witherspoon	Fanny
Frank Reicher	Dr. Mathews
Gus Glassmire	Dr. Martin
Rex	Moxie

PRODUCTION CREDITS

Associate Producer	Sol C. Siegel
Director	Sidney Salkow
Screenwriter	Joseph Moncure March

original story
by Alice Altschuler and Miriam Geiger

Photography	Ernest Miller
Musical Director	Cy Feuer

Metro-Goldwyn-Mayer

Young Dr. Kildare

US (1938)

81 min, No rating, Black & White, Available on videocassette

See chapter 3

CAST LIST

Performer	Character
Lew Ayres	Dr. James Kildare
Lionel Barrymore	Dr. Leonard Gillespie
Lynne Carver	Alice Raymond
Nat Pendleton	Joe Wayman
Jo Ann Sayers	Barbara Chanler
Samuel S. Hinds	Dr. Stephen Kildare
Emma Dunn	Mrs. Martha Kildare
Walter Kingsford	Dr. Walter Carew
Pierre Watkin	Mr. Chanler
Monty Woolley	Dr. Lane Porteus
Phillip Terry	Vickery
Don "Red" Barry	Collins
James Mason	Lodger

PRODUCTION CREDITS

Producer	Lou Ostrow
Director	Harold S. Bucquet
Screenwriters	Harry Ruskin
	Willis Goldbeck
	based on characters
	created by Max Brand
Cinematographer	John Seitz
Composer	David Snell

Universal Artists

The Young Doctors

US (1961)
102 min, No rating, Black & White

See chapter 3

CAST LIST

Performer	Character
Fredric March	Dr. Joseph Pearson
Ben Gazzara	Dr. David Coleman
Dick Clark	Dr. Alexander
Ina Balin	Cathy Hunt
Eddie Albert	Dr. Charles Dornberger
Phyllis Love	Mrs. Alexander
Edward Andrews	Bannister
Aline MacMahon	Dr. Lucy Grainger
Arthur Hill	Tomaselli
Rosemary Murphy	Miss Graves
Barnard Hughes	Dr. Kent O'Donnell
George Segal	Dr. Howard
Dick Button	Operating Intern
Ronald Reagan	Narrator
Gloria Vanderbilt	Elizabeth Alexander
James Broderick	Dr. Alexander

PRODUCTION CREDITS

Producers	Stuart Millar
	Lawrence Turman
Director	Phil Karlson
Screenwriter	Joseph Hayes

based on the novel *The Final Diagnosis*
by Arthur Hailey

Cinematographer	Arthur J. Ornitz
Composer	Elmer Bernstein

Sources of Photographs

Photofest, New York, provided all photographs except as specifically noted below.

The Alan Mason Chesney Medical Archives of the Johns Hopkins Medical Institutions, Introduction, Figure 1

Author's collection, Chapter 10, Figure 6

Beacon Communications, Inc., Chapter 7, Figure 10

Castle Rock Entertainment, Chapter 5, Figure 11

Cinergi Productions, Inc., and Cinergi Productions N.V. Chapter 4, Figure 10

Columbia Pictures, Inc., Chapter 5, Figure 10

Orion Pictures, Chapter 8, Figure 6

Tate Picture Library, Introduction, Figure 2

Touchstone Pictures, Chapter 7, Figure 8

Trimark Pictures, Chapter 6, Figure 6

TriStar Pictures, Chapter 8, Figure 7

Turner Entertainment Co., Chapter 9, Figure 1 and Figure 2

Universal City Studio Productions, Inc., Chapter 1, Figure 7

Index

A

Abel, Walter 235, 236, 328
Adams, Hunter 22, 26, 357
Adams, Nick 78, 335
Addy, Wesley 212, 368
Adler, Luther 49, 337
Albert, Eddie 75, 373
Alda, Alan 202
Allan, Elizabeth 58, 350
Allen, Vera 32, 313
Allen, Woody 241
Allyson, June 134, 136, 137, 327
Altman, Robert 199, 242, 347
Anderson, Judith 181, 336
Andrus, Mark 218, 302
Anson, A. E. 85, 300
Appel, Anna 231, 366
Arizmendi, Yareli 263, 338
Arkin, Alan 15, 162, 163, 331
Arness, James 137, 327
Arquette, Patricia 145, 146, 304
Arrowsmith 83, 84, **85–92**, 103,
    151, 173, 236, 283, 286, 289,
    292, 297, 300
Article 99 209, **214–218**, 301
As Good As It Gets **218–220**, 302
Atwill, Lionel 84, 316
Auberjonois, René 242, 347
Awakenings **276–280**, 303
Ayres, Lew 67, 68, 69, 71, 73,
    287, 320, 321, 372
Azzara, Candy 250, 333

B

Bacon, Irving 318, 334, 364
Bacon, Kevin 19, 21, 325
Bailey, John 302, 324
Baker, Lenny 203, 332
Baldwin, Alec 193, 194, 284, 344

Baldwin, William 20, 21, 325
Ballhaus, Michael 356, 370
Bancroft, Anne 192, 195, 226, 309,
    344
Barnes, George 362, 364
Barrat, Robert 35, 308
Barringer, Emily Dunning 327
Barrymore, Lionel 66, 68, 69, 287,
    320, 321, 372
Basserman, Albert 102, 318, 341
Beatty, Ned 250
Bellamann, Henry 179, 336
Bellaver, Harry 156, 353
Benjamin, Richard 250, 333
Bennett, Richard 87, 300
Bergman, Ingrid 132, 133, 182, 364
Berman, Pandro S. 354, 366
Bernstein, Elmer 361
Beyond Rangoon 143, **145–147**, 304
Bickford, Charles 14, 290, 352
Bissell, Whit 295, 352
Blackmer, Sidney 46, 358
Blanke, Henry 328, 365
Blossom, Roberts 311, 332
Bogarde, Dirk 8, 314
Bogart, Humphrey 182
Bogle, Donald 151
Bondi, Beulah 300, 362
Bosco, Philip 224, 309
Bovasso, Julie 301, 368
Bowe, David 193
Boyle, Peter 98
Bracco, Lorraine 111, 348
Branagh, Kenneth 96, 97, 285, 345
Brand, Max 64, 240, 320, 321,
    334, 372
Bridges, Lloyd 6, 351
Brooks, Albert 225, 309
Brooks, Clarence 90, 151, 300

Brooks, James 218, 302
Bruce, Virginia 61, 288, 363
Bucquet, Harold S. 320, 321, 372
Bujold, Genevieve 139, 142, 186,
    187, 188, 307, 310
Burghoff, Gary 202, 347
Burke, Billie 60, 63, 363
Byington, Spring 234, 328
Byrde, Edye 51, 52, 311

C

Callan, Michael 78, 335
Cambridge, Godfrey 48, 337
Carey, MacDonald 37
Carlin, George 360
Carney, Art 250, 251, 333
Carnovsky, Morris 8, 351
Carrasco, Ada 263, 338
Carroll, Diahann 170, 323
Carson, Lisa Nicole 168, 323
Carter, Helena Bonham 96, 345
Castle Rock Entertainment 304,
    324, 344
Caulfield, Joan 7, 41, 42, 288,
    351, 369
Cavazos, Lumi 262, 338
Cecil, Nora 32, 33, 313
Chaney, Jr., Lon 11, 352
Chaplin, Geraldine 261, 317
Chapman, Michael 311, 326
Chayefsky, Paddy 203, 209, 332
Chevret, Lita 232, 366
Christie, Julie 261, 262, 317
Citadel, The 173, **173–178**, 182, 199,
    209, 239, 283, 285, 290, 305
City of Joy **270–275**, 306
Clark, Dick 75, 289, 373
Clough, John Scott 15, 329
Coburn, Charles 179, 182, 336
Coleman, Nancy 180, 336
Collins, Pauline 272, 306
Colman, Ronald 85, 86, 89, 300
Columbia Pictures 303, 325, 330,
    335, 337, 360
Coma 20, 79, 139, **139–143**, 173,
    242, 245, 246, 307
Connery, Sean 111, 348
Conroy, Pat 143, 360
Cook, Robin 78, 139, 242
Cooperman, Harold O. 138

Coppola, Francis Ford 345, 361
Cortez, Ricardo 231, 366
Cotten, Joseph 257, 260, 367
Country Doctor, The 31, **34–
    37**, 46, 308
Courtenay, Tom 261, 317
Cozzens, James Gould 32, 313
Craig, Nell 320, 321
Crain, Jeanne 44, 151, 358
Crawford, Broderick 10, 11, 352
Crawford, Joan 123
Crichton, Michael 139, 307
Crisp, Donald 104, 318
Critical Care 29, 81, **222–227**, 243,
    285, 287, 290, 291, 294, 309
Cronenberg, David 186, 310
Cronin, A. J. 173, 176, 239, 305
Cronyn, Hume 43, 358
Crosby, Bing 40, 42, 369
Crothers, Scatman 355
Cummings, Robert 179, 336
Currie, Finlay 46, 358

D

Damon, Matt 220, 222, 361
Danner, Blythe 143, 360
Darnell, Linda 157, 353
Davenport, Harry 318, 336
David, Keith 214, 301
Davis, Bette 3, 4, 123, 173, 354
Day, Laraine 71, 72, 320, 321
De Havilland, Olivia 10, 12, 287,
    352
De Mille, Cecil B. 201
De Niro, Robert 97, 277, 296, 303,
    345
De Vito, Danny 220, 355, 361
De Wolfe, Billy 7, 55, 351
Dead Ringers 186, **186–189**, 197,
    310
Dee, Frances 5, 354
Dell, Barbara Wood 40, 315
Denny, Reginald 3, 4, 354
Destination Tokyo 41, 295, 296
Devine, Andy 32, 313
Dieterle, William 100, 318, 322, 365
Dionne Quintuplets 34, 308
Doc Hollywood 31, **51–53**, 290, 311
Doctor Bull 31, **32–33**, 37, 38,
    290, 297, 313

Doctor in the House 2, **8–9**, 284, 285, 294, 314

Doctor Jim **39–40**, 315

Doctor, The **189–192**, 209, 292, 294, 312

Doctor X **84**, 173, 316

Doctor Zhivago **260-262**, 317

Dodd, Claire 130, 371

Donat, Robert 173, 174, 175, 239, 305

Dooling, Richard 222, 309

Douglas, Lloyd C. 233, 237, 328, 342, 343

Douglas, Michael 139, 307, 325, 355, 361

Douglas, Susan 153, 340

Dr. Ehrlich's Magic Bullet **101–107**, 151, 292, 297, 318

Dr. Jekyll and Mr. Hyde 84, **93–96**, 319

Dr. Kildare's Crisis **70–71**, 320

Dr. Kildare's Wedding Day **72–73**, 288, 321

Dr. Monica **127–129**, 130, 286, 291, 322

Dreyfuss, Richard 254, 255, 370

Duchovny, David 195, 196, 295, 359

Dunn, Emma 320, 321, 322, 372

Dunne, Irene 232, 237, 238, 239, 342, 366

Dunning, Emily 134, 286

Dunnock, Mildred 134, 297, 327

Duvall, Robert 200, 242, 347

Dysart, Richard 205, 208, 332

E

Ebsen, Buddy 77, 335

Edwards, Bill 6, 351

Elfman, Danny 301, 324

Elliott, Stephen 203, 332

Ellis, Maurice 152, 340

Erbe, Kathryn 255, 370

Erwin, Stuart 40, 315

Esquivel, Laura 262, 338

Eve's Bayou 167, **168–170**, 297, 323

Extreme Measures 84, 117, 173, 243, **243–247**, 324

F

Farrell, Glenda 124, 346

Farrell, Mike 202, 357

Ferrer, Mel 151, 152, 154, 340

Field, Betty 179, 336

Field, Todd 15, 329

Film Classics, Inc. 340

First National Pictures 316

Fitzgerald, Barry 40, 42, 369

Flatliners 2, 3, **19–20**, 242, 325

Fletcher, Louise 211, 355

Flynn, Errol 234, 236, 328

Folsey, George 321, 350

Forbstein, Leo F. 316, 322, 346, 365

Ford, Harrison 267, 326

Ford, John 32, 85, 242, 300, 313

Ford, Wallace 350, 364

Foster, Preston 84, 316

Fox, Michael J. 51, 52, 277, 311

Francis, Kay 108, 123, 124, 125, 127, 128, 322, 346

Freeman, Morgan 164, 165, 167, 356

Fugitive, The **265–270**, 270, 326

G

Gable, Clark 56, 57, 350

Garson, Greer 108, 109, 341

Gazzara, Ben 74, 75, 373

Gelbart, Larry 202

Girl in White, The 122, 123, **134–138**, 239, 284, 286, 291, 295, 297, 327

Gish, Lillian 5, 6, 351

Glover, Danny 221, 361

Goldbeck, Willis 320, 321, 372

Goldsmith, Jerry 307, 344, 348

Goldwyn, Samuel 300

Good, Meagan 168, 323

Gooding, Jr., Cuba 164, 166, 218, 241, 302, 356

Gordon, Ruth 102, 318

Gould, Elliott 200, 347

Gould, Jason 144, 360

Grahame, Gloria 14, 352

Grant, Cary 42, 43, 45, 244, 296, 358

Grant, Hugh 243, 245, 246, 324

Greaves, William 153, 340

Green Light, The 233, **234–237**, 236, 286, 290, 291, 328

Greenburg, Zack O'Malley 112, 339

Greene, Graham 257, 367
Grisham, John 220, 361
Gross Anatomy 2, 3, **15–19**, 22,
    283, 284, 329
Guess Who's Coming to Dinner
    160, **160–161**, 330
Guinness, Alec 317
Gunton, Bob 22, 357

H

Hackman, Gene 245, 324
Hagerty, Julie 254, 370
Hall, Irma P. 23, 357
Hall, Vondie Curtis 169, 323
Hamilton, George 53, 311
Hamilton, Margaret 43, 358
Harareet, Haya 81, 138, 335
Hardwicke, Cedric 234, 328
Harrelson, Woody 52, 311
Harrison, Rex 176, 305
Harvey, Paul 349, 364
Hayes, Helen 85, 86, 300
Head, Edith 369
Heart is a Lonely Hunter, The **162–**
    164, 292, 331
Hecht, Ben 132, 364
Helm, Anne 80, 335
Hepburn, Katharine 161, 330
Hersholt, Jean 34, 35, 37, 39, 57,
    308, 349, 350
Hilton, James 202
Hinds, Samuel S. 321, 350, 372
Hitchcock, Alfred 132, 133, 195,
    244, 364
Hobart, Rose 93, 319
Hobbes, Halliwell 93, 319, 365
Hoffman, Dustin 165, 356
Hoffman, Philip Seymour 23, 357
Holden, Fay 321, 334
Holland, Anthony 252, 333
Hollywood Pictures 348
Holmes, Wendell 152, 340
Hooker, Richard 200, 347
Hopkins, Miriam 94, 319
Hopton, Russell 89, 300
Hospital, The 194, **203–209**, 211,
    242, 285, 290, 332
Houghton, Katharine 160, 161, 330
House Calls **250–252**, 256, 297, 333
Houseman, John 5, 351

Howard, James Newton 325, 326,
    356, 360
Howard, Leslie 3, 4, 354
Howard, Trevor 258, 367
Howe, James Wong 318, 331, 336,
    337
Hudson, Rock 238, 343
Hughes, Barnard 51, 242, 311,
    332, 373
Hughes, Bernard 204
Hulce, Tom 285, 345
Hunt, Helen 218, 219, 302
Hurst, Fannie 230, 366
Hurt, William 189, 192, 312
Huston, John 318
Hutton, Timothy 196, 359
Hylton, Richard 153, 154, 340

I

Inescort, Frieda 130, 131, 371
Internes Can't Take Money 55, **64–**
    66, 196, 283, 290, 292, 295,
    334
Interns, The 74, **76–81**, 123, 138,
    239, 285, 292, 294, 335
Irons, Jeremy 186, 187, 310

J

J. Arthur Rank 8, 314
Jackson, Glenda 250, 333
Jackson, Samuel L. 168, 169, 323
Jagger, Dean 183, 362
Jalan, Shyamanand 273, 306
James, Rian 334, 346
Janssen, David 265
Jarré, Maurice 261, 317
Jason, Sybil 130, 371
Joffe, Roland 306
Johnson, Dotts 155, 353
Johnson, J. Louis 5, 6, 351
Johnson, Kay 5, 354
Johnson, Van 68, 341
Jolie, Angelina 197, 359
Jones, Tommy Lee 266, 270, 326
Justice, James Robertson 9, 285,
    294, 314

K

Kalisch, Beatrice 66
Kalisch, Philip 66
Karas, Anton 257, 367

Karloff, Boris 95
Keach, Stacy 162, 331
Keen, Geoffrey 9, 314, 317
Keighley, William 322, 346
Kellaway, Cecil 161, 330
Kellerman, Sally 200, 347
Kemper, Victor J. 307, 332
Kennedy, Arthur 135, 327
Kesey, Ken 210, 355
Kidman, Nicole 344
King, Claude 88, 300
Kings Row **179–182**, 291, 336
Kingsford, Walter 320, 321, 365, 372
Kingsley, Sidney 56, 350
Kinnear, Greg 218, 220, 302
Knox, Alexander 183, 184, 362
Kolker, Henry 60, 328, 363
Kopelson, Arnold 326, 356
Korda, Alexander 257, 367
Korsmo, Charlie 254, 312
Krabbé, Jeroen 326, 360
Kramer, Stanley 10, 330, 352
Krasker, Robert 257, 367
Krasner, Milton 353, 358
Kruger, Alma 320, 321
Kruger, Otto 58, 102, 238, 318, 343, 350

L

Lahti, Christine 16, 17, 191, 312, 329
Lake, Veronica 7, 351
Lanchester, Elsa 95
Lang, June 35, 308
Langevin, Paul 110
Lapierre, Dominique 270, 306
Lardner, Jr., Ring 200, 347, 349
Last Angry Man, The 30, 31, **48–51**, 174, 209, 222, 290, 292, 337
Lean, David 260, 317
Lee, Bernard 258
Lee, Canada 154, 340
Leonardi, Marco 263, 338
Lewis, Sinclair 85, 92, 300
Like Water for Chocolate **262–265**, 338
Lindsay, Margaret 235, 328
Liotta, Ray 216, 301

LIVE Entertainment 309
Locke, Sondra 162, 331
Lombard, Carole 291
London, Daniel 24, 357
Lorenzo's Oil **112–117**, 339
Lost Boundaries 151, **152–154**, 340
Louise, Anita 234, 235, 236, 328, 365
Love, Montagu 36, 102, 308, 318
Love, Phyllis 76, 373
Loy, Myrna 58, 90, 300, 350
Luke, Keye 68
Lumet, Sidney 29, 30, 31, 214, 222, 309, 368

M

M*A*S*H 164, 199, **199–202**, 200, 210, 216, 242, 296, 347
MacArthur, James 77, 79, 240, 335
MacMahon, Aline 76, 373
Macollum, Barry 66, 334
Madame Curie **107–110**, 138, 341
Madison, Noel 232, 366
Magnificent Obsession (1935) **237**, 342
Magnificent Obsession (1954) **238–242**, 343
Mahoney, John 216, 301
Maille, Claudette 264, 338
Malice **193–195**, 284, 285, 294, 344
Malkovich, John 266
Maltin, Leonard 134, 261
Mamoulian, Rouben 94, 319
Mancini, Henry 333
Mandel, Johnny 347, 368
Mankiewicz, Joseph L. 155, 353, 358
March, Fredric 74, 75, 93, 94, 319, 373
Marchand, Nancy 203, 332
Marshall, Penny 279, 303
Martindale, Margo 223, 309, 339
Martinez, Mario Iván 264, 338
Marvin, Lee 10, 11, 352
Mary Shelley's Frankenstein **96–97**, 284, 285, 345
Mary Stevens, M.D. 55, **124–126**, 127, 139, 239, 283, 284, 286, 291, 292, 346
Mason, James 212, 368, 372

Matthau, Charles 250, 333
Matthau, Walter 250, 251, 333
Maugham, Somerset 3, 354
Max Factor 316
Maxwell, Morton 10
McCormick, Myron 14, 352
McCrea, Joel 65, 295, 334
McCullers, Carson 162, 331
McDormand, Frances 145, 304
McNally, Stephen 155, 289, 353
McNeil, Claudia 48, 337
Meara, Anne 303
Medicine Man **111-112**, 348
Meek, Donald 318, 363
Meet Dr. Christian 30, 31, **37–38**, 290, 297, 349
Men in White 56, **56–58**, 59, 64, 134, 173, 239, 286, 290, 291, 292, 295, 350
Merivale, Philip 183, 184, 362
Merrill, Gary 135, 327
Metro-Goldwyn-Mayer 305, 307, 316, 317, 319, 320, 321, 327, 341, 350, 363, 372
Metty, Russell 335, 343
Miller, George 112, 339
Mirren, Helen 223, 309
Miss Susie Slagle's 2, **5–8**, 53, 55, 130, 234, 283, 284, 286, 288, 291, 294, 351
Mitchum, Robert 10, 11, 289, 290, 352
Modine, Matthew 15, 17, 329
Mokae, Zakes 19, 329, 356
Moore, Gar 136, 327
Moorehead, Agnes 343
More, Kenneth 8, 314
Morgan, Harry 202, 352
Morgan, Ralph 32, 313, 342
Morris, Chester 60, 63, 363
Morton, Gregory 77, 335
Moser, Hugh 114, 116, 117
Muir, Jean 128, 322
Muni, Paul 49, 99, 100, 292, 337, 365
Murray, Bill 218, 253, 255, 370

N

Nelligan, Kate 143, 360
Newman, Alfred 300, 353, 358

Newman, Paul 212, 213, 368
Nicholson, Jack 210, 218–220, 302, 355
No Way Out 155, **155–159**, 209, 285, 286, 289, 297, 353
Nolan, Lloyd 66, 334
Nolte, Nick 112, 115, 143, 145, 339, 360
Not As a Stranger 2, **10–13**, 16, 74, 209, 284, 285, 286, 287, 288, 289, 290, 291, 293, 295, 296, 297, 352

O

Of Human Bondage 2, **3–4**, 288, 354
One Flew Over the Cuckoo's Nest **210–211**, 355
O'Neill, Henry 234, 236, 318, 328, 365
Orion Pictures 301
Orth, Frank 320, 321
Ouspenskaya, Maria 105, 179, 318, 336
Outbreak 164, **165–167**, 356
Owen, Reginald 341, 354

P

Palmer, Betsy 337
Palmer, Michael 243, 324
Paltrow, Gwyneth 344
Paramount Pictures 334, 351, 361, 369
Parker, Cecil 177, 305
Parker, Sarah Jessica 244, 324
Parker, Suzy 79, 240, 335
Parsons, Percy 177, 305
Pasternak, Boris 260, 317
Patch Adams 2, 3, **21–27**, 279, 357
Patinkin, Mandy 190, 312
Pearson, Beatrice 152, 154, 340
Peck, Gregory 132, 133, 258, 364
Pendleton, Nat 320, 372
People Will Talk **42–48**, 74, 284, 358
Perkins, Elizabeth 191, 192, 312
Peterson, Dorothy 308, 362, 363
Pflug, Jo Ann 200, 347
Phelan, Pat 6, 351
Pidgeon, Walter 108, 109, 341
Platt, Oliver 21, 325

Playing God **195–197**, 293, 295, 359
Poitier, Sidney 155, 157, 159, 160, 161, 297, 330, 353
Potter, Monica 22, 357
Powers, Stefanie 78, 335
Preston, Richard 167
Prince of Tides, The 132, 143, **143–144**, 360
Pullman, Bill 194, 344
Puri, Om 270, 271, 274, 306

Q

Quinn, Aidan 96, 345

R

Rainmaker, The **220–221**, 361
Rains, Claude 179, 336
Rampling, Charlotte 214, 368
Ratoff, Gregory 230, 231, 366
Reagan, Ronald 180–182, 336, 373
Reed, Carol 257, 367
Reicher, Frank 35, 308, 318, 362, 365, 371
Republic Pictures 130, 355, 371
Richards, Beah 161, 330
Richardson, Ralph 174, 305, 317
Ridges, Stanley 156, 334, 353
Rigg, Diana 205, 208, 332
RKO Radio Pictures 349, 354, 362, 366
Roberts, Desmond 4, 354
Roberts, Julia 19, 20, 21, 325
Robertson, Cliff 77, 240, 335
Robinson, Edward G. 101, 105, 318
Rodriguez, Percy 162, 163, 331
Rogers, Will 32, 33, 292, 313
Rosenbaum, Edward E. 189, 312
Rosenberg, Charles 91
Roueché, Berton 164
Rourke, Mickey 220, 361
Rozsa, Miklos 132, 364
Rumann, Sig 102, 318
Ruskin, Harry 320, 321, 372
Russell, Rosalind 175, 184, 305, 362
Russo, Rene 165, 356

S

Sacks, Oliver 276, 303
Sage, Michael 6, 351
Samuel Goldwyn 300
Sanford, Isabel 160, 330

Sarandon, Susan 113, 115, 339
Saunders, Rai 152, 340
Savalas, Telly 77, 138, 294, 335
Scott, George C. 194, 200, 202, 203, 205, 208, 332, 344
Seale, John 304, 312, 339
Sedgwick, Kyra 223, 309
Seitz, John 308, 320, 372
Selleck, Tom 307
Selzer, Richard 231
Selznick, David O. 257, 364, 367
Seneca, Joe 213, 368
Sevalas, Telly 81
Shadyac, Tom 26, 357
Sharif, Omar 261, 262, 317
Shawn, Wallace 224, 309
Sheppard, Sam 265
Sheridan, Ann 180, 182, 336
Siegel, Sol C. 369, 371
Sinatra, Frank 10, 11, 285, 287, 352
Sister Kenny **182–186**, 199, 287, 362
Skelton, Red 72, 321
Skerritt, Tom 200, 347
Slezak, Walter 46, 358
Smollett, Jurnee 168, 323
Snell, David 320, 372
Society Doctor 41, **59–62**, 64, 173, 285, 288, 292, 295, 363
Sommer, Josef 344, 357
Spacey, Kevin 166, 356
Spader, James 223, 227, 309
Spellbound **132–133**, 295, 364
Stanwyck, Barbara 65, 123, 334
Steiger, Rod 261, 317
Steiner, Max 104, 232, 234, 318, 328, 354, 366
Sternhagen, Frances 311, 332
Stewart, Jimmy 244
Stiers, David Ogden 53, 202, 311
Stockwell, Dean 221, 361
Story of Louis Pasteur, The **98–100**, 151, 283, 297, 365
Streisand, Barbra 144, 145, 360
Struss, Karl 94, 319
Sutherland, Donald 165, 200, 202, 216, 347, 356
Sutherland, Kiefer 19, 20, 21, 216, 301, 325
Swayze, Patrick 270, 274, 306

Symphony of Six Million 29, **230–233**, 289, 366

T

Talbot, Lyle 124, 346
Taylor, Robert 60, 237, 239, 285, 342, 363
Teasdale, Vernee 127, 322
Third Man, The **256–259**, 367
Thompson, Lea 216, 301
Thompson, Morton 10, 352
Todd, Ann 318, 336
Toomey, Regis 362, 364
Torn, Rip 140, 307
Torne, Regina 263, 338
Touchstone Pictures 312, 329, 359, 370
Tracy, Spencer 160, 161, 330
Treacher, Arthur 342
Trimark Pictures 323
TriStar Pictures 302, 306, 345
Tucker, Augusta 5, 234, 351
Tufts, Sonny 5, 284, 288, 351
Turow, Joseph 240
Twentieth Century Fox 308, 310, 313, 347, 353, 358, 368
Tyson, Cicely 48, 162, 331, 337

U

United Artists 316, 332, 352, 364
Universal Artists 373
Universal City Studios 333
Universal Pictures 339, 342, 343, 357
Ustinov, Peter 113, 116, 164, 339

V

Valli, Alida 258, 367
Vanderbilt, Gloria 373
Verdict, The 164, **212–213**, 221, 222, 368
Verne, Kaaren 181, 336
Voight, Jon 221, 361

W

Walburn, Raymond 60, 363
Walker, Robert 108, 341
Wallach, Eli 216, 217, 301
Warden, Jack 212, 368
Warner Bros. 311, 318, 326, 328, 331, 336, 346, 354, 356, 365
Warner, Julie 52, 311

Waterston, Sam 250
Watkin, Pierre 328, 334, 372
Wayne, David 50, 337
Welcome Stranger **40–41**, 52, 295, 369
Welles, Orson 260, 367
West, Mae 58
Westmore, Wally 94, 319
Whalen, Michael 35, 308
What About Bob? 218, **253–256**, 370
White, Jesse 327, 352
White, William 151, 340
Whitfield, Lynn 169, 323
Widmark, Richard 140, 155, 157, 159, 186, 246, 307, 353
Wilcoxon, Henry 130, 371
William, Warren 127, 322
Williams, Billy Dee 48, 50, 337
Williams, Robin 21, 22, 25, 241, 276, 277, 279, 303, 357
Williamson, Fred 164, 200, 347
Willis, Bruce 214, 368
Woman Doctor **130-132**, 283, 371
Wray, Fay 316
Wright, Jeffrey 224, 309
Wright, Teresa 221, 361
Wyman, Jane 238, 240, 343

Y

Young Doctors, The 74–76, 138, 285, 286, 289, 373
Young Dr. Kildare 67–70, 286, 287, 292, 293, 372
Young, Freddie 261, 317
Young, Robert 37, 320

Z

Zanuck, Darryl F. 308, 353, 358
Zanuck, Richard D. 368
Zimmer, Hans 302, 304
Ziskin, Laura 312, 370
Zuniga, Daphne 15, 329